Prosecutors, Voters, and the Criminalisation of Corruption in Latin America

Lava Jato, a transnational bribery case that started in Brazil and spread throughout Latin America, upended elections and collapsed governments. Why did the investigation gain momentum in some countries but not others? The book traces reforms that enhanced prosecutors' capacity to combat white-collar crime and shows that *Lava Jato* became a full-blown anti-corruption crusade where reforms were coupled with the creation of aggressive taskforces. For some, prosecutors' unconventional methods were necessary and justified. Others saw dangerous affronts to due process and democracy. Given these controversies, how did voters react to a once-in-a-generation attempt to clean politics? Can prosecutors trigger hope, conveying a message of possible regeneration? Or does aggressive prosecution erode the tacit consensus around the merits of anti-corruption? *Prosecutors, Voters, and the Criminalisation of Corruption in Latin America* is a study of the impact of accountability through criminalisation, one that dissects the drivers and dilemmas of resolute transparency efforts.

EZEQUIEL A. GONZALEZ-OCANTOS is Associate Professor and Fellow of Nuffield College at the University of Oxford. He is the author of *Shifting Legal Visions: Judicial Change and Human Rights Trials in Latin America* and *The Politics of Transitional Justice in Latin America*.

PAULA MUÑOZ is Associate Professor at the Universidad del Pacífico. She is the author of *Buying Audiences: Clientelism and Electoral Campaigns When Parties are Weak*.

NARA PAVÃO is Associate Professor in the Political Science department at the Federal University of Pernambuco, Brazil. Her research focuses on political behaviour and comparative politics.

VIVIANA BARAYBAR HIDALGO is a DPhil student in the Department of Politics and International Relations at the University of Oxford and a member of Nuffield College. Her research focuses on the study of corruption and political behaviour.

T0382237

Cambridge Studies in Law and Society

Founded in 1997, Cambridge Studies in Law and Society is a hub for leading scholarship in socio-legal studies. Located at the intersection of law, the humanities, and the social sciences, it publishes empirically innovative and theoretically sophisticated work on law's manifestations in everyday life: from discourses to practices, and from institutions to cultures. The series editors have longstanding expertise in the interdisciplinary study of law, and welcome contributions that place legal phenomena in national, comparative, or international perspective. Series authors come from a range of disciplines, including anthropology, history, law, literature, political science, and sociology.

Series Editors

Mark Fathi Massoud, *University of California, Santa Cruz*
Jens Meierhenrich, *London School of Economics and Political Science*
Rachel E. Stern, *University of California, Berkeley*
A list of books in the series can be found at the back of this book.

Prosecutors, Voters, and the Criminalisation of Corruption in Latin America

The Case of Lava Jato

EZEQUIEL A. GONZALEZ-OCANTOS
University of Oxford

PAULA MUÑOZ
Universidad del Pacífico

NARA PAVÃO
Universidade Federal de Pernambuco

VIVIANA BARAYBAR HIDALGO
University of Oxford

Shaftesbury Road, Cambridge CB2 8EA, United Kingdom

One Liberty Plaza, 20th Floor, New York, NY 10006, USA

477 Williamstown Road, Port Melbourne, VIC 3207, Australia

314–321, 3rd Floor, Plot 3, Splendor Forum, Jasola District Centre, New Delhi – 110025, India

103 Penang Road, #05–06/07, Visioncrest Commercial, Singapore 238467

Cambridge University Press is part of Cambridge University Press & Assessment, a department of the University of Cambridge.

We share the University's mission to contribute to society through the pursuit of education, learning and research at the highest international levels of excellence.

www.cambridge.org
Information on this title: www.cambridge.org/9781009329804

DOI: 10.1017/9781009329835

First published 2023
First paperback edition 2024

A catalogue record for this publication is available from the British Library

ISBN   978-1-009-32984-2   Hardback
ISBN   978-1-009-32980-4   Paperback

Cambridge University Press & Assessment has no responsibility for the persistence or accuracy of URLs for external or third-party internet websites referred to in this publication and does not guarantee that any content on such websites is, or will remain, accurate or appropriate.

Contents

Figures

Tables

Acknowledgements

This project started with a casual conversation between Nara and Ezequiel during a conference at Oxford in 2017. They wondered how they could finally realise their graduate school dream of working together. Given Nara's interest in corruption and public opinion and Ezequiel's interest in judges and prosecutors, an obvious starting point would be to field a short survey to examine the impact of *Lava Jato* on voters' attitudes towards corruption and politicians. At the time, the *Lava Jato* (or Car Wash) Operation, the largest anti-corruption push in Brazilian history, was in full swing and ravaging politics. Both soon realised that given the complexity of the phenomenon, it would not be possible to explore the relationship between judges, prosecutors, and voters rigorously in a one-off survey or experiment; they needed to dig deeper into citizens' attitudes and emotional reactions to *Lava Jato*. This would require multiple studies and a multi-method approach. It was also becoming increasingly clear that *Lava Jato* would not remain a strictly Brazilian phenomenon. Indeed, throughout 2017 the investigation gained traction in other countries too, most notably in Peru, where it wreaked havoc on the political establishment, and would quickly become the largest foreign bribery case in history. Discussions with Paula, who was already investigating attitudes towards corruption in Peru, and Viviana, who was starting her graduate studies at Oxford, suggested the project had to expand its geographical and substantive scope.

This is how the four of us came together to address a series of questions about one of the most significant shocks to Latin American politics in recent times. What made an investigation like *Lava Jato* possible in a part of the world where impunity for grand corruption used to be the norm? Why did it expand beyond Brazil and why did prosecutors prove effective in some countries but not in others? For some members of the elite, the aggressive and unconventional methods deployed to uncover grand corruption were necessary and perfectly justified. Others instead saw dangerous affronts to the rule of law and democracy. Given these controversies, how did voters in contexts with different levels of partisan polarisation and aversion to politicians react to a once-in-a-generation attempt to clean politics? Did they instinctively back anti-corruption or did this zealous and unorthodox form of anti-corruption prove too difficult to support despite the longstanding and majoritarian yearning for a different kind of politics? Are anti-corruption crusades like *Lava Jato* capable of building strong and durable anti-corruption coalitions, or do the methods and outcomes of anti-corruption sooner or later become fatally contested?

We presented the book's main findings at Stanford University, Harvard University, MIT, Universidad de Barcelona, Universidad Carlos III de Madrid, University of Utah, McGill University, Sciences Po, Universidad del Rosario, University of Oxford, Columbia University, and King's College London, as well as at meetings of the American and Brazilian Political Science Associations. We are grateful to all present at these seminars and conferences for their excellent feedback. Manuel Balan, Santiago Basabe, Alisha Holland, Melis Laebens, Marcelo Leiras, Matthew Taylor, Pablo Valdivieso, and Laurence Whitehead deserve special thanks for their feedback on different parts of the manuscript. Isabella Cantoni, Mats-Philip Ahrenshop, Moshe Ben Hamo Yager, Maria Bahia, Diego Quesada, Andrea Tafur, and Wendy Adrianzen provided invaluable research assistance at different stages. Finally, we are indebted to the journalists, prosecutors, judges, civil society activists, politicians, and lawyers, who agreed to be interviewed for this project and shared their insights on the ins and outs of corruption prosecutions.

This book would not exist without the financial support we received from various institutions. Ezequiel would like to thank the Leverhulme Trust for awarding him the 2018 Philip Leverhulme Prize in Politics and International Relations. The prize funded field trips, several rounds of public opinion data collection, and a year of sabbatical leave to write the book. He would also like to thank the John Fell Fund at the University of Oxford for a grant that paid for surveys, focus groups, and research assistant hours. Paula is grateful to the Office of the Vice-President for Research at the Universidad del Pacifico for supporting the survey we conducted in Peru jointly with Proetica. Nara thanks the Dean's Office for Research at the Universidade Federal de Pernambuco for supporting our data collection in Brazil.

Ledda Narvaez, Manuel Cañas, Camila Arruda Vidal Bastos, and Silvania Moura did a terrific job organising and moderating the focus groups in Lima and Recife. Samuel Rotta and his colleagues at Proetica helped us design our survey in Peru, and generously allowed us to include questions in their XI National Survey of Corruption Perceptions in Peru.

At Cambridge University Press, Sara Doskow and Rachel Blaifeder generously championed our project from the start and provided outstanding editorial guidance throughout. We also thank two anonymous reviewers for excellent comments and the editors of Cambridge Studies in Law and Society for agreeing to include our book in their prestigious series. Jadyn Fauconier-Herry,

Becky Jackaman, Anshu Sinha, and Anoop Kumar helped us get the manuscript across the finish line. Victoria De Negri did a wonderful job with the index.

Some passages in Chapter 3 originally appeared in V. Baraybar and E. Gonzalez-Ocantos (2022), "Prosecutorial Agency, Backlash and Resistance in the Peruvian Chapter of *Lava Jato*," in *The Limits of Judicialization: From Progress to Backlash in Latin America* edited by S. Botero, D. Brinks, and E. Gonzalez-Ocantos, New York: Cambridge University Press.

1

Introduction

Anti-corruption Crusades

INTRODUCTION

News of multinational companies bribing foreign public officials to secure market access sometimes breaks out and leads to scandal. In the mid-2000s, Siemens was forced to overhaul its management board and pay millions in fines in the United States and Germany after prosecutors discovered it had engaged in corrupt practices for years (Berghoff 2018). In 2012, a series of *New York Times* articles revealed that Walmart executives had similarly bribed officials in Mexico, Brazil, China, and India. Following a long investigation, the company settled the case with a US$282 million fine.[1] When it comes to the judicial and political repercussions of this kind of revelations, however, no scandal comes close to the one that engulfed Brazilian construction giant Odebrecht starting in 2014. This book analyses how a relatively minor inquiry that began in Curitiba, a city in the south of Brazil, evolved into an investigation of continental proportions known as Operation *Lava Jato*, and upended politics throughout Latin America. The pages to come explain why prosecutors successfully criminalised Odebrecht's corruption in some countries but not others. We also explore what voters make of these zealous corruption probes, documenting their emotional reactions and prognoses about the future of politics. In so doing, we identify the obstacles that resolute prosecutorial campaigns face when it comes to building broad, engaged, and hopeful coalitions in support of unprecedented anti-corruption efforts. The book thus contributes to debates about the determinants of strong law enforcement institutions, the (de)merits of accountability through criminalisation, and the complicated relationship between corruption, anti-corruption, and public opinion in contemporary democracies.

[1] Nandita Rose, "Walmart to Pay $282 Million to Settle Seven-year Global Corruption Probe," *Reuters* (20 June 2019).

A group of Brazilian prosecutors and police officers launched Operation *Lava Jato* in March 2014. Within months they were able to map the contours of a prolific corruption scheme at the heart of Petrobras, the state-owned oil company. Petrobras executives allegedly received bribes in exchange for contracts and relied on intermediaries to launder the money so that it could reach their political bosses, who in turn used the cash to finance elections. By November 2014 it was clear that at least eleven of the country's largest companies, including Odebrecht, were involved in Petrobras's fraudulent bidding practices. Between 2014 and 2020, prosecutors and judges in the cities of Curitiba, Rio de Janeiro, and São Paulo signed 278 leniency and plea bargain agreements with individuals and corporations; arrested at least 546 suspects; conducted 1,864 searches throughout the country; issued 195 indictments; imposed millions of dollars in fines; and convicted 219 defendants. Among those implicated in the scandal was former president Luiz Inácio "Lula" Da Silva of the Workers' Party (hereafter, PT), and congressional leaders, former ministers, and advisors belonging to twenty-eight political parties. *Lava Jato* thus helped catalyse a political crisis that had been brewing since the protests of June 2013, when citizens took to the streets to repudiate corruption and demand better public services (Alonso and Mische 2017). The investigation complicated, but did not thwart, President Dilma Rousseff's (PT) re-election bid in the second half of 2014. As the case snowballed, it did however contribute to her downfall two years later. Most dramatically, Lula's arrest and conviction transformed the 2018 race and facilitated the rise to power of far-right populist Jair Bolsonaro, whose party went from obtaining a single congressional seat in 2014 to winning fifty-two seats and the presidency (Hunter and Power 2019).

Lava Jato is not only unique in terms of its scope within Brazil; its regional implications are equally unprecedented. In fact, according to the BBC, it amounts to "the largest foreign bribery case in history."[2] The turning point for the internationalisation of *Lava Jato* came in December 2016, when Odebrecht struck a deal with authorities in the United States. It emerged that the company had offered kickbacks to public officials all over the world in exchange for preferential treatment in the allocation of large infrastructure projects. US Department of Justice documentation indicates that between 2001 and 2016, Odebrecht "paid approximately $788 million in bribes in association with more than 100 projects in 12 countries, including Angola, Argentina, Brazil, Colombia, Dominican Republic, Ecuador, Guatemala, Mexico, Mozambique, Panama, Peru and Venezuela" (United States Department of Justice 2016: 7). The company "funded an elaborate, secret financial structure that operated to account for and disburse corrupt bribe payments to, and for the benefit of foreign officials, foreign political parties, foreign political party officials and foreign political candidates" (ibid.: 7–8). At the heart of the scheme was the Division

[2] Linda Pressly, "The Largest Foreign Bribery Case in History," *BBC* (20 April 2018).

TABLE 1.1 *Estimated cost of Odebrecht's bribes per country and returns on investment*

Country	Total bribes (millions of US$)	Return to the company (millions of US$)	Return per 1 US$ in bribes
Argentina	35	278	7.94
Colombia	11	50	4.54
Dominican Republic	92	163	1.77
Ecuador	33.5	116	3.46
Mexico	10.5	39	3.71
Panama	59	175	2.97
Peru	29	143	4.93
Venezuela	98	N/A	N/A

Source: United States Department of Justice, DOCKET NO. 16-CR-643 (2016), www.justice.gov/criminal-fraud/fcpa/cases/odebrecht-sa (accessed 1 November 2018).

of Structured Operations, a clandestine unit within Odebrecht responsible for bribe payments and money laundering. US authorities estimate the company spent approximately $439 million outside Brazil, securing a return of around $1.4 billion (ibid.: 16; Table 1.1).

Given the source of the allegations, judges and prosecutors outside Brazil were immediately forced to open local chapters of *Lava Jato*. This event therefore worked as an exogenous shock. In countries like Argentina and Mexico, investigators made little or no progress, while in others, such as Ecuador and Peru, the legal and political repercussions have been far-reaching. In Peru, for example, the investigation started with a narrow focus on bribes paid to secure three public works projects, but quickly expanded its remit and wreaked havoc on the political class. Five former presidents, as well as leading opposition figures, capital city mayors, and regional governors, have been investigated and ordered to spend time in detention. Most tragically, former president Alan García committed suicide the morning the police arrived in his house to arrest him. If one looks carefully, it is not hard to see how *Lava Jato* also contributed to a presidential resignation in 2018, the shutdown of Congress in 2019, the repudiation of the establishment in the legislative elections of January 2020, and the impeachment of yet another president a few months later.

That corruption around large infrastructure projects is rampant in Latin America is little surprising. If we take Transparency International's Corruption Perception Index for 2015, the year before the internationalisation of *Lava Jato*, only three countries, Uruguay, Chile, and Costa Rica, scored above 50 per cent.[3]

---

[3] The CPI uses a standardised scale of 0–100 where 0 equals the highest level of perceived corruption and 100 equals the lowest level of perceived corruption.

TABLE 1.2 *Ranking of Latin American countries in Transparency International's 2015 Corruption Perceptions Index*

Country	Ranking (out of 167 countries)	Country	Ranking (out of 167 countries)
Uruguay	21	Dominican Republic	102
Chile	23	Argentina	106
Costa Rica	40	Ecuador	106
Cuba	56	Honduras	111
El Salvador	72	Mexico	111
Panama	72	Guatemala	123
Brazil	76	Nicaragua	130
Colombia	83	Paraguay	130
Peru	88	Haiti	158
Bolivia	98	Venezuela	158

Source: Transparency International, www.transparency.org/en/cpi/2015/index/ven (accessed 19 February 2021)

The rest ranked rather poorly in a list of 167 nations (Table 1.2). What is indeed surprising is that prosecutors in some of these countries were able to launch ambitious investigative efforts with unprecedented zeal. This is even more remarkable if we consider that the kind of corruption at the heart of the Odebrecht scandal is incredibly hard to prove, even for the most politically independent and professional prosecution services (Hilti 2021). Crimes orchestrated at the highest levels of government leave behind opaque evidence trails. Moreover, criminals exploit their institutional prerogatives to lash back against investigators and mount sophisticated cover-ups, deploying intricate mechanisms to camouflage the proceeds of corruption (Della Porta 2001; Bertossa 2003; Joly 2003; Klinkhammer 2013; Martini 2015).

What are the origins of this newfound prosecutorial zeal? And what explains why *Lava Jato* gained momentum in some countries, becoming a full-blown anti-corruption crusade, but stalled in others? Our answer looks at the legacy of the reforms to criminal justice institutions that swept Latin America during the 1990s and 2000s. These reforms, however, were not adopted to the same degree across the board, leading to important cross-country differences in the autonomy and organisational structure of the prosecution services, as well as in the legal frameworks governing corruption investigations. In addition to long-term processes of institutional change, our explanation emphasises prosecutorial agency. We argue that tactical decisions associated with the design of investigative efforts, most crucially the creation of specialised task forces, ultimately determined whether the initial allegations snowballed into a much bigger affair. Prosecutorial teamwork in small groups nurtured legal innovation, aggressive fact-finding, and the shrewdness needed to plough through hostile political landscapes.

For many observers, *Lava Jato* anticipates a new era of accountability and may serve as a strong deterrent for those who would otherwise not think twice before engaging in corruption. Critics, by contrast, think that the criminalisation of politics at this scale is a devil in disguise. By casting doubt on the integrity of politicians and putting some of them in jail, courts distort the normal course of democratic processes. Moreover, even when inquiries gain momentum like in Brazil or Peru, success on the criminal legal front always remains uncertain and precarious. Generalised disappointment in accountability institutions, as well as establishment backlash against them are latent possibilities throughout. Finally, and perhaps more importantly, prosecutorial zeal usually comes at the expense of strict respect for the due process rights of defendants. As we shall discuss at length in this book, investigators sometimes deploy aggressive and unorthodox strategies relentlessly. Without this approach, it is hard to imagine how transnational corruption networks could ever be uncovered or punished. The problem is that this same toolkit provides the perfect ammunition for corrupt actors to cry foul. Denouncing "lawfare"[4] while experiencing the wrath of daring prosecutors is obviously an attractive proposition. But this conflict over the legality of the inquiry between prosecutors and defendants can also make less impassioned observers question the merits of the enterprise. As a result, what in principle is a noble cause can in practice backfire.

Such debates consume the political agenda and capture voters' imaginations. To be sure, very few citizens approve of corruption. In fact, Latin Americans are quite concerned about this issue (Table 1.3). For example, in Transparency International's 2019 Global Corruption Barometer, 86 per cent of respondents in the region considered that corruption was "quite a big" or "a very big" problem. But because of the tense relationship between aggressive anti-corruption probes, due process, and open democratic competition, positive public reactions to these shocks are by no means guaranteed. Prosecutors, who often feel the need to "go public" to protect their work from backlash, can therefore struggle to build support and thus ensure the legitimacy and sustainability of anti-corruption efforts. With this in mind, the book also explores how crusades impact mass opinions, in particular, how the criminalisation of corruption by zealous prosecutors affects voters' relationship with institutions and their representatives. Do prosecutions trigger system satisfaction and hope, conveying a message of possible political regeneration? Or do they signal further decay, exacerbating cynical and defeatist views about the nature and future of politics? Are these investigations capable of galvanising

---

[4] "Lawfare" is the strategic use of courts and the law to delegitimise, weaken, or neutralise political opponents. According to Comaroff and Comaroff (2006: 30) it refers to "the resort to legal instruments, to the violence inherent in the law, to commit acts of political coercion, even erasure." The term has been invoked by leftist leaders in Latin American since 2016 to accuse the "right" of resorting to questionable judicial proceedings to thwart progressive agendas (Smulovitz 2022).

TABLE 1.3 *How serious is the problem of corruption for Latin Americans?* *(2019)*

Country	No problem at all (%)	Fairly small (%)	Quite big (%)	A very big problem (%)	Don't know (%)
Argentina	1	5	41	52	1
Brazil	1	2	32	58	7
Chile	2	12	48	37	1
Colombia	1	4	43	51	1
Costa Rica	12	5	34	48	0
Dominican Rep	1	6	54	39	1
El Salvador	1	5	46	47	0
Guatemala	3	7	49	41	0
Honduras	3	5	44	46	1
Jamaica	5	13	28	50	4
Mexico	3	5	49	41	1
Panama	5	4	48	42	0
Peru	0	3	40	56	1
Trinidad & Tobago	2	10	24	62	3
Venezuela	2	4	26	68	2
Guyana	8	28	21	38	5
Barbados	11	27	28	25	9
Bahamas	5	12	23	57	3
Average	4	9	38	48	2

Source: Transparency International, www.transparency.org/en/gcb/latin-america/latin-america-and-the-caribbean-x-edition-2019 (accessed 9 March 2021)

the public against corruption, or do they turn anti-corruption from a valence issue into a one that is deeply divisive? Our original public opinion data suggests that the sui generis prosecutorial tactics that propel ambitious anti-corruption efforts interact with voter preferences, including partisanship, in ways that make it difficult for hope to take root. When it does, hope tends to be short-lived because investigations quickly accumulate controversies that polarise and disappoint. As a result, political cynicism usually wins the day.

ANTI-CORRUPTION CRUSADES

If you spend some time among corruption experts, you will not be surprised to find that one key question drives their advocacy and research: what is the best way to curb the misuse of public office for personal or political gain?[5] Or to paraphrase Alina Mungiu-Pippidi (2015), how does a society get to Denmark?

---

[5] This is the definition of corruption initially proposed by the World Bank (1997) and later adopted in most academic work on the topic. For a discussion of the difference between grand and petty corruption, see Uslaner (2008).

Not everyone, however, agrees on what the central focus of anti-corruption efforts should be. There are two competing paradigms, one that emphasises prevention and gradual norm-building, and another that highlights the need for eradication via targeted law enforcement (Rothstein 2011; Mungiu-Pippidi 2015; Fisman and Golden 2017; Rotberg 2017; Taylor 2018). These paradigms are, of course, not mutually exclusive, but the differences in emphasis are important. While the former camp puts a premium on long-term processes of holistic institutional and cultural overhaul that make both society and state "self-restraining" (Schedler et al. 1999), the latter prioritises the strengthening of *ex post* punishment mechanisms, usually those associated with criminal justice systems. In this book we intervene in the normative and policy debate about the merits and complementarities of prevention and enforcement approaches. We do so by studying what one might think of as enforcement "on steroids": *anti-corruption crusades*.

Anti-corruption crusades consist of widespread efforts by judges and prosecutors to investigate, prosecute, and punish corruption through the courts. We borrow the term "crusades" from Matthew Taylor (2018: 65). It is used here in its more general acceptation to refer to a big push or offensive against corruption, in the form of an "organized campaign concerning a political, social, or religious issue, typically motivated by a fervent desire for change."[6] The focus is on white-collar crimes involving high-level public officials and businessmen.[7] These crimes are often listed in penal codes as crimes "against the public administration," and include graft, the supply and receipt of bribes, influence-peddling, embezzlement, illicit enrichment, and money laundering, among others.

Four characteristics set these crusades apart from routine judicial anti-corruption cases. The first and most important of these is the sheer *zeal* with which judges and prosecutors approach the investigation. The courts and prosecution services cease to behave in a reactive fashion. No longer do they merely respond to the odd media exposé or accusation against a member of the political class. Instead, judges and prosecutors become much more proactive anti-corruption agents. This zeal is on display on a variety of fronts. One is the frenzy of investigative and punitive measures adopted during the inquiry. Judicial actors engage in waves of evidence-gathering activities, often in a spectacular fashion. For example, they execute search warrants in party headquarters or politicians' homes, and stage televised depositions and plea bargain negotiations with high-profile informants. Crusades also consist of waves of pretrial detentions, indictments, and convictions targeting a variety

---

[6] This definition comes from the *New Oxford American Dictionary*, available at www.oxfordreference.com/view/10.1093/acref/9780195392883.001.0001/acref-9780195392883

[7] The term "white-collar crime" was coined by Sutherland in the 1930s. He defined it as a "crime committed by a person of respectability and high social status in the course of his occupation" (Sutherland 1983: 7).

of establishment figures, many previously considered "untouchable," such as powerful businessmen, officials in prominent executive and legislative posts, and high-ranking ministers, advisors, and civil servants. A second manifestation of zeal is the creative interpretation of the legal framework with the goal of easing procedural and evidentiary constraints. This includes the unorthodox use of criminal definitions; the redefinition (critics say relaxation or breach) of evidentiary standards via unconventional theories of criminal liability; and heavy reliance on plea bargains. Finally, zeal is on display in the rhetoric of moral certainty and virtue often used to justify aggressive and unorthodox tactics. Judges and prosecutors present themselves as custodians of integrity who have been called upon to fight against a class of "evil" public officials. They argue for the need to go above and beyond their formal terms of reference because the crimes in question are simply too elusive and hard to prove, rendering traditional uses of the law ineffective. In so doing, crusaders declare no room for compromise in pursuit of this mandate.

Second, is the high level of *coordination* between and within various law enforcement agencies, including the courts, the police, and prosecution services (Da Ros 2014). Most notably, anti-corruption crusades tend to be driven by teams of prosecutors, sometimes even special ad hoc prosecutorial task forces set up to investigate specific allegations. Team members pool resources to gather troves of information, connect the evidence to attribute individual criminal responsibility in complex networks, recover stolen assets, force a large number of witnesses and defendants to parade through the courts, campaign to amass public support, and jealously guard the case from political intrusions. As we will argue extensively in Part I of the book, task forces are uniquely suited to catalyse the legal innovations, sense of purpose, and political dexterity that help crusades gain and maintain momentum.

Third, crusades consist of a bundle of sequenced prosecutorial and judicial decisions that trigger a *snowball effect*. Cases usually start with a narrow focus on minor or highly targeted allegations, but quickly grow in scope, producing multiple spin-offs. In this regard, they are rather different from other instances of judicialisation of interest to political scientists, which tend to be more discrete phenomena (e.g., rulings on the constitutionality of a law). As a result, we are challenged to think differently about the determinants of judicial and prosecutorial decision-making. In addition to antecedent conditions external to the judicial process – the relative power of defendants, formal institutional arrangements, or the ideational make-up of the courts – we ought to take seriously more endogenous factors, especially the internal dynamics of the investigation. For this is crucial to understand what enables or thwarts the snowballing process (Bakiner 2020). A related implication is that the protracted nature of these affairs means there is ample room for contingency and error. And as the stakes rise, those who are threatened by criminalisation have incentives to deploy resources to orchestrate backlash against the investigators and the entire justice system. The process therefore looks more like a battle, and its resolution is invariably uncertain. This high level of uncertainty underscores a key puzzle. Why would investigators embark in such an ambitious and risky enterprise? And when they do so, how do they deal with obstruction? It also raises normative questions. If at the end of the day effectiveness is so elusive and the courts and prosecutors can be compromised, is this the best way to fight corruption?

Finally, the zeal, scope, visibility, and subject matter of anti-corruption crusades give them *eventful* qualities (Meierhenrich and Pendas 2017). William Sewell conceptualises "events" as historical occurrences that are "remarkable in some way" and "have momentous consequences" (Sewell 1996: 841–842). Events can be deeply disruptive and transformative of political processes, social structures, and mass attitudes. Some national chapters of *Lava Jato* are interesting precisely because of this kind of impact beyond the courtroom. The political implications are the most obvious: political careers destroyed, presidential races rebooted, governments collapsed, publics polarised. In some contexts, investigations also had economic ramifications. For instance, they produced a complete paralysis of the construction sector, a key engine of growth in Latin America. This was because major infrastructure projects were put on hold, and banks became wary of lending to local companies for fear they could also end up implicated in the scandal. Finally, in line with the aforementioned rhetoric of virtue, judges and prosecutors sometimes launched campaigns with the explicit goal of mobilising citizens and transforming institutions. These campaigns galvanised the attention of multiple actors, including the media. For example, *Lava Jato* prosecutors in Brazil collected over two million signatures in support of a legislative package designed to tackle the problem of corruption.

Until recently, the canonical example of anti-corruption crusades was the "Clean Hands" operation, which overhauled Italian politics in the 1990s. A handful of magistrates had investigated a non-trivial percentage of parliamentarians since the 1940s. The number of corruption investigations and prison sentences, however, soared between 1992 and 1994 (Della Porta 2001; Fisman and Golden 2017: 217). As a result, the issue salience of corruption skyrocketed, re-election rates plummeted, and old political parties collapsed. This debacle subsequently led to the rise of anti-establishment sentiments and outsider politicians. Today there are more examples of anti-corruption crusades. One is the work of Nigeria's Economic and Financial Crimes Commission (EFCC) during the 2000s. Created to appease the international demand for greater transparency, the commission quickly became a nightmare for the establishment. Between 2003 and 2008, under its first and most autonomous chief prosecutor, the EFCC convicted over 250 individuals and recovered billions of dollars (Adebanwi and Obadare 2011). Also established in response to international pressures, and sponsored by the UN, the Commission Against Impunity in Guatemala (CICIG) worked closely with a handful of local prosecutors to punish systemic corruption. Until it was dismantled in 2019, the

CICIG identified seventy criminal organisations and judicialised dozens of cases. This resulted in more than 400 convictions, including some against extremely high-profile defendants.[8] A fourth example is the work of Colombia's Supreme Court in the so-called parapolitics case. While involving a different kind of corruption – illegal connections between legislators and paramilitary groups rather than big business – it followed a similar snowballing trajectory and had a seismic effect on local politics. According to Bakiner (2020: 620, ft. 1), "37 of the 102 senators who were elected for the term 2006–2010 were under investigation [...] As of March 2014, there were 41 sentences, 18 ongoing trials, 126 preliminary investigations, and 5 acquittals."

This book deepens our understanding of this kind of phenomena in developing democracies, integrating in one study an analysis of the drivers, public reactions to, and merits of anti-corruption enforcement "on steroids." We focus on a spectacular crusade that transcended national borders to upend the politics of an entire region: Operation *Lava Jato*.

Part I: The Causes of Anti-corruption Crusades

Why do some anti-corruption investigations gain momentum, expanding beyond their original remit to become crusades, but others stall? Part I of the book tackles this question. In Chapter 2 we introduce a framework that helps us think systematically about the nature and dynamics of these inquiries. Chapters 3 and 4 use the framework to explain why *Lava Jato* snowballed into a much bigger affair in some Latin American countries but not in others.

Some scholars and many politicians (especially those subject to exacting corruption probes) endorse the view that the criminalisation of corruption is nothing but "politics by other means." In other words, the criminal legal process is not autonomous from the political dynamics that unfold outside the courtroom. At best, judges and prosecutors cautiously respond to indirect political signals to know when they can act and against which groups. At worst, those in power directly weaponise prosecutions to attack their rivals. Chapter 2 discusses why we consider that this perspective is not entirely satisfactory when it comes to explaining anti-corruption crusades like *Lava Jato*, and why we need an account that puts investigators centre stage. Three reasons stand out.

First, seeing judicial actors as purely reactive or mere puppets does not square well with reality. Crusades are full of twists and turns that result from the decisions of those immediately in charge, sometimes to the benefit and sometimes to the detriment of the overall effort. This defies the notion of a perfect principal/agent relationship, or of top-down planning from behind the scenes, with prosecutors serving as pawns in someone else's political ploy.

---

[8] For the CICG's Final Report, visit: www.cicig.org/cicig/informes_cicig/informe-de-labores/informe-final-de-labores/ (accessed 25 February 2021).

Moreover, crusades are defined by widespread targeting, including of influential establishment figures, which goes counter to the assumption that judicial actors are necessarily cautious or manipulated by those in power. Quite the contrary: as the snowball effect gains momentum, investigators embrace risk and expose themselves to retaliation, not only from defendants but also from their own superiors. Second, during ambitious corruption probes judges and prosecutors have high autonomous damage potential and defensive capabilities that enable them to challenge the dictates of *realpolitik*. As a result, the criminalisation process need not respond to the preferences and warnings of powerful elites. Third, even when investigators go after weak actors or pursue lines of inquiry that favour the interests of those in office, criminalising grand corruption is hard. Accounts that assume external actors can easily manipulate law enforcement to undermine their rivals are therefore too voluntaristic. They fail to problematise the process through which prosecutors acquire the resources to expose corruption and how they go about doing so in specific cases. Overcoming the many obstacles that emerge along the way requires investigators with very specific legal and non-legal skills. On the one hand, the crimes leave behind opaque evidence trails. On the other, the targets of these investigations, even when relatively weak, are never passive bystanders who let prosecutors collapse their political careers. And as the investigation escalates into a much bigger affair, even those who are not directly threatened by it are likely to join this backlash out of an abundance of caution.

Going back to our characterisation of anti-corruption crusades, a more satisfactory framework is one that understands these crusades as an open-ended battle between, on the one hand, a handful of maverick rank-and-file investigators, and on the other, politicians and their allies in senior judicial and prosecutorial roles. In particular, the framework ought to locate the origins of the zeal and skills that fuel these investigations and explain how an inquiry comes to exhibit autonomous snowballing dynamics that defy the limits of political possibility. To this end, Chapter 2 engages in what Michael Coppedge calls "stylized induction" (2012: 96). We combine general theoretical intuitions about the drivers of autonomous bureaucratic and prosecutorial behaviour with a detailed analysis of well-documented cases of crusades (in particular, Italy's Mani Pulite and Brazil's *Lava Jato*). This allows us to induce a model that we then probe with other cases in Chapters 3 and 4. The argument specifies the motives and incentives guiding small groups of rank-and-file prosecutors, with attention to the structure of rules, procedures, and organisations within which they are trained and selected (and within which they operate), and to their agency and the place of contingency in the unfolding of specific inquiries. The story consists of a long-term *process* of institutional and organisational change, and three *moments*.

The figure of the prosecutor-hero, deep-rooted in the US legal tradition, and a proven route to power and prestige in that country, is less established in many parts of the globe, including Latin America. This is because the tools and professional role conceptions that enable and predispose prosecutors to play that role (control over the criminal investigation, prosecutorial selectivity, plea bargains, etc.) are recent transplants. What led, then, to the emergence of the hyper-active, daring, and effective prosecutors responsible for various national chapters of *Lava Jato*? How did these individuals come to defy bureaucratic routines (and often superior orders), embracing aggressive fact-finding tactics, innovating with creative interpretations of the law, and nurturing informal relations with witnesses, foreign judicial authorities, and the media to trigger productive evidentiary flows and build defensive shields?

Our answer starts by identifying three streams of *institutional and organisational change* since the 1980s: the removal of prosecution services from the orbit of executive branches; overhauls to criminal justice systems, including the transition from inquisitorial to prosecutor-centered accusatorial models; and the legal translation of fledging international anti-corruption norms. These reforms created the necessary space for the emergence of the maverick prosecutors that engineer crusades. They provided minimum levels of political insulation and fostered greater internal independence for the rank-and-file. Furthermore, the reforms made available a better legal framework to tackle macro-criminality, including more precise criminal definitions, the introduction of plea bargains, and the formalisation of channels for international penal cooperation. Finally, and more importantly, reforms led to bureaucratic differentiation within the prosecution services via the creation of units dedicated to white-collar crime. This specialisation nurtured expertise, a certain espirit de corps, and greater autonomy vis-à-vis senior members of the organisation.

Where these reforms were more fully implemented, the likelihood of observing anti-corruption crusades became much higher. Institutions, however, did not overdetermine the emergence of, or the momentum behind, *Lava Jato*. Finding the necessary evidence to prosecute remained a central challenge. Moreover, reforms never fully eliminated slackers within prosecutorial bureaucracies, insulated zealots from undue pressures, or broke ties between politicians and senior law enforcement agents. A lot could therefore still go wrong after the various inquiries started, both in terms of evidence-gathering and obstructionist shenanigans. To understand how seemingly minor revelations snowballed into crusades, we must get closer to the events in question. Here is where we introduce our three "moments." The goal is to recognise the role of contingency and prosecutorial agency in the story.

First is the *moment of serendipity*, during which chance discoveries enable some prosecutors to light the investigative fire and start their politically inexpedient poking. One can therefore easily imagine counterfactual worlds in which the inquiry never happens, even when institutional and political conditions are ripe.

Second is the *moment of agency* during which prosecutors make strategic choices to unravel complex criminal networks in hostile and information-poor environments, ultimately operationalising the potential created by institutional change. The key at this stage, we argue, is the deployment of aggressive strategies on a variety of fronts: pretrial detentions, plea bargains, international cooperation, the selection of criminal definitions, and public outreach. This involves plenty of controversial decisions that sometimes redraw the boundaries of due process to secure evidence and pre-empt attacks. Prosecutors therefore need to proceed with great care. A lot hinges on the knowledge endowments and professional role conceptions nurtured by the aforementioned reforms, as well as on individuals' predisposition to accept risk. But one factor that conditions the adoption of a zealous approach capable to setting the snowball effect in motion is the extent to which investigators operate under the umbrella of a *task force*. We draw from theories of small group dynamics in economics and psychology to explain why this kind of teamwork leads to more adequate conceptualisations of the criminal phenomenon, evidentiary economies of scale, innovation, a strong sense of purpose, and the building of protective shields. Task forces trigger positive feedback loops, optimising investigative strategies, cementing commitment to the case, and increasing leverage vis-à-vis powerful defendants.

Last is the *moment of backlash*. Establishment actors almost invariably react to the prosecutorial threat. Prosecutorial zeal, that is, aggression and unorthodoxy, invites *and* legitimises attempts to stop the inquiry. While backlash is clearly a consequence of the case gaining momentum, it also affects the sustainability of that momentum over time. Put differently, the presence of backlash, and the extent to which prosecutors manage to diffuse attacks, is part and parcel of the process that makes crusades. This renders the outcome of the anti-corruption effort highly precarious because it becomes contingent on how the legal and political battles that break out along the way are resolved.

In sum, we argue that a combination of greater institutional autonomy, expertise attained via processes of bureaucratic differentiation and specialisation, and strategic cooperation in small investigative task forces allowed some prosecutors to decisively challenge the political establishment. This challenge, however, triggered fierce resistance among interested parties and more neutral observers, turning criminalisation into a conflictive and fragile phenomenon.

Empirical Strategy

One of the highlights of this book is to compare cases of crusades with cases of investigations that stalled. This allows us to better understand the conditions under which the synergies responsible for the snowball effect flourish, and where exactly things can go terribly wrong, as they often do. To do so, we leverage important similarities between the national chapters of *Lava Jato* outside Brazil, including the fact that they all started simultaneously following the same exogenous shock, or "moment of serendipity," in December 2016.

Chapter 3 relies on official documentation, rich institutional analysis, and elite interviews, to process trace Peru's *Lava Jato*, arguably the most ambitious branch of the inquiry after the Brazilian one. We show that a sequence of institutional and organisational changes consistent with those discussed in Chapter 2 created a more hospitable environment for proficient and innovative anti-corruption investigations. We identify a process of bureaucratic differentiation within the prosecution services that created interstices of autonomy for the development of investigative capabilities. All of this despite the persistence of corruption and political obsequiousness at the top of the institution. Crucially, however, *Lava Jato* struggled to take off until all lines of inquiry were placed under the purview of a unified task force. We thus exploit within case variation in this key aspect of the prosecutorial strategy to show the benefits of teamwork on the evidentiary and defensive fronts. One important consequence of the decision to pool together investigative resources was the signing of a comprehensive cooperation agreement with Brazilian authorities and Odebrecht, which made available the evidence needed to crack the case. Finally, Peru shows that while prosecutorial zeal and innovation were critical for the progress of the case during the "moment of agency," they also invited backlash and jeopardised the legitimacy and survival of the inquiry at various stages.

Some might argue that the destructive force of *Lava Jato* in Peru had little to do with institutions or prosecutorial agency and is more parsimoniously explained with reference to the structural weakness of Peruvian parties.[9] In other words, investigators were hunting lions in the zoo. To assess this alternative view and further probe our account, Chapter 4, which similarly relies on official documentation and elite interviews, takes us further afield in Latin America. This allows us to explore how *Lava Jato* unfolded under different political conditions. Ecuador, another positive case, shows the heuristic value of our explanation when defendants are much stronger than those in Peru. We document how institutional change nurtured bureaucratic capacity to investigate corruption, and again establish the critical role that task force creation plays in engineering crusades. For example, the Ecuadorian task force displayed great dexterity in securing international penal cooperation, a cornerstone of prosecutorial success. Mexico and Argentina are our negative cases. They both lack the type of autonomy-enhancing and capacity-building reforms we see elsewhere. One consequence of a partial or deficient reform process is that corruption investigations rarely fall in expert hands, easily fall prey to political shenanigans, and struggle to acquire autonomous dynamics. Importantly, Argentina demonstrates that without the synergies associated with teamwork inside a task force, prosecutors were unable to break the walls of silence that haunt anti-corruption inquiries. As a result, the "moment of agency" never materialised. The case failed to gain momentum despite initially benefiting from a generous window of political opportunity.

---

[9] On Peru's democracy "without parties," see Levitsky and Cameron (2003) and Muñoz (2019).

Part II: Public Reactions to Anti-corruption Crusades

One of the main lessons of Part I is that the aggressive and unorthodox prosecutorial tactics that propel crusades also make them extremely controversial, for example, by creating tensions between accountability and due process. Part II shifts gears to investigate what voters make of these controversies. Do crusades cement or complicate the construction of a strong consensus in support of anti-corruption? Public reactions to crusades matter not only because they condition the sustainability of the prosecutorial effort amidst elite backlash; they also create more (or less) favourable environments for a cleaner type of politics. If anti-corruption becomes contested, with its findings and methods put into question, societies may easily decant into a dangerous spiral of division and disenchantment.

While other scholars tend to study the impact of corruption allegations on voting behaviour, we build on this work to look at how crusades shape general dispositions at the heart of accountability choices. Recovering the concept of "political cynicism" (Agger et al. 1961), that is, the sense of futility that comes with a generalised lack of trust in politics, and incorporating emotions to the analysis, we ask if crusades signal to voters further political decay or put political regeneration within sight. Do they make citizens anxious, worried, and more cynical about the innately crass nature and future of politics, or enthusiastic and hopeful about the possibility of political redemption? We posit that the road to either cynicism or a more productive engagement with the political system is mediated by complex interactions between pre-judicialisation attitudes – for example, partisanship, trust in (judicial) institutions – and the spectacle that unfolds in the courts.

Voters generally dislike corruption and should in principle welcome its criminalisation. But the meaning of crusades is likely ambiguous, complicating prosecutors' ability to build broad coalitions in support of their project and, in turn, the extent to which the anti-corruption push can become a reason for hope in politics. Chapter 5 introduces a framework to think about these issues, which further reveals the political precarity and potentially divisive nature of anti-corruption crusades.

We begin by identifying two stylised prognoses, one optimistic and the other pessimistic. On the one hand, citizens could interpret criminalisation as a sign of the system's ability to disrupt "business as usual." In other words, crusades dramatise a country's potential for political regeneration. Courts and prosecutors are better positioned than other anti-corruption agents to convey this message. Their rituals and procedures endow them with a kind of symbolic capital that projects what scholars call "the myth of legality" (Scheb and Lyons 2000), namely the impression that accountability efforts are even-handed and driven by seriousness of purpose. Anti-corruption crusades can therefore elicit feelings of system satisfaction that generate hope and enthusiasm, undermining cynical attitudes towards politics and producing a virtuous cycle of critical engagement.

One the other hand, by disclosing authoritative evidence of wrongdoing on a grand scale, and often crafting a strong anti-politics message to justify their actions, judges and prosecutors could actually reinforce cynicism. A system shown to be rotten at its core inspires emotions such as anger, fear, or worry, and the generalised feeling that little can be done to change reality. This cynicism may ultimately lead to greater tolerance for corruption, political withdrawal, or support for extra-systemic alternatives. In addition, optimists are perhaps too naïve in believing citizens will buy into the "myth of legality." Even if judicial actors are above good and evil, so to speak, some voters will repudiate measures taken against politicians they support as biased, thus rationalising or ignoring corruption allegations. Among other groups, the selectivity at the heart of these inquiries (e.g., plea bargains, leniency agreements), coupled with the uncertainty of the legal process, could quickly produce disillusionment, and reinforce a sense of futility. Finally, courts and prosecutors are not always above good and evil precisely because the zeal that fuels the crusade is far from a standard or universally accepted trait of the judicial role. This can undermine the "myth of legality" and erode support for crusades as a legitimate tool to fight corruption.

Our argument in Chapter 5 indicates that the optimistic prognosis can materialise, but only partially and under a restrictive set of conditions. Prosecutorial efforts interact with local political contexts and voter preferences, and this interaction conditions system satisfaction, emotional reactions, and cynicism. First, the extent to which the public conversation is dominated by a discussion of the crimes (i.e., what prosecutors reveal about the nature of politics) matters a great deal. A crime-focused conversation becomes a negative information shock and a breeding ground for cynicism. If, by contrast, voters also pay attention to the investigative effort (i.e., the judicial attempt to solve these problems), other possibilities arise. Because judicial actors *qua* crusaders possess distinct forms of symbolic capital, a focus on the investigation has the potential to activate hope and other mechanisms of system satisfaction associated with the optimistic account. Whether crime or investigation-centric orientations dominate the conversation, we argue, is a function of how the media reports on the crusade, but also of baseline attitudes that induce voters to pay attention to certain aspects of the phenomenon more than others, including preexisting levels of cynicism and trust in the criminal justice system.

Second, when citizens discuss the investigative effort, how do they evaluate its fairness and effectiveness? Levels of satisfaction with the work of the prosecutors, in particular perceptions of fairness and effectiveness, matter because they support the construction of the myth of legality, determining whether attention to the judicial effort ultimately elicits hope and enthusiasm about the future of politics, or diametric reactions. We contend that these evaluations are shaped by attitudes such as voters' partisan attachments to defendants, meaning, for example, that in polarised societies crusaders can easily haemorrhage support. This is true even when, objectively speaking, prosecutors engage in widespread or unbiased targeting. Furthermore, short-term developments also determine procedural evaluations. The prosecutorial toolkit characteristic of crusades is prone to controversy. In some cases, selectivity via the use of plea bargains leads to the charge that not everyone is being treated equally. Similarly, unorthodox interpretations of the evidence or an aggressive treatment of defendants raise rule of law considerations that sound alarm bells among partisan and non-partisan observers alike. As a result, enthusiasm may easily fade as the inquiry progresses. All in all, when voters see procedural failures, for whatever reason, the space for optimism narrows and they likely revert to cynicism.

Empirical Strategy

Anti-corruption crusades are messy and protracted affairs. Their effects on voters are also likely conditional and heterogenous. This means there are no silver bullets to assess impact. We therefore adopt a multipronged empirical strategy that subjects the argument to various partial tests based on original focus group and (experimental) survey data from Brazil and Peru. Importantly, this comparative approach allows us to probe how crusades play out in a context featuring higher levels of polarisation (Brazil) and one characterised by generalised political disaffection (Peru). Such contrasting environments potentially lead to important cross-country differences in how voters think about anti-corruption efforts and their implications for politics. The main takeaway is that even if crusades mount a fight against a phenomenon that most would like to see eradicated, their effect is not straightforwardly positive, and when optimism does surface, it is far from universal and usually short-lived. What we ultimately see is an exacerbation of existing trends towards either division or disenchantment. If anything, hope as an outcome of criminalisation appears more robust in places where polarisation is relatively more intense, leading some portions of the electorate that derive partisan satisfaction from seeing their figures of hate parading through the courts.

In Chapter 6 we rely on focus groups to map the contours of the public conversation around *Lava Jato*. First, the focus group protocols included questions and activities (e.g., emotion mapping, personification games) to explore whether voters associate the *Lava Jato* "brand" with the problem of corruption (the crimes) or its solution (the judicial effort), and how those associations are linked to emotional and attitudinal reactions. We find that Peruvians focus mainly on the crimes, what some of them called the "cockroaches" lurking in the backstage of politics. Brazilians, however, are more evenly divided between both orientations, with some seeing judicial "superheroes" capable of instigating change. This is accompanied by a contrast in emotions and attitudes: Peruvians overwhelmingly voice negative emotions and cynicism; reactions in Brazil are more mixed. Descriptive survey statistics and text analysis of newspaper headlines suggest these differences in the orientation of the overall conversation may be due to (a) contrasting patterns of media coverage, with newspapers in Peru paying more attention to the crimes relative to the crusaders, and (b) pre-crusade levels of trust in judicial institutions, which were higher in Brazil.

Second, Chapter 6 dives deep into voters' fairness and effectiveness evaluations. The debate about these issues is more intense in Brazil due to higher levels of political polarisation (Samuels and Zucco 2018). Supporters of the PT feel victimised by *Lava Jato*; their rivals passionately defend it. Diverging assessments of the prosecutorial effort thus separate those who find reasons for hope from those who derive little satisfaction from criminalisation. This shows that when hope takes root, it may come at the expense of nasty partisan feuds. By contrast, Peru features no partisan fervour and universal political distrust. As no one feels victimised, Peruvians talk little about judicial bias; instead, they focus on the crimes. When prompted to discuss the judicial process, participants do not see prosecutorial efforts through partisan lenses. They cannot, however, get past their cynicism, and are deeply sceptical of the merits and potential of *Lava Jato* as an anti-corruption probe. In particular, voters are critical of the trade-offs at the heart of the prosecutorial strategy, especially leniency agreements. Peruvians smell the scent of betrayal. In the end, a citizenry that is hopelessly cynical to begin with is reluctant to give the crusade the benefit of the doubt, and consequently prone to stick to its priors about the irredeemably crass nature of politics.

In Chapter 7 we use observational and experimental survey data from Brazil to continue probing our framework. The effects of *Lava Jato* are unlikely to be straightforward or uniform across the electorate and are especially likely to become quite heterogenous as the inquiry's progress triggers multiple controversies. First, we explore the evolution of Brazilians' attitudes towards *Lava Jato* at the aggregate level, showing that they indeed became divided over time. We then use individual level data that measures public support for the operation, as well as perceptions of its fairness and effectiveness, to shed light on these rifts and their correlates at different points in time. In line with the debates between focus group participants in Chapter 6, all regression analyses show that attitudes towards the crusade are sensitive to partisan preferences. In particular, PT supporters tend to be more critical of *Lava Jato*'s effectiveness and fairness. Taken together, both sets of results point to the precarity of optimism and the importance of voters' priors in assessing the merits of prosecutorial zeal.

Second, we use a vignette experiment fielded in April 2021 that allows us to study more directly the impact of *Lava Jato* on public opinion, all other things being equal. We investigate whether putting crusades at the forefront of narratives of Brazilian corruption elicits emotions and attitudes in a more optimistic direction, compared to narratives that focus exclusively on the dark side of politics. The results show that when voters fixate on the crimes, as opposed to considering decisive efforts to punish them, they are more likely to experience strong negative emotions about politics and more likely to be dissatisfied with the democratic system. However, we also find that contrary to the argument put forward in Chapter 5 and the focus group data presented in Chapter 6, a crime-oriented narrative increases respondents' external political efficacy, whereas an investigation-oriented one has the opposite effect, deepening citizens' sense of political futility. This suggests that the attitudinal impact of *Lava Jato* is far from being uniformly in line with the optimistic story. Under certain conditions, pessimists might be right in warning that the anti-political message that crusaders espouse does more harm than good to the view that politics is perfectible and redeemable.

Finally, Chapter 8 takes us back to Peru. The first part assesses whether evaluations of the prosecutorial effort condition cynicism and alter the accountability equation. We use original survey data to probe whether levels of satisfaction with the *Lava Jato* task force correlate with more (or less) intense positive and negative emotions, as well as with more (or less) optimistic prognoses about the future of politics. The results indicate that satisfaction with the investigation shapes emotional reactions and expectations about future corruption, with positive evaluations leading to greater enthusiasm and less cynical forecasts. We also study if emotional reactions of varying intensity are associated with voters' propensity to tolerate corruption, finding that more intense positive emotions resulting from *Lava Jato* are linked to greater severity vis-à-vis corrupt politicians, and more intense negative ones to cynicism in the form of leniency and resignation. A conjoint experiment then allows us to assess whether the *Lava Jato* task force, by virtue of its visibility and reputation, indeed induces voters to impose penalties on politicians to a greater extent than other sources of corruption allegations. Optimists maintain that crusaders have special qualities that enhance their pro-social effects. If optimists are right in thinking that criminalisation efforts undermine cynicism or lead voters to engage constructively with the system, accusations that benefit from the prestigious *Lava Jato* "brand" should elicit tougher sanctions. The experiment shows that they do.

The second part of Chapter 8 leverages another conjoint experiment to document how voters respond to the trade-offs at the heart of the prosecutorial effort, and thus better understand why these controversial choices complicate citizens' relationship with the crusade, making hope and enthusiasm rather precarious. As we show in Chapter 3, Peru's *Lava Jato* gained momentum after prosecutors made a series of concessions to sign an agreement with Odebrecht. The cost of the deal was quite high: immunity for executives, a cap on the fines imposed on the company, and the green light to continue contracting with the state. The conjoint experiment reveals that Peruvians are quite reluctant to endorse such concessions. Together with additional descriptive survey statistics measuring reactions to other controversies triggered by *Lava Jato*, the experimental results underscore how hard it is for prosecutors to effectively dramatise the "myth of legality" and cement any hope they may have originally generated.

All three empirical chapters support a broader point we make in Chapter 5, namely that as the crusade unfolds, anti-corruption ceases to be a valence issue.

Far from universally celebrating these exacting probes, citizens eventually come to interpret anti-corruption efforts in different ways, depending on their attitudinal and political priors as well as on the behaviour of law enforcement agents. Quite tragically, at least from the perspective of prosecutors, the kind of investigative tactics that make crusades possible, sooner or later prove too controversial in the eyes of many voters. This limits the extent to which aggressive law enforcement is conducive to building broad and stable support coalitions, despite prosecutors' multiple attempts to court public opinion. By implication, it also limits the sustainability of the pro-transparency push, especially during the moment of backlash, as well as crusaders' ability to contain political cynicism and reconcile citizens with the system.[10]

WHAT CAN WE LEARN FROM THE STUDY OF *LAVA JATO*?

The virulent political and legal battles over criminalisation we describe in Part I, together with the divisive impact of prosecutorial efforts documented in Part II, suggest that anti-corruption crusades are likely to scar politics and society. Importantly, crusades spur debates about what the boundaries of legal possibility ought to be when it comes to attacking corruption. In so doing, they pose the question of how much corruption we should tolerate in the name of democratic stability and the rule of law. The conundrum can be summarised as follows: while a zealous and aggressive prosecutorial *modus operandi* is essential to give teeth to abstract legal frameworks, and thus dismantle criminal networks backed and obscured by state power, it can also polarise and disappoint, and often stands in tension with important liberal values, including respect for due process.

Chapter 9 concludes the book with a discussion of these normative issues. The goal is to identify the merits and demerits of criminalisation as a pro-transparency tool, zeroing in on the challenges we face to strike a balance between, on the one hand, horizontal accountability and justice, and on the other, political stability, due process, and competitive elections. A comparison with human rights prosecutions, an area that in Latin America was once marred by similar politico-legal debates, points to the importance of engaging in efforts to "norm" prosecutorial zeal. We suggest what this "norming" exercise could look like and why it is needed to lower the political voltage of crusades, render prosecutions less controversial, and by implication, their outcomes less precarious. In other words, the focus is on how investigators could still make the rules bite without simultaneously compromising the kind of political order they seek to promote.

---

[10] See the Appendix for a discussion of our multi-method approach to questions about the causes and consequences of anti-corruption crusades, including a word on the reasons why the empirical strategy is so eclectic. The Appendix can be found on http://www.narapavao.com/book.html

We bring the Introduction to an end anticipating parts of this normative evaluation and outlining the book's contributions to three literatures. First, our analysis of the drivers and impact of *Lava Jato* in Latin America contributes to debates about best practices in the struggle against corruption. While there is a consensus that corruption is a serious threat to economic well-being and democratic quality, scholars often disagree in their conceptualisation of the problem and its solutions (Rothstein and Varraich 2017). Democratic theory, for example, expects that elections will serve as an effective antidote, simply because voters seek to maximise government efficacy over time (Fearon 1999). Unfortunately, however, a large body of research shows that electoral accountability for corruption is weak and inconsistent (see below). In light of this disappointing evidence, most commentators have come to favour more comprehensive fixes, in part because they see corruption not as a problem of individual agents overriding their principals, but one of collective action. In other words, systemic corruption generates norms and incentives that reinforce perverse equilibria (Rose-Ackerman and Palifka 2016; Fisman and Golden 2017). For some, changing the course of history therefore requires shocks that radically modify elite behaviour and preferences for reform, such as severe economic crises or military defeats (Rothstein 2011). This recipe is unsatisfactory from a policy-making perspective because shocks of this kind are not only costly, but also extremely rare and fortuitous. Others place their hopes in enlightened leadership, but once again, societies could just end up "waiting for Godot" or simply embracing highly precarious transformations (Rotberg 2017). Finally, yet another group points to the importance of incremental reforms that strengthen oversight capacity and reduce both motives and opportunities for graft (Gingerich 2013; Mungiu-Pippidi 2015; Taylor 2018). While this approach can deliver holistic transformations, the piecemeal introduction of institutional change is often incoherent and quickly loses steam in contexts of systemic corruption.

We examine one additional fix that combines several characteristics of the aforementioned approaches. Anti-corruption crusades, a strategy of radical enforcement, are fuelled by an unorthodox prosecutorial *modus operandi* that gives bite to institutional reforms. Importantly, investigators succeed when they cease to see corruption as the result of circumstantial moral failure and conceptualise it as a systemic deficit. Moreover, the snowball effect gives crusades the shock-like qualities that some analysts prefer. This shock, however, is not dependent on rare historical junctures like military defeats or the rise to power of exceptional personalities. Instead, it is firmly anchored in pre-existing horizontal accountability institutions.

Unlike other country-specific studies of anti-corruption crusades (Della Porta 2001; Della Porta and Vannucci 2007; Chang et al. 2010; Manzi 2018; Taylor 2018; Lagunes and Svejnar 2020; Da Ros and Taylor 2022a; Mota-Prado and Rodriguez-Machado forthcoming), ours is explicitly comparative. This allows us to provide a more comprehensive conceptualisation of the nature and dynamics of the phenomenon, identifying what needs to obtain for a crusade to happen and realise its potential as a remedy for corruption. We do this with an eye on the evidentiary and political challenges that make these inquiries so difficult, and another on the conditions that favour the human and institutional capital required to overcome such obstacles. We conclude that the autonomy of the prosecution services, as well as bureaucratic differentiation and specialisation within them are central pre-conditions for success. So too are certain short-term decisions, such as the creation of task forces or the activation of formal and informal channels of international cooperation. In addition, through a careful reconstruction of corruption probes in several countries, and analyses of original public opinion data, we dissect the dilemmas at the heart of enforcement approaches in deeply corrupt societies, shedding light on the political precariousness of such efforts, as well as on the complicated relationship between prosecutorial zeal, due process, and democratic representation. The analysis thus identifies plausible pathways to strong horizontal accountability bodies but also calls attention to the perils of building institutional strength.

Second, the book contributes to the comparative judicial politics literature. As Julio Ríos-Figueroa eloquently put it, "the bulk of social science research on judicial institutions focuses on courts and judges forgetting the prosecutorial organ and the prosecutors – as if scholars working on these topics had never watched *Law & Order*" (2015: 196). Colleagues may be forgiven for this oversight. After all, hyperactive and involved *Law & Order*-type prosecutors are quite new to many legal cultures, including those of Latin American countries. But as the role of these prosecutors is gradually redefined, and their behaviour becomes more consequential and disruptive, unpacking the make-up and dynamics of the prosecution services has never been more relevant. The zealous prosecutors driving crusades are perhaps an extreme manifestation of this transformation and its significance. The fact that prosecutors are now the protagonists of spectacular dramas foreshadows an era of intense battles over their autonomy, including struggles over institutional resources and prerogatives, as well as over who the prosecutors are and how they think. We hope that his book will equip us for the analysis of these developments.

We build on existing work (notably, Langer 2004; Tonry 2012; Michel 2018a, 2018b) to locate the institutional roots of prosecutorial empowerment, with a substantive focus on corruption investigations in Latin America. We trace how constitutional autonomy from the executive and the judiciary, the introduction of adversarial proceedings, and the adoption of new criminal definitions and procedural tools sharpened the institutional lens through which some rank-and-file prosecutors understand, plan, and execute their horizontal accountability functions. Scholars who have turned their attention to prosecutorial organs advance explanations for empowerment and greater effectiveness that emphasise formal external and internal independence, international pressure and assistance, and synergies with civil society (Brinks 2008; Michel and

Sikkink 2013; Burt 2016; Gonzalez-Ocantos 2016a; Gallagher 2017; Michel 2018a; Ríos-Figueroa 2019). A lot of this research is on human rights violations, hence the central role of civil society. As we explore in more detail in Chapter 9, corruption cases are different in that there are no "victims," narrowly defined, that can jolt prosecutors into action. Our account is therefore more similar to those that concentrate heavily on institutional overhaul. But rather than reducing change to improvements in formal arrangements, we explore the endogenous mechanisms of empowerment that follow these reforms. We are particularly interested in understanding how gains in independence translate into effectiveness: what Hilbink (2012) calls "positive independence". The focus is then on organisational changes, including processes of bureaucratic differentiation and specialisation that nurture interstices of investigative capacity and professional resolve. This analysis therefore has general implications for debates about the determinants of institutional strength (Brinks et al. 2019).

In so doing, we also engage broader theories of judicial behaviour, taking them for a spin in the world of prosecutors. We join those who argue that we cannot understand the interactions between judicial actors and politicians without considering the effect of bureaucratic environments on the production and reproduction of professional ideologies and role-conceptions (Hilbink 2007; Woods and Hilbink 2009; Couso 2010; Arantes 2011; Ingram 2015; Gonzalez-Ocantos 2016a). In other words, the politics around judicial and prosecutorial decision-making are not just a game between rational, utility-maximising actors; they are also a function of organisationally embedded individuals who develop, and abide by, institutional norms, standards, and missions (Gillman 1999; cf. Segal and Spaeth 1993; Epstein and Knight 1998; Helmke 2005). This helps explain why relatively weaker players, such as judges and prosecutors, sometimes "irrationally" collide with the establishment. Specifically, we trace changes to prosecutorial institutions with attention to the ways in which those changes altered the outlook of a new generation of law enforcement actors, making available the tools required to live up to those values.

Unlike other historical or sociological institutionalist accounts of judicial behaviour, however, we go beyond factors that are purely external and temporally prior to the court proceedings of interest, including judicial ideologies and role conceptions, formal rules, the incentives induced by the relative power of defendants, or the inputs of litigation. Together with recent work (Bakiner 2020), we note that the power and personal resolve to decide in sensitive cases is also a function of experiences and developments *during* the course of a legal battle. Specifically, judicial or prosecutorial choices, can, in the short term, transform the conditions of political possibility for difficult outcomes. This could be the consequence of evidence-gathering, penal or public relations efforts that weaken adversaries or reinforce investigators' commitment to obtaining particular results. The book thus highlights the complexity and contingency of the conditions that favour the effective exercise of judicial and prosecutorial power, with an eye on how operating in small groups akin to combat cells allows prosecutors to fearlessly advance exacting anti-corruption probes.

Third, the pages to come intervene in debates among political behaviour scholars about the relationship between corruption and public opinion. Over the last decade or so, political scientists have increasingly deployed sophisticated methods of causal inference to explore whether voters punish corruption or acquiesce. The results suggest that the electoral punishment of corruption is inconsistent at best and non-existent at worst (for reviews, see de Vries and Solaz 2017 and Chapter 5; for a meta-analysis, see Dunning et al. 2019). Accountability chains involve a number of complicated steps, from information acquisition to blame attribution, so a lot can go wrong in the process. But these disappointing results could also conceal the more worrying sign that citizens in many parts of the world have simply come to normalise corruption (Pavão 2018). To think systematically about this possibility, we recover the concept of "political cynicism," which used to be central to debates about disaffection and trust in American politics (Agger et al. 1961; Citrin 1974; Miller 1974). Exposure to systemic corruption may turn voters into cynics who conclude that the exercise of accountability functions is futile, and either tolerate wrongdoing or withdraw system support. A resolute drive to enforce anti-corruption norms, we speculate, may unleash forces that counter this vicious cycle. This is especially true in the new era of social media. In contrast to previous crusades, for example, Italy's Mani Pulite, the active use of social media during daily citizen interactions magnified the salience of *Lava Jato's* sweeping horizontal accountability push.

The book is the first attempt to study the conditions under which ambitious anti-corruption enforcement may alter the accountability equation in this way. Rather than offering yet another test of the limits of elections as an antidote for corruption, we look at how criminalisation efforts impact the attitudinal foundations of existing channels of political representation, and of the relationship between voters and corruption. In so doing, we integrate various methodological tools, and crucially, incorporate the role of emotions, exploring how voters feel about these shocks and whether those feelings are associated with more or less cynical perspectives and expectations about the future of politics. This is in line with recent work that sees political attitudes and behaviour as shaped not only by resources and socialisation, but also by more immediate forms of cognition (Valentino et al. 2011; Albertson and Kushner Gadarian 2015; Webster 2020). The conclusion is that cynicism most likely deepens when voters experience crusades, either because crusades confirm negative priors about politics or because prosecutorial efforts prove less than credible (and effective) attempts to eradicate corruption. This offers new perspectives on the vexing puzzle of why anti-corruption instincts not always lead to the proactive repudiation of wrongdoing, with transparency concerns carrying limited weight in voting decisions.

PART I

CAUSES

2

The Drivers of Prosecutorial Zeal

Institutional Change and Three "Moments" (with Stories from Brazil, Italy, and Beyond)

INTRODUCTION

Politicians investigated for corruption tend to dismiss the charges as politically motivated (Smulovitz 2022). For them, these proceedings amount to nothing more than a form of intimidation. For example, Cristina Kirchner, who served as Argentina's president between 2007 and 2015, has been the subject of numerous investigations. In response to the accusations, her lawyers filed a complaint before the Inter-American Commission on Human Rights denouncing "political discrimination and persecution." The brief also mentioned "lawfare" as a major threat to democracy in Latin America.[1]

The view that judicial efforts to investigate corruption are driven by actors and processes outside the courtroom is also common among political scientists. There are three versions of this argument. First, scholars of authoritarian regimes see "lawfare" as one of the tools that autocrats use to strengthen their rule (Bueno de Mesquita and Smith 2011). Pei (2018), for instance, shows that corruption prosecutions in China tend to coincide with the arrival of a new leader eager to assert authority. Similarly, Shen-Bayh (2018) documents the use of judicial rituals to legitimise repression against insider-challengers in Africa. While these are usually "show trials" in which defendants do not stand a chance, they help autocrats justify attacks against rivals because the line between legality and farce is "fuzzy." And even if court manipulation ultimately proves too obscene, what matters is that the regime displaces conflict to a controlled environment, relying on judges to "propagate narratives of incumbent strength and challenger weakness" (ibid.: 322).[2]

---

[1] "Cristina Kirchner Files 'Lawfare' Writ with the IACHR," *BA Times* (20 May 2020).
[2] Carothers (2022) shows that dictators also champion anti-corruption to improve state capacity when, for example, facing foreign threats.

Moving beyond the theatrical world of autocratic rule, a second group sees political leadership as the key driver of anti-corruption efforts. Robert Rotberg writes,

Political will is the single most critical variable in any effective campaign against corruption ... In each of the significant positive sustained examples in this book, the executive believed in the anticorruption objective and used investigative commissions, prosecutors, attorney generals, and the courts to advance, not to frustrate, that mission (2017: 297).

To understand why judicial institutions stand up to the establishment, triggering cycles of aggressive law enforcement, we must look outside the judiciary, particularly at presidents' determination to champion transparency. In an exhaustive survey of anti-corruption policies in the United States, Cuéllar and Stephenson (2020) make a similar point. During the Progressive Era, for example, "a new generation of leaders ... made anticorruption central to their agendas" (ibid.: 25). Most notably, "Roosevelt's administration ramped up federal criminal prosecutions of bribe-payers and bribe-takers [beginning] a 'new era of criminal enforcement'" (ibid.: 26). Political will also explains the criminalisation of corruption after Georgia's Rose Revolution. Partly out of conviction and partly to ensure survival, "the new government would not tolerate the rampant bribery that had discredited the old elite" (Kupatadze 2016: 120).

A final group looks at resources in addition to political will to identify likely targets of corruption prosecutions. The work of Popova and Post (2018) on Eastern Europe finds that prosecutions are more common against politicians whose parties are not strong enough to negotiate impunity, including junior coalition partners, concluding that these are not independent anti-corruption efforts. Political resources also account for prosecution patterns in Latin America. Conaghan (2012) shows that Ecuadorian presidents who resigned or underwent impeachment were more vulnerable to judicial proceedings instigated by their successors. But ousted presidents were not always powerless. In fact, their lingering political clout helps explain why some managed to delay or neutralise prosecutions. Similarly, Helmke et al. (2019) find that Latin American presidents are more likely to end up in jail if their successors are political outsiders who are not afraid to politicise corruption, or if irregular exits severely damage the electoral competitiveness of outgoing presidents and their parties.

The conclusion that emerges from these studies is that corruption prosecutions are "politics by other means." To understand who is targeted and why, one need not spend too much time studying the evidence, the law, or court behaviour. Instead, the explanation lies in the balance of power between non-judicial actors. The judiciary is merely a conveyor belt for the imperatives of *realpolitik*. At best, judges and prosecutors respond to indirect political signals (e.g., changes in the balance of power) to know when to act and against which groups. At worst, prosecutions are weapons purposefully manipulated by incumbents. In both cases, only those who fall out with the powerful or fall from grace suffer the consequences.

To be sure, the assumption that partisan or regime politics plays a dominant role in determining the fate of these proceedings has its merits. This is especially true in authoritarian contexts, where courts tend to be an appendage of the leader. Courts' political calculations possibly affect criminalisation processes in democracies too. Of all the ways in which judges or prosecutors can intervene in the life of a democracy, the decision to launch a corruption investigation against a serious contender for power is particularly consequential. If certain politicians end up in jail, prosecutions can upend electoral races or fatally damage major parties. Moreover, investigations targeting powerful defendants are likely to face a backlash. Precisely because the stakes are so high, it makes sense to expect the "least dangerous branch" to carefully consider when it is wise to challenge the establishment. Judicial actors will therefore behave with caution, picking battles they can realistically win or for which they can extract some form of compensation.

Given that our goal in this book is to explain the origins of anti-corruption crusades, as opposed to isolated or compartmentalised corruption prosecutions, there are limitations with this approach. All of them point to an underlying problem: it is not entirely accurate to see the courts and prosecution services that take part in these crusades as perfect agents of political principals or as fully responsive to the dictates of *realpolitik*.

The first shortcoming is empirical. The sheer scope of crusades challenges the notion of careful top-down planning by powerful politicians from behind the scenes. Anti-corruption crusades are full of twists and turns, often expanding in ways that from the establishment's point of view are both unexpected and inexpedient. As such, crusades are not narrowly focused on members of weak opposition parties or specific politicians. Quite the contrary: they tend to target quite aggressively a wide range of actors, including incumbents. Nigeria's Economic and Financial Crimes Commission (EFCC) is a case in point. As Adebanwi and Obadare (2011: 192) note, "for many highly placed Nigerians ... the unprecedented manner" in which the EFCC "went about its work created fear and panic." While critics depicted it as the legal arm of President Obasanjo, some of those investigated during the 2002–2008 prosecutorial frenzy "were the president's political friends, allies, or wards," including his own daughter (ibid.: 196). Similarly, Italian prosecutors at the forefront of Mani Pulite uncovered corruption networks that involved members of all major political parties (Della Porta 2001).

When politicians struggle to contain and survive anti-corruption crusades, it is tempting to conclude that they were not very powerful to begin with, thus confirming explanations that emphasise political resources or the balance of power. For example, with regard to Mani Pulite, one could argue that widespread prosecutions were only possible because the collapse of communism had loosened the Christian Democrats' grip over the political system (Nelken 1996: 103–104). A similar point can be made about the conditions that enabled Brazil's *Lava Jato*. After twelve years in office and debilitated by protests and an economic downturn, the incumbent Workers' Party was a shadow of its former self (Alonso and Mische 2017; Samuels and Zucco 2018: 2–3). If taken too far, however, this claim leads to a fallacy of retrospective determinism. It downplays the fact that in pursuing such broad lines of inquiry, crusaders always embrace risk and incur massive personal and professional costs. Even when defendants show signs of weakness, they almost always retain the capacity to retaliate. Moreover, the relentless pursuit of punishment tends to pit rank-and-file law enforcement actors against their superiors, who sometimes favour impunity or disagree with the methods chosen to infer culpability.

Emphasising the contingent, widespread, and risky nature of crusades should not imply that investigators are never biased or calculating; it simply reminds us that they have agency and cannot be considered reactive, epiphenomenal, or mere puppets. Consequently, and in contrast to analyses that do not incorporate judicial actors into accounts of corruption prosecutions, focusing instead on politicians, their preferences and resources, we take the dispositions, capabilities, and choices of judges and prosecutors very seriously. What they do, and how they think, matters in determining whether an investigation gains momentum and becomes a crusade.

Second, observers who maintain that external political factors are the main drivers of prosecutions depict the balance of power courts and prosecutors supposedly respond to as exogenous to the judicial process. This in turn leads them to assume that criminal inquiries merely serve to reinforce existing power distributions. As Bakiner (2020: 606, our emphasis) astutely points out, however, "courts sometimes go against seemingly powerful actors, *sometimes even weakening them in the process.*" In other words, judicial and prosecutorial behaviour, with or without intention, can have an impact on the resources that politicians have at their disposal to condition the outcome of prosecutions. We should therefore not necessarily expect investigators to always be subservient or perfect agents of powerful principals. Judicial decisions can expand what a priori look like rather narrow limits of political possibility. And if these limits narrow due to fierce backlash, judges and prosecutors are not helpless. Their damage potential and defensive capabilities ought to be taken seriously because both help explain why exacting probes snowball into crusades that leave the establishment in disarray.

Third, even when operating under politically permissive circumstances, investigating corruption is no small feat. Voluntaristic accounts are therefore problematic. In addition to eliciting scrutiny, the cases at the heart of anti-corruption crusades are technically complex. Corruption crimes leave behind opaque evidence trails. Proving intent in contexts where corruption is systemic is notoriously difficult because explicit quid pro quo between bribe-payers and bribe-takers is uncommon. Under such conditions, corruption tends to be the outcome of implicit collusion rather than outright extortion (Della Porta 2001). Complicating things further, criminals exploit their institutional prerogatives to mount cover-ups, block the disclosure of evidence, or weaken the legislative framework that governs prosecutions (Bertossa 2003). The mechanisms used to camouflage the proceeds of corruption are also quite convoluted (Joly 2003; Klinkhammer 2013; Martini 2015). Crimes are transnational in nature, involving the use of figureheads, offshore accounts, and intricate asset ownership structures. Uncovering these schemes can only be done with sophisticated financial investigations based on information supplied by other jurisdictions. International cooperation, however, is "slow and cumbersome" (Roht-Arriaza 2009: 69).

Due to the elusive nature of this type of criminality, the templates developed for regular investigations are not easily transferable to corruption inquiries. A highly bureaucratic modus operandi is not fit for purpose because it cannot produce the cascade of evidence and indictments necessary to build momentum, break the *omerta* that defendants rely on to secure impunity, or ignore calls by superiors or politicians to abandon politically inexpedient investigations. Instead, crusaders act in unconventional ways, without the aid of pre-established and widely accepted templates. They learn how to outfox establishment figures and are prepared to stretch the boundaries of legal possibility, often playing at the margins of the law. As we shall see, successful prosecutors make innovative use of corporate leniency regimes and plea bargain legislation, as well as pretrial detentions. They also sometimes come up with creative (and therefore controversial) interpretations of criminal law to justify evidentiary standards that lower the burden of proof, and actively pursue new, informal relations with informants, foreign authorities, and the press. In so doing, the only experiences crusaders can fall back on are those associated with similarly exceptional cases of macro-criminality such as human trafficking, money laundering, or human rights violations, which also require political finesse to fend off intense third-party pressures, as well as special savoir faire to reconstruct convoluted criminal organisations backed (and obscured) by state power.[3]

To explain why corruption prosecutions sometimes gain momentum amidst a variety of obstructionist forces and evidentiary gaps, it is critical to pay attention not just to the incentives and possibilities afforded by politics, but also to processes inside the criminal justice system through which judicial

---

[3] In the case of human rights prosecutions, for example, the diffusion of legal doctrine anchored in international human rights law, as well as the abandonment of inadequate investigative routines, enabled judges and prosecutors in some Latin American countries to conduct trials against former military officers. By contrast, in countries where judges did not acquire new technical capabilities, prosecutions failed (Gonzalez-Ocantos 2016a). Similarly, Lessa (2019) shows that unprecedented levels of international cooperation between South American prosecutors were crucial for the success of the investigation into the *Operación Cóndor*, a multinational repressive venture orchestrated by Southern Cone dictatorships in the 1970s.

actors develop the skills to become crusaders, defying orthodoxy and embracing aggressive evidence-gathering tools. To this end, we focus on the institutional origins of the skill set, personal resolve, and professional dispositions required to make a success of corruption investigations. We also zoom in on the micro-dynamics of the inquiry, with emphasis on investigators' choices and defendants' reactions.

Under what conditions, then, are anti-corruption crusades likely to thrive? Our framework sees anti-corruption crusades as a battle between, on the one hand, zealous investigators, usually rank-and-file prosecutors, and on the other, powerful defendants and their allies in senior roles in the judiciary and prosecution services. Rather than providing an account of the ultimate effectiveness of the criminalisation effort, for instance, whether there are convictions and whether these stand the test of the appeals process, we are more interested in explaining why and how an investigation gains momentum and expands its target pool, snowballing into a crusade. It is in the blossoming part of the story where rank-and-file prosecutors make a difference, determining whether an intriguing revelation leads to the convincing exposure of systemic corruption or to a lethargic investigation, one limited in scope and largely innocuous.

Our explanation of the origins of crusades begins with a long-term *process of institutional change*. We focus on the history of reforms that increased the external and internal independence of rank-and-file prosecutors in Latin America, upending traditional, passive professional role conceptions. These reforms also improved the framework that governs anti-corruption efforts, especially via the legal translation of international anti-corruption norms and processes of bureaucratic differentiation that facilitated specialisation in white-collar criminality among some prosecutors. We thus account for how gains in formal independence translate into effectiveness.

We then explore short-term factors associated with the investigation that affirm the professional commitment and the evidentiary basis necessary for prosecutions to gain momentum and take on politicians en masse. These include, first, a *moment of serendipity*, during which chance discoveries are responsible for igniting the investigative fire. This part of the argument is important because it reminds us of the role that contingency plays in bringing about crusades. One can easily imagine a world in which they do not happen, even if the political conditions are ripe or the institutional environment favours prosecutorial zeal.

Second, the process involves a *moment of agency* during which prosecutors make strategic choices that trigger (or not) the snowball effect. What is required at this stage is the design of a zealous prosecutorial campaign, one that is relentless and unorthodox. This depends on prosecutors holding certain professional attitudes, knowledge endowments, and personality traits that are in part nurtured by institutional reforms. But the decisions that trigger the snowball effect also stem from the creation of *task forces* dedicated exclusively to all aspects of the case. Crusades thrive thanks to the evidentiary economies of

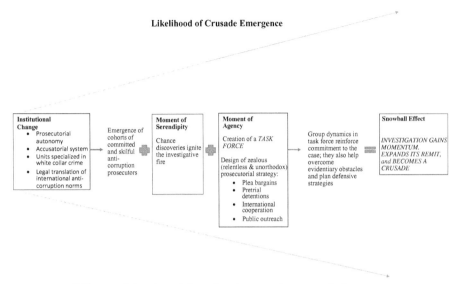

FIGURE 2.1 What explains the origins of anti-corruption crusades?

scale, as well as innovation- and commitment-reinforcing dynamics, made possible by work in small, cohesive groups. Our emphasis on agency therefore does not imply endless possibility or total contingency; the kind of agency conducive to crusades is structured by long-term, as well as more tactical, organisational factors. Overall, the moment of agency shows that in addition to institutional variables and a dose of good luck, the prosecutorial decisions taken during the day-to-day proceedings of the inquiry matter. Intentionally or not, they shape outcomes by narrowing (or expanding) the limits of possibility and weakening (or reinforcing) investigators' commitment to the cause.

Figure 2.1 summarises our core argument about how institutional change coupled with moments of serendipity and agency give rise to anti-corruption crusades.

The story we tell in this chapter has one additional moment: the *moment of backlash*. This is when the establishment tries to thwart the inquiry or undermine the institutions and personnel responsible for it. Backlash is in many ways a consequence of the crusade becoming a threat to elite interests, so discussing it in a chapter dedicated to the causes or origins of the phenomenon may seem misplaced. We maintain, however, that the moment of backlash is an integral part of the process because it moderates how far crusades can go. It especially helps explain why the snowball effect is usually not sustainable over time. The chapter thus highlights a paradox: the prosecutorial zeal that makes anti-corruption crusades possible is also the likely source of their undoing. Zealousness not only invites reactions from defendants and their allies by elevating the level of threat; the unorthodoxy at the heart of these tactics also legitimises the "lawfare" narrative that accompanies elite backlash. At the end of the day, this means that the criminalisation of corruption is always conflictive and highly precarious. The fate of the investigative effort rests on the contingent and uncertain outcome of those battles.

We are not ashamed to admit that we derived this account looking for similarities between well-documented anti-corruption crusades. The chapter is therefore guilty of what Michael Coppedge calls "stylized induction." We sought to produce a framework "that classifies the actors and key steps" in the criminalisation process and identifies "conditions, relationships, and choices that tend to lead to one outcome or another. The result is a partially integrated body of inductively generated concepts and propositions that lies somewhere between a checklist and a theory" (2012: 96). In fact, the reader will find that we illustrate the different stages with examples from crusades such as Italy's Mani Pulite and Brazil's *Lava Jato*. In the next two chapters we use out-of-sample cases, namely four national chapters of the *Lava Jato* investigation launched in 2016 outside Brazil, to probe the framework.

LAYERING INVESTIGATIVE CAPACITY

At the heart of anti-corruption crusades are a small group of prosecutors (and sometimes judges) that stand out among their colleagues for their commitment to fighting corruption. In doing so they risk backlash from political actors as well as from their superiors, who are sometimes aligned with establishment interests or reject the use of unorthodox legal tactics. Where do these maverick prosecutors come from? What motivates them to defy establishment actors? How do they acquire the skills needed to launch far-reaching investigations? The emergence of these figures is somewhat puzzling because in the contexts we study, the "prosecutor-hero" role is not as established as it is in the United States (Boyd et al. 2021), where Hollywood celebrates it and is a proven passport to power and prestige. Behavioural innovation is therefore quite risky, as there are few local models to emulate.[4] Moreover, as we shall see throughout the chapter, success in this role is uncertain. In fact, zealous prosecutors almost always incur heavy personal and professional costs.

According to public administration scholars, a survey of any bureaucracy likely reveals that routine-oriented and highly formalistic "slackers," who operate strictly within the narrow boundaries of their institutional prerogatives, coexist alongside activist, pro-social, and policy-motivated "zealots," who, by contrast, are inclined to go far beyond their terms of reference (Gailmard and Patty 2007; see also Banuri and Keefer 2013; Metz-McDonnell 2017; Abers 2019). James March (1991: 71), for instance, distinguishes between two bureaucratic orientations: "the exploration of new possibilities and the exploitation

---

[4] We thank Laurence Whitehead for this point and for helping us articulate it more effectively.

of old certainties." The former "includes things captured by terms such as search, variation, risk taking, experimentation, play, flexibility, discovery, innovation," whereas the latter "includes such things as refinement, choice, production, efficiency, selection, implementation, execution." The regularity of this duality suggests that it is not entirely surprising for prosecutorial agencies to occasionally produce actors who break with bureaucratic inertia and formalistic rule-following, developing the necessary drive and capabilities to accept risk, innovate, and carry out difficult tasks such as prosecuting a wide range of politicians.

Even if these disruptive individuals tend to be present in most bureaucracies, we also know that gradual changes to regulatory frameworks, organisational structures, and operational remits, as well as social mobilisation processes, sometimes transform incentives, inject resources, and articulate new missions, tilting the zealots/slackers ratio in favour of the former (Pires 2010; Gallagher 2017; Bersch 2019; Rich 2019). Our job here is therefore to identify institutional transformations that nurtured the human capital necessary for the emergence of anti-corruption crusades. We argue that the presence of risk-accepting and competent prosecutors has its roots in processes of institutional change that increased the political insulation of prosecutorial agencies and improved their structural capacity to combat corruption. These processes were in part exogenous to the prosecution services because they were the product of reforms championed by elected officials and international donors. But to some extent they were also endogenous: formal institutional change triggered positive feedback mechanisms that expanded anti-corruption capabilities, mainly through internal bureaucratic differentiation.

The story has three parts. First, we discuss autonomy-enhancing reforms that overhauled prosecution services in Europe and Latin America. Second, we survey more recent changes to Latin American criminal justice systems, especially the transition from inquisitorial to prosecutor-centred adversarial systems. Finally, we look at the legal translations inspired by the consolidation of the international anti-corruption regime in the 1990s and 2000s. One important lesson is that in addition to greater political insulation, these reforms pushed prosecutorial bureaucracies to adapt their structures to pay more attention to white-collar crime *and* improved the tools available for prosecutors to do so effectively. Institutional change was therefore far from merely formal; in some contexts, it was operationalised in ways that had very concrete consequences.

Enhancing the External and Internal Autonomy of Prosecutors

One crucial set of reforms were those designed to improve the autonomy of the prosecution services charged with investigating crimes (van Aaken et al. 2004). Following the centralisation of prosecutorial authority, most modern constitutions placed those functions under the orbit of the executive branch and envisioned hierarchical bureaucracies (Michel 2018a). This setup reduced the likelihood that prosecutors would seriously scrutinise incumbents' behaviour. The outcome was a prosecution service oriented towards law enforcement in private disputes, and in more authoritarian settings, one biased against the opposition (Aguiar Aguilar 2019). In Europe, changes to this arrangement gained momentum after World War II, whereas in Latin America the reformist trend accelerated during the third wave of democratisation. In both cases, the implications for horizontal accountability of decoupling prosecutorial and executive roles, and of diffusing power within the prosecution services, were huge. On the one hand, prosecutorial authorities were now able to determine criminalisation priorities independently. On the other, reforms afforded rank-and-file prosecutors greater autonomy. It thus became possible to imagine law enforcement officers going after the ruling elite or defying the wishes of their superiors. In fact, de Sousa-Santos (1995: 20) explicitly links prosecutorial reform to a new phenomenon: the "criminalization of political responsibility."

For example, scholars locate the origins of Mani Pulite in reforms that increased the independence of judicial and prosecutorial bureaucracies. The 1948 constitution transformed the Higher Council of the Judiciary, created in the early twentieth century to administer the courts in the name of the King, into an autonomous entity. In addition to distancing proceedings associated with the appointment, promotion, and disciplining of judges and prosecutors from partisan politics, the reform gradually "flattened" the courts and prosecution services (Manzi 2018), that is, it reduced the power of the upper echelons over the professional fates of the rank-and-file (Guarnieri 2003). Among prosecutors, higher levels of internal independence gave rise to a "polycentric setting" in which "each unit – if not each prosecutor – is more or less free to run a proceeding" (ibid.: 233). This means that behaviour is not necessarily governed by a bureaucratic logic whereby those at the bottom follow the instructions of those at the top. A more horizontal structure, in turn, creates space for mavericks, which are precisely the kind of prosecutors that engineer anti-corruption crusades.

Apart from changing professional incentives, these reforms had a sociological and cultural impact (Della Porta 2001). Sociologically, they allowed for greater diversity in the kinds of individuals reaching positions of authority. As a result, the dominance of anti-communist hardliners typical of the 1950s diminished, and by the late 1970s there was a critical mass of progressive voices. Greater diversity, coupled with autonomy, inspired successful investigations into complex criminal networks. Formative experiences against the mafia and terrorism in turn transformed the institutional culture of judges and prosecutors. According to Della Porta and Vannucci (2007: 845), "a new generation of judges began ... increasing its own *espirit de corps*." In other words, *de jure* autonomy allowed for bolder behaviour, producing a series of success stories that further cemented de facto autonomy. Importantly, judges and prosecutors learnt how to use new tools to punish wrongdoing at the highest level. For instance, they exploited plea bargain legislation introduced in 1979 in response to the rise in domestic terrorism cases. But they went further. As Manzi (2018: 141) explains, judges and prosecutors "asked Parliament to pass additional legislation" to increase the effectiveness of plea bargains. This proactive approach leads some to conclude that "Italian judges started to perceive themselves as charged by a civic mission of responsibility towards society" (Sberna and Vannucci 2013: 582), one that would later inspire Mani Pulite.

Independence-enhancing reforms that create space for formative investigations into high-level macro-criminality, and in so doing sharpen the anti-corruption resolve of prosecutors, are not unique to Italy. At the onset of the third wave of democratisation, throughout Latin America either presidents or judges exercised control over prosecutorial careers. Most countries eventually changed the law to grant greater autonomy to the prosecution services. While the type of political insulation varies, especially as a function of the mechanisms devised to appoint the chief prosecutor, it is now harder for any faction, in particular for the presidency, to capture this sensitive part of the state apparatus (Michel 2018b). Consequently, the chances of seeing serious corruption investigations that target a wide range of actors, including incumbents, are much higher than before. One notable exception is Mexico, where the attorney general serves at the pleasure of the president. As we shall see in Chapter 4, this had important implications for the fate of the local chapter of *Lava Jato*. In sharp contrast, Peru's Council of Supreme Prosecutors has total control over the selection of the chief prosecutor, making it one of the most formally insulated agencies in the region. In Chapter 3 we discuss how this setup favoured the anti-corruption crusade.[5]

It is probably no accident that *Lava Jato* started in Brazil, a country that is often celebrated for having one of the most powerful prosecution services in the world. For most of the twentieth century, prosecutors were not only "held in lesser regard and prestige," but their legal mandate focused on defending "the interests of the State and its respective officeholders" (Sadek and Cavalcanti 2003: 205). A new constitution approved three years after the 1985 democratic transition changed this. Like Italy, Brazil illustrates how independence-enhancing reforms open space for risky investigations, and help unleash endogenous processes of institutional change that over time reprogram the mission that orients the work of public prosecutors. As Praça and Taylor (2014: 28) explain, "[t]he evolution of accountability institutions has been marked [...] by transformative processes, whereby new resources and roles have been constructed via daily institutional changes."

The 1988 constitution granted the *Ministério Público Federal* full autonomy from the executive and judicial branches. The president needs an absolute

---

[5] In between are cases where Congress oversees the nomination/appointment process (e.g., Bolivia, El Salvador) and those where the Executive needs qualified congressional majorities to appoint/remove the head of the prosecution services (e.g., Argentina, Brazil).

majority in the Senate to confirm his or her nominee for chief prosecutor, and since 2003, the nominee usually comes from a list of senior prosecutors proposed by members of the *Ministério Público*. It is therefore unlikely that outsiders with links to specific partisan factions end up heading the institution. In addition to providing insulation, the priority given to bureaucratic insiders aids the reproduction of a certain espirit de corps. The new constitution also changed the mandate of the prosecution service to one explicitly oriented towards the protection of fundamental rights. Prosecutors are now tasked with controlling officeholders and upholding the interests of the vulnerable, rather than the other way around. Furthermore, the reform put in place new arrangements that guarantee the internal independence of the rank-and-file. As a result, individual prosecutors need not follow instructions and are guarded against attempts to move them around should they poke in the wrong places (Silva 2000). Scholars agree that this package amounted to "the most significant reform" of the 1988 constitutional moment because it resulted in the creation of something akin to a "fourth" branch of government (Sadek and Cavalcanti 2003: 208; Arantes 2011).

The 1988 constitution thus enshrined a legal mandate that zealots within the *Ministério Público* could exploit in pursuit of substantive agendas (Aguiar Aguilar 2019). Taking stock of the progress achieved during the first decade, one prosecutor stated: "we are extending the law to areas that were previously untouched, punishing privileged groups, and increasing the access to justice of excluded groups" (cited in Sadek and Cavalcanti 2003: 212). In fact, a critical mass started to ascribe to a new professional role conception that Arantes (2011) aptly refers to as "political voluntarism." This includes,

1) a pessimistic assessment of society's ability to defend itself; 2) a pessimistic view of political representatives and political institutions, which are seen as corrupt and/or unable to fulfil their duties; and 3) an idealized conception of the MP as the preferred representative of a weak society, especially in contrast to inept bureaucracies that fail to enforce the law (Ibid.: 188).

Studies show that these zealous "prosecutors have built a parallel, overlaid, and covert organization" (Coslovsky 2011: 78) that helps them reproduce like-minded voices within the institution. They mentor and socialise aspirants and newcomers; create professional associations such as the *Ministério Público Democrático*;[6] and form alliances with civil society actors that champion similar causes. Moreover, aided by other changes to the "accountability complex" (Power and Taylor 2011), such as capacity-building in the Federal Police (Arantes 2011), Brazilian prosecutors went through a series of formative experiences that further cemented their commitment to values such as transparency. For example, prosecutors quickly ramped up corruption investigations against

---

[6] This is modelled on the Italian *Magistratura Democratica*, another progressive organisation (Coslovsky 2011).

mayors (Arantes 2011; Da Ros 2014). In fact, during the 1990s some within the *Ministério Público* began to see the fight against white-collar crime as an institutional priority. A few jurisdictions even made use of their newly acquired autonomy to create prosecutorial units specialised in this type of wrongdoing, starting a process of bureaucratic differentiation that nurtured the investigative expertise necessary for anti-corruption investigations to succeed. One of these jurisdictions was Parana, home to *Lava Jato*, where prosecutors created a white-collar crime unit as early as 1992.

The Adoption of American-Style Prosecutorial Tools

Apart from improving the structural autonomy of the prosecution services, Latin American reformers also pushed for the adoption of American-style prosecutorial tools. These reforms, which constitute the second leg of our story of institutional change, further empowered the prosecution services, in particular vis-à-vis the courts, and created new professional scripts that facilitated the emergence of zealous anti-corruption enforcers.

In the 1980s, a group of scholars and practitioners joined forces to align criminal justice systems with the aspirations of the region's fledgling democracies. The main goal was to abandon authoritarian practices and enhance accountability and efficiency (Bischoff 2003; Langer 2007). To this end, they published the Model Code of Criminal Procedure for Iberoamerica (Binder 2000), which promoted the adoption of oral proceedings and greater protections for the accused. Crucially, the proposal championed a transition from the inquisitorial criminal justice systems in place since independence (Michel 2018a), to accusatorial or adversarial systems.[7]

One important feature of the adversarial setup is that it transforms the role of prosecutors, and in so doing, generates incentives for them to make sure investigations are run as smoothly as possible. In the inquisitorial system, judges and prosecutors are jointly responsible for pursuing an "absolute" truth in an impartial fashion. In the accusatorial world, by contrast, prosecutors have full control over the investigation and the truth becomes a relative concept (Langer 2004). The adversarial structure of the proceedings thus encourages the prosecutorial zeal we often see in American legal dramas. Put differently, prosecutors have much more at stake in a game in which they are expected to produce, on their own, a version of events that competes with, and seeks to prevail over, the story put forward by the defence. These conditions, coupled with the greater flexibility afforded by oral proceedings, encourage zealousness. Furthermore, under accusatorial codes of criminal procedure, judges become due process "generalists" who oversee the legality of the inquiry and determine

---

[7] This reformist wave also affected European countries. For example, Italy changed its code of criminal procedure in 1989 (Sberna and Vannucci 2013: 582).

guilt. The prosecution services, on the other hand, can be restructured so that prosecutors specialise in different kinds of crimes and are ready to be put in charge of investigations that match their expertise. In fact, as we shall see in the case studies, the creation of permanent units exclusively dedicated to specific forms of macro-criminality enhanced the effectiveness of Latin American prosecution services in this critical area. As Bischoff (2003: 44) puts it, "expert prosecutorial units should be better able to deal with the sophisticated and well-financed criminal organizations."

A second relevant feature of the paradigm shift is that it empowers and motivates prosecutors not only by separating investigative from adjudication functions and fostering specialisation, but also by inserting greater discretion in the exercise of criminalisation prerogatives (Pulecio-Boek 2015). At the macro-level, the so-called opportunity principle allows prosecutors, especially chief prosecutors, to allocate personnel and institutional resources to prioritise some forms of criminality over others. This is, in part, what enabled the creation of the aforementioned expert units. At the micro-level, those in charge of specific investigations are given greater leeway in deciding whether to go after individual defendants and to what extent. This is reflected, for example, in the introduction of variants of American-style plea bargain legislation, especially for cases involving complex criminal organisations (e.g., drug trafficking, money laundering, etc.).[8] Enticing insider confessions is usually the only way to understand how these criminal networks work and collect incriminating evidence. It is important to note that until the 1990s most of these alternative dispute resolution mechanisms, which proved critical in cases such as *Lava Jato*, were absent from Latin American penal codes (Langer 2004).

The movement in favour of greater prosecutorial control over criminal investigations led Latin American countries to either formally embrace adversarial proceedings or enshrine in law many of the tools that prosecution services have at their disposal in accusatorial systems. In practice, however, the transition was far from straightforward, with many governments pursuing slow and territorially patchy adoption trajectories.[9] The process also faced resistance

---

[8] One example is Argentina's "*procedimento abreviado*," added to the Federal Code of Criminal Procedure in 1997 (Langer 2004: 54). Legislation passed both before and after the introduction of the "*procedimiento abreviado*" also allows plea bargains for certain crimes, including drug trafficking (article 29bis, Law 23.737, 1989), terrorism (Law 25.241, 2000), money laundering (article 31, Law 25.246, 2000). Peru also introduced plea bargains in cases of macro-criminality in 2000.

[9] Chile created a new *Ministerio Público* from scratch (Michel 2018b: 208). Peru opted for a phased introduction of the accusatorial system in 2004. At the time of writing, the process is near completion (see Chapter 3). Several Argentine provinces transitioned to the accusatorial system, but the federal jurisdiction, in charge of complex crimes, including corruption, is still inquisitorial. This is despite the introduction of oral trials at the federal level in the early 1990s (Chapter 4). In Mexico, a constitutional reform passed in 2008 adopted some aspects of the accusatorial model, but implementation has been slow and fraught with difficulties (Chapter 4).

from those who lost power as a result of the regulatory changes (Cavise 2007; Hammergren 2008). And perhaps more importantly, the transition required a revolution in the legal cultures of criminal justice institutions, one that could not happen overnight. Actors had to adjust, internalise new roles, and learn to deploy new tools. A prosecutor used to lethargic "desk-oriented" routines was all of a sudden expected to assume a much more proactive, "street-oriented" role. Similarly, because truth became a more relative concept and the opportunity principle was placed at the heart of investigative routines, prosecutors had to become comfortable with the idea of selective punitivism and master the art of striking deals with witnesses or defendants.

To ease frictions, reform packages were accompanied by multi-million dollar re-socialisation initiatives. An expert who spent time training Latin American legal professionals recalls: "[T]he transfer of power from the judge to the lawyers in the presentation of the case required a very substantial retooling for judges, prosecutors, defense lawyers and civil litigants" (Cavise 2007: 790–791). These initiatives were usually funded by the United States and the World Bank (Langer 2007; Hammergren 2008). The international community wanted to ensure the effectiveness of judicial reforms because it considered them essential for human rights and democratic consolidation. But donors also pursued more prosaic goals. In particular, many were guided by the belief that prosecutorial capacity, coupled with more insulated institutions of horizontal accountability, would help secure a friendlier investment environment at a time when Latin American countries were beginning to embrace neoliberalism. In their view, the project of retrenching the state would not be complete without a parallel effort to punish white-collar crime and restrain politicians and bureaucrats from engaging in the old rent-seeking practices associated with large public sectors. Furthermore, increasing the competitiveness of Latin American economies required eliminating the burden of corruption-induced costs.

In this context, prosecutorial and criminal justice reforms met the anticorruption rhetoric at the heart of the Washington Consensus. This leads us to the third and final leg of our journey: the consolidation of the international anti-corruption regime in the 1990s and 2000s.

The International Anti-corruption Regime

The 2015 United Nations Sustainable Development Goals include a commitment to "significantly reduce illicit financial and arms flows, strengthen the recovery and return of stolen assets and combat all forms of organized crime," alongside a commitment to "substantially reduce corruption and bribery."[10]

Finally, Brazil and Uruguay stand out for being the two countries that display the least progress in transitioning to an accusatorial system (Michel 2018b). This being said Brazil has introduced many of the instruments and regulations typical of adversarial proceedings.

[10] See www.un.org/sustainabledevelopment/peace-justice/ (accessed 4 March 2021).

These goals respond to the widespread view that corruption is a global problem in need of global solutions. Curbing the demand for bribes requires the diffusion of prevention standards and enforcement capabilities across a broad range of countries, especially in the developing world. It also calls for the harmonisation of legal frameworks in the developed countries where bribe-paying multinational companies are based, and where the proceeds of corruption usually end up.

This consensus, however, is relatively new. It wasn't until the 1990s that policymakers came to think of corruption as a systemic problem (Eilstrup-Sangiovanni and Sharman 2022: 125–127). As Moisés Naím (1995) puts it, that decade experienced a "corruption eruption" and the rise of the international anticorruption regime. The United States played an important role. In 1977 Congress passed the Foreign Corrupt Practices Act (FCPA), which conferred law enforcement agents the power to prosecute American companies involved in corruption abroad. For many years, the United States was alone in holding its corporations to such standards, a situation that put them at a disadvantage vis-à-vis companies registered in other countries. The problem became more acute as economic globalisation intensified following the end of the Cold War. The Clinton administration therefore made it a priority to export the FCPA model (Carr and Outhwaite 2008). Pressures directed at Organization for Economic Cooperation and Development (OECD) countries resulted in the 1997 Convention on Combating Bribery of Foreign Public Officials in International Business Transactions. The OECD Convention, which entered into force in 1999, requires parties to criminalise companies' supply of bribes to foreign public officials.

Developing nations were subject to similar pressures. Inspired by the Washington Consensus of the late 1980s, a variety of governmental and nongovernmental actors, including the World Bank and the International Monetary Fund, started to promote financial and commercial liberalisation, as well as the downsizing of public sectors. In their assessment, large states were breeding grounds for rent-seeking and therefore key enemies of growth. When it came to the third world, the "corruption eruption" of the 1990s thus fixated on corruption as a problem of the state, that is, of bribe-receivers. This, in turn, laid the ideological foundations for the popular definition of corruption as the abuse of public office for private gain (Gathii 2019). Little surprising that, armed with this worldview, former World Bank officials went on to create Transparency International in 1993 (Eilstrup-Sangiovanni and Sharman 2022: 152). Those who stayed at the bank similarly turned anti-corruption into an institutional priority, leading, for example, to the introduction in 1996 of new corruption prevention standards, or an alliance with the OECD to create the Global Corporate Governance Forum, with a heavy emphasis on corporate practices in emerging markets (McCoy and Heckel 2001).

The rise of this practitioner community, and the concomitant problematisation of corruption, catalysed the diffusion of anti-corruption reform templates.

In particular, there was a push for convergence across legal systems in order to better criminalise wrongdoing and foster inter-jurisdictional cooperation during corruption investigations (Jackson and Summers 2012). The spread of internationally sanctioned templates for defining corruption in criminal codes is especially relevant for our story. First, it created a language or technical script that led states, via their law enforcement agents, to start seeing and thinking about the patterns of behaviour we now associate with grand corruption in a new light. More precise definitions single out certain phenomena as "criminal," creating clearer obligations and gearing the quest for evidence in more specific directions. One way in which reformed criminal codes transformed the institutional vision of the prosecution services was the creation of specialised units dedicated to newly codified macro-criminal behaviour. When coupled with tools that allow for prosecutorial discretion (e.g., individual and corporate leniency regimes), those now tasked with enforcement were empowered even further. Second, isomorphism created communities of enforcers with comparable terms of reference and responsibilities. These individuals attend summits where they share best practices and develop similar ways of operationalising their duties. Importantly, the convergence of formal legal infrastructures, international commitments, and professional dispositions facilitates cooperation during complex inquiries. For example, during our many interviews with Latin American prosecutors we heard anecdotes about how informal contacts during the meetings of the OECD Bribery Convention or the EU's Eurojust initiative helped build trust, led to agreements to strengthen institutional links, or even allowed them to begin drafting information-sharing agreements for specific investigations.

An early trigger of this trend was the aforementioned OECD Bribery Convention. Another was the 1996 Inter-American Convention Against Corruption, also brokered by the United States. Signatories agreed to put in place mechanisms to enhance public sector transparency, protections for whistle-blowers, and oversight agencies. The Convention also provides a comprehensive list of acts of corruption, encouraging the criminalisation of the supply, demand, and acceptance of bribes, and sets the basis for international cooperation, including the relaxation of banking secrecy and clearer standards for extraditions. The United Nations spearheaded additional milestones in the juridification of corruption. One was the 2000 Convention Against Transnational Organized Crime. Building on these efforts, in 2003 more than 100 nations signed the UN Convention Against Corruption, which commits parties to the criminalisation of bribery and embezzlement. It further highlights the importance of cooperation for repatriating the proceeds of corruption. Finally, developing countries seeking to sign trade agreements or admission to the OECD have been under pressure to create corporate liability regimes that provide incentives for companies to cooperate with anti-corruption investigations, mirroring the FCPA model. As Jorge (2019: 321) explains, the "paradigm seeks to calibrate" enforcement "in a context of scarce investigative resources, the transnational nature of 'grand corruption,' and the difficulties of identifying individual wrongdoers within complex, usually multinational corporations."[11]

Brazil is a good example of how international obligations spread locally (Da Ros and Taylor 2022a). Laws passed in the 1990s, most notably the 1992 Law on Administrative Impropriety, the 1995 Law on Criminal Organizations, and the 1998 Law on Money Laundering, were part of a package to signal adherence to emerging global standards at a time when the country was undergoing an ambitious economic liberalisation process. These innovations had spillover effects, further enhancing the state's preventive and enforcement capabilities. For example, the money laundering law inspired the creation of "a specialized financial crime unit in the Central Bank, and specialized courts for money-laundering" (Praça and Taylor 2014: 39). In turn, the actors empowered by these changes championed "a long list of reform proposals, including revisions to the money-laundering law, creation of a financial asset recovery committee, implementation of a national registry of bank accounts, and better integration of criminal justice databases" (ibid.). Further down the line, Brazil ratified the OECD (2000), Inter-American (2002), Palermo (2004), and UN (2005) conventions, as well as the Inter-American Convention on Mutual Assistance in Criminal Matters (2008). Finally, in reaction to massive anti-corruption protests in 2013, and also to comply with the OECD Convention, Congress passed the Anti-Corruption Law and reformed the Law on Criminal Organizations allowing for "the possibility of collaboration agreements between criminal authorities and suspects, and of leniency agreements with civil effects" (Sanchez-Badin and Sanchez-Badin 2019: 327). In other words, the new legislation allows prosecutors to strike deals with individuals and companies. Following the spirit of OECD guidelines, companies are now liable for corruption perpetrated both in Brazil and abroad. This latest innovation played a critical role in *Lava Jato*.

In sum, the international anti-corruption regime consists of a multilayered juridical structure and community of practice. The consolidation of this regime has important implications for states' capacity to combat corruption. Two are particularly noteworthy. First, the regime complements the reforms discussed in previous sections, making available to domestic anti-corruption agents a set of tools specifically conceived with transnational corruption crimes in mind. Second, the efforts of international norm entrepreneurs raised the salience of corruption at the local level. One obvious channel were the pressures exerted on national governments during trade negotiations. Another was the incorporation of local enforcers to a transnational specialist network that debates templates of best practices, validates juridical

---

[11] See below for recent innovations in corporate liability legislation in Latin America.

innovations, and offers protection to those who decide to take on powerful interests. The zeal incentivised by other reforms thus finds a clearer sense of purpose (and external legitimacy), putting "accountability" at the heart of new prosecutorial role conceptions.

***

The process of institutional change discussed thus far is a key source of the legal prerogatives, skills, and professional resolve that make anti-corruption crusades possible. Thanks to these reforms, Latin America is now a more hospitable place for serious enforcement. As we shall see in Chapters 3 and 4, variation in internal and external prosecutorial autonomy, in the introduction of sharper anti-corruption legislation, and in levels of bureaucratic differentiation conducive to specialisation in macro-criminality help explain why *Lava Jato* advanced at a different pace in different countries. But this type of institutional change does not overdetermine the emergence or the momentum behind crusades; a more hospitable environment is not the same as an anti-corruption paradise. As we shall also see in our case studies, reforms never eliminate slackers within prosecutorial bureaucracies, break ties between politicians and senior law enforcement agents, or fully insulate the rank-and-file from undue pressures. Moreover, even with the right legal tools in place and motivated prosecutors in charge of sensitive investigations, punishing corruption is still extremely hard. A lot can go wrong, both in terms of evidence-gathering and fending off the political attacks that inevitably ensue.

In order to complete the "causal chain" and arrive at a more satisfactory account of why prosecutors sometimes become anti-corruption crusaders, we need to get closer to the events in question. This requires recognising that there is room in the story for contingency and prosecutorial agency.

THE MOMENT OF SERENDIPITY

There is always a moment of serendipity at the inception of criminal investigations that eventually become anti-corruption crusades. For they are rarely planned. Instead, they tend to be triggered by fortuitous discoveries that are merely suggestive of grand corruption or implicate only peripheral figures. A few examples help illustrate the role that chance plays in the initial stages.

The discovery that gave birth to Mani Pulite was rather serendipitous. Luca Magni, the manager of a Milanese cleaning company that had dealings with the local government, filed a lawsuit against Mario Chiesa, at the time in charge of a retirement home. Chiesa, who was also a Socialist Party member with lofty career ambitions, had demanded a bribe in exchange for a contract. To prove the crime, Prosecutor Antonio Di Pietro convinced Magni to record a private conversation. This led to Chiesa's arrest. In the meantime, investigators found Swiss bank accounts that they could trace back to the defendant (Barbacetto et al. 2012: 1–10). That Di Pietro then seized the opportunity to go after Chiesa's multiple connections in the establishment was certainly not a coincidence. After all, the prosecutor belonged to a new generation of law enforcers nurtured by the process of institutional change summarised in the previous section. Like some of his colleagues, Di Pietro had made the fight against corruption a key institutional priority. By leveraging the detention and mounting evidence to force Chiesa to cooperate with the authorities in exchange for penal compensation, Di Pietro sought to fulfil this mission and triggered "a snowball effect which quickly expanded investigations into the whole country" (Vannucci 2016: 63). The point, however, is that the presence of a motivated prosecutor did not by itself initiate the case; Di Pietro also needed a dose of good luck. And as we shall see, the snowball effect was by no means guaranteed once this initial evidence came to light. It was rather a function of strategic choices and creative interpretations of the law following Chiesa's arrest.

The origins of Brazil's *Lava Jato* bear some resemblance to those of Mani Pulite, although the case needed two moments of serendipity to take off. Alberto Youssef was a currency trader with a history of involvement in high-level corruption schemes. After following him for years, the authorities intercepted an email in which he mentioned the purchase of an expensive car for Paulo Roberto Costa, a former Petrobras executive. Armed with this suggestive evidence of bribery, the authorities arrested Youssef in the state of Maranhão on 17 March 2014. Three days later, they captured Costa. As these key suspects pondered whether to cooperate with the prosecutors, they likely concluded that the case would soon stall. Chemin (2017) explains that similar anti-corruption efforts had failed in the past because higher courts had decided they ought to be shelved. Why would *Lava Jato* be any different? In fact, shortly after Costa's arrest, the Supremo Tribunal Federal (STF), the highest court in the land, ruled that the judge assigned to the case had no jurisdiction. The ruling also ordered the Federal Police to release Costa, a decision that put the inquiry in jeopardy because it reduced his incentives to enter a plea deal.

But this time things would be different. It certainly boded well for the case that *Lava Jato* was in the hands of law enforcement agents with a strong anti-corruption drive, partly nurtured by the institutional developments we discussed earlier in the chapter. Most notably, Curitiba Judge Sergio Moro had been thinking about how to tackle systemic corruption for a long time. In the early 2000s he wrote a thesis on the main lessons that investigators should draw from the Italian experience, including the use of pretrial detentions to facilitate plea bargains and the need to leverage relations with the media to protect the inquiry (Moro 2004). Moro also attended courses on money laundering in the United States. Furthermore, as a member of a unit specialised in white-collar crime, he had participated in several high-profile corruption cases, including Banestado and Mensalão.[12] On the prosecutors' side, interest in complex financial crimes was similarly high. For instance, Deltan Dallagnol wrote his Harvard thesis on the importance of rethinking the evidentiary standards applicable to money laundering. Together with other members of the *Lava Jato* team, he also published a book on the subject (de Carli et al. 2011).

Given their resumes, it is not hard to see why neither the judge nor the prosecutors were content with the STF's decision to release Costa. Chief Prosecutor Rodrigo Janot was equally disappointed, and successfully petitioned the high court to allow the Curitiba authorities to resume the inquiry.[13] As they continued to investigate, the prosecutors got lucky for a second time when they found that Costa had a secret Swiss account. This second discovery was critical because it allowed them to put Costa back in jail. Faced with mounting evidence against him, in August 2014 the former Petrobras executive decided to cooperate. Three weeks later, Youssef, who had earlier warned his lawyers that if he talked the "Republic is going to fall," also signed a plea deal.[14] Both confessions set the *Lava Jato* team in a collision course with the establishment. But as well shall see, the evidentiary chain reaction was by no means guaranteed and still required a further "moment of agency."

Given the role that serendipity plays at the onset, it is important to accept that our crusades defy neat, generalisable theoretical accounts. Put differently, when or where they start, and why they gain initial momentum, is partly due to chance. One can easily imagine a counterfactual world in which that sudden witness tells a different version of events, a suspect is a bit more careful with his emails, or a police raid arrives a few minutes too late. In that world, investigators fail to experience the same level of alarm, and even if they do want to pursue the inquiry further, they are deprived of arguments to request more wiretappings, arrest warrants, and so on. As a result, the investigation stalls and the crusade never happens.

Moreover, nothing guarantees that minor but intriguing findings will snowball. Apart from being highly contingent, the initial evidentiary spark has to fall in the hands of the right agents for it to light a fire. Not all prosecutors, for

---

[12] *Banestado* was a large-scale money laundering and tax avoidance case involving dozens of politicians and bureaucrats, including Petrobras officials. The investigation started in the late 1990s and languished in the 2000s. *Mensalão* was another famous case involving forty defendants, including prominent politicians from the Workers' Party and its coalition partners. The term *Mensalão* refers to the monthly payments by the party to congressional allies in return for support (Paiva 2019). Moro participated in *Mensalão* as part of the team that advised one of the STF justices.

[13] In June 2014, the STF split the case, keeping the parts of the inquiry that involved defendants with "foro privilegiado," that is, officeholders with the constitutional right to be tried at the STF. The rest of the case returned to Curitiba.

[14] David Segal, "Petrobras Oil Scandal Leaves Brazilians Lamenting a Lost Dream," *New York Times* (7 August 2015).

example, have the experience required to understand the implications, or see potential in seemingly minor revelations. Similarly, not all prosecutors have the necessary curiosity or resolve to pull from the thread to find out if there are indeed more worms in the can. Some would much rather return to routine cases than embark on a battle with the establishment that will most certainly upend their lives. Compounding things further, even if the case does fall in zealous hands, rank-and-file prosecutors usually need the support of their superiors. For example, senior prosecutors can release resources to assemble a team dedicated exclusively to the case, or as in the Brazilian case, petition judicial authorities to allow the investigation to continue. If whoever happens to be the chief prosecutor at the time is not interested in fighting corruption, has close relations with members of the political class, or is simply not daring enough, the investigation is also likely to stall.

To be sure, the reforms discussed in the previous section improve the odds. They modify the zealots/slackers ratio among career prosecutors and make available better legal tools to investigate corruption. When combined, these changes make it more likely that at any given time some law enforcement agents will be actively looking for the moment of serendipity that allows them to finally live up to their new role conception. When the breakthrough evidence is not the product of ongoing investigations but comes to light as an exogenous shock, these reforms also make it more likely that cases will be assigned to committed prosecutors or that chief prosecutors will have fewer incentives to sabotage further discoveries.

There is, however, ample room for obstruction and inefficiency following the moment of serendipity. The way investigations are subsequently run matters a great deal. Prosecutors must innovate and make strategic decisions to put the anti-corruption toolkit to good use.

THE MOMENT OF AGENCY

Explaining anti-corruption crusades requires an account of how prosecutorial actors leverage the moment of serendipity to trigger a snowball effect. We therefore ought to look at the subsequent "moment of agency," tracing the decisions that allow law enforcers to expand the evidentiary basis for justifying further investigative measures and broaden the inquiry to incrementally target more defendants. Securing productive evidentiary flows is not only important from a legal (probative) point of view; it also likely cements investigators' commitment to the case, helps them defend their efforts in public, and motivates the quest for additional information. In other words, the snowball effect likely triggers self-reinforcing dynamics. For instance, a succession of hardly sought smoking guns will persuade investigators that they are on the right track and might turn the case into something of a personal battle. Under those circumstances, prosecutors will find it difficult to self-censor further progress or passively surrender in the face of external pressures. Impunity or inaction is now harder to justify and would imply professional defeat, with strenuous efforts going to waste. Finally, in addition to momentum-inducing evidence-gathering strategies, we must also trace efforts to build defensive shields as the case becomes a threat to political elites.

This section takes a closer look at these choices. We explain why the design of zealous investigations that stand out for the relentless deployment of innovative tools is necessary for a case to become a crusade, even though there are risks involved in using aggressive and unorthodox tactics. Our argument further suggests that investigators are more likely to come up with these zealous strategies if they create task forces dedicated exclusively to the case. Teamwork within task forces catalyses the kind of prosecutorial agency that makes crusades, exploiting the promises of institutional change to their full potential.

From a theoretical point of view, the argument is that we should think of agency during the judicial process as an explanatory factor in its own right. With the exception of scholars who study the impact of strategic litigation (Epp 1998, 2009; Brinks 2008; Gonzalez-Ocantos 2016a; Gallagher 2017; Michel 2018a), the literature on judicial behaviour tends to emphasise "independent" variables that are external to judicial proceedings. For instance, scholars look at environmental conditions such as the balance of power between political forces to estimate how daring judges are likely to be (Epstein and Knight 1998; Helmke 2005; Ríos-Figueroa 2007). Others look at judges' pre-existing ideological and professional values to account for decisions in specific cases (Segal and Spaeth 1993; Hilbink 2007; Couso 2010; Teles 2012; Hollis-Brusky 2015). But as recent work suggests, judicial power to decide certain things, or the professional/personal disposition to do so, may be a function of more immediate experiences associated with the legal battle itself (Bakiner 2020).

The key point is quite simple: what happens during the day-to-day of an investigation matters because, intentionally or not, it conditions the outcome of cases, both by narrowing/expanding the evidentiary basis and limits of political possibility, and by altering judicial actors' commitment to guaranteeing certain results. This insight is particularly applicable to anti-corruption crusades. Crusades are different from, say, rulings on the constitutionality of a law. Crusades do not consist of a one-off decision, but of a bundle of interrelated choices in a cluster of cases. As a result, there is room for attitudinal or strategic shifts during the process. For instance, prosecutors may learn that standard techniques fail to yield strong evidence and therefore become more willing to embrace innovation. Attempts to sabotage their efforts at any given point may also feel like a personal affront, strengthening prosecutors' determination to find evidence against their detractors. In addition, because of the protracted nature of the phenomenon, decisions made at time t can alter the resources and resolve of the actors at $t + 1$. After a convincing indictment, hitherto powerful politicians may lose firepower and prosecutors may become highly popular. Finally, precisely because we are dealing with a sequenced bundle of decisions, often one that drags on, there is ample room for mistakes or other eventualities that derail the process. A lot can still go wrong even when investigators develop the necessary zeal or defendants fall from grace. This further heightens the impact of agency and short-term developments during the day-to-day of the inquiry, in addition to pre-existing environmental or attitudinal factors.

An emphasis on prosecutorial agency does not mean that possibilities are boundless. As already argued, the kind of behaviour that is likely during these investigations is structured by changes to the institutional environment in which prosecutors are trained and operate. It is also structured by more tactical organisational factors such as the creation of dedicated task forces. All that an agency-minded account encourages us to do is pay closer attention to the actual legal battle, focusing on the microcosm of seemingly minor twists and turns. While not a recipe for parsimony, this is what will ultimately allow us to explain how we get from serendipity to crusades.

Prosecutorial Zeal: Relentless and Unorthodox Investigative Tactics

Corruption investigations, as do investigations into other forms of state-sponsored macro-criminality, present a series of challenges related to how to secure evidence in hostile and information-poor environments (Anti-corruption Center 2009; Okonjo-Iweala 2018). In the absence of "smoking guns," it is simply too difficult (and too risky) to go after high-profile defendants. This is why most cases flounder (e.g., Hilti 2021). Given the inherent difficulties in investigating corruption, the key during the "moment of agency" is the adoption of a zealous prosecutorial strategy.

Zeal refers, in part, to a type of prosecutorial style, for instance, the one associated with prosecutors' role in accusatorial systems. Instead of passive "desk" prosecutors who take little to no initiative during criminal investigations, or have a limited say over the proceedings, crusades need involved "street" prosecutors. We also use "zeal" more narrowly to refer to the management of specific criminal investigations. In this sense, the term applies not so much to isolated decisions or the use of individual tools, but to an overall approach. Zeal denotes a *sustained* set of actions on the part of prosecutors, and contrasts sharply with spasmodic investigations. Apart from being *relentless*, zealous prosecutors are willing to innovate in the legal tactics they use to obtain incriminating evidence (e.g., they use new tools like plea bargain legislation and reinterpret the boundaries of what is allowed by that legislation). They also innovate when it comes to the use of extra-legal tactics, usually to strengthen their hand vis-à-vis powerful defendants (e.g., they nurture relations with journalists or court public opinion).

Because innovation is such a central aspect of a zealous investigative strategy, we associate zealousness with a certain degree of *unorthodoxy*. The tools that our prosecutors must rely on are different from those relevant for ordinary criminal cases, and therefore require investigators to abandon bureaucratic routines, step outside their comfort zones, and learn new skills, sometimes on the spot. As with any form of unorthodoxy in established fields of professional practice, zealous investigative approaches generate controversy. For some, especially anti-corruption crusaders, innovation is required to make the law bite. For others, innovation is a synonym of illegality or professionally inappropriate behaviour. These tensions between prosecutorial effectiveness and strict respect for due process are often difficult to resolve and provide the perfect ammunition for those with an interest in stopping the investigation.

Rotberg (2017: 78–79) neatly summarises the paradox at the heart of zealous investigations that seek to strengthen transparency and the rule of law while using aggressive and unorthodox legal tactics:

> The more legal provisions curtail (unfortunately) a potential defendant's civil liberties, the easier it is for the prosecutors. Indeed, in several nations that have successfully reduced corruption, prosecutors have possessed broad powers of search and seizure, have been permitted to enter hearsay evidence, and have been allowed by law and judicial practice to infer guilt merely from suspicious actions or appearances.

What is interesting about prosecutions that snowball into crusades is that investigators themselves shape these rules as they try to uncover highly elusive criminal activity. On a practical level, moving from serendipity to crusade tends to be a function of the expansive deployment of five tools – pretrial detentions, plea bargain agreements, international cooperation, criminal definitions, and public outreach – and the dexterous management of potential fallouts.

First, prosecutors must decide whether to use pretrial detentions. Grand corruption cases target well-connected defendants capable of derailing the investigation. Pretrial detentions are useful precisely because they help neutralise the firepower of such actors. In addition, pretrial detentions enable investigators to extract confessions. Despite these benefits, not all judicial actors, even those highly motivated to eradicate corruption, will be comfortable with pretrial detentions, especially if they adhere to liberal conceptions of criminal law. Legal preferences aside, the benefits of pretrial detentions are conditional on the extent to which they are used with caution, as they can quickly decant into accusations of political "revanchism" or lack of respect for due process. And instead of neutralising powerful defendants, they may up the ante in ways that awaken the beast. In other words, if not used (and explained) carefully, pretrial detentions can damage the perceived integrity of the investigation and backfire. This is particularly true if they are used strategically, for instance, to extract confessions when the evidence is still thin, because critics can convincingly cry foul. In those circumstances, investigators also risk embarrassing setbacks if judges exercise by-the-book legality control.

Second, investigators must consider using plea bargains. Existing accounts of anti-corruption investigations show that balancing carrots and sticks is what allows law enforcement agents to obtain incriminatory evidence. When dealing with such intricate criminal networks, it is very difficult to proceed without the collaboration of those involved. For some, this is a completely legitimate tactic:

exchanging benefits for information helps investigators fulfil a higher-order mission. But the use of carrots can also prove problematic even for the most committed law enforcement agents. Some may refuse to consider plea bargains on principled grounds; they want to punish the guilty, not reward them. Others may not feel comfortable building a case primarily based on confessions as opposed to hard evidence. And because in some legal cultures the very notion of prosecutorial selectivity is an alien one, plea deals are not a routine, "go to" tactic that will be used as a matter of course. Professional or moral dilemmas aside, these negotiations ought to be planned and executed with care. Trading immunity for information can be unpopular, and lead to the charge that investigators are acting unlawfully, abdicating their role, or revealing their biases (see Chapters 6 and 8). In fact, plea bargains and offers of immunity provide the perfect ammunition for those who wish to cast doubt on the impartiality and effectiveness of the inquiry.

Third, investigators need to nurture unusual relations with companies, banks, and foreign authorities that possess critical information about transnational corruption networks. Judges and prosecutors are not always well-versed in these practices, which involve venturing into the worlds of international relations and penal cooperation. Crucially, to build these new associations, investigators must do more than just issue formal information requests. Unfortunately, judicial authorities cannot directly compel foreign banks or prosecution services to hand over evidence. Instead, investigators must work behind the scenes to establish bonds of trust that make comprehensive cooperation agreements possible. This informal approach is the best way to secure productive exchanges rather than barren or sluggish responses. In addition to certain personality traits (e.g., the willingness to travel abroad), crafting agreements calls for a great deal of creativity in the interpretation of domestic law and international anti-corruption conventions to make the resulting evidence admissible in court. Any political or procedural mistake incurred while navigating these waters can prove fatal, as it may alienate crucial sources or trigger byzantine battles over admissibility. Finally, and especially when it comes to cooperation agreements with the companies responsible for bribing politicians, prosecutors must be willing to offer penal *and* economic benefits. These could range from granting immunity to top executives to lifting sanctions that limit companies' ability to do business with the state. Deals of this sort not only present similar professional dilemmas to those associated with pretrial detentions and plea bargains; they are also a legal novelty. In fact, in most Latin American countries corporate liability regimes were introduced shortly before the start of *Lava Jato* (e.g., Brazil, 2013) or as the case gained momentum (e.g., Peru, 2018). Law enforcement agents were quite literally experimenting with the law.

Fourth, investigators must decide how they conceptualise and define the crimes. Like with the other aspects of the investigative strategy, making conceptualisation choices is no small feat as even the best ones involve trade-offs.

Studies of organised crime show that the way law enforcement agents frame criminal activity affects how they prosecute it (Sergi 2016). In other words, legal categories act like lenses that produce different versions of reality and send the quest for evidence in different directions. This has implications for whether an investigation becomes a crusade. For example, accusing a business executive of false accounting may leave the investigation short of uncovering the more serious bribery schemes that lead to the dodgy accounts in the first place. In some instances, this is justified because relatively minor offences are easier to prove and allow investigators to deliver results quickly (Dervan and Podgor 2016). In addition, precisely because they are easier to prove, minor accusations may be enough of a threat to encourage defendants to cooperate. But there is always the risk that penal shortcuts create scapegoats, only scarring the tip of the iceberg. This is particularly true if investigators operate with tunnel vision, compartmentalising individual cases and not seeing them as part of a bigger network.

One of the key contributions of the international anti-corruption regime is the introduction of criminal definition templates that more precisely identify behaviour constitutive of corruption. For example, templates single out the demand, acceptance, and supply of bribes as criminally liable, thus allowing prosecutors to attack networks from different angles. If prosecutors follow this multipronged strategy, they are more likely to strike plea bargains, trace the full trajectory of the money, and thus obtain the incriminating evidence they need to transform an investigation into a crusade. But even if they opt for criminal definitions that help reveal the systemic nature of corruption, there are still important choices ahead. One is whether to select definitions that allow for longer periods of pretrial detention (but that may be harder to prove), in order to buy time or pressure defendants to confess. Another is how to interpret the evidentiary standards applicable to each criminal definition. On this front, rather than turning to the dry letter of the criminal code for answers, prosecutors must rely on precedent, doctrine, and their own jurisprudential virtuosity to come up with theories of criminal liability that ease the burden of proof for highly elusive forms of wrongdoing. As with other choices, decisions on evidentiary standards entail two types of risk. First, they invite accusations of "lawfare" because prosecutors are essentially changing the rules as they go along. Second, even if they do not invite political controversy, such choices are likely to be legally controversial, jeopardising the viability of the prosecution's case in the trial and appellate stages.

Finally, prosecutors must usually engage in public outreach efforts. Cultivating a strong presence in the media or close personal relationships with trusted journalists is a good way to enhance visibility and build defensive shields that help pre-empt or respond to political attacks. Furthermore, it provides a platform to lobby for regulatory or legislative reforms designed to facilitate the prosecution of complex crimes. Moreover, carefully timing leaks to the press or official press releases with details about the evidence that is beginning to surface can tarnish defendants' reputation and weaken them. It may also keep corrupt actors on tenterhooks. Signalling that progress is being made can, for instance, incentivise confessions. More generally, because deploying tools like pretrial detentions or plea bargains tends to generate tensions between prosecutorial effectiveness and strict respect for due process, it is crucial that investigators manage how various audiences perceive the crusade. A sound public relations strategy helps explain the need for unortho-dox methods and thus secure the support of opinion leaders, civil society organisations, and ordinary citizens. Whether these PR strategies make pros-ecutors' zeal infectious and bring together broad anti-corruption coalitions is far from guaranteed. In fact, it is a question we study in detail in Part II. The point we make here is simply that moving from serendipity to a crusade requires a type of media presence that adds an element of spectacle to the evidentiary momentum.

Well-known anti-corruption crusades reveal that the adoption of aggressive and innovative tactics is the key to success. For instance, the zeal of Nigeria's EFCC was made explicit early on in the bellicose language chosen to publicly brand its mission:

[C]urb the menace of the corruption that constitutes the cog in the wheel of progress; protect national and foreign investments in the country; imbue the spirit of hard work in the citizenry and discourage ill-gotten wealth; identify illegally acquired wealth and confiscate it (Adebanwi and Obadare 2011: 193–194).

As they put this mission into practice, investigators were indeed implacable. In fact, when the inaugural prosecutor stepped down in 2009, his successor, a lawyer aligned with establishment interests, promised to steer away from a "Gestapo approach where if you want to arrest one person, you go with 40 mobile policemen. You go to newspapers and radio, calling people thieves" (ibid.: 201–202).

Similarly, Italian judicial actors in charge of Mani Pulite innovated to produce a snowball effect. The creative use of plea bargains played a central role. Prosecutors "encouraged" cooperation "by sowing suspicions that others had already 'talked' and holding out the prospect of a period of preventive custody in prison if they remained silent … Isolation in prison forced those charged with political corruption to face a true-life 'prisoner's dilemma'" (Della Porta 2001: 14). When doing so, magistrates came up with "informal rules that afforded defendants who pleaded guilty fewer years of prison the more infor-mation they provided about the corruption network" (Manzi 2018: 200).

This strategy stemmed from the novel way in which investigators conceptu-alised the crimes. They realised that the usual focus on politicians in corruption cases did not generate incentives for private sector actors to cooperate. Business would therefore carry on as usual, with companies continuing to offer kick-backs and politicians continuing to escape prosecution due to lack of evidence. To shift the focus (and the pressure) from bribe-receivers to bribe-payers, and thus obtain confessions, magistrates had to come to see corruption as a system, as opposed to a problem of greedy or immoral politicians. They also had to find a legal path to use existing criminal legislation against companies. Key to enabling this were links to anti-corruption NGOs that promoted a new understanding of corruption as a form of macro-criminality akin to mafia activities (Manzi 2018: 176–188). In the early 1990s, some judicial actors translated these insights into legal doctrine. Most notably, Prosecutor Antonio Di Pietro came up with the notion of "dazione ambientale," depicting corruption as an "environmental condition" that makes participation of all parties, including businessmen, a matter of routine praxis, completely voluntary and criminally liable (ibid.: 189). He applied this doctrine in the wake of Chiesa's arrest. The focus of the plea deal were the names of the company managers that kept the supply of bribes going, not other politicians (ibid.: 197–198; Barbacetto et al. 2012). This tactic led to the arrest of several businessmen, thus setting in motion a chain reaction that upended Italian politics.

The judges and prosecutors involved in Brazil's *Lava Jato* applied similar tactics, many of which were without precedent. The deals signed in Curitiba courts with Yousseff and Costa allowed investigators to quickly discover a large corruption operation in which Petrobras executives received bribes to award contracts to other companies at higher than market prices. By November 2014 it was clear that at least eleven of the country's largest companies, including construction giants Odebrecht and Camargo Correa, were involved in the scheme (Moro 2018: 160). Initially, however, investigators were careful not to expand the tentacles of the inquiry too much. They wanted to maintain a narrow focus on individuals who could be tried in lower courts. This is because the law mandates that criminal cases involving certain officials in the executive and legislative branches belong to the STF. According to one commentator, every time Judge Moro interviewed someone, he would interrupt the testimony if he thought the witness was about to implicate a "deputy, minister or senator" (Moreira Leite 2015: 31).

As prosecutors started to make their way up the chain of command, this strategy became untenable. In fact, in March 2015 Chief Prosecutor Janot asked the STF to investigate forty-eight elected politicians "including the sitting speakers of both the House and the Senate, as well as long-time leaders of various political parties" (Da Ros and Taylor 2022b: 252). The following year, Sergio Machado, former Transpetro executive, signed a plea deal that further stretched the remit of the case, implicating the then president Michel Temer (PMDB), sitting and former federal legislators from half a dozen parties, and the deputy governor of Rio de Janeiro (Chemin 2017: 104–105). Following this confession, the STF appropriated some lines of inquiry and ordered the remaining cases to be divided between Curitiba, Rio de Janeiro, and São Paulo.[15]

---

[15] The Rio de Janeiro and São Paulo legs started in July and August 2015, respectively.

There were several driving forces behind this snowball effect. First, aware of the risk of backlash, investigators were determined to keep the political class on tenterhooks, applying an aggressive strategy that left little time for them to plan effective responses. A key pillar of this "shock and awe" approach was to make sure every move received ample media coverage. As Moro wrote with reference to Mani Pulite:

> The publicity given to the investigations had the salutary effect of alerting those under investigation about the growing mass of information in the hands of the magistrates, favouring new confessions … More importantly, it guaranteed public support for legal actions, preventing public officials from obstructing the work of the magistrates (2004: 59, our translation).

While the focus on public relations was justified in the name of transparency, it sometimes dovetailed with illegality and therefore proved rather controversial. Never more so than when Moro leaked the recordings of a conversation between President Dilma Rousseff and her predecessor Lula Da Silva, at a time when Rousseff planned to appoint Da Silva as her chief of staff. The former president was being investigated in Curitiba, so his prospective appointment meant his case would need to be surrendered to the STF. The release of the wiretaps triggered widespread criticism, not only because it stank of political opportunism, but also because the conversation was recorded after the warrant had expired. While the move did block Lula's appointment, it lent credence to the narrative that *Lava Jato* was a conspiracy against the Workers' Party.

The media strategy also involved dividing the operation into what the investigators called "phases." Each new phase was given a catchy name to maximise publicity, and consisted of a new wave of arrests, plea bargains, and indictments that captured the public's imagination. As Figure 2.2 shows, investigators in Curitiba and Rio de Janeiro, where the two largest arms of *Lava Jato* unfolded, were relentless. During the period covered by the analysis, there was a new phase (and often more than one) every month. Prosecutors also turned *Lava Jato* into a broader anti-corruption campaign with the goal of further galvanising public opinion and putting pressure on defendants. For example, they proposed a legislative package consisting of "10 measures against corruption." The campaign collected more than two million signatures.[16]

Another force driving the snowball effect were the 256 plea bargains and 22 corporate leniency agreements struck between 2014 and 2020. In Moro's assessment of Mani Pulite, Milanese prosecutors relied heavily on these tools because they rightly concluded that "corruption involves someone who pays and someone who gets paid; if both shut up, we won't ever find out." For him this was completely legitimate, even if it required a high degree of punitive selectivity: luring confessions "is in fact collaborating with the law and with the

---

[16] Julia Affonso, Mateus Coutinho, and Ricardo Brandt, "Completo descomprometimento com o combate à corrupção, diz procuradora," *O Estado de S. Paulo* (30 November 2016).

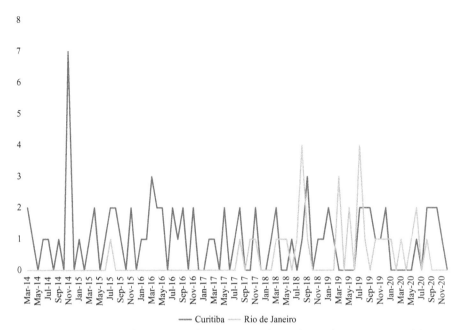

FIGURE 2.2 Number of *Lava Jato* phases in Curitiba and Rio de Janeiro (monthly).
Source: Authors' dataset based on information published by Brazil's *Ministério Público Federal*.
Data on phases is not available for São Paulo

application of the laws of a country" (Moro 2004: 58). As we saw previously, Brazilian legislation on this front is new, meaning that investigators had to proceed with caution to make sure these deals survived judicial scrutiny.[17] In fact, they often had to defend the strategy. Prosecutor Dellagnol, for example, reminded critics that deals were necessary and not signed on a whim:

> If we had not done any collaboration, probably all we would know would be the receipt of bribes by Paulo Roberto Costa, an amount lower than R$ 100 million. Today we have proven bribes in the billions and have already recovered R$500 million. The prosecutor's office is open to agreements. However, most of the companies that came to us either did not want to deliver new facts or were not willing to pay a reasonable sum in compensation.[18]

The investigative effort also relied heavily (and relentlessly) on sticks, particularly searches, *conduçoes coercitivas*, and pretrial detentions (Figure 2.3). As Moro puts it, "given the presumption of innocence, pretrial detentions should be exceptional; but the extraordinary nature of systemic corruption

[17] High courts green-lighted 140 of the deals struck in Curitiba.
[18] Mario C. Carvalho, "Procurador da *Lava Jato* quer revisão de leis," *Folha de S. Paulo* (15 March 2015).

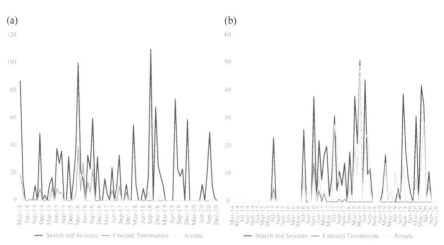

(a)   (b)

FIGURE 2.3 Arrests, *conduções coercitivas*, and searches in Curitiba and Rio de Janeiro (monthly). (a) Curitiba; (b) Rio de Janeiro.
Source: Authors' dataset based on information published by Brazil's *Ministério Público Federal*

demands strong and urgent measures by criminal justice to break the vicious circle" (2018: 164). This ruthless approach, however, drew criticism as it potentially violated due process. Some accused *Lava Jato* of using pretrial detentions to pressure defendants. These objections were not without merit. Investigators usually timed detentions with search operations that provided them with the necessary evidence to interrogate (and negotiate with) defendants. Prosecutors countered with the claim that the courts scrutinised their actions and rejected the vast majority of habeas corpus writs filed by defence lawyers (372 were filed between 2014 and 2019). Even more controversial was the use of *conduções coercitivas* to compel individuals to appear in court to answer questions against their will and often without time to prepare. When the STF declared the tactic unconstitutional in 2018, "Justice Toffoli referred to coercive questioning ... as a 'creative interpretative move' that was not supported by the law ... Justice Mendes, in turn, argued that the 'ingenious interpretation' was built on a fallacy that it was less intrusive than temporary or preventive detention" (Mota-Prado and Rodriguez-Machado forthcoming). As Figure 2.3 shows, the measure was not used after 2018, but the STF decision spoke volumes about the experimental nature of some aspects of *Lava Jato*'s strategy.

One final aspect of this aggressive approach was the creative use of criminal definitions and evidentiary standards to justify convictions. The key challenge in most corruption cases is to find evidence of each aspect of the bribing process, including the intention of both parties to exchange benefits. Most notably, in his ruling against former president Da Silva, Moro circumvented these difficulties by lowering the standard of proof. He relied on the *Mensalão* precedent to argue he did not need to demonstrate that the defendant had indeed given the company something in return for the bribe. As Mota-Prado and Rodriguez-Machado (forthcoming) explain in detail, Moro went further than the STF's decision in *Mensalão* because here "there was no gift but mere indicia that construction companies were planning to give him [Lula] a beach condo."[19] Similarly, in other cases the courts imported the doctrine of "wilful blindness" from US and Spanish jurisprudence to conclude that there is criminal liability when a public official had the opportunity to scrutinise potentially illegal conduct by third parties but chose not to. In other words, it is not necessary to prove that the defendant had knowledge of the crime or participated in it. While these decisions were usually confirmed on appeal, they still elicited controversy (see below). Critics point out that rather than applying the law, judges were creating law in an ad hoc manner, thus violating defendants' due process rights (ibid.).

The Attitudinal and Organisational Foundations of Zeal

Why do prosecutors choose to be relentless and unorthodox? Our answer is in part attitudinal, but we also look at how small group dynamics within prosecutorial task forces reinforce commitments and facilitate the efficient deployment of the anti-corruption toolkit.

The willingness to make use of aggressive tactics, innovate, and accept risk reflects specific professional role conceptions and personality traits. As Rotberg (2017: 83) puts it, when it comes to crusades "legal frameworks are less important ... than are the attitudes of those who administer and utilize those instruments." What our law enforcement agents have in common, apart from being daring and happy to break the mould, is a higher-order commitment to fighting corruption. One pillar of this worldview is a negative perception of politicians as inherently corrupt, and of criminal justice institutions as disruptors of rotten political ecosystems. This does not mean they are impartial or rule-abiding, and most certainly does not turn them into saints. Quite the contrary: another pillar of their worldview is the belief that law enforcers have the responsibility to ensure the law bites, whatever it takes. This not only implies that prosecutors think they ought to go the extra mile to apply existing laws; they also maintain that legal formalisms (and occasionally the law itself) should not stand in the way of punishment.

The Brazilian case illustrates both dimensions of this mantra. A recurrent theme in the public statements of *Lava Jato* judges and prosecutors is the characterisation of corruption as a system in which politicians, bureaucrats, and business collude to defraud the public. This is an extreme expression of the ideology that took root among some Brazilian prosecutors after the

---

[19] See footnote 20 for a summary of the *Mensalão* case.

1988 constitutional reform. As we noted earlier, Arantes (2011) refers to this ideology as "political voluntarism." For example, Prosecutor Dellagnol described the object of the investigation as "a multi-party phenomenon, which corroborates the widely held view that our politics is in the midst of a moral crisis."[20] Elsewhere, he stressed the need for "systemic changes in organizational structures," and argued that corruption "must be punished more firmly than homicide because it kills many people. It also steals schools, running water, medicine and the safety of millions."[21] Furthermore, Dellagnol invoked medical metaphors to describe corruption as a metastasising cancer,[22] and invoked religious rhetoric (he is a committed evangelical) to ascertain that "God is clearing the way for change."[23]

If this is the nature of the beast, taming it requires extraordinary efforts; prosecutorial business as usual will not cut it. This is why *Lava Jato* officers pushed for legislative reforms that would have made it easier to punish corruption. For them, allowing for more effective investigations was an obvious starting point to try to disrupt a corrupt ecosystem. As Dellagnol puts it, "the widespread perception that corrupt people are not punished [...] due to [...] 'loopholes in the law,' is certainly one of the main conditions that favour corruption."[24] But responsibility for closing these loopholes lies not only with legislators; it is also legitimate for judges and prosecutors to look for ways to interpret existing regulations in ways that facilitate the anti-corruption struggle. Most of the controversial innovations described above were in fact justified with reference to this duty. For some observers, this type of zealousness produces "a 'political grammar' that is closer to illiberalism" because it strips defendants of their rights and arbitrarily changes the rules of the game (de Sa e Silva 2020: 4). For those in charge of *Lava Jato*, by contrast, "special investigative methods," "strong judicial measures," and "exceptional remedies" are necessary to "break a vicious cycle."[25] Judge Marcelo Bertas refused to accept the view that *Lava Jato* amounted to a form of "judicial dictatorship": "The dictatorship that we work for and defend is the one of honesty."[26] Dellagnol

---

[20] Ibid.

[21] Fausto Macedo and Ricardo Brandt, "'Maior parte das acusações ainda Virá,' diz procurador," *O Estado de São Paulo* (16 March 2015).

[22] "Corrupção no país está em metástase, diz procurador da *Lava Jato*," *Uol Noticias* (28 July 2015); Rafael Moraes Moura, "*Lava Jato* trata de um câncer, mas sistema brasileiro favorece a corrupção, diz Dallagnol," *O Estado de São Paulo* (10 August 2015).

[23] "Dallagnol: A Lava-Jato trouxe esperança, mas precisamos da sua ajuda," *O Globo* (28 July 2015).

[24] Fausto Macedo and Ricardo Brandt, "'Maior parte das acusações ainda virá,' diz procurador," *O Estado de São Paulo* (16 March 2015).

[25] Cleide Carvalho, "Moro defende remédios excepcionais no combate à corrupção sistêmica," *O Globo* (29 September 2016).

[26] Paula Bianchi, "Juiz da *Lava Jato* no Rio nega 'ditadura do Judiciário' e celebra 'cruzada contra corrupção," *Uol* (12 June 2017).

went further, advancing a doctrinal case for innovation rather than a conse-quentialist vindication of legal breaches.[27] He attacked "hipergarantismo," a liberal conception of criminal law that prioritises defendants' rights (see also Moro 2004: 61). In his view, this legal philosophy is highly problematic when applied to corruption because it invariably leads to impunity. Instead, Dellagnol advocates a "garantismo integral," that is, a more balanced approach to due process that respects both defendant rights and the "rights of society" to eradicate corruption.

It is unlikely that this zealousness simply predates the investigation as the mere product of socialisation under changing institutional environments and international anti-corruption scripts. We think it is also fuelled by discovery, enemy fire, and group work *during* the inquiry. In other words, investigators become more committed as they become more invested in the case. Moreover, one thing are verbal diatribes against the political class, and another is the actual use of aggressive prosecutorial tools in a sustained fashion. This requires planning and smart implementation. We therefore argue that beyond attitu-dinal factors, zeal is also a function of the organisational characteristics of the investigative effort. The kind of creativity and resolve that propels the case forward is partly the product of the establishment of *task forces* in which prosecutors operate as a team. The decision to assign the case to a specialised task force, as opposed to leaving different aspects of the inquiry in the hands of isolated or ordinary prosecutors, triggers productive synergies: it reinforces commitments and unleashes forces of innovation and mutual protection. In the absence of a task force, the case is more likely to stall.[28]

As we discussed in earlier sections, one of the consequences of the various streams of institutional change since the 1980s is the specialisation of cohorts of prosecutors in various forms of macro-criminality. Specialisation creates what Metz-McDonnell (2017) calls "interstitial bureaucracy," that is, islands of efficiency and motivation in otherwise deficient organisations. Via different

---

[27] Luis Carvalho, "'É preciso um garantismo integral,' diz procurador Deltan Dallagnol," *Estadão* (5 February 2017).

[28] *Watergate* is a good example of how teamwork can be commitment-reinforcing, and how task forces can build protective shields. The first special prosecutor appointed to investigate the scandal, Archibald Cox, quickly became Nixon's worst nightmare. The White House went to great lengths to try to fire him. Achieving that goal was certainly not easy, not least because of the terrible optics of seeking to dismantle a dedicated task force. When this finally happened on the so-called Saturday Night Massacre, it was the result of an extremely blunt political man-oeuvre that cost the president a great deal. Weakened, but unrelenting, Nixon replaced Cox with Leon Jaworski, a Texas lawyer thought to be more reliable. But as soon as Jaworski was exposed to the evidence contained in the infamous White House tapes and the pressure of the strongly committed junior prosecutors who had been working on the case for a long time, the new special prosecutor turned against Nixon. It helped that Jaworksi felt offended and upset by the adminis-tration's stalling tactics. Pushing the case forward became a personal matter for him. Jaworksi subsequently showed strong determination to force Nixon to surrender additional tapes, includ-ing the one containing the well-known "smoking gun" that destroyed his presidency.

informal tactics of boundary control, these units avoid the pathologies dominant in the wider environment and cultivate their own ethos. The task force model takes this form of bureaucratic differentiation to the next level. It certainly benefits form pre-existing specialised units as it is easier to recruit suitable personnel. But full-time dedication to a specific case enhances the benefits of "interstitiality" in important ways.

The literature on group dynamics in economics and psychology is useful to think theoretically about the role of task forces. When it comes to improving performance during complex tasks, groups have a key advantage over individual decision-makers: they are able to pool together diverse viewpoints and resources (Levine and Moreland 1998; Wittenbaum and Moreland 2008). This is similar to the effects of firm clustering on innovation. Co-location of R&D and manufacturing, for example, facilitates knowledge production and sharing (Buciuni and Finotto 2016). In groups of professionals, co-location also improves levels of "tacit knowledge," that is, the skills that individuals learn inadvertently by working alongside one another (Iversen and Soskice 2019). There are additional benefits if groups are relatively small. While small groups can be plagued with well-known decision-making pathologies such as "groupthink" (Janis 1982), low internal diversity reduces the probability of rifts or inaction. Moreover, smaller groups are better able to solve coordination problems and avoid free riding. This is because such groups can ensure higher levels of individual member engagement (Patterson and Schaeffer 1977), as well as lower levels of status differentiation, which can in turn lead to greater commitment (Diehl and Stroebe 1987; Widmeyer et al. 1990; Spink and Carron 1992). In this sense, smaller groups are usually more cohesive, acquiring the proprieties of discrete entities (Forsyth 2014). While cohesion often depends on the presence of good leadership (Piper et al. 1983; Smith 2003), small groups tend to be better at deploying socialisation tactics to engineer cohesion and propagate a collective ethos (Levine et al. 2001).

It is not hard to see how these insights apply to crusades. First, if corruption is a systemic problem, it needs to be investigated as a system. Detecting macrocriminality is only possible when information about different actors is pooled together and investigators take a comprehensive look at the overall network. Compartmentalising cases derails the prosecutorial effort because it blocks the transfer of evidence and leads investigators to adopt a tunnel vision approach. After "the moment of serendipity," when prosecutors start pulling from the thread, the lines of inquiry suddenly multiply. Having a dedicated group not only guarantees greater efficiency and celerity in processing this new evidence, but also generates evidentiary economies of scale. Even if the crimes perpetrated by different actors are technically distinct, they tend to be part of one single structure of criminal activity. This means that evidence from one case is useful to solve others.

Second, task forces are favourable environments for the kind of deliberation conducive to adaptation and innovation. Having professionals with diverse backgrounds working together brings to the table different personalities, skills, and types of expertise, opening the door to unexpected alchemies. For example, not all prosecutors have the charisma required to become a media darling and give the task force a friendly face on television. Similarly, if the corruption scheme extends across the country, it helps to have prosecutors with knowledge of territorially based criminal networks. The presence of other skills and traits across members, including connections to certain social circles, proficiency in foreign languages, or experience with different types of criminality may also prove handy, for example, to build rapport with witnesses, negotiate with foreign authorities, or prosecute different aspects of the case. Finally, when it comes to jurisprudential innovation, new ideas can be refined as part of a group effort. And because these ideas do not emerge from the mind of a single individual, unorthodoxy can appear less idiosyncratic.

Third, creating a task force facilitates the development of a collective identity that endows members with the sense of purpose required to investigate elusive corruption crimes perpetrated by powerful defendants. This is why the international community has been so adamant to diffuse the "anti-corruption commission model." As Popova and Post (2018: 236) put it, "an anti-corruption agency sees the task as its *raison d'être* and its employees can be socialized into a stronger commitment to the anti-corruption cause." This is also true for ad hoc task forces dedicated to a single case like *Lava Jato*. Ordinary prosecutors all of a sudden become anti-corruption prosecutors with a very clear mission. As the group becomes more cohesive and endures attacks, this commitment likely extends to most members. This is important because the investigation thus becomes less dependent on the zeal of any particular individual.

Fourth, in addition to multiplying zeal and facilitating innovation, task forces have defensive advantages. There is strength in numbers when it comes to protecting a controversial investigation both from powerful defendants and superior prosecutors whose interests might be threatened by the investigation or who disagree with the use of unorthodox tactics. Cohesive task forces are better equipped to construct a brand of their own and a meta-narrative explaining their goals and methods. This heightens their visibility and prestige among certain sectors of the public, thus increasing the costs if politicians try to disband them. While task force termination is always a latent possibility, especially for ad hoc teams, having to explain the decision to abort an initiative with a clearly defined anti-corruption mandate can put judicial and political leaders in an awkward position, allowing rank-and-file investigators to fight back. Moreover, coordinating public relations strategies to disseminate information about how the case is progressing or respond to backlash is much easier under the umbrella of a task force. This is important not just to build momentum but also to champion broader causes that may facilitate the prosecutorial effort, such as legislative reform packages. Finally, task forces lower the risk of *kompromat*, making it harder (or perhaps unthinkable) for individual members to relent in the face of undue pressures. This can be achieved via socialisation and internal surveillance. And if some members do succumb to temptation, the presence of other committed investigators means the case does not have to stop entirely.

Italian judges and prosecutors learnt the importance of teamwork during anti-mafia and terrorism investigations in the 1970s. In a lecture delivered in 1982, two veteran judges summarised the key lessons they took from this experience. On task forces, they wrote:

[J]udicial inquiries of immense proportions ... can be managed with a certain agility if they are fragmented and guided with rigorous coordination by a pool of investigative magistrates equally distributed in the regions most affected by the phenomenon and operating in close functional relationship with specialized judicial police units (Falcone and Turone [1982] 2015: 129).

Apart from allowing investigators to combine resources and coordinate decisions on related cases, teamwork served more mundane purposes. In particular, given the latent risk of assassination, it ensured that if any one magistrate was murdered, the case would not die with her. Manzi (2018: 121–124) brilliantly describes the origins of this "egalitarian judicial governance" model in Turin, as well as its diffusion to other jurisdictions, in particular Milan, where it played a critical role in Mani Pulite.

Brazilian judges and prosecutors took note of this important aspect of the Italian case. In fact, after studying Mani Pulite and reflecting on his own experience during *Lava Jato*, Judge Moro listed task forces as the first of a series of prosecutorial tactics required to transform investigations into crusades (2018: 166). Curitiba was not a stranger to this type of prosecutorial specialisation, being one of the first jurisdictions in the country to create a white-collar crime unit within the local *Ministério Público* in 1992. When *Lava Jato* took off, Chief Prosecutor Janot followed this tradition, appointing a special task force in each state where *Lava Jato* had ramifications, as well as one dedicated to cases litigated before the STF. According to Da Ros and Taylor (2022b: 249), "as of the end of 2019, a total of fifty-nine prosecutors – 5.1% percent of federal prosecutors nationwide – were participating in different task forces linked to Lava Jato."

Reflecting on the reasons why *Lava Jato* gained momentum, Prosecutor Dellagnol highlights the importance of expertise and coordination:

The *Lava Jato* case is the product of a series of factors that were concatenated in an extraordinary way and produced a positive result. Among these factors are the experience and synergy of the teams from the Public Ministry, the Police and the Internal Revenue Service ... , the responsible handling of cooperation agreements by professionals who have accumulated knowledge in this matter ... , the creation of the *Lava Jato* Task Force by the Attorney General ... There are so many random circumstances that many would call it a fluke, a conspiracy of the universe. Because of my Christian worldview, I believe that God … gives us a unique historic opportunity to bring about structural change.[29]

As we shall see in the next section, however, while coordination among task force members helped engineer momentum, other forms of coordination, especially between the Curitiba prosecutorial team and Judge Moro, proved more problematic. In that case, cooperation morphed into collusion, providing strong grounds for defendants to successfully challenge the legality of the inquiry.

***

An aggressive, relentless, and unorthodox prosecutorial strategy is the key to unleashing the snowball effect. Task forces make the effective deployment of this modus operandi more likely. In fact, when looking at the non-Brazilian chapters of *Lava Jato* later in the book, we will see that the presence or absence of specialised teams explains why some investigations expanded and others stalled.

Task forces tend to be the product of a decision made in the face of mounting evidence that a larger than usual case is looming. The move usually responds to practical considerations (e.g., the need to pursue multiple lines of inquiry), but also to the conviction that the investigation constitutes a priority for the prosecution services. The willingness of a country's chief prosecutor to support the anti-corruption cause is therefore critical.[30] Institutional factors also affect the ease with which task forces can be created. For example, chief prosecutors that enjoy greater autonomy are better positioned to determine their priorities. Furthermore, in fully accusatorial systems the investigation is completely in the hands of the prosecution services, which means there is more flexibility to decide how to proceed. Where judges still have a say over the investigative phase, forming task forces is harder because cases are assigned to judges depending on jurisdictional criteria, and prosecutors have no option but to work with them.

We do not maintain that every decision taken by these task forces is necessary for the success of the anti-corruption push. In fact, some decisions implemented to trigger the snowball effect can backfire and jeopardise momentum. After all, an unorthodox strategy is bound to cause controversies along the way, for example, among legal experts and commentators. Moreover, moving from relatively weak defendants to those higher up in the chain of command implies exposing the crusade to ever more effective forms of retaliation. Our argument is simply that the adoption of a zealous investigative approach that combines, in a sustained fashion, various legal and extra-legal elements is

---

[29] "Procurador diz que maior parte das acusações na *Lava Jato* ainda virá," *Amazonas Atual* (15 March 2015).

[30] The Italian case is perhaps an exception because the decision to work as a team did not come from the top. It was something local judicial bosses chose to do. This is why the move triggered byzantine legal discussions. See Manzi (2018: 124).

critical for a case to gain momentum following the "moment of serendipity," and for it to maintain that momentum and continue expanding its remit further down the line. Without this resoluteness and creativity, corruption cases involving transnational criminal networks and high-flying defendants are most likely dead upon arrival.

There are a host of reasons why prosecutors may take decisions that ultimately prove counterproductive, even when the overall approach is adequate. Investigators sometimes become convinced that their tactics, however unorthodox, ought to be perfectly acceptable to anyone who is genuinely interested in fighting corruption, and therefore mistakenly assume there are no risks in pursuing daring measures. In addition, prosecutors sometimes read too much into earlier victories, or fail to build broad support coalitions in the aftermath of those victories, miscalculating their strength as they move on to more resourceful defendants. Finally, they often have no choice but to try their luck against higher profile targets because that is what the evidence dictates. All of this means that zeal is inherently risky, making prosecutors quite vulnerable to their own fallibility and biases, and ultimately makes it difficult to ensure the sustainability of the crusade.

THE MOMENT OF BACKLASH

We began this chapter with the observation that anti-corruption crusades should be seen as the product of autonomous processes within the prosecution services, rather than a mere reflection of extra-judicial power struggles or "lawfare." Put differently, politicians and party politics do not fully dictate who prosecutors go after; it is institutional change coupled with a dose of good luck and astute investigative decisions that mostly explain why an ordinary criminal investigation snowballs into an extraordinary anti-corruption crusade.

Having said this, it is important to recognise that politicians do play a role in the story. The snowball effect characteristic of crusades is always conditioned by their reactions, which include attempts to pass legislation that makes the criminalisation of corruption harder to pursue or of little consequence, and together with their allies in senior prosecutorial/judicial roles, attempts to remove zealous prosecutors. These forms of backlash are obviously a result of the crusade becoming a real threat, but they are also a factor that moderates how big the snowball gets and how far it goes. For example, if backlash takes the form of ploys to dismantle task forces, it can have direct implications for whether a crusade survives to uncover more evidence.

Defendants are rarely passive bystanders. They do not just let prosecutors collapse their governments, sully their reputations, or demolish their electoral chances. Quite the contrary: in addition to defending themselves in court, they resort to ruthless tactics to delegitimise, block, or dismantle the investigative effort. This is also true for politicians who are not directly targeted. To be sure, they may rejoice at the sight of their rivals parading through the courtroom and may even be able to benefit politically from prosecutions. More often than not, however, they are also worried that the crusade will eventually come to haunt them. If a seemingly minor revelation could grow exponentially to become an epic affront to establishment interests, what guarantees that prosecutors will not expand the remit of the inquiry even further and reach new shores? This means that even after a crusade has inflicted damage on the establishment – weakening or destroying hitherto powerful actors – the list of enemies is never fully exhausted.

Prosecutorial unorthodoxy further complicates the picture because it often stands in tension with strict standards of legality. As a result, the very nature of these tactics helps legitimise backlash. First, and most immediately, aggressive and innovative prosecutorial manoeuvres give defendants the arguments they need to cry foul. The "lawfare" narrative is never more credible than when prosecutors toy with legal orthodoxy. Under those circumstances, the line between due process and farce becomes dangerously blurry. The claim that the investigation amounts to a noble effort to strengthen the rule of law thus clashes against counterclaims that the rule of law is being sacrificed in the altar of putative corruption and that prosecutions are driven by ulterior motives and obscure forces. Second, unorthodoxy makes the sustainability of the snowball effect quite uncertain. When prosecutors use pretrial detentions strategically or champion novel interpretations of evidentiary standards, they often do so without the backing of a robust corpus of precedent or doctrine. The case is consequently vulnerable to deadly setbacks when scrutinised by senior prosecutors and judges in the appellate stages. More worryingly, such tactics may lead chief prosecutors to conclude that the task force has gone too far and decide to terminate it. These concerns could be a pretext to protect political allies and patrons, or stem from a genuine worry about the implications of overzealousness. Third, because at the heart of the crusader's manual is the use of carrots to obtain confessions, prosecutors often have a hard time justifying selectivity and dodging accusations of ineffectiveness and bias. These charges are particularly problematic when coming from independent journalists or the mass public, crucial allies in the face of political backlash. In other words, the tactics that make crusades possible risk poking the beehive too harshly, but also risk not quenching the punitive thirst of key constituencies decisively enough to secure their permanent support.

Balancing prudence and zeal so that no one is sufficiently angry or disappointed can become an impossible game. Indeed, the momentum behind the crusades reviewed in this chapter dwindled because of this tension. Nigeria's President Obasanjo, who created the EFCC, left power in 2007. The coalition that supported Obasanjo's successor included figures who had been targets of the anti-corruption effort and therefore wanted to take the agency down. Undeterred by the changing political environment, in December 2007 prosecutors arrested one of these disgruntled actors. A few weeks later, the lead prosecutor was removed from his post and replaced with someone closer to the regime. As we saw earlier, the new boss promised to put an end to the EFCC's "Gestapo approach," effectively transforming it into a paper tiger. Reflecting on the unusually aggressive approach of the original EFCC, some of its members reportedly regretted "strategic choices" that were necessary to succeed in an "ocean of corruption," but which created a "moral platform for rogues" (Adebanwi and Obadare 2011: 201).

Backlash was similarly fierce in Italy. According to Della Porta (2001: 10) "corrupt politicians often used their informal contacts in the senior ranks of the judiciary to intimidate those magistrates who pierced the circle of political illegality." Magistrates suffered more overt forms of backlash after 1994, when Italian voters repudiated establishment parties and ushered in a new political era dominated by media mogul and hitherto outsider Silvio Berlusconi (Chong et al. 2010). Soon after taking office, Berlusconi, who also became the target of corruption investigations, promoted acts of intimidation against Milanese judicial authorities and pushed to reform plea bargain legislation and pretrial detention rules with the goal of weakening prosecutorial zeal (Della Porta 2001: 7). Judges' professional associations and public opinion questioned these measures, some of which never came into effect. The political establishment was nevertheless determined to eliminate the judicial threat. To this end, Berlusconi accused judges of being biased against the right ("red judges"). This rhetoric inspired laws that constrained the anti-corruption toolkit, including restrictions on the admissibility of evidence obtained abroad, the strengthening of parliament's gate-keeping role in investigations against certain authorities, and shorter statutes of limitations for corruption crimes (Vannucci 2009: 254–255). As Della Porta and Vannucci (2007: 844) put it, "this 'revolution of the judges' appears to have been succeeded by a 'counter-revolution' of the political class."

Brazil's *Lava Jato* experienced a similar pattern of attacks. In his 2004 analysis of Mani Pulite, Judge Moro had already warned that "it is naïve to think that effective criminal prosecutions against powerful figures such as government officials or businessmen can be conducted normally, without reactions" (2004: 57, our translation). Moro was on to something. Two failed congressional inquiries launched in 2014 and 2015 into the crimes perpetrated within Petrobras were an early sign that the establishment was willing to go to great lengths to protect itself (Limongi 2017). Attacks intensified after Dilma Rousseff's impeachment in 2016.[31] On the legislative front, for example, the Senate approved a bill that criminalised "abuses of power" by prosecutors, explicitly targeting some of the tactics used during *Lava Jato*. A watered-down version finally passed the lower chamber in 2019 (Law 1389/2019), putting a Damocles' sword over the head of zealous investigators. Similarly, between

---

[31] The decision to impeach President Rousseff was partly taken when some allies realised she was proving unable to stop *Lava Jato*. Rousseff's successor, Michel Temer, was informally mandated with finishing the job (Limongi 2017; Da Ros and Taylor 2022b).

2016 and 2017, during a flurry of leniency agreements that put politicians from all parties on high alert, Congress debated, and on occasion approved, bills that sought to decriminalise corruption (Chemin 2017). Importantly, during this period legislators showed no interest in approving the reform package that the *Lava Jato* task force campaigned for.

On the judicial front, the STF proved to be an unreliable ally. Given the partisan background of some justices, and the court's historic inclination to cooperate with the other branches on policy (Kapiszewski 2012), its ultimate alignment with establishment interests is little surprising. Some instances of prosecutorial overreach did not help either. To be sure, during the initial years of *Lava Jato*, the STF issued rulings that favoured the inquiry. For example, a 2015 decision backed prosecutors' investigative prerogatives. The following year, the STF ruled that convictions could be enforced before they were confirmed on appeal. This meant, for instance, that Moro's judgments alone could send someone to prison, allowing the *Lava Jato* task force to show palpable results relatively quickly. It also strengthened prosecutors' hand during plea bargain negotiations because it made punitive threats more credible.

But the love affair between the STF and *Lava Jato* would not last. In the wake of Lula's indictment in 2016, for example, Justice Dias Toffoli warned that the judiciary risked becoming a dangerous tutelary force within the democratic system, akin to the military in the 1960s:

> If you criminalise politics and think that the judicial system will solve the problems of the Brazilian nation with moralism, ... destroying the Brazilian nation and the political class ... [i]s it the judicial system the one that will save the Brazilian nation?[32]

In line with this scepticism about the merits of *Lava Jato*, in 2019 the STF reversed the 2015 decision that allowed the enforcement of convictions before the end of the appeals process. Another 2019 ruling annulled a conviction against a former Petrobras president, arguing that Moro's interpretation of plea bargain legislation breached due process.[33] Since lower courts applied Moro's doctrine widely, the STF ruling puts other convictions in jeopardy. Finally, apart from making it harder for prosecutors and lower court judges to investigate and punish wrongdoing, the high court has largely dragged its feet when it comes to the *Lava Jato*-related cases over which it has original jurisdiction. This means that several prominent figures have been largely safe.

Lava Jato judges and prosecutors made strategic choices (mistakes?) that further emboldened their opponents. Most notably, investigators expended valuable political capital, first when they released the famous wiretaps of Rousseff's conversations with Lula to pre-empt what they thought was yet

---

[32] "Toffoli: 'Judiciário pode cometer o mesmo erro de militares em 1964'," *O Globo* (16 September 2016).

[33] Felipe Bächtold, "Decisão do STF pode anular quase todas as sentenças da *Lava Jato*, diz força-tarefa," *Folha de São Paulo* (19 August 2019).

another obstructionist manoeuvre, and also during the onslaught that followed the presentation of the thin evidence used to charge the former president. The narrative associating *Lava Jato* to a conspiracy against the Workers' Part received another boost in 2018 after Moro accepted the position of minister of justice in President Bolsonaro's inaugural cabinet. His departure deprived the case of a zealous, committed judge with high levels of name recognition and prestige, and cast additional doubt on the impartiality of the affair. Compounding things, a few months into Moro's ministerial adventure *The Intercept* published WhatsApp conversations between the then judge and the prosecutors. Excerpts from these exchanges, which continued to surface throughout 2020 and 2021, revealed that the prosecutors did not just coordinate among themselves but also with the judge, violating due process.[34] As we shall see below, President Lula took this complaint to court and fatally wounded the entire *Lava Jato* operation.

Bolsonaro reached the presidency in 2018 riding on the coattails of *Lava Jato*. By appointing Moro as minister of justice, he signalled his intention to become the investigation's strongest ally. This, however, proved to be a mirage. The new president would go to great lengths to try to obstruct corruption investigations against family members, triggering clashes with Moro, who eventually resigned in 2020. Furthermore, Bolsonaro promoted Augusto Aras to the position of chief prosecutor. In doing so, he broke with a long-standing tradition that saw presidents since 2003 select their nominees for the role from a list of candidates submitted by senior federal prosecutors. Aras reciprocated by moving decisively against *Lava Jato*. After withstanding multiple personal attacks, Prosecutor Dellagnol resigned. The members of the São Paulo task force followed suit. On the back of these developments, Bolsonaro declared that "*Lava Jato* is dead."

Facing these changes in the political environment and in the leadership of the prosecution services, deprived of its most committed members, and marred by controversies stemming from an aggressive (and dubiously legal) strategy, at the time of writing Brazil's *Lava Jato* faces a very uncertain future.[35] For instance, the STF issued a decision in March 2021 annulling Moro's investigation against Lula. The court argued that the former Curitiba judge had overstepped the limits of his jurisdiction. Two weeks later, the court voted in favour of a motion filed by Lula's lawyers to declare Moro "partial." The former president relied on *The Intercept's* exposé to accuse the judge of due process violations.[36] By finding fault in the way Moro coordinated with the prosecutors, the STF's

[34] Andrew Fishman et al., "Breach of Ethics," *The Intercept* (9 June 2019).
[35] Celso Rocha, "How *Lava Jato* Died – And What Comes Next," *Americas Quarterly* (15 October 2020).
[36] "Defesa de Lula: Processos em que Moro atuou devem ser anulados desde investigacão," *JOTA* (9 March 2021).

ruling implies the case against Lula has to be reinvestigated in another jurisdiction.[37] Other lines of inquiry may follow the same path.

These examples of the "moment of backlash" make the decision to engage in anti-corruption efforts quite puzzling. Why take on the establishment if the consequences can be so dire and results so uncertain? Institutional changes are important because they nurture a different kind of prosecutor, one that is endowed with a role conception and tools that improve the odds when taking on white-collar criminals. As the most recent developments in Brazil show, however, the insulation afforded by these reforms is not bullet proof. Institutional change never amounts to a complete overhaul, meaning that there are still strong incentives that conspire against risk-taking by the rank-and-file. To understand why prosecutors go the extra mile, we must therefore also pay attention to individual attitudes and the internal dynamics of task forces, which cement resolve, facilitate innovation, and sometimes provide (temporary) protection. This is the principal lesson that emerges from "the moment of agency."

Backlash against anti-corruption crusades renders the snowball effect responsible for expanding the remit of the investigation highly precarious. In other words, even though a crusade against powerful political actors may indeed materialise, how far it goes is at the mercy of the contingencies introduced by elite reactions. What direction the saga will take as this final moment kicks in is difficult to predict, although experience tells us that prosecutorial adventures usually come to ignominious ends. Backlash need not be a death sentence, but sometimes all it takes for the establishment to eviscerate momentum is for a prosecutor to cross a line too many or make one fatal mistake.

This points to the tragedy of prosecutorial zeal. A relentless and creative approach allows prosecutorial task forces to expand the political, evidentiary, and legal space required to take on high-profile defendants. The irony is that while this makes anti-corruption crusades possible it is also the source of their undoing. Zealousness invites reactions from defendants and their allies *and* legitimises attempts to derail the prosecutorial effort.

Including the moment of backlash in the explanatory framework is therefore important because it helps account for the high level of uncertainty regarding how much an investigation can expand after it blossoms. It is also important because the presence and virulence of backlash directly affects the dynamics of the investigation, particularly the tone that crusaders adopt in public and the strategies they deploy to manage conflict and defend their work. In this regard, the regularity of elite backlash puts into sharper focus the centrality of public outreach efforts in the overall prosecutorial strategy. As our case studies in the next two chapters will show, backlash is more "survivable" when

---

[37] "Entenda efeitos do julgamento no STF que declarou Moro parcial em caso de Lula," *Folha de São Paulo* (23 March 2021).

prosecutors successfully go public, both exposing specific attempts to thwart the investigation, and more generally, campaigning to build broad anti-corruption coalitions. Crusaders need to explain why their zeal, while controversial, is necessary, and why objections miss the mark. PR efforts of this kind were an effective antidote against fierce backlash at critical moments during the crusades in Peru and Ecuador. But as we will also discuss in greater detail in Part II of the book, amassing broad and durable support for a project that is legally controversial, affects powerful interests, puts in tension citizens' partisan commitments with their preference for accountability, and rarely delivers resounding successes, is hard. Those who spearhead backlash sooner or later gain the upper hand.

CONCLUSION

In this chapter we put forward a framework that identifies the dynamics that characterise judicial anti-corruption crusades. In so doing, we are now closer to understanding why and how seemingly minor corruption revelations sometimes snowball into criminal cases of historic proportions. The main takeaways are as follows:

- It is important to look beyond partisan and regime politics, taking the behaviour of judges and prosecutors seriously. We should expect politicians to talk about "lawfare," depicting investigators as puppets of spurious interests and the crusade as an overdetermined political ploy. But as analysts, we should not fall into the same temptation, denying agency to the law enforcement agents involved. Their choices and skills, the legal environment in which they operate, and how they conceptualise their role, all matter. Conceptually, we are better off seeing the crusades as an open-ended battle between, on the one hand, a handful of zealous and autonomous rank-and-file investigators, and on the other, politicians and their allies in senior judicial and prosecutorial roles.
- Investigating corruption at the highest level is hard. Inquiries take place in hostile and information-poor environments. Long- and short-term factors account for the prosecutorial savoir faire that is instrumental in helping overcome these obstacles and produce crusades. Processes of institutional change set the stage by introducing the key actors in these dramas, that is, zealous, risk-taking, and maverick investigators, and some of the legal tools required to unpick complex criminal networks backed and obscured by state power. But whether this produces a crusade is highly contingent on luck and a series of strategic choices made during the investigation, especially those that prioritise aggressive and unorthodox tactics on a variety of fronts.
- Crucially, we argued, cementing the zeal required to produce a snowball effect, and translating zeal into effectiveness, is more likely in the presence of specialised task forces.

• A lot can go wrong (and goes wrong) during anti-corruption crusades. Zeal is threatening and controversial, leading to backlash. Consequently, results, for instance, in the form of convictions, always stand on precarious foundations.

In the next two chapters we probe this framework beyond the cases that inspired it. In Chapter 3, we offer an in-depth look at the Peruvian *Lava Jato*, the largest crusade in Latin America outside Brazil. In Chapter 4 we introduce a series of shadow cases from across the region where outcomes vary dramatically. Later in the book we return to some of the themes that run through this chapter when we explore how anti-corruption crusades impact public attitudes towards corruption and politics. In particular, while cases like *Lava Jato* could in principle be seen as a noble attempt to eliminate the most vicious side of politics, we discuss and evaluate how the controversies triggered by unprecedented levels of prosecutorial zeal condition public reactions and complicate the building of broad and stable anti-corruption coalitions.

3

Lava Jato in Peru

Taking on the Political and Judicial Establishments

INTRODUCTION

Since 1979 Odebrecht undertook numerous infrastructure projects commissioned by the Peruvian government (Durand 2018). While Peru was never the company's most lucrative market – in 2012 it only accounted for 3 per cent of global revenues – Odebrecht had ambitious plans to expand its operations.[1] These plans suffered a blow in December 2016 when its executives told US prosecutors that between 2005 and 2014 Odebrecht handed over approximately US$29 million in corrupt payments to Peruvian officials (US Department of Justice 2016). Within days of these revelations, *Lava Jato* started in earnest with a focus on bribes paid to secure three major infrastructure projects: a segment of the Inter-Oceanic Highway, built during Alejandro Toledo's presidency (2001–2006); an electric train line in Lima, built during Alan García's administration (2006–2011); and a coastal infrastructure project in Callao (2013–2014). The investigative effort soon snowballed to include an inquiry into campaign finances, which targeted, among others, former president Ollanta Humala (2011–2016) and his wife, Nadine Heredia; opposition leader and several times presidential candidate, Keiko Fujimori; and former Lima mayors, Susana Villarán and Luis Castañeda.

The scandal erupted six months into President Kuczynski's administration. With the Fujimorista opposition in total control of Congress (73 out of 130 seats), inter-branch relations were tense from the start of the new presidency.[2] Keiko Fujimori had been defeated in the second round of the 2016 election by a razor-thin margin, and quickly turned her legislative caucus into an

---

[1] "Odebrecht: 'Concentraremos nuestras inversiones en energía en Perú más que en Brasil'," *Gestión* (3 May 2013).
[2] For an account of the tumultuous relationship between Kuzcynski and Fujimori, see below, but also Sifuentes (2019) and León (2019).

obstructionist force (Dargent and Muñoz 2016). At first, *Lava Jato* seemed to be centred on some of Fujimori's figures of hate, especially former presidents Toledo and Humala. Fujimoristas therefore saw the scandal as an opportunity to discredit them. Given that Kuczynski had served as Toledo's Chief of Staff, it also offered the chance to try to implicate the sitting president. With help from García's party, Alianza Popular Revolucionaria Americana (APRA), the Fujimoristas launched a congressional investigation. During these proceedings, Fujimoristas and Apristas went to great lengths to ensure the scandal maintained its initial narrow focus and protect their respective leaders (Roca 2019). Unfortunately for them, while the spectre of *Lava Jato* did eventually come to haunt Kuczynski, precipitating his resignation in March 2018, the investigation ended up implicating Fujimori and García too. When this happened, Fujimoristas enlisted allies in the judiciary and the prosecution services to attack the prosecutorial task force appointed to investigate the case. Interestingly, these efforts backfired and prompted President Vizcarra, Kuczynski's successor, to dissolve Congress, thus depriving Fujimori of her institutional stronghold. In the election called to appoint a new legislature in January 2020, the performance of the main political parties was dismal, further weakening some of the defendants.

Various political actors enmeshed in this drama tried to weaponise *Lava Jato* but were never perfectly able to control the task force in charge of the case. As a result, *Lava Jato* quickly expanded beyond its original remit, implicating politicians both in and out of power and across all branches of government. In so doing, a handful of little-known prosecutors served to exacerbate the political crisis still further. Indeed, in one the latest instalment of the saga, a leak to the press indicated that investigators were negotiating a deal that could potentially link President Vizcarra to *Lava Jato*. Specifically, the rumours suggested he had accepted bribes when he was regional governor of Moquegua between 2011 and 2014. Vizcarra was subsequently impeached, causing yet another constitutional crisis in November 2020.

The prosecutors were relentless from the start. By December 2017, just a year into the inquiry, they had identified 64 bank accounts and 50 offshore companies involved in the bribery scheme, reviewed more than 2,000 wire transfers, and conducted searches of 50 addresses.[3] Between December 2016 and July 2019, they convinced judges to order at least fifty-one pretrial detentions. These detentions incentivised some defendants to confess and reduced the firepower of those determined to obstruct the crusade. Furthermore, the prosecutors secured a deal with Odebrecht in which the company agreed to pay S./ 610 million (over US$170 million) in penalties and surrender vital information about the crimes. This allowed the task force to

---

[3] See www.mpfn.gob.pe/equipo_especial/logros/ (accessed 19 April 2019).

expand the case even further. While at the time of writing the inquiry is still ongoing and only a few defendants have seen their cases progress to the trial stage, there is no denying that prosecutors inflicted incalculable damage on the political establishment.

Peru's *Lava Jato* is fascinating not only because of the unprecedented reach of the inquiry, but also because the task force had to deal with obstructionist political forces working hard to derail the investigation. Complicating things further, prosecutors operated within a hierarchical institution, the *Ministerio Público*, in which some of those at the top – highly corrupt actors in their own right – tried to stop the crusade. As we argued in Chapter 2, to understand why these rank-and-file prosecutors were able to devise a successful investigative strategy, stretching the tentacles of the inquiry, we need to pay attention to two factors: a long-term process of institutional change and prosecutorial decisions following the December 2016 "moment of serendipity."

First is the history of institutional change within the prosecution services. The *Ministerio Público* is by no means close to the ideal of bureaucratic autonomy or corruption-free. Moreover, its structure and rules generate career incentives that to some extent conspire against innovators or mavericks. Despite these characteristics, a series of changes dating back to 1979 – but most importantly to the immediate aftermath of President Alberto Fujimori's resignation in the early 2000s – nurtured an environment favourable for the emergence of interstices of autonomy populated by cohorts of driven and daring investigators with the necessary skills to tackle complex macro-criminality. When the opportunity arose following the release of information by US authorities, there were actors within the *Ministerio Público* capable of understanding what was at stake and ready to seize the moment.

Institutional change does not overdetermine crusades; it only makes them more likely. In line with our framework, to fully account for Peru's *Lava Jato* we must take prosecutorial agency seriously. The decisions taken during the day-to-day of an investigation matter, intentionally or not, condition the outcome of controversial cases by narrowing or expanding the limits of political possibility. It is therefore necessary to trace the choices that enabled prosecutors to generate and maintain momentum as *Lava Jato* dragged on. As we shall see, a series of unexpected developments over which prosecutors had little control played a role in engineering this momentum. No explanatory framework can easily incorporate these factors. But also central to the process were prosecutorial decisions conducive to a zealous strategy. While the professional disposition and skills to adopt a relentless and unorthodox approach can be partly attributed to the legacy of institutional change within the *Ministerio Público*, the creation of a unified prosecutorial task force exclusively dedicated to *Lava Jato* played a critical role. The task force triggered productive synergies and helped unleash dynamics of innovation and mutual protection, enabling prosecutors to push the inquiry forward and defend it from backlash.

In what follows we analyse how the investigation unfolded in Peru. After Brazil, Peru stands out as the country where investigators have been able to stretch the tentacles of *Lava Jato* the most. Interestingly, they did so in what at times was a hostile environment and following an initial period in which the investigation stalled. We begin by tracing the history of institutional change that led to the emergence of pockets of prosecutorial capacity and bureaucratic autonomy in the *Ministerio Público*. As a result of this trans-formation, groups within the institution acquired the resources and professional repertoires needed to make a success of corruption investigations. To trace these developments, we rely on interviews with high-level prosecutors, journalists, and civil society actors, as well as governmental and non-governmental organisation (NGO) reports. The chapter then reconstructs the nitty-gritty of the prosecutorial effort that started in 2016 using myriad primary sources such as news reports, official documents, and confidential interviews with key players. The narrative highlights how strategic inter-actions between the prosecutors, and between them and other political, economic, and judicial elites, allowed the "moment of agency" to materialise. We show that the choices they made cannot be fully explained by the institutional or political environments. Instead, they are better explained as the product of small group dynamics within the task force, prosecutors' personality traits, and occasionally, good luck. These choices determined whether enough evidence came to light, widening windows of opportunity for ever more ambitious investigative efforts, and also whether attacks could be diffused.

LAYERING INVESTIGATIVE CAPACITY IN THE *MINISTERIO PÚBLICO*

In Chapter 2 we showed that the presence of risk-accepting and competent prosecutors has its roots in gradual processes of institutional change that increase the political insulation of prosecutorial agencies and improve their capacity to combat corruption via bureaucratic differentiation and the legal translation of international anti-corruption norms. We discussed, for example, how following the most recent democratic transition, Brazilian elites created a robust accountability complex. This included a far-reaching reform of the prosecution service, today one of the most autonomous in Latin America. The success of *Lava Jato* owes much to this process of empowerment. The Peruvian *Ministerio Público* (hereafter, MP) never experienced the same type of major overhaul. This, however, does not mean that it has not experienced its fair share of independence and capacity-enhancing reforms.

The constitution approved during the 1979 democratic transition removed the Peruvian MP from the orbit of the Executive branch and gave it full auton-omy. The 1993 constitution drafted in the aftermath of Fujimori's self-coup kept this arrangement in place. At the helm of the MP is the chief prosecutor (*Fiscal de la Nación*), who presides in consultation with the Council of Supreme Prosecutors (*Junta de Fiscales Supremos*). Importantly, while not always free from connections to politicians, the leaders of the MP are not political appointees. They are all appointed, evaluated, and removed from office by a judicial council, which does not include representatives of the legislative or executive branches.[4] Below them sit a series of Superior and Provincial prosecutors with jurisdiction over different "prosecutorial districts." Collectively, Chief and Supreme Prosecutors have ample degrees of freedom to determine the organisation's internal structure and policy priorities (Cubas 2003: 17). For example, they can create new positions, appoint (or dismantle) task forces to investigate specific crimes, and establish (or close down) units specialised in certain types of criminal activity. Moreover, rank-and-file prosecutors are autonomous agents on paper, but the internal rules also specify that members must abide by the instructions of their superiors.

The MP is therefore an autonomous but hierarchical institution. In practice, this means that those at the top can condition the course of an investigation and micro-manage the career trajectories of their subordinates. To be sure, like Supreme Prosecutors, Superior and Provincial prosecutors are appointed, ratified, promoted, or fired by the judicial council. Ratification and promotion, however, are conditional on performance and reputation, so if a high-level prosecutor initiates internal disciplinary proceedings against one of his underlings, the career prospects of the latter could suffer. Furthermore, until 2018 the judicial council could start impeachment proceedings only at the request of the MP's governing bodies, effectively granting great sanctioning powers to the chief prosecutor. And even when ratified or promoted, individual prosecutors are still largely at the mercy of their bosses. For instance, the chief prosecutor can move prosecutors around the organisation, deploying them to, or removing them from, a district or case. Finally, the chief prosecutor can unilaterally expand or reduce the number of positions in any district, thus rewarding or punishing those in charge of specific jurisdictions.

Constitutional autonomy is obviously far from trivial: it created an institutional environment in which investigations against powerful politicians are at least imaginable. To put it bluntly, the MP is no longer the legal arm of the president or minister of justice. But the prerogatives of Chief and Supreme Prosecutors mean that there are weak incentives for the rank-and-file to take

---

[4] Between 1993 and 2018, the judicial council was known as the Consejo Nacional de la Magistratura. It had seven members: the chief prosecutor; two Supreme Court Justices; one representative from the National Federation of Lawyers; one representative from Lima's Chamber of Lawyers; and two academics (Law No. 26397). After evidence of corruption and nepotism surfaced in 2018, it was replaced by the Junta Nacional de Justicia, which has more disciplinary prerogatives. See below.

the initiative in attacking establishment actors against the wishes of their bosses. In addition, ratification and promotion evaluations consider the quality of prosecutorial briefs and the average length of proceedings. As a result, experimenting with unorthodox legal interpretations (as is often required in complex corruption cases) or committing to potentially protracted investigations (instead of relying on formalisms to quickly close them down) without the explicit support of the chief prosecutor can be unwise.

Under these conditions, aggressive prosecutorial initiatives against any form of organised crime, including high-level corruption, struggle to take root without the support of the upper echelons of the MP. Having said this, a series of reforms to the structure of the organisation introduced since the early 2000s enabled the development of internal pockets of autonomy, which make such criminalisation efforts less dependent on the preferences of the chief prosecutor. These changes were adopted in response to domestic political crises and international pressures. The fact they were reactive and piecemeal rather than part of a masterplan to institutionalise anti-corruption capabilities means that progress, while highly consequential, is still precarious. Pockets of autonomy coexist with networks of prosecutors that are either indifferent to the problem of corruption or are part of the problem. Let us review these innovations and their implications for prosecutorial zeal.

Bureaucratic Differentiation and the Autonomy of the Rank-and-File

According to the final report of the Truth and Reconciliation Commission, during the 1980s Peruvian judges and prosecutors abdicated their prerogative to investigate the crimes perpetrated by all parties involved in the armed conflict. For example, prosecutors delegated investigative duties to the police, systematically failing to check the legality of their actions. In the 1990s, judicial actors also passively endorsed and applied Fujimori's draconian anti-terrorism legislation in flagrant violation of due process. The report therefore characterises the judiciary as an "agent of violence" (Truth and Reconciliation Commission 2003: Volume III, chapter VI, 249–250). Furthermore, following Fujimori's 1992 self-coup, the intelligence services subjected the MP and the courts to a process of institutional capture. Fujimori placed staunch supporters at the helm of both institutions and promoted a surge in untenured positions to keep the rank-and-file under control. This setup allowed the regime to put a lid on any attempt to implicate the ruling elite in serious crimes. For instance, the chief prosecutor often assigned loyalists to sensitive cases (Comisión Andina de Juristas 2003).

Fujimori's regime collapsed in November 2000. One immediate trigger was the release of the *Vladivideos*, a series of recordings that showed the president's closest aide and intelligence advisor, Vladimiro Montesinos, negotiating bribes with politicians, military officers, media moguls, and judges. Initially, Fujimori responded by appointing José Ugaz, a regime outsider, as anti-corruption czar (*procurador ad hoc*) to go after Montesinos.[5] This move, however, was not enough to save himself. After Fujimori resigned and fled to Japan, the caretaker government gave Ugaz additional resources. It also expanded his prerogatives so he could investigate other corrupt actors, including the now former president.

Armed with the flexibility afforded by the aforementioned autonomy-enhancing reforms, the MP, no longer in the hands of Fujimori's cronies, mirrored the executive's anti-corruption push almost immediately. Years of institutional capture and atrophy, coupled with the difficulties that haunt high-level corruption investigations, made it apparent that existing institutional structures would not have the capacity to rise to the occasion. Beyond the likely lack of political commitment among current prosecutors, the authorities also understood that failing to place all corruption cases under the supervision of a dedicated group of MP officials would be a recipe for inaction and inefficiency. Here they took lessons from the creation of task forces during Italy's Mani Pulite. Consequently, Chief Prosecutor Nelly Calderón signed a resolution creating six prosecutorial units with exclusive jurisdiction over the cases involving Fujimori and Montesinos, and two months later appointed Superior Prosecutor Pablo Sánchez Velarde to coordinate all efforts. According to the MP, the Vladivideos pointed to "the need to group together existing investigations [...], and given the severity and complexity of these cases, to [put] specialized prosecutors" in charge.[6]

This move kicked off a process of bureaucratic differentiation with the goal of nurturing greater specialisation in various forms of macro-criminality. For instance, in 2001 the MP created provincial prosecutorial units dedicated to drug trafficking. Furthermore, that same year Peru signed an agreement with the Inter-American Commission on Human Rights in which it acknowledged responsibility for 160 cases of human rights violations perpetrated during the armed conflict. As part of the agreement, starting in April 2002 the MP installed prosecutorial units specialised in forced disappearances and extrajudicial executions in Lima and other provinces, and appointed a superior prosecutor as coordinator. The following year the chief prosecutor continued this journey of organisational overhaul, creating more units, this time to investigate terrorism cases (i.e., the crimes of the Shining Path). These were later merged with the human rights units so that all conflict-related cases shared a docket.

In addition to revealing the need to nurture capacity via specialisation, the Fujimori-Montesinos affair inspired a package of regulatory changes that enhanced the ability of the prosecution services to investigate corruption, all of which would come in handy during *Lava Jato*. As we argued in Chapter 2, those implicated in state crimes tend to make use of their institutional positions

---

[5] *Procuradores* are government attorneys who represent the interests of the state. They are not prosecutors.
[6] Resolution 020-2000-MP-FN.

to engineer cover-ups, and in corruption cases, deploy intricate asset ownership structures (often offshore) to hide illegally obtained funds. Evidence against them is therefore incredibly hard to collect. One way around this opaqueness is to encourage some of those involved to confess. With this in mind, the *procurador ad hoc* and the prosecutors investigating the scandal since December 2000 successfully lobbied Congress to pass a law authorising plea bargains (Law No. 27378). The MP then moved swiftly to draft resolutions that regulated their use.[7] Another law passed in December 2000 (Law No. 27379) empowered prosecutors to request pretrial detentions, travel bans, and asset embargoes to prevent powerful defendants from fleeing or obstructing the investigation. Furthermore, the Constitution stipulates that to indict certain high-level officials it is necessary to seek congressional approval. This can cause delays, so another legislative change passed in early 2001 (Law No. 27399) allowed prosecutors to request pretrial detentions or travel bans without the authorisation of Congress. Finally, alongside these regulatory changes, the National Police set up a special anti-corruption division to work alongside the new prosecutors, and the government created a Financial Intelligence Unit to boost capacity to investigate money laundering (Law No. 27693).[8]

On the anti-corruption front, the performance of specialised prosecutors was remarkable. Between 2000 and 2006, they launched 246 cases against 1,743 defendants and wired over 140 extradition requests against 64 individuals to 14 countries. By December 2006, 58 per cent of these cases were still under investigation, 11 per cent were in the trial stage, and 31 per cent either had a final ruling or one pending appeal (Justicia Viva 2007: 30–46). Crucially, by this date courts had already handed down 112 convictions, including several against Vladimiro Montesinos. In addition to securing high-profile convictions, prosecutors were able to recover some of the proceeds of corruption. Specifically, they repatriated over US$170 million from accounts in the United States, Switzerland, and the Cayman Islands, and managed to freeze accounts worth another US$46 million (Justicia Viva 2007: 47). Victories on this front were instrumental in further strengthening investigative capacity: part of the money was handed over to anti-corruption prosecutors via a fund created in 2001 to administer recovered assets.[9]

Institutional autonomy gave the MP both the organisational flexibility to respond decisively to changing circumstances and address societal demands for greater accountability. Reflecting on his experience as a member of the *Procuraduría Ad Hoc*, which worked closely with the prosecutors, Eduardo Dargent explains:

The key factor to ensure greater judicial effectiveness was to recognize institutional weakness from the start [...] Facing a delegitimized judiciary [the authorities] chose to

---

[7] Resolution 070-2001-MP-FM.   [8] Resolution RM 100-2001-IN/PNP.
[9] Decreto de Urgencia 122-2001.

make sure institutions within the system counted with an adequate structure and with the legal tools necessary to confront organized crime [...] Had they scattered the cases across multiple criminal courts and prosecutorial units in Lima [...] the process would have probably failed [...] Aware of these limitations, [the authorities] chose to put in place a *shielding* system (2005: 390–391; our translation).

Beyond providing some level of political insulation and boosting capacity, bureaucratic differentiation had other benefits. Crucially, it entrusted cohorts of judicial actors with a clear mission and allowed them to study a small and highly related set of cases in detail. As a result, they were suddenly motivated to go to great lengths to deliver results. Investigators soon realised that an orthodox approach would represent a major obstacle, leading several judges and prosecutors to champion innovations that gave additional bite to existing laws. For example, they endorsed the view that certain criminal definitions traditionally applied exclusively to public officials could also be used against private citizens (Dargent 2005: 396). By extending the reach of criminal responsibility beyond state actors in this way, the criminalisation effort could now go after media moguls or businessmen, and therefore paint a more comprehensive picture of Fujimori's corruption machine. Like in Italy, these creative interpretive moves put pressure on corporate actors, extracting confessions that paved the way for convictions against high-profile politicians.

One key shortcoming of this process of institutional adaptation, however, was that it was not part of a grand anti-corruption strategy. Quite the contrary, it was highly reactive. For instance, there was little coordination between the MP and the judiciary, which undermined the effectiveness of the new anti-corruption system. Both institutions often played cat and mouse to catch up with organisational changes introduced in the courts or prosecution services, respectively (Defensoría del Pueblo 2008, 2017).[10] Moreover, the lack of an overarching plan opened the door to legal challenges. Specifically, some defendants questioned the authority of specialised prosecutors or judges, arguing that these organisational innovations violated due process (specifically, the *principio de juez natural*).[11] It wasn't until the Constitutional Court settled these issues, concluding that the nature of "governmental criminality" justified *post hoc* criminal specialisation, that investigations and trials could proceed in earnest.[12]

Perhaps more importantly, this unprecedented institutional thrust was highly dependent on leadership turnover in the MP and the judiciary after 2000. This was in turn a function of highly unusual transparency "spring" following Fujimori's collapse. But the political bargain struck after the

---

[10] The judiciary also created courts specialised in corruption, terrorism, and human rights violations.

[11] The idea behind this principle is that there should be a predetermined judge with jurisdiction over a case. Who will judge a case should not be established *ex post*. This is meant to provide legal certainty and ensure impartiality.

[12] Ruling 1073-2003-HC/TC.

democratic transition did not last long. As the anti-corruption consensus cracked, so did the effectiveness of criminalisation efforts. On the electoral front, APRA's Alan García returned to the presidency in 2006 and formed an informal congressional alliance with an equally resurgent Fujimorismo. Since García's first term (1985–1990) had coincided with the peak of conflict-related violence, he shared with Fujimoristas an interest in blocking the judicialisation of human rights violations and other high-profile cases. This changing balance of power also made it possible for judicial actors with links to both parties (and a preference for impunity) to regroup and reach influential positions in the MP and the Supreme Court. Given the strong prerogatives of the chief prosecutor and the chief justice, including their role in the judicial council, the institutional incentives for the rank-and-file to continue investigating and punishing the crimes of the past weakened. Moreover, these judicial authorities were responsible for jurisprudence that undermined the criminalisation effort both on the human rights and corruption fronts.[13] The MP also started disciplinary proceedings against a few prosecutors to deter others from defying the new political settlement.[14]

This precarity notwithstanding, the move towards bureaucratic differentiation did begin to institutionalise a new prosecutorial modus operandi in the area of macro-criminality. In particular, it engrained the view that assigning cases involving powerful political and economic actors to ordinary prosecutors was simply not the correct way to proceed. Specialisation, sometimes via the creation of task forces, became the go to template to deal with such cases. After the precedent set in response to the Fujimori-Montesinos affair, it would prove hard for the powers that be to force a return to a pre-specialisation state of affairs in which judges and prosecutors inhabited an organisational environment that made inaction and lack of expertise the default position. This kind of reversal would have not only encountered resistance from a significant cohort of prosecutors with a stake in preserving the new elite units; it would have also gone against the MP's modified internal logic of behavioural appropriateness. In other words, even with changing political winds and the empowerment of a pro-impunity coalition, re-engineering bureaucratic *incapacity* was not a viable path. In fact, the inertia behind the process of internal specialisation continued, expanding to crimes of the present, not just the past. Starting in 2007, for instance, the MP appointed new prosecutors specialised in organised crime, corruption, money laundering, crimes against the environment, human trafficking, tax fraud, and customs and intellectual property crimes. In addition, several existing special prosecutors with provincial jurisdiction were given national jurisdiction to enhance their ability to coordinate investigative efforts.

---

[13] For a discussion of jurisprudence that complicated the judicialisation of corruption cases, see Justicia Viva (2007: 56).

[14] For a discussion of other attacks against judges and prosecutors see Gonzalez-Ocantos (2016a).

The fact that starting in 2006 some politicians and their high-ranking allies in the judiciary and prosecution services felt they had to openly intervene to stop human rights and corruption prosecutions shows that things were indeed changing among sectors of the rank-and-file. By this stage, specialised prosecutors had developed a sense of mission and acquired the skills to act in ways that complicated more subtle attempts to dictate and control their behaviour. Going forward, while the judicialisation of human rights and corruption crimes perpetrated during the armed conflict and Fujimori's regime did slow down, it never stopped completely and continued to yield victories against impunity. Importantly, participation in armed conflict cases as well as in less salient – and less politically charged – ones involving contemporary crimes constituted a truly formative experience for specialised prosecutors. Those experiences nurtured a different, more effective way of conceptualising and investigating macro-criminality, and strengthened their resolve to take on powerful actors. Greater capacity and resolve emerged through a variety of channels.

One of the advantages of specialisation was that the new prosecutorial units became the focal point of pedagogical interventions by external groups with an interest in boosting investigative capacity. For example, in the early 2000s Peruvian NGOs launched an ambitious training programme that targeted prosecutors and judges overseeing human rights cases (Gonzalez-Ocantos 2016a). According to the civil society and judicial actors we interviewed for this book, NGOs did not design a similar strategy for corruption cases. But the authorities of the MP did accompany the move towards greater specialisation with their own pedagogical initiatives. As one prosecutor with two decades of experience in coordinating specialised units told us, these training opportunities, coupled with stable career paths, consolidated investigative capacity:

[Specialised units] are key because they bring together prosecutors from all levels. And you can give them very specific training. It is our policy to train the prosecutors that make up these units. Also, belonging to a specialized unit allows you to build up experience in the investigation of complex cases. This has professionalizing consequences for those prosecutors who want to pursue a more specialized career. Specialization guarantees that prosecutors are not moved around as much as it happened in the past. In fact, calls to fill in vacancies are organized by area of specialization, which means that those with prior experience in a topic have more chances of getting the job (Authors' interview, August 2020).

In addition to the professionalising impact of specialisation, these small groups developed an elite unit mentality. Several of our informants relied on military language to describe them as "combat cells" with high levels of institutional autonomy, operational flexibility, and cohesion. This is also how prosecutors see themselves. For example, we had access to the content of a presentation that the prosecutorial unit specialised in organised crime prepared for an external audience. In one of the slides, they described the "main characteristics" of their unit in the following terms:

- Highly specialised system, with experience in the investigation of mega-cases and serious crimes;
- Agile system for quickly mobilising interventions with national reach;
- Collaborative work. High flexibility to form task forces;
- Own computer system [to monitor] prosecutorial performance;
- Strength of the [unit]: probity and *mística* [collective identity] of its members.

The ability to move fast and effectively as a unit using their own resources is critical because in difficult cases it helps build both investigative and political momentum. If prosecutors are able to gather incriminating evidence quickly, for instance, it becomes costlier for their superiors to force them to backtrack. Furthermore, the development of a strong sense of collective purpose makes these prosecutors harder to manipulate.

Relatedly, our sources pointed out that the reduced size and high visibility of elite units allow them to develop a series of protection mechanisms. According to an NGO official who monitors developments in the MP since the mid-2000s:

Honest prosecutors are certainly not in the majority, but they are there. In addition to not being in the majority, they do not always coordinate among themselves. In the MP everything is an uphill battle. There's opacity in the selection of authorities, there are all kinds of conflicts of interest, resources are scarce, and there's political intervention [...] [But] some prosecutors are able to survive, overcome obstacles, train themselves, and protect others. Some do coordinate to plan their careers and protect themselves. This is obviously something you see among the "bad" and the "good" types. Among the good ones, there are various survival strategies [...] They work as a team. If you want to change things you have to do it as a team; individual prosecutors cannot change anything. So for example they apply together for certain positions. Or they plan which member of their group will apply for a leadership position. This allows them to secure the protection of a friendly superior [...] [Furthermore] they make alliances with members of the police, who offer them protection and allow them to investigate effectively [...] Information management is also important. Many prosecutors become well-known among journalists and lean on these contacts to control the flow of information to protect themselves (Authors' interview, August 2020).

A high-ranking prosecutor described additional mechanisms of internal protection. He highlighted the role of group leaders and internal socialisation processes in consolidating internal cohesion and commitment to hard cases:

Courage is something that develops daily. In that sense, the heads of these units play a very important role. I always tell my prosecutors: "I'm the boss and I'll answer for what you do." The boss filters external pressures and protects his subordinates. What gives you strength is the team; we remain united. You also have to close ranks to avoid influence peddling. So the socialization of those who join the team is critical. We alert them to all the extorsion maneuvers they will be exposed to (Authors' interview, August 2020).

Socialisation and internal monitoring are easier in small groups, and because these mechanisms forge a strong esprit de corps, specialised units sometimes muster the courage to defy the dictates of those in command of the MP, which otherwise remains a hierarchical institution. According to another prosecutor with similar leadership experience, the stabilisation of specialised professional career paths consolidates tight groups in which members can protect each other as well as strategise when things turn sour:

In the team, we advise one another and collectively design strategies. This is key because when you are dealing with complex crimes there are always political groups and high-ranking members of various state institutions [NB: the MP and the judiciary] who are protecting the other side. This was the case in the Montesinos case, and it is also the case today with Cuellos Blancos and *Lava Jato* [NB: see next section]. So it is important to see these cases with different eyes, and now and then collectively reflect on the overall strategy (Authors' interview, August 2020).

One final and perhaps elusive element that emerges from our interviews with specialised prosecutors is the sense of efficacy that they developed after being part of a successful wave of investigations in the aftermath of Fujimori's downfall. This experience expanded their horizons of possibility and defined them as the generation that went after powerful actors. When asked to describe their careers in the MP, for instance, most of the graduates of this anti-corruption push usually started by mentioning they had been part of the team that prosecuted Montesinos and other high-profile defendants in the 2000s. Prestige is not just a source of pride; it can also shield them from the darker side of Peruvian judicial politics. In this sense, another recurrent theme during interviews was the notion that by developing an anti-corruption reputation, prosecutors are less likely to receive questionable "instructions" from their superiors. As one of them told us: "Acquiring prestige is key. If a prosecutor is regarded as honest, the corrupt ones won't come to pressure them because they know he or she won't be responsive" (Authors' interview, August 2020).

It is hard to find visible examples of the kind of group-level strategic planning or resistance described in the interviews. This is because defensive moves are orchestrated informally, behind closed doors. One episode that took place in 2010, during the peak of the backlash against the human rights units in the MP and the judiciary, however, is illustrative of how cooperative dynamics in these interstices of bureaucratic autonomy afford the rank-and-file greater freedom. President García was determined to stop armed conflict-related cases that implicated him and his allies. To do so he relied on delegated legislative powers to issue Legislative Decree No. 1097. The decree was essentially an amnesty in disguise, which included a series of guidelines for judges and prosecutors.[15] One mandated the immediate closing of all prosecutions that had been ongoing for more than fourteen months. Another told judicial actors to stop giving certain international treaties retroactive effects. These were

---

[15] It was later revealed that the minister of defence received advise from Fujimori's lawyers when drafting the decree.

precisely the legal instruments that had enabled authorities to ignore statutes of limitations and proceed with the investigation of crimes perpetrated decades earlier. A few days after the publication of the decree, members of the anti-corruption and human rights units in the judiciary and the MP repudiated the Executive's decision decisively, even though the decree had the backing of the chief prosecutor. For example, prosecutors issued a joint press release explaining why they refused to apply the decree. They emphasised that if cases were closed, the country would be contravening its international legal obligations. Following this rebellion, the judges of the First Criminal Chamber of the anti-corruption unit in Lima handed down a unanimous decision declaring the decree unconstitutional. This collective response, likely the product of internal deliberations, allowed specialised judges and prosecutors to prevail. Indeed, the public outcry they helped fuel forced the president to backtrack and fire the ministers responsible for the decree.

This episode shows that even if the incentives to go after powerful political actors weakened in the mid-to-late 2000s, the institutional environment continued on a capacity-building trajectory. The preservation of this built-in capacity and resolve to prosecute complex crimes despite changing political winds was possible because of organisational changes following the post-Fujimori spring. But other factors also played a role in pushing for additional changes in the legal framework that complemented those at the organisational level.

First was the transition to an accusatorial criminal justice system via the adoption of a new Code of Criminal Procedure in 2004. While implementation has been slow and uneven across the territory, the code applies nationally to corruption cases since 2011. This is critical because it shifts power away from judges and towards prosecutors (Langer 2004). The code affords prosecutors full control over investigations and more time for the preliminary investigation of complex crimes (up to thirty-six months). Furthermore, it regulates a series of abridged proceedings in cases in which defendants seek to cooperate with the authorities. These changes reinforced the positive effects of organisational specialisation, especially when it comes to corruption cases.

Second, Peru engaged in the legal translation of international anti-corruption standards. For instance, to abide by commitments such as those enshrined in the UN Convention Against Corruption, the new Code of Criminal Procedure created the Office of International Judicial Cooperation and Extraditions. This agency plays a key role assisting prosecutors in cases of money laundering or bribery because the proceeds of corruption are almost invariably stashed in offshore accounts. Furthermore, the international anti-corruption regime encourages countries to modify legislation to criminalise all forms of corruption. The Peruvian criminal code has undergone several reforms in line with these standards. Notably, to comply with the conditions set by the United States for a free trade agreement, between 2009 and 2010 Congress passed laws criminalising international bribery (the new criminal types include *cohecho pasivo* and *cohecho activo internacional*). Complementing prior legislation on

plea bargain agreements, in 2010 Peru also passed a law to protect whistle-
blowers.[16] Finally, following recommendations made by the OECD, Peru
approved laws that specify the administrative responsibility of legal entities,
including companies, in cases involving active transnational bribery and thus
make it possible to negotiate leniency agreements.[17] This last piece of legislation
played a key role in *Lava Jato* (see below).

The weight of formative criminalisation experiences following the collapse
of Fujimorismo, coupled with gradual organisational and regulatory changes,
conditioned how the MP responded to *Lava Jato*. Due to the enormity of the
case, however, the relative success of the investigation launched in December
2016 cannot only be explained by this legacy of institutional change. It is also
important to look at the micro-dynamics of the inquiry to trace how prosecutorial choices, as well as prosecutors' personality traits and a good dose of luck,
shaped the trajectory of *Lava Jato*. To be sure, those choices were in part made
possible by the presence within the MP of prosecutors who were by now quite
seasoned in cases of macro-criminality, felt protected within specialised units,
and could rely on more adequate legislation. But as we shall see, a lot
could have still gone wrong; indeed, at times a lot did go wrong. The network
of prosecutors committed to fighting corruption coexisted with a powerful
group of colleagues with diametric preferences. And not all committed prosecutors behaved in ways that were equally effective in triggering the "moment
of agency." This suggests that inherited institutional structures did not do all
the work.

LAVA JATO ARRIVES IN LIMA: THE MOMENTS OF SERENDIPITY AND AGENCY[18]

We have thus far discussed how changes to the institutional context set the
ground for the development of prosecutorial experience and organisational
repertoires without which the Peruvian MP would not have been able to
effectively engineer the largest anti-corruption probe in history. However, as
Chapter 2 highlights, to explain anti-corruption crusades we also need to
explore short-term factors associated with the day-to-day of an inquiry that
affirm the professional commitment and the evidentiary basis necessary for

[16] Decreto Supremo 038-2011-PCM.
[17] Law 30424 in 2016 and DL 1352 in 2017. For an example of Peru's receptivity to international
standards, especially the need to adopt a special institutional and legal framework to investigate
and prevent grand corruption, see the Presidencia de Consejo de Ministros's Anti-Corruption
Plan for the period 2012–2016.
[18] A lot of the "behind-the-scenes" details we discuss in the rest of the chapter come from confidential interviews with the protagonists of Peru's *Lava Jato*. To preserve their anonymity, we cannot
identify our sources or note which parts of the story are derived from the interviews. Details
about informal meetings for which there is no official record have been checked with at least two
sources, usually direct participants.

prosecutions to gain momentum. As we shall see, after a double "moment of serendipity," choices made during the "moment of agency" and the "moment of backlash" played a particularly important role in Peru, both to push (and block) progress along the way.

Two Strokes of Luck

Peru's *Lava Jato* started with an exogenous "moment of serendipity." Rather unexpectedly, in December 2016 authorities in the United States made public the testimonies of Odebrecht executives detailing a bribery scheme of continental proportions. To be sure, it was not the first time Peruvian authorities had heard of allegations linking Odebrecht to high-level politicians. For example, a congressional commission created earlier that year had looked into *Lava Jato's* possible connections to local elites but failed to reach a consensus, instead producing three reports – a majority and two minority reports. A multiparty coalition then refused to debate (or approve) any of the reports, effectively boycotting the commission's work (Pari 2017). The exogenous shock coming from Washington forced Peruvian authorities to take the allegations more seriously, putting an end to inaction.

Lava Jato benefited from a second stroke of luck. In April 2014, Carlos Ramos Heredia, a cousin of Nadine Heredia, the first lady at the time, was chosen to become the next chief prosecutor. While originally expected to serve until 2017, less than a year into his term the judicial council suspended him. It emerged that in a previous role, Ramos had unlawfully obstructed an investigation into a corruption network in the Ancash region, removing four provincial prosecutors from the case. César Alvarez, governor of Ancash between 2007 and 2014, had allegedly set up a bribery and intimidation machine akin to the one that Montesinos ran from the headquarters ("central") of the National Intelligence Services in the 1990s, and colluded with Ramos to save his skin. Because the scale of this illegal venture was regional rather than national, the case came to known as *La Centralita* (Spanish diminutive of "central").[19] Years later, the *Lava Jato* inquiry would reveal that Alvarez was one of Odebrecht's clients in Peru.

This second story is important for two reasons. First, it shows the ties that bind some high-ranking members of the MP with politicians, as well as the lengths to which they are willing to go to protect allies implicated in corruption scandals. Second, this episode matters because Pablo Sánchez, the man chosen to replace Ramos, belonged to a very different network of prosecutors. Most notably, Sánchez had served for many years in specialised anti-corruption units. This is how, almost by chance, a graduate of the Montesinos investigation, as

---

[19] On 25 January 2021, Alvarez was sentenced to thirty-five years in prison for the murder of a political opponent.

opposed to an accomplice of a *Montesinesque* corruption network, was in charge of the MP when *Lava Jato* arrived in Lima in December 2016. Had the reverse been the case, it is unlikely that the organisational capital accumulated since 2000 would have been deployed as effectively to investigate Odebrecht and its local clientele. This speaks to the precarity of institutional change and highlights the impact of contingent developments on the outcome of the investigation. In this sense, the Ramos affair underscores a basic distinction between prosecutors who have no intention to fight corruption and others who have a long history of doing just the opposite. Despite the initial momentum of the case under Sanchez's leadership, the tug of war between these two networks conditioned, and at times jeopardised, the trajectory of *Lava Jato* in Peru.

Creating a Task Force

In December 2016, Chief Prosecutor Sánchez received a call from anti-corruption prosecutor Hamilton Castro. Castro wanted to discuss a case that had just landed on his docket: *Lava Jato*. During their conversation, Sánchez reasoned by analogy and instinctively set in motion what by now was a well-entrenched modus operandi to deal with complex crimes. In his experienced eyes, the case looked awfully like the Montesinos one, but seemed to have the potential to become a much bigger affair. This meant that while the case definitely needed to be in the hands of specialised prosecutors, it probably required an even greater degree of specialisation than that afforded by existing anti-corruption units. After all, it included allegations against three former presidents – Toledo, García, and Humala. Castro, who had also investigated Montesinos, agreed.

Making use of one of his prerogatives as chief prosecutor, on 26 December Sánchez created a task force to focus exclusively on this investigation.[20] Castro was given carte blanche to select his team, but Sánchez recommended a few names, including young prosecutors he knew from prior informal interactions and in his capacity as professor of criminal law at various provincial universities. When selecting the members of the task force, it was little surprising that the two men tapped into their networks within specialised units of the MP and thus made use of the capacity amassed over the previous two decades in interstices of bureaucratic autonomy.[21]

According to official records, the initial *Lava Jato* task force consisted of twenty-one prosecutors from Lima, Piura, Cusco, and Ancash. Territorial diversity was important because the targets of the investigation were both national and regional elites. Being part of a task force allowed these prosecutors

---

[20] Resolution 5050-2016-MP-FN.
[21] For an excellent discussion of how networks bound by shared professional role conceptions may enhance judicial power and influence, see Ingram (2015).

TABLE 3.1 *Initial results of Peru's* Lava Jato *(December 2016–December 2017)*

Stage of the Investigative Process	Preliminary proceedings	9
	Preliminary investigation	11
	Preparatory investigation	11
	No. of defendants	237
Evidence-seeking Measures	No. of raids	115
Coercive Measures	No. of international travel bans	16
	No. of pretrial detentions	12
	No. of "*cauciones*" (embargoes)	3
Leniency Measures	No. of cases with plea bargains	11
	No. of cases with requests for international cooperation	22

Source: Ministerio Publico

to focus exclusively on *Lava Jato*, deploying their rich knowledge of local networks while working shoulder to shoulder on interrelated cases. Prosecutors were divided into smaller groups, each one responsible for specific lines of inquiry. Table 3.1 shows the main outcomes of their efforts between December 2016 and December 2017.

At the start, the focus was on allegations that Odebrecht had bribed public officials to secure the construction of the Inter-Oceanic Highway during Alejandro Toledo's presidency (2001–2006); an electric train line during Alan García's administration (2006–2011); and a coastal infrastructure project sponsored by the regional government of Callao (2013–2014). As the evidence mounted, Castro's inquiry produced a series of spin-offs, expanding its remit.[22] For example, witness testimonies indicated that Odebrecht had also made off-the-books contributions to political campaigns. The most salient allegations were those against former president Ollanta Humala and former first lady Nadine Heredia, and opposition leader Keiko Fujimori.[23] In addition, the prosecutors trained their eyes on bribes allegedly paid to secure the construction of a gas pipeline during the Humala years (2011–2016), and local infrastructure projects in Lima and Cusco. And there were yet other cases that looked at possible collusion between Peruvian construction firms, and illegal payments by Odebrecht to a consultancy firm linked to President Kuczynski while he was a member of Toledo's cabinet. In short, no one was spared as the case snowballed into a crusade.

Instead of assigning the new cases to members of the task force, Castro decided to trust some of them to prosecutors based in a pre-existing unit specialised in

[22] Resolution 2683-2017-MP-FN.
[23] Keiko's case originated from information provided by Marcelo Odebrecht, former CEO of the company. In one of his diaries, he wrote: "Aumentar Keiko para 500 e eu fazer visita." This strongly suggested that Odebrecht had funded her 2011 congressional bid.

money laundering. Like Castro, the prosecutor in charge of this unit, Rafael Vela, was a veteran of the crusade against Montesinos/Fujimori and before joining the MP in 2013 had served as an anti-corruption judge for seven years. One of Vela's closest aides was Prosecutor José Domingo Pérez. While he was younger and did not take part in those formative investigations, Pérez was no stranger to difficult cases. For example, in 2008 he secured a conviction against a former governor in the *Moqueguazo* case.[24]

As we shall see, Vela and his team also made quick progress initially. In fact, they managed to secure high-profile pretrial detentions and ground-breaking confessions earlier than Castro, and thus gained greater notoriety. But the division of labour between two prosecutorial teams made it harder for all involved to understand the complexities of *Lava Jato* and approach the investigation in a coordinated fashion. This introduced frictions that complicated the prosecutorial effort, adding internal obstacles to those already posed by politicians fighting for survival. Put differently, Castro's decision conspired against furthering "the moment of agency."

The clashes between Vela and Castro suggest that internal cohesion *within* small groups does not necessarily guarantee cohesion *between* them. In particular, Vela and Perez, on one side, and Castro, on the other, had very different leadership and working styles, and at times, diametric views of how best to deploy the anti-corruption toolkit. For example, a high-ranking prosecutor who knows all of them well explained that while Castro usually follows formalistic, by the books, and orthodox investigative strategies, Pérez is more "dynamic," standing out as a "riot squad prosecutor" who favours more aggressive tactics. From a research design perspective, this is interesting because it allows us to see how despite following similar professional trajectories and having equally impeccable anti-corruption credentials, the choices Castro and Vela/Perez made once in control of their respective teams played a role in determining the investigative and political momentum behind different lines of inquiry.

In what follows we zoom in on two crucial dimensions of the investigative strategy. First, we look at the use of pretrial detentions and innovative applications of criminal definitions. On this front, Vela and Castro worked in a similar fashion, but Vela ended up issuing more pretrial detentions due to productive synergies between different investigative techniques. His line of inquiry therefore gained momentum faster. This is consistent with our claim in Chapter 2 that the zealousness that makes crusades has less to do with the use of specific tactics or with specific decisions, and more with an overall approach that relentlessly and creatively combines legal and non-legal tools. Second, we look at how each team approached negotiations with Odebrecht and information

---

[24] "Conoce la carrera de José Domingo Pérez, el fiscal que investiga a Alan García y Keiko Fujimori," *RPP Noticias* (22 December 2018). On the *Moqueguazo*, see Meléndez and León (2009).

exchanges with Brazil. Here preferences diverged quite dramatically, with implications for the speed at which each team produced quality evidence. Crucially, Castro's reluctance to agree to make concessions in exchange for evidence precipitated his downfall in July 2018, at which point Vela, who was always more daring and willing to negotiate better terms for the company, took over both teams and accelerated the discovery. In other words, the "moment of agency" materialised in earnest only after all lines of inquiry were placed under the umbrella of a single task force. This supports our argument regarding the importance of teamwork for optimising investigative strategies.

Pretrial Detentions: Victories and Controversy

Defendants in grand corruption cases are well-connected and therefore have the means to derail the investigative effort. Pretrial detentions are useful precisely because they help neutralise the firepower of such actors. Pretrial detentions also enable investigators to extract confessions. But despite these benefits, they are controversial from a legal standpoint (e.g., they rely on subjective assessments of flight risks, etc.), and raise the stakes of an inquiry quite dramatically, inviting retaliation (e.g., accusations of "lawfare," revanchism, overzealousness) or exposing prosecutors to embarrassing setbacks if decisions are overturned on appeal.

According to an analysis of corruption investigations carried out between 2014 and 2017, for every 100 cases there were 2 individuals serving time in prison. Considering that a case often has more than one defendant, the use of pretrial detentions was relatively rare in Peru (Defensoría del Pueblo 2017). In *Lava Jato*, by contrast, the investigative teams did not hesitate to use of this tool aggressively. During interviews, sources mentioned that both teams strategically planned these requests. It was of course entirely possible that while vital for neutralising obstructionist forces or extracting confessions, some judges could consider the requests excessive, risky, or politically inexpedient. To circumvent such obstacles, it was common for the prosecutors to time the requests to make sure they landed on the desks of sympathetic judges.[25] Regardless of the veracity of these claims, the prosecutors certainly found echo in the courts.

Table 3.2 shows the list of pretrial detentions approved by the courts between 2017 and 2020. Unfortunately, we were not able to access the entire universe of detention requests, so we cannot establish prosecutors' success rates. In any case, the kind of defendants that spent time in jail is indicative of the boldness of the strategy. For example, at Castro's request, personalities such as Miguel Angel Navarro and Jorge Cuba, both deputy ministers under Alan García, went to prison for eighteen months. Only two months into the inquiry, national and international arrest warrants were issued against

---

[25] One in particular: Judge Richard Concepción Carhuancho.

TABLE 3.2 *Pretrial detentions: Peru's* Lava Jato *(2017–2020)*

Date	Name	Time	Case	Team
24/01/2017	Jorge Cuba (former cabinet minister)	18 months	Metro de Lima	Castro
24/01/2017	Edwin Luyo (former ministerial aide)	18 months	Metro de Lima	Castro
25/01/2017	Miguel Navarro (former ministerial aide)	18 months	Metro de Lima	Castro
03/02/2017	Jessica Tejada (Jorge Cuba's partner)	18 months	Metro de Lima	Castro
04/02/2017	Mariella Huerta (former ministerial aide)	18 months	Metro de Lima	Castro
09/02/2017	Alejandro Toledo (former president)	18 months	Interoceanic Highway	Castro
23/03/2017	Juan Zevallos (former ministerial aide)	18 months	Interoceanic Highway	Castro
08/04/2017	Felix Moreno (former governor)	18 months	Costa Verde	Castro
28/05/2017	Jorge Acurio (former governor)	18 months	Vía Evitamiento Cusco	Castro
28/05/2017	Gustavo Salazar (businessman)	18 months	Vía Evitamiento Cusco	Castro
13/07/2017	Ollanta Humala (former president)	18 months	Campaign financing (Humala)	Vela
13/07/2017	Nadine Heredia (former first lady)	18 months	Campaign financing (Humala)	Vela
29/09/2017	Víctor Muñoz Cuba (former cabinet minister)	18 months	Metro de Lima	Castro
04/12/2017	José Graña (businessman)	18 months	Interoceanic Highway	Castro
04/12/2017	Hernando Graña (businessman)	18 months	Interoceanic Highway	Castro
04/12/2017	Fernando Camet (businessman)	18 months	Interoceanic Highway	Castro
04/12/2017	José Castillo (businessman)	18 months	Interoceanic Highway	Castro
22/12/2017	Santiago Chau (former ministerial aide)	18 months	Metro de Lima	Castro
25/01/2018	Rodolfo Prialé (businessman)	18 months	Club de la Construcción	Castro
25/01/2018	Paul Tejada (businessman)	18 months	Club de la Construcción	Castro
25/01/2018	Félix Málaga (businessman)	18 months	Club de la Construcción	Castro
25/01/2018	Luis Prevoo (businessman)	18 months	Club de la Construcción	Castro
25/01/2018	Carlos García (businessman)	18 months	Club de la Construcción	Castro

July 2018: Vela replaces Castro as task force leader and teams are merged

Date	Name	Time	Case	Team
06/10/2018	Magdalena Bravo (former ministerial aide)	12 months	Metro de Lima	Vela
06/10/2018	Jesús Munique (former ministerial aide)	12 months	Metro de Lima	Vela
31/10/2018	Keiko Fujimori (opposition leader)	36 months	Campaign financing (Fujimori)	Vela
10/11/2018	Vicente Silva (Fujimori's advisor)	36 months	Campaign financing (Fujimori)	Vela
15/11/2018	Pier Figari (Fujimori's advisor)	36 months	Campaign financing (Fujimori)	Vela

Date	Name	Time	Case	Team
15/11/2018	Ana Herz (Fujimori's advisor)	36 months	Campaign financing (Fujimori)	Vela
16/11/2018	Luis Mejía (Fujimori's advisor)	36 months	Campaign financing (Fujimori)	Vela
20/11/2018	Giancarlo Bertini (contributor to Fujimori's campaign)	36 months	Campaign financing (Fujimori)	Vela
23/11/2018	Jaime Yoshiyama (former minister and Fujimori's advisor)	36 months	Campaign financing (Fujimori)	Vela
31/01/2019	Felix Moreno (former governor)	18 months	Costa Verde	Vela
12/03/2019	Jaime Yoshiyama (former minister and Fujimori's advisor)	36 months	Campaign financing (Fujimori)	Vela
12/03/2019	Gonzalo Monteverde (businessman)	36 months	Financial Operator	Vela
12/03/2019	Jorge Salinas (businessman)	36 months	Financial Operator	Vela
12/03/2019	María Carmona (businesswoman)	36 months	Financial Operator	Vela
17/04/2019	Pedro Pablo Kuczynski (former president)	36 months	Pedro Pablo Kuczynski	Vela
30/04/2019	Luis Nava (former cabinet minister)	36 months	Financial Operator	Vela
14/05/2019	Susana Villarán (former mayor of Lima)	18 months	Campaign financing (Villarán)	Vela
15/05/2019	José Castro (former Lima mayoralty official)	18 months	Campaign financing (Villarán)	Vela
16/05/2019	Luis Gómez (Villaran's former aide)	18 months	Campaign financing (Villarán)	Vela
21/05/2019	José Paredes (former cabinet minister)	18 months	Club de la Construcción	Vela
11/07/2019	Antonio Palomino (former Callao government official)	18 months	Costa Verde	Vela
11/07/2019	Eber Ramírez (former Callao government official)	18 months	Costa Verde	Vela
25/07/2019	Felix Moreno (former governor)	18 months	Costa Verde	Vela
07/08/2019	Juan Sánchez	18 months	Costa Verde	Vela
07/08/2019	Nancy Suito (former Callao government official)	18 months	Costa Verde	Vela
07/08/2019	Víctor Suelpres (former Callao government official)	18 months	Costa Verde	Vela
07/08/2019	Roberto Sandobal (former Callao government official)	18 months	Costa Verde	Vela
07/08/2019	Helberth Barrera (former Callao government official)	18 months	Costa Verde	Vela
04/11/2019	Humberto Abanto (lawyer)	18 months	Arbitrations	Vela
04/11/2019	Fernando Cantuarias (lawyer)	18 months	Arbitrations	Vela

(*continued*)

TABLE 3.2 *(continued)*

Date	Name	Time	Case	Team
04/11/2019	Alejandro Alvarez (lawyer)	18 months	Arbitrations	Vela
04/11/2019	Randol Campos (lawyer)	18 months	Arbitrations	Vela
04/11/2019	Luis Prado (lawyer)	18 months	Arbitrations	Vela
04/11/2019	Frank Kundmüller (lawyer)	18 months	Arbitrations	Vela
04/11/2019	Richard Tirado (lawyer)	18 months	Arbitrations	Vela
04/11/2019	Weyden Garcia (lawyer)	18 months	Arbitrations	Vela
04/11/2019	Mario Castillo (lawyer)	18 months	Arbitrations	Vela
04/11/2019	Marcos Espinoza (lawyer)	18 months	Arbitrations	Vela
04/11/2019	Luis Pebe (lawyer)	18 months	Arbitrations	Vela
04/11/2019	Ramirez Rivera (lawyer)	18 months	Arbitrations	Vela
04/11/2019	Daniel Linares (lawyer)	18 months	Arbitrations	Vela
04/11/2019	Alfredo Zapata (lawyer)	18 months	Arbitrations	Vela
11/12/2019	César Villanueva (former governor and cabinet member)	18 months	Construction work San Martin	Vela
11/12/2019	Marco Diaz (former ministerial aide)	18 months	Construction work San Martin	Vela
28/01/2020	Keiko Fujimori (opposition leader)	15 months	Criminal organization	Vela
04/02/2020	Rómulo Peñaranda (businessman)	18 months	Interoceanic Highway	Vela
14/02/2020	Luis Castañeda (former mayor of Lima)	24 months	Campaign financing (Castañeda) and OAS	Vela
21/08/2020	Werner Guevara (businessman)	18 months	Construction work in Loreto	Vela
09/10/2020	Victor Belaúnde (lawyer)	36 months	Construction work in Loreto	Vela

Source: Various newspapers and official reports

Alejandro Toledo.[26] Shortly after, former governor of Callao, Félix Moreno, was similarly handed a pretrial detention.[27] In this initial phase, however, the most headline-grabbing detentions were those secured by Vela's team against Ollanta Humala and his wife, accused of receiving US$3 million from Odebrecht to fund the 2011 presidential campaign.[28] After Vela took over from Castro in July 2018, his team continued to shoot for the stars. In October of that year, prosecutor Pérez requested a pretrial detention against the then opposition

---

[26] "Interpol confirma la orden de captura y alerta roja por Alejandro Toledo," *Radio Programas del Perú* (8 May 2017). At the time of writing, Toledo still awaits a final decision on an extradition request. He was apprehended in California in July 2019.

[27] See timeline of Félix Moreno's case at: https://idehpucp.pucp.edu.pe/observatorio-de-casos-antic orrupcion-y-lavado-de-activos/casos-materia-corrupcion/felix-moreno/ (accessed 31 October 2022).

[28] Jacqueline Fowks, "Ollanta Humala y su esposa, Nadine Heredia, salen de la cárcel después de nueve meses," *El País* (1 May 2018).

leader Keiko Fujimori for thirty-six months.[29] Months later, Alan García[30] and Pedro Pablo Kuczynski (already out of power) were banned from leaving the country. Kuczynski was eventually placed in detention in April 2019 after he asked for permission to travel abroad,[31] and was later put under house arrest.[32] Most tragically, when the police arrived in García's home to execute a pretrial detention order that same month, the former president committed suicide.

In some cases, pretrial detentions made a difference. For example, after the authorities captured businessman Gil Shavit in April 2017, Castro traded immunity for information.[33] This agreement was instrumental to determine that Odebrecht had paid US$4 million in bribes to former governor Félix Moreno.[34] Similarly, in December 2017 his team placed the top executives of Peruvian construction conglomerate Graña & Montero in pretrial detention for eighteen months. They were suspected of facilitating bribe payments in the Inter-Oceanic Highway case. While the detentions were cut short in March 2018, the decision to "turn the heat" on Graña & Montero forced a restructuring of the company's management team. The new chief executives were eager to mitigate the damage inflicted on their reputation and agreed to sign a cooperation agreement.[35] And when the prosecutors, this time under Vela's leadership, threatened Graña & Montero's former executives with another stint in jail for their alleged participation in the Metro de Lima case, they quickly agreed to a plea deal. Finally, Susana Villarán, former mayor of Lima, was accused of receiving money from Odebrecht to fund the 2013 recall referendum campaign and her 2014 re-election bid, and immediately placed behind bars in May 2019. This move persuaded a witness to sign an agreement with the prosecutors in which s/he corroborated the charges. Days later, Villarán confessed to the crimes despite having previously denied the charges during a congressional hearing.[36]

While both teams used pretrial detentions, with Vela in charge of a unified task force from late July 2018, the tactic became more frequent. When comparing a similar time frame of eighteen months (Castro's full term and Vela's

[29] Jacqueline Fowks, "Un juez peruano impone 36 meses de prisión preventiva a Keiko Fujimori," *El País* (1 November 2018).
[30] "Alan García tiene impedimento de salida del país por 18 meses," *El Comercio* (3 December 2018).
[31] "Poder Judicial ordena la detención preliminar de Pedro Pablo Kuczynski," *Gestión* (10 April 2019).
[32] "Kuczynski seguira con arresto domiciliario pese al pedido de carcel de un fiscal," *Agencia EFE* (23 August 2019).
[33] Hence why his name does not appear in Table 3.2.
[34] "Odebrecht: Coima de Félix Moreno se obtuvo de los sobrecostos de la obra Costa Verde Callao," *Gestión* (20 February 2019).
[35] "Graña y Montero inicia colaboración eficaz," *IDL Reporteros* (3 May 2019).
[36] "Siempre supe que los aportes de la NO revocatoria eran de Odebrecht y OAS, confiesa Villaran," *Gestion* (12 May 2019).

tenure from August 2018 to December 2019), we observe twenty-one pretrial detentions under Castro and forty-four under Vela. It is also noticeable that prosecutors asked for longer pretrial detentions under Vela. His prosecutors asked the courts to grant orders that would last for more than eighteen months in fifteen of the forty-nine requests filed until October 2020. This never happened under Castro's leadership. Various factors may account for the pattern. First, they probably reflect Vela and Perez's preference for harsher and more unconventional tactics. For instance, they chose to frame the offences using less orthodox criminal definitions that allowed for longer periods of pretrial detention (see below). Second, we must also consider the combined effect of deploying various tools in the arsenal. As we will discuss in the next section, the ways in which Vela and Castro approached plea bargain negotiations and information exchanges with Brazil differed widely. Vela's approach proved more effective in securing evidence from abroad. With this evidence in hand, he not only had better reasons to request pretrial detentions but could also more effectively use the threat of long stints in jail to extract confessions.

Despite the benefits, the use of pretrial detentions was not without costs. For example, Prosecutor Pérez believed that Odebrecht's off-the-books contributions to Keiko Fujimori's 2011 campaign were part of a money laundering scheme because the cash had originated from the company's secret accounts. He also suspected that Fujimori was working behind the scenes to obstruct the investigation. On that basis, in August 2018 he put her in jail for thirty-six months. The decision, which relied on an expansive interpretation of the crime of money laundering,[37] was a smart one because under the new criminal code prosecutors are allowed more time to investigate this offence. The code also authorises longer pretrial detentions (up to thirty-six months). But as we know, creative legal interpretations are controversial, and since they are not grounded in established jurisprudence, they can prove quite feeble on appeal. In fact, Perez's decision became the subject of a byzantine legal battle that put prosecutors on the defensive.

It all started months before Keiko's case was even on the table, when one of her allies in the Supreme Court anticipated the direction that the inquiry was taking and came to her rescue. In an August 2017 decision on an unrelated case, the judge established tougher evidentiary standards for money laundering charges.[38] Fortunately for the *Lava Jato* prosecutors, this triggered a public outcry: it was clear the judge was trying to protect Keiko. The Supreme Court subsequently rectified the decision in a plenary ruling.[39] Attempts to derail the case against Fujimori did not end there and intensified following her arrest.

---

[37] The prosecutors had already applied a similar theory in Humala's case in 2017.
[38] Segunda Sala Penal Transitoria, Casación N. 92/2017 Arequipa. Justice Hinostroza was responsible for this ruling. It later emerged that he was part of a corruption network. See the analysis of *Cuellos Blancos* below.
[39] Sentencia Plenaria Casatoria, Casación N. 1-2017/CIJ-433.

After all, she was the leader of an opposition party that controlled Congress. Many lawyers maintained that the claim that the cash Keiko had allegedly received from Odebrecht could be classified as "money laundering" was a stretch. Some went further, reasoning that her actions did not match any criminal definition listed in the penal code; it was merely an "administrative offence."[40] Citing some of these arguments, the Supreme Court eventually ruled to reduce the prison term from thirty-six to eighteen months.[41]

The fallout from García's suicide in April 2019 compounded these problems. The tragedy served as the perfect ammunition to raise charges of overzealousness and recklessness against the prosecutors. Echoing these criticisms, Apristas and Fujimoristas in Congress tabled bills to reform the rules on pretrial detentions.[42] Moreover, according to some of our sources, after hearing these criticisms, judges became more reluctant to agree to pretrial detention requests. While these claims are hard to corroborate, we did find that between April and June 2019, at the height of the controversy, the courts rejected at least six pretrial detention requests.

By upping the ante with high-profile pretrial detention orders and innovative interpretations of the criminal code, prosecutors made headlines, carved legal and evidentiary avenues to go after important targets, and potentially neutralised resourceful enemies. But in so doing they also risked undermining their case against defendants like Fujimori, and also the viability of future pretrial detention requests. For example, in September 2019 the Supreme Court devised a new set of stricter guidelines for issuing pretrial detentions.[43] This illustrates the central dilemma that haunts the criminalisation of corruption: investigations cannot take off, or indeed survive, without prosecutors willing to make bold, controversial moves. Those same decisions, however, can also foreshadow their undoing because they open the door for opponents in politics and the judicial system to lash back. This dilemma was also centre stage when it came to negotiations with Odebrecht over a leniency agreement. The remaining sections tell that story, which was critical for the momentum behind Peru's *Lava Jato*.

---

[40] Concerns about the legal void regarding the illegal financing of electoral campaigns led President Vizcarra to propose a constitutional amendment, which was approved via referendum in December 2018. This change established that illegal financing carries a criminal sanction. In August 2019, following recommendations from an expert-led commission tasked with operationalising new constitutional provisions, Congress approved a law creating the lesser crime of "illegal financing of electoral campaigns," one which fits Keiko's case quite neatly. Judges could therefore eventually apply the principle of retroactivity of the most favourable criminal law and change the prosecutors' theory of this and other cases.

[41] "Corte Suprema reduce a 18 meses la prisión preventiva contra Keiko Fujimori," *RPP Noticias* (12 September 2019).

[42] Martin Hidalgo, "Congreso suma 5 proyectos de ley que buscan modificar la prision preventive," *El Comercio* (27 April 2019).

[43] Acuerdo Plenario N. 1-2019/CIJ-116.

To Deal or Not to Deal?

In addition to planning pretrial detentions and dealing with their consequences, Peruvian prosecutors also engaged in plea bargain negotiations. As we discussed in Chapter 2, first-hand accounts of anti-corruption investigations invariably make the case that balancing carrots and sticks is the only way to obtain incriminatory evidence. But carrots are not uncontroversial. Investigators must decide what degree of prosecutorial selectivity they are willing to live with. For Peruvian prosecutors, this was hard because their main interlocutor was a company based in a foreign country, not an individual based in Peru. This was a situation they had not encountered in past investigations, and therefore raised unique technical, logistical, and ethical questions. For instance, in addition to navigating the intricacies of international judicial cooperation, the prosecutors had to coordinate with government lawyers (*procuradores*), whose primary goal was to make sure the company paid reparations for the money the state had lost to inflated project costs. Excessive demands on this front would not help the prosecutors ensure the company's cooperation. And even after agreeing on a common strategy with government lawyers, any benefits prosecutors exchanged to lock-in a leniency agreement would be quite literally unprecedented. As a result, defending them in front of a judge and the mass public could prove hard. Trading immunity for information is often unpopular and helps legitimise the charge that investigators are acting unlawfully, abdicating their role, or simply biased (see Chapters 6 and 8). In fact, as we shall see, offers of immunity helped opponents cast doubt on the impartiality and effectiveness of the *Lava Jato* task force.

When it came to negotiating with Odebrecht, Castro and Vela provided very different answers to the question of prosecutorial selectivity.[44] As early as January 2017, the company expressed willingness to collaborate in exchange for immunity for the executives implicated in the scandal. Odebrecht was also after a broader deal that would allow it to resume operations in Peru. Vela's team welcomed this overture. He and Alonso Peña Cabrera, head of the international cooperation division of the MP, quickly negotiated a preliminary agreement with Jorge Barata, former head of Odebrecht in Peru, and two other Brazilian executives, including Marcelo Odebrecht. In the deal signed on 8 June 2017, Peruvian prosecutors agreed to refrain from bringing charges against them. This was an important concession not only because it generated goodwill among key witnesses, but also because Brazilian judicial authorities refused to release relevant case files if this risked double jeopardy (i.e., prosecuting executives in two jurisdictions for the same crimes).[45] The agreement permitted access, among other things, to the video recording of the confession that

---

[44] Gustavo Gorriti, "Entre el Silencio y la Confesión," *IDL-Reporteros* (22 February 2018).
[45] Gustavo Gorriti, "¿Quieres la Información? Firma Primero," *IDL Reporteros* (12 June 2017).

Marcelo Odebrecht made in Curitiba in May 2017. It also made it possible to further interrogate him in November 2017, and thus obtain new evidence about illegal donations to Keiko Fujimori and Ollanta Humala's campaigns. Barata corroborated these accusations in February 2018 and confessed to off-the-books donations to other politicians, including Toledo, Kuczynski, García, and Villarán.[46] In other words, this initial agreement was instrumental in allowing Vela and his associates to make quick progress on their side of the crusade.

By contrast, Castro proved more reluctant to grant immunity to those willing to assist the case. This was a major problem for everyone involved. First, it hampered progress on the more significant line of inquiry, the one focused on large public works projects. Second, because Castro's cases involved bribes that cost the state millions in overpriced infrastructure, he held the keys to the broader agreement the company was after, that is, an affordable damages bill and an end to the ban on future contracts with the state. Without these benefits, Odebrecht executives had few incentives to continue cooperating with Vela's team. Moreover, the company was the one in a position to supply hard documentary evidence. A corporate deal, not just plea bargains with individual executives, was therefore of the essence.

Castro's relationship with Odebrecht was very tense from the start. Despite signing a preliminary agreement in January 2017, in which the company promised to assist the work being done in the Inter-Oceanic Highway and Metro de Lima cases[47] and thus establish its reliability as an informant, Castro opened a formal investigation against Odebrecht. Castro also refused to entertain the possibility of closing a pre-existing investigation into Odebrecht's participation in a case not included in the original agreement (the gas pipeline case), in exchange for additional cooperation. More importantly, while Barata cooperated with Castro from the beginning, enabling some of the pretrial detentions ordered by members of his team, Castro never offered him full immunity from prosecution or asset embargoes.[48] Castro's decision to spend several months testing Barata's good intentions with numerous requests for additional information eroded trust, limited the flow of evidence, and stalled the negotiations. At one point, Castro concluded that Barata had withheld information from his team, so he opened a formal investigation against the star witness and asked a court to freeze Barata's assets.[49] The implications of this decision were huge, as it violated the terms of existing cooperation agreements and therefore jeopardised

---

[46] "*Lava Jato*: El escándalo de corrupción de Odebrecht en el Perú," *La Republica* (17 February 2019).

[47] "Caso Odebrecht: la Fiscalía de Perú logra el primer acuerdo de entrega de ganancias ilícitas," *CNN Español* (5 January 2017).

[48] Gustavo Gorriti, "Hablaste, te fregaste," *IDL Reporteros* (14 June 2018).

[49] "¿Qué significa que Jorge Barata haya sido excluido del delito de colusión en el caso Odebrecht?" *Peru 21* (28 November 2017).

the admissibility of the evidence that Barata and other collaborators had provided thus far to Vela's team. The relationship reached a breaking point in July 2018, when Odebrecht decided to stop talking to Peruvian prosecutors.

As a result of these contrasting strategies, the two streams of the *Lava Jato* inquiry eventually started to move at very different paces. This illustrates the importance of securing confessions to build momentum in grand corruption investigations. Factors such as the legal framework governing plea bargain negotiations can obviously not explain such contrasting approaches between the prosecutors. Moreover, during most of the initial period, Castro and Vela had the support of Chief Prosecutor Sánchez. And, of course, they were both clearly skilful and experienced. So, what explains such different negotiating positions?

The one answer we got from our sources, both those with direct participation in the negotiations and those who followed them closely, was consistently underwhelming: it all came down to prosecutorial "styles." We were eventually persuaded that these sources were on to something; leadership mattered. The difference in approaches boiled down to the fact that Vela was a pragmatic and intrepid "street" prosecutor, and therefore more relentless and aggressive in orientation. For example, he was more willing than Castro to make regular visits to Brazil, and thus forged a personal relationship with Brazilian authorities and witnesses. This resulted in higher levels of mutual trust: greater willingness to make concessions on the part of Vela and to hand over better information (both through formal and informal channels) on the part of the Brazilians. Vela quickly realised that this symbiosis would help him with another key pillar of his approach, one he learnt from Brazilian Judge Moro: a fluid relationship with the media. In fact, he became well-known for feeding the information supplied by his international partners to journalists, thus raising his profile, showing results to the public, and consolidating his anti-corruption credentials. Castro, by contrast, was a "desk" prosecutor, more reticent to engage in informal transnational adventures or public relations strategies. He therefore never developed the same rapport with, or trust in, his Brazilian counterparts, and never fully saw the importance of exploiting juicy witness testimonies to add momentum to the case. Our sources, including civil society actors who approached him with offers to support the investigation, indicated that he consistently eschewed those alliances.

Contrasting degrees of zealousness were also reflected in how both Vela and Castro understood the role of plea bargains. Corporate plea bargains were unprecedented so relying on them required a certain openness to experimentation and unorthodoxy. Castro was extremely cautious and tried to make sure he extracted as much information as possible before agreeing to any deal. And even if this high informational threshold was ever met, Castro never seemed persuaded of the value and appropriateness of offering exceptional monetary benefits on top of immunity from prosecution. For example, he showed little interest in coordinating strategies with government lawyers tasked with estimating the fines to be imposed on the company. Partly as a result of this lack of coordination, government lawyers pursued a maximalist strategy, at one point asking for S./3000 million in reparations. This clearly undermined the chances of the prosecutors reaching a deal.[50] Odebrecht was not in a position to pay such an exorbitant sum. Moreover, if as a result of having to pay a large amount in damages the company filed for bankruptcy or left the country, all efforts to extract additional information would be doomed. By contrast, Vela and his team showed a greater willingness to take risks. This was in line with other aspects of their strategy, for example, their decision to rely on expansive interpretations of "money laundering." In their view, without a deal there would be no information, and without information, no case against the politicians. If a deal meant being accused of "rewarding" a corrupt company, so be it. Furthermore, Vela was prepared to accept that the company had no incentives to provide access to all the evidence it had about corruption in Peru, so at some point, his team would have to stop asking for more, agree to grant generous criminal and commercial benefits, and trust that in the future Odebrecht would prove more forthcoming.

Victim of his orthodox approach, Castro became increasingly isolated and the target of media criticism. The company's July 2018 decision to stop conversations, further pushed Castro into the wilderness. Odebrecht made it clear that with him leading the main task force, the company would not come back to the negotiating table.[51] If the inquiry was to recover its initial momentum and truly snowball into an anti-corruption crusade, it became apparent that what the case needed was a new leader willing to change course.

An Unexpected Revelation

One unexpected and completely unrelated event injected the oxygen required to jump-start the negotiations. This could be thought of as another "moment of serendipity." Since 2014 a team of provincial prosecutors had been investigating a drug trafficking organisation based in the port city of Callao. During that inquiry, based largely on wiretaps, they stumbled upon evidence of influence peddling by members of the judiciary and the MP. Investigators had strong reasons to believe that a network of judicial clientelism, which involved several Supreme Court Justices and Supreme Prosecutors, members of the judicial council, provincial judges and prosecutors, and influential lawyers and politicians, worked behind the scenes to place allies in key positions and micromanage the outcome of cases. By now it should not come as a surprise that the prosecutors who discovered this belonged to a unit specialised in organised crime. According to our confidential interviews with actors linked to the case, it

---

[50] "Fiscalía considera 'extrema' postura de procurador frente a Odebrecht," *El Comercio* (30 January 2018).

[51] Romina Mella, "Zona de naufragio," *IDL Reporteros* (2 July 2018).

is largely because of this expertise, the support of a committed unit leader, and close links with the police, that they were able to make progress without attracting the attention of the targets of the inquiry, who obviously had the power to shut down the case. This was bureaucratic boundary control at its best.

In July 2018 a reporter published a high impact exposé with transcripts of the wiretaps that formed the cornerstone of the investigation.[52] The revelations, which came to be known as the *Cuellos Blancos del Puerto* (While Collars of the Port) scandal, sent shockwaves across the judiciary and MP. The impact on the *Lava Jato* case was twofold.

First, *Cuellos Blancos* exposed a network of judicial and prosecutorial authorities with links to those implicated in *Lava Jato* and the power to help them out. As a result, the ability of this network to openly derail the investigation diminished. For example, Supreme Court Justice Hinostroza, who was the one who had previously tried to shield Keiko Fujimori from the money laundering charges, was fired. At least six additional Supreme Court Justices and two Supreme Prosecutors were also severely compromised. Despite initially remaining in post due to the protection they received from Fujimoristas in Congress,[53] these actors would no longer be able to disguise their obstructionist moves in technical legalese as effectively. Furthermore, the judicial council, the institution at the heart of the new scandal, was disbanded. In the absence of a functioning disciplinary body, *Lava Jato* prosecutors now had greater degrees of freedom to make risky moves (Table 3.3).

Second, these shocking revelations coincided with the election of a new chief prosecutor. Prosecutor Pedro Chávarry replaced Pablo Sánchez in June 2018. Although later on he would also end up embroiled in *Cuellos Blancos*, for the moment Chávarry's goal was to repair the image of the MP. To divert the attention away from judicial corruption and back to the politicians, there was no better alternative than to jump-start *Lava Jato*. In an effort to change the narrative and show the system's commitment to fighting corruption, Chávarry removed Castro as the head of the *Lava Jato* task force and appointed Vela.[54] Both streams of the inquiry would now benefit from greater coordination and Vela's zeal.

The Deal with Odebrecht

Determined to get a deal, Vela departed radically from Castro's approach. Instead of compartmentalising negotiations by line of inquiry (e.g., one for each public works project), or negotiating separately with each executive and

---

[52] "Corte y corrupcion," *IDL Reporteros* (7 July 2018).
[53] Congress has the prerogative to authorise indictments against high-level judicial actors.
[54] "Fiscalía de la Nación unifica el equipo especial del Caso *Lava Jato*," *El Comercio* (21 July 2018).

TABLE 3.3 *Judicial authorities implicated in* Cuellos Blancos

No.	Name	Position	Status of disciplinary process	Congressional decision	Notes
1	César Hinostroza Pariachi	Supreme Court Justice	Suspended by CNM* (07/16/2018)	Removed and banned from holding public office for 10 years (4/10/2018)	
2	Aldo Figueroa Navarro	Supreme Court Justice	Removed by JNJ* (02/03/2021)		
3	Martín Hurtado Reyes	Supreme Court Justice	Suspended by JNJ (07/20/2020); suspension extended (01/27/2021)		
4	Duberlí Rodríguez Tineo	Supreme Court Justice			Left after reaching retirement age (25/09/2019)
5	Ángel Romero Díaz	Supreme Court Justice	JNJ launched a preliminary investigation (02/20/2020)		
6	Vicente Walde Jáuregui	Supreme Court Justice	JNJ launched a preliminary investigation (02/20/2020)		Left after reaching retirement age (27/11/2019)
7	César San Martín Castro	Supreme Court Justice	Suspended by JNJ for 30 days (02/05/2021)		
8	Pedro Chávarry Vallejos	Chief Prosecutor	Removed by JNJ (02/02/2021)		
9	Tomas Gálvez Villegas	Supreme Prosecutor	Suspended by JNJ (14/07/2020)		
10	Victor Rodríguez Monteza	Supreme Prosecutor	JNJ launched a preliminary investigation (3/07/2020)		
11	Orlando Velásquez Benites	Member of the judicial council (CNM)		Removed (20/07/2018)	

(continued)

TABLE 3.3 (continued)

No.	Name	Position	Status of disciplinary process	Congressional decision	Notes
12	Guido Águila Grados	Member of the judicial council (CNM)		Removed (20/07/2018)	Resigned (16/07/2018)
13	Iván Noguera Ramos	Member of the judicial council (CNM)	CNM asked Congress to remove him (10/07/2018)	Removed (20/07/2018)	
14	Herbert Marcelo Cubas	Member of the judicial council (CNM)		Removed (20/07/2018)	
15	Julio Gutiérrez Pebes	Member of the judicial council (CNM)	CNM initiates removal proceedings (10/07/2018)	Removed (20/07/2018)	
16	Baltazar Morales Parraguez	Member of the judicial council (CNM)		Removed (20/07/2018)	
17	Maritza Aragón Hermoza	Member of the judicial council (CNM)		Removed (20/07/2018)	
18	Walter Ríos Montalvo	Justice, Superior Court of Callao	Suspended by the OCMA** (02/05/2020); OCMA recommended removal (02/27/2020)		
19	Víctor León Montenegro	Former Justice, Supreme Court of Callao	He was no longer in office when the audio recordings were released.		
20	Ricardo Chang Racuay	Justice, Superior Court of Lima	Suspended by the OCMA. Later on, he resigned		Pleaded guilty to the crime of active bribery and was sentenced to 5 years and 7 months in prison. First conviction in the *Cuellos Blancos* case.

Source: Various newspapers. *The CNM (Consejo Nacional de la Magistratura) is the old judicial council disbanded as a result of *Cuellos Blancos*. JNJ (Junta Nacional de Justicia) is the name of the new council. ** Oficina de Control de la Magistratura is the judiciary's internal audit division

the company, Vela brought all discussions under the same umbrella. This had one key objective: speed up the process of corroborating the evidence, establish the credibility of the witnesses, and seal the deal. Without this, no judge would approve the final agreement. While the company could supply hard evidence of the illicit payments, only the individual executives could provide the necessary context to fully grasp the dynamics of the bribery scheme and assign individual criminal responsibility. For example, the executives were the only ones who could reconstruct the sequence of informal meetings or decipher the pseudonyms used in the company's parallel accounting system to identify each client. It therefore made sense to unify both sets of negotiations and corroboration exercises. After all, as discussed in Chapter 2, uncovering systemic corruption requires a systemic approach, not a fragmented one.

As negotiations resumed, Vela further benefited from a legislative change introduced in March 2018. Law 30.373 created a formula to calculate fines for companies implicated in corruption. The formula replaced the subjective criteria hitherto outlined in the Civil Code. *Lava Jato* was severely damaging the economy. The construction sector had come to a stop: payments along the supply chain were at a standstill and companies had trouble securing loans to fund operations as banks feared that existing and future corruption allegations could cripple their clients' finances. The government therefore hoped that more objective criteria to estimate fines would avoid excessive penalties, bring certainty to balance sheets, and reassure the banks. The new law also had the potential to provide a clear focal point for negotiations between Odebrecht and government lawyers, which until now had been marred by massive disagreements over the amount due in reparations.

Armed with this new set of incentives, Vela opened a new chapter in the relationship between the *Lava Jato* task force and government lawyers. By law, any deal on the criminal front had to be accompanied by a deal on the civil front (i.e., the fine). This called for coordination between branches, something which had been missing under Castro. The prosecutors agreed that government lawyers would be solely responsible for negotiating the fine and the payment scheme. While the law allowed prosecutors to take over this aspect of the process, the job was simply too complex. Vela recognised his team lacked the time or technical expertise. He also understood that government lawyers had stronger cards to reach a viable deal. On the one hand, because government lawyers were now constrained in what they could demand from Odebrecht, they were likely to agree on a fine that would not bankrupt the company. On the other, given that the prosecutors' main goal was to extract information, not money, their threats to the company regarding the lowest fine they were prepared to offer would be less credible. Government lawyers, whose main interest was the money, had more leverage to agree on a sum high enough to withstand public scrutiny. Government lawyers, for their part, came to terms with the idea that negotiating the fine in the context of a plea deal with the prosecutors was the best way to make sure the company paid. Moreover, with the new formula in place, government lawyers needed the information obtained by the prosecutors to estimate damages. Cooperation was therefore essential. This alignment of interests made it possible to agree on a joint strategy.

Government lawyers estimated damages for S./ 610 million and refused to budge. The company protested and turned to Vela. But in line with the strategy agreed beforehand, Vela and his team told Odebrecht that they would not get involved with the financial negotiations. Vela asked the company to sort things out with government lawyers, and only then come back to negotiate immunity from prosecution and an end to the ban on the company's ability to do business with the state. Odebrecht, now in a corner, agreed to pay the full S./ 610 million. While much lower than the amounts floated in the previous months, it was still a debilitating figure. To make sure the company could pay, the state accepted a proposal for a flexible payment plan and removed an asset embargo hanging over the company's head. The prosecutors in turn agreed to offer full immunity from prosecution and to lift the aforementioned ban. They also agreed to a dynamic deal, whereby the benefits would not be automatically suspended should the investigators discover new crimes. In doing so, unlike Castro before him, Vela accepted that the company would not and could not disclose everything at once. Finally, Odebrecht agreed to give information about the corruption scheme mounted to secure four major infrastructure projects (Vía Evitamiento in Cusco, Costa Verde in El Callao, Inter-Oceanic Highway, and Metro de Lima), and to surrender the information saved in company servers, which included (among other things) details about the payments made through Odebrecht's infamous Division of Structured Operations.[55]

The Moment of Backlash

Because the company had to establish credibility and reliability, the flow of information accelerated as the final negotiations progressed. With new evidence in hand, in October 2018 prosecutor Pérez, with Vela's support, filed the already discussed pretrial detention request against Keiko Fujimori. He also conducted an unprecedented search in her party's headquarters, which was widely covered in the press. This was certainly a daring move: Fujimori's party still controlled Congress and was well-known for having allies in the upper echelons of the judiciary and prosecution services. *Cuellos Blancos* had revealed that much. The pretrial detention, coupled with the imminence of a deal, put the establishment on high alert. A fierce backlash ensued. This showed that while securing productive evidentiary flows was critical to gain momentum, it did not guarantee the sustainability of the crusade. As argued in Chapter 2, politicians' reactions are yet another obstacle that has to be overcome for the snowball effect to materialise in earnest.

---

[55] This was the division set up to manage relations with politicians and government officials across Latin America.

When Chief Prosecutor Chávarry promoted Vela back in July as a gesture to weather the Cuellos Blancos storm, he expected to be able to control the new team. Chávarry, whose links to Fujimori and the network of judicial clientelism eventually came to light, had hoped *Lava Jato* would not move too far away from its initial focus and implicate Keiko. In so doing, he fatally underestimated the prosecutors' autonomy and commitment. By mid-December 2018, his relationship with the prosecutors reached breaking point. Vela made use of a court hearing to publicly accuse the chief prosecutor of obstructing the investigation.[56] In his view, Chávarry sought to undermine the relationship between the task force and Brazilian authorities.[57] Vela was not mistaken: on New Year's Eve, Chávarry dismissed him and Pérez, accusing them of mishandling negotiations with Odebrecht.[58]

What followed was an impressive display of political dexterity and media savviness on the part of the embattled prosecutors. Starting in 2016, Vela and his team took great care in forging tacit alliances with journalists and civil society organisations. These would prove invaluable when news of their dismissal broke. For example, a few months earlier, the Instituto de Defensa Legal, an NGO that houses public interest lawyers as well as investigative journalists, had filed a complaint before the Inter-American Commission on Human Rights denouncing threats to the autonomy of *Lava Jato* prosecutors.[59] As one IDL lawyer told us:

Whenever we see news indicative of physical or disciplinary threats against some prosecutors, we tend to 'judicialize' them. We file information requests or denounce the relevant disciplinary bodies for trying to intimidate prosecutors. Regarding *Cuellos Blancos* and *Lava Jato*, we approached the Inter-American Commission. This was meant to deter those who posed a danger to sensitive investigations and thus protect the prosecutors (Authors' interview, August 2020).

Deterrence clearly did not work in this case, but the Inter-American Commission did join the chorus of voices demanding the MP to reinstate Vela and his team.[60] By going public, Vela and Pérez also managed to engineer support among the mass public. This support became particularly visible on 2 January 2019, three days after they were fired. A huge group of protesters marched towards the headquarters of the MP to demand Chávarry's resignation.[61] This was a truly unprecedented display of mass support for judicial actors in Peru. It worked: the

[56] "Fiscal Vela: 'Jose Domingo Perez y yo hemos sido permanentemente hostilizados'," *RPP Noticias* (15 December 2018).
[57] Vela also complained that someone had accused Pérez of plagiarising his post-graduate thesis.
[58] "Pedro Chávarry remueve a fiscales Vela y Pérez del Equipo Especial del Caso *Lava Jato*," *El Comercio* (1 January 2019).
[59] "Fiscal Jose Domingo Perez no realizo tramite ni participo en solicitud del IDL ante CIDH," *Instituto de Defensa Legal* (12 December 2018).
[60] "CIDH expresa preocupacion por remocion de fiscales Vela y Perez," *Andina* (1 January 2019).
[61] "Caso Chávarry: Así fue la marcha que llegó hasta el Ministerio Público," *El Comercio* (3 January 2019).

Council of Supreme Prosecutors asked Chávarry to tender his resignation. While he first tried to save face by reinstating Vela and Pérez, a few days later he ignominiously stepped down.

A reinvigorated *Lava Jato* task force sealed the deal with Odebrecht on 15 February 2019 at the Peruvian consulate in São Paulo. Immediately after, Jorge Barata confirmed that Odebrecht had funded one of Alan García's campaigns, corroborated the existence of a cartel in the construction sector, proved that Odebrecht bribed Toledo to secure the Inter-Oceanic Highway project, and showed that former Lima Mayor Villarán knew of Odebrecht's contributions to her campaign coffers. In other words, no one was spared. The prosecutors thus confirmed that they had been right to see the deal as the main pillar of the investigative strategy.

Unfortunately for the prosecutors, the establishment would not surrender that easily. While big chunks of the network of judicial corruption revealed by Cuellos Blancos were dismantled surprisingly fast (see Table 3.3), key members remained as Supreme Prosecutors and Supreme Court Justices and were prepared to protect some defendants. Most notably, in July 2019 the Supreme Court was reportedly getting ready to revoke Fujimori's pretrial detention. The timely publication of additional wiretaps that further implicated the justices in Cuellos Blancos forced them to delay the decision.[62] This gave the *Lava Jato* team some breathing space because the Supreme Court would have most certainly torpedoed their efforts to deepen the campaign finances stream of the inquiry, and with it, the most productive pillar of the entire investigation.

The task force narrowly survived, but there was more to come. Fujimoristas felt increasingly threatened by the flurry of new allegations and trained their eyes on the Constitutional Court, which had to rule on a writ of habeas corpus filed by Keiko Fujimori's lawyers. The goal was to make sure the Court established a precedent against pretrial detentions and the classification of the *Lava Jato* crimes as "money laundering." An opportunity came in September 2019 when Congress initiated proceedings to appoint new Constitutional justices. Fujimoristas tried to manipulate the process to their advantage, but like previous efforts to control judicial institutions, the move failed spectacularly. Their tactics were too blunt and their ulterior motives too obvious. Meddling with Constitutional Court appointments triggered clashes with the Executive, now in the hands of President Vizcarra.[63] This ended with the

---

[62] One Supreme Court justice recused himself. The Supreme Prosecutor in charge of the case, who days earlier had urged the court to release Fujimori, was also implicated in the scandal.

[63] President Kuczynski resigned in March 2018 following a period of severe inter-branch clashes with Fujimoristas. When the *Lava Jato* revelations implicating Kuczynski came to light in 2017, Fujimoristas tried to impeach him on 21 December but failed. After a brief summer truce, Congress moved again to impeach the president, this time precipitating his departure from office (Vergara 2018).

dissolution of Congress, Fujimori's only remaining institutional stronghold.[64] Vizcarra's move, while not without controversy, was quite popular.[65] In fact, in the January 2020 legislative elections called to form an interim Congress, the performance of Fujimori's party was truly dismal: the Fujimorista bloc went down from 72 legislators to just 15 (out of 130).

While Vela and Perez's public outreach efforts were the key to diffuse Chávarry's initial threat, as other actors joined the backlash the sustainability of the crusade became more dependent on the contingent outcome of clashes with politicians, and therefore more precarious. It certainly helped that Fujimoristas relied on unscrupulous tactics that backfired. *Lava Jato* thus benefited from cannibalising dynamics, which saw members of the establishment destroy each other. The constant onslaught did, however, take its toll. This is because not all avenues chosen to lash back against the task force were equally clumsy.

Discursively, opponents of the investigation put forward fairness and "rule of law" arguments to discredit the prosecutors. First, critics framed the deal with Odebrecht as a capitulation to foreign business interests. The focus was almost invariably on the fine, which they deemed too low. According to Luz Salgado, a member of the Fujimorista parliamentary group, "[the prosecutors] don't know how the debts are going to be paid [. . .] [W]hat I see is mostly a concern for the interests of the company instead of our [country's]." Her colleague Rosa Bartra agreed: the prosecution is "giving everything to a criminal organization that has perverted our system."[66] Second, shortly after the courts had reviewed and approved the deal, reporters revealed that the documentation that Odebrecht surrendered contained records of bribes that the company had failed to confess. This was the perfect ammunition for those trying to depict the prosecutors as naïve at best, or biased in favour of the company, at worst. As we shall see in Chapters 6 and 8, many of these criticisms strongly resonated with the public and dented support for the task

---

[64] The Fujimorista attempt to manipulate the appointment of new Constitutional Court justices was widely criticised, prompting the Executive to file a "confidence motion." The reasoning was that the selection process affected the principle of separation of powers. Congress ignored the motion, which the Executive interpreted as a de facto rejection. This was the second time that Congress had rejected a confidence motion since 2016. According to the Constitution (article 134), two failed confidence motions allow the president to dissolve Congress.

[65] At the time, Vizcarra's popularity was sky high, partly because he resolutely embraced the anti-corruption cause, hoping to ride the coattails of *Lava Jato* and Cuellos Blancos. For example, Vizcarra proposed four constitutional changes – a reform to the judicial council, the introduction of term limits for national legislators, stricter campaign financing regulations, and the return to bicameralism. The first three proposals were decisively approved in a December 2018 referendum.

[66] "Fuerza Popular reitera criticas al acuerdo con Odebrecht tras su homologacion," *El Comercio* (19 June 2019).

force. The effectiveness of the critique underscores the precarity of a prosecutorial strategy heavily reliant on unorthodox tactics.

Subsequent developments further point to the limited ability of the prosecutors to emerge unscathed from relentless backlash or ensure the sustainability of the crusade and its snowballing trajectory. To be sure, the task force showed great skill in diffusing threats during this first round of attacks, especially when Chávarry tried to remove Vela and Pérez from the case. They were also lucky that *Cuellos Blancos* undermined the firepower of obstructionist forces in the upper echelons of the MP and the judiciary, and that the political crisis that followed hardened Fujimorismo's self-destructive instincts. But as the investigation progressed, prosecutors took a series of steps that ended this streak. As we argued in Chapter 2, zealousness can at times jeopardise the integrity of the inquiry and its momentum. A process that is fuelled by agency and contingency is also vulnerable to actors' inherent fallibility and biases. We can see this very clearly in how the task force became embroiled in yet another inter-branch crisis.

In September 2020, the Congress elected in January attacked Vizcarra.[67] Parliamentarians resorted to a constitutional provision that allows the legislature to remove the president on the grounds of "permanent moral incapacity." The argument was that Vizcarra had conspired to hide his role in the irregular hiring of singer Richard Swing in the Ministry of Culture. While the impeachment failed, it did weaken Vizcarra, who up to this point had tried hard to burnish his transparency credentials. It did not take long for Congress to find another pretext to file a second impeachment request in November 2020. This time the trigger were rumours that the *Lava Jato* task force was negotiating a plea deal with someone who claimed that Vizcarra had received bribes during his tenure as governor of Moquegua (2011–2014). Vizcarra's involvement in *Lava Jato* was the reason Congress needed to finally oust him. Because the legal grounds were again rather dubious,[68] citizen indignation ensued, leading to mass protests across the country. Demonstrators were met with violence, leaving two dead and thousands injured. A victim of the ensuing domestic and international outcry, the government chosen to replace Vizcarra resigned within a week and Congress elected another interim president.

Amid this political turmoil, journalist César Romero published an exposé in which he argued that "the statement of the would-be informants against former president Martín Vizcarra for alleged acts of corruption in Moquegua was not spontaneous. It was suggested, conditioned, and promoted by the team of prosecutors in the *Lava Jato* case."[69] Given the tenor of the accusation,

---

[67] Vizcarra refrained from fielding his own congressional candidates so his position in the legislature was fragile.

[68] A total of 105 congressmen voted in favour of the motion.

[69] Cesar Romero, "Declaracion contra Martin Vizcarra fue un pedido del equipo *Lava Jato*," *La Republica* (22 November 2020).

backlash against the task force was inevitable. This time, however, it was not just the usual suspects turning against the prosecutors; figures who had previously been staunch supporters of the investigation made devastating critiques, accusing *Lava Jato* of "playing politics" or "playing dirty" instead of pursuing justice. Some even suggested that the prosecutors were themselves involved in corrupt deals.[70] This came at a time when the task force was getting ready to wrap up various lines of inquiry, and initiating new ones, for example, against Vizcarra.[71]

This haemorrhage of public trust, which we document more extensively in Chapter 8, highlights the precarity of crusades. Prosecutors are always a mistake (or gamble) away from losing it all. While Peru's *Lava Jato* is still ongoing at the time of writing, backlash at various junctures compromised the sustainability and credibility of the anti-corruption effort, reducing its legitimacy, scope, and speed.

PROSECUTORIAL AGENCY OR POLITICAL PRECARIOUSNESS?

In line with scholarship that emphasises political resources as a determinant of corruption prosecutions (Conaghan 2012; Popova and Post 2018; Helmke et al. 2019), some might argue that the momentum behind *Lava Jato* in Peru had little to do with more robust criminal justice institutions, the creation of task forces, or prosecutorial agency, and is more parsimoniously explained with reference to the structural weakness of Peruvian parties. Peruvian political actors are so weak in comparative perspective that they do not actually constitute a serious threat. They backtrack or fail too easily, allowing prosecutors to do their job relatively unconstrained. In other words, the emergence of a crusade is not puzzling; investigators were hunting lions in the zoo. Indeed, the prosecutors went after politicians without robust party support, including former presidents Toledo and Humala. And the defendants that at different stages had more power (Kuczynski, Fujimori, García, Vizcarra), always stood on precarious grounds. Even those with institutional resources were weak in an

---

[70] Luis Pasara, "Los fiscales han jugado sucio," *La Mula* (17 November 2020).

[71] In May 2019, the prosecution finished the investigation against Humala and his wife. They sent the case to a trial court, asking for a twenty-year sentence against the former president. Between July 2019 and February 2021, the courts held hearings to evaluate the accusation ("audiencias de control de acusación"). The trial started in February 2022. In March 2021, Prosecutor Perez finished the investigation against Keiko Fujimori and also sent the case to a trial court. At the time of writing, the prosecutors' accusation against Fujimori is still being scrutinised by the courts. If given the green light, there will be a trial. Cases against former Lima mayor Susana Villaran and former presidents Kuczynski and Vizcarra, by contrast, are still in the preliminary investigation phase. In the case of Vizcarra, the prosecutors filed a pretrial detention request in early 2021. While the courts denied it, they did agree to imposing a ban on international travel.

organisational sense and lacked robust links with loyal groups of voters. As we will further discuss in Chapters 6 and 8, partisan identification barely exists in Peru and public opinion has a strong aversion for politicians.

Although not without merits, an exclusive focus on political resources is unsatisfactory. To begin with, the idea that all establishment actors implicated in the *Lava Jato* scandal were weak is simply not accurate. If anything, the ongoing political crisis in Peru has its roots in the growing strength of Fujimorismo as a parliamentary force. This renewed strength resulted from a fruitful congressional coalition with APRA starting in the mid-2000s and excellent performances in the 2011 and 2016 elections (Vergara 2018; Muñoz 2021). All of this contributed to the emergence of Congress as a central institution in Peruvian politics (Dargent and Rousseau 2021). Fujimoristas were of course aware that their power was on the rise. Since at least 2015, still during Humala's presidency, the so-called fuji-aprismo acted as a confrontational force in Congress, successfully attacking the Executive at various points, boycotting reform attempts, and shielding themselves and their allies from investigations. Most notably, they blocked the work of the commission set up to investigate *Lava Jato* before the arrival of explosive information from the United States. And they subsequently kept the country on edge for more than two years after Fujimoristas gained full control of Congress in 2016, censoring cabinet ministers and shielding various senior members of the judiciary and the MP, including Chief Prosecutor Chávarry, despite mounting evidence of their participation in *Cuellos Blancos*. The institutional power of "*fuji-aprismo*" was therefore real *and* significant. They had the means (votes in Congress and allies in the criminal justice system) to obstruct the work of the task force.

Where a focus on political resources is more fruitful is in trying to understand why nominally strong actors ultimately failed to wield their power more effectively. Organisational weakness impacts decision-making capacity because it does not allow Peruvian parties to lengthen their time horizons (Levitsky 2013; Levistky and Zavaleta 2016; Meléndez 2019). And the huge disconnect with voters further complicates the calculation of the political costs of certain actions. In other words, organisationally weak parties lacked strategic vision and made too many mistakes along the way, ultimately making it easier for the prosecutors to do their job. Indeed, several observers have highlighted the electoral "irrationality" of various attempts by Fujimoristas to derail the investigation. These attempts, which ultimately cost them their congressional majority, have been explained with reference to the fact that throughout this period, Fujimorismo continued to behave not like a robust party organisation, but like a vehicle for its leader to achieve short-term goals, including the presidency and favourable court outcomes, often resorting to desperate tactics (Vergara 2018). This personalistic and self-serving approach opened a wedge between the party and the electorate, partly because voters did not appreciate living in constant crisis mode.

While bad decisions may be a function of organisational weakness, they cannot be fully attributed to political weakness. In fact, one might argue exactly the opposite. When *Lava Jato* started, Keiko Fujimori and those orbiting around her were very confident that their position following the 2016 elections meant they would not have to face the wrath of daring prosecutors. Consider, for example, how she publicly supported the pretrial detentions ordered in July 2017 against former president Humala and his wife Nadine Heredia. In her twitter account, Fujimori wrote: "the judicial system has shown signs of independence"; "justice continues in search of the truth that we all deserve to know."[72] A Fujimorista congressman also sounded bullish when he told the press that "justice slowly makes its way, and the truth comes to light." APRA leaders were similarly confident that what happened to Humala would not happen to them. APRA's general secretary, Omar Quesada, for instance, commented that this should be a lesson for the Peruvian people to never again elect "improvised and adventurous" leaders.

That Fujimorists and Apristas could lash back so aggressively when the investigation came to haunt them is a further sign that they had the means to do so. At the end of the day, however, their capital sin was to overestimate the power of their network of cronies in the courts and prosecution services to control everything that went on inside those institutions, as well as their own political capacity to shield themselves from prosecution. In particular, they overestimated how certain subterranean organisational changes in the prosecution services, coupled with smart tactical investigative decisions, would allow *Lava Jato* to take a life of its own, resisting external pressures and weakening hitherto resourceful defendants. When political actors struggle (or fail) to survive crusades, it is tempting to conclude that they were not very powerful to begin with. But the truth is that had the investigation been managed differently or by less experienced law enforcement agents, it would have probably been possible for Fujimoristas and others to contain it.[73]

Finally, avoiding political reductionism, and paying close attention to the role of prosecutorial institutions and choices in the story, is also important simply because those choices help explain not only why *Lava Jato* gained momentum in the way it did, but also why it sometimes lost it. As discussed, backlash was perhaps more damaging not when the political establishment overtly pointed its guns at the prosecutors, but when Vela and his team made controversial decisions that fatally undermined their reputation.

---

[72] "Ollanta Humala y Nadine Heredia a prision preventive: Estas fueron las reacciones," *El Comercio* (14 July 2017).

[73] At the height of the backlash, it obviously helped that newly appointed president Vizcarra put his popularity and the bully pulpit at the service of the anti-corruption cause. Vizcarra's quick unravelling, however, suggests we cannot explain *Lava Jato's* survival only with reference to politicians' resources and behaviour.

CONCLUSION

After Brazil, Peru stands out as the country where prosecutors have been able to expand the *Lava Jato* investigation the most. This was partially the result of a process of institutional change in the MP, starting with the autonomy granted by the 1979 and 1993 constitutions. Autonomy from external political actors notwithstanding, the structure of the MP still generated few incentives for rank-and-file prosecutors to take the initiative in attacking establishment actors. Since the early 2000s a series of piecemeal reforms changed this, enabling the development of pockets of internal autonomy and investigative capacity. The first set of reforms took place following the collapse of Fujimori's authoritarian regime in late 2000, enabling bureaucratic differentiation. Coupled with the adoption of American-style prosecutorial tools, this enhanced the ability of the prosecution services to investigate macro-criminality. The institutional environment and the legal framework continued on a capacity-building trajectory in the mid-2000s after the democratic transition. In particular, the MP benefited from the adoption of the accusatorial model in 2004. Groups within the institution thus acquired the resources and professional repertoires needed to make a success of corruption investigations. One of these repertoires was the tendency to create task forces dedicated to particularly challenging cases, a modus operandi that proved critical during *Lava Jato*.

Institutional change was not sufficient to guarantee the crusade. Contingency played a role. We showed, for example, that the story could have played out differently had the United States not made such shocking revelations, or had certain networks been in control of the MP. Importantly, institutional change did not fully do away with corruption at the top of the institution or sever the links between senior prosecutors and the political class. In fact, *Lava Jato* unfolded against the backdrop of a tug-of-war between those who had no intention to fight corruption and others who had a long history doing just the opposite. The choices pro-transparency prosecutors made along the way to deal with these obstructionist forces mattered for the trajectory of the case. The decisions taken during the day-to-day of the inquiry carry further weight when explaining how the evidence needed to prosecute politicians came to light. In this regard, we leveraged within-case variation in the pace of the *Lava Jato* investigation to show that different professional role conceptions led otherwise equally committed prosecutors to make more or less aggressive uses of the anti-corruption toolkit and therefore more or less progress during the "moment of agency."

We also showed that the type of decision-making that transforms investigations into crusades is greatly facilitated by the small group dynamics typical of task forces. It was only when one team of experienced prosecutors monopolised all lines of inquiry that the case really took off. After Vela monopolised all proceedings and signed a comprehensive deal with Odebrecht, evidence became forthcoming, allowing for a more aggressive approach to pretrial detentions and strategic partnerships with a variety of actors. The snowball effect could now begin in earnest. Prosecutorial zeal, however, was responsible for a dangerous dialectic in which the more the investigation moved forward, the more controversial it became. This invited backlash from defendants but also criticisms from more impartial observers concerned about the legality and opportunism of certain decisions. As a result, zeal carried with it the seeds of *Lava Jato's* political precarity and possible demise.

4

One Crusade and Two Failed Inquiries

Ecuador, Argentina, and Mexico

INTRODUCTION

The Peruvian chapter of *Lava Jato* largely followed the trajectory of the framework we developed in Chapter 2. The prosecution services underwent autonomy-enhancing reforms in the early 2000s, as well as processes of internal bureaucratic differentiation that led to the creation of units specialised in white-collar crime. Coupled with the introduction of the accusatorial system, these changes not only improved the capacity of the institution to fight corruption but also triggered organisational dynamics that allowed zealous prosecutors to put in place informal mechanisms to insulate their work from external encroachments. Armed with these new tools, know-how, and professional identities, the prosecutors in charge of *Lava Jato* were able to translate the "moment of serendipity" into a "moment of agency." Crucially, however, the case only truly gained momentum when all lines of inquiry were unified under a single task force. This catalysed more effective forces of innovation and mutual protection.

Does the argument apply to other national chapters of *Lava Jato*? The information made public by US authorities in December 2016 pointed to the involvement of high-profile politicians and businessmen from many Latin American countries in Odebrecht's corruption scheme. Following this common "moment of serendipity," we see some level of judicialisation in all countries mentioned in the documents. Importantly, judges and prosecutors had to deal with analogous crimes and case facts and grapple with comparable evidentiary challenges. Moreover, they had the chance to leverage unparalleled opportunities for transnational cooperation with Brazil, where the main evidence is located, and thus ride the coattails of the *Lava Jato* brand. These shared characteristics allow us to craft a systematic multinational comparison of very similar and contemporaneous anti-corruption efforts to assess how political,

FIGURE 4.1 Investigative measures per month in Mexico, Ecuador, Peru, and Argentina (January 2017–December 2018).
Source: Authors' database based on newspaper articles. Measures include: indictments, pretrial detentions, international travel bans, leniency agreements (individual and corporate), and convictions by lower courts. Bigger bubbles indicate more measures; the absence of a bubble indicates no measures

agentic, and institutional factors play out in a variety of national contexts, leading to higher or lower levels of investigative momentum.

We chose to study three additional national chapters of *Lava Jato* as "shadow" cases. As Soifer (2020) points out, shadow cases are not merely illustrative of a hypothesised correlation between dependent and independent variables, that is, they do not just qualitatively "score" cases along relevant dimensions. Instead, they rely on the techniques of qualitative research to assess the portability of process-oriented theories, alternative explanations, and scope conditions in depth (albeit more superficially than in core cases). In line with this approach, we reconstruct the trajectory of *Lava Jato* in Ecuador, Argentina, and Mexico using interviews with experts and key protagonists, as well as engaging in a close analysis of newspaper articles, official press releases, and court documents.

Our shadow cases provide variation in the intensity of the snowball effect following a common "moment of serendipity." Figure 4.1 plots original data showing that while prosecutors in Ecuador (and Peru) adopted a zealous approach, leading to extremely active investigations, those in Argentina and Mexico were more lethargic and engaged in spasmodic criminalisation efforts. Each bubble in the figure shows the number of investigative measures adopted each month during the first two years of the inquiry. Unfortunately, there isn't a single reliable or official source of information for each country as there is for Brazil (see Figures 2.2 and 2.3 in Chapter 2). Our dataset therefore likely underestimates the number of events. This is especially true for Peru and Ecuador because we cannot precisely date some of the decisions taken by the *Lava Jato* task forces in those countries. In any case, the evidence points to the presence of a crusade in some cases and failed or limited inquiries in others.

Ecuador, Argentina, and Mexico are also instructive because they offer different "theoretical contexts" to probe the portability of our framework and its merits relative to alternative accounts. One possible objection to the argument about institutions and prosecutorial agency, is that these factors matter far less than power politics. Put crudely, the only reason why the Peruvian *Lava Jato* acquired autonomous dynamics and snowballed, sending shockwaves across the establishment, is because political actors in that country were too weak to mount a serious retaliatory or obstructionist effort. Prosecutors therefore had ample room for manoeuvre. The political sensitivity of corruption cases is of the highest order, so when investigations seek to target more powerful figures, including strong incumbents or politicians with robust party and legislative support, judges and prosecutors are likely to face credible threats, encounter informational roadblocks, and ultimately achieve much less. For example, strong incumbents can rely on their appointees in the judicial system to moderate the impact of prosecutorial activism or, in more extreme circumstances, rely on these allies to ensure a more selective and narrow investigation against political opponents. And, of course, where elites are more resourceful, rank-and-file prosecutors may altogether shy away from zealous behaviour, engaging in strategic self-restraint out of fear of retaliation. By contrast, the space for investigating a wide array of high-level politicians, and thus engineer a crusade, is much greater when targets belong to weak executives, do not command the backing of electorally competitive parties, or no one in the political system is sufficiently powerful to weaponise, and thus condition, the scope of the investigation.

The shadow cases show that there is some truth to this alterative view. For example, Mexico is a case in which the main target of the inquiry (at least initially) was the sitting president. This complicated the investigative effort. But our analysis also reveals that the failure of the investigation cannot be fully understood without taking into account the absence of the kind of independence-enhancing and capacity-building efforts that improved the quality of prosecution services in other countries. Even if the political will had been there, so to speak, Mexico simply did not have the cast of law enforcement actors needed to trigger the "moment of agency." As a result, corruption prosecutions in that country are perennially exposed to political shenanigans as opposed to having the potential to acquire more autonomous dynamics.

By contrast, Ecuador underwent prosecutorial reforms since the 1990s, including during Rafael Correa's presidency, which was otherwise character-ised by the stifling of horizontal accountability institutions. This meant that when the Odebrecht confessions became public towards the end of his presi-dency, there were prosecutors with enough capacity and flexibility to follow up on them. Interestingly, investigators successfully targeted very powerful figures, including a sitting vice president and key members of Correa's inner circle, who continued to gravitate heavily on Ecuadorian politics even after Correa stepped down in 2017. In other words, the political status and resources of the defendants did not fully condition the outcome of the case. Furthermore, we show that like in Peru and Brazil, the creation of a task force played a critical role, cementing prosecutorial zeal, ensuring productive evidentiary flows, and ultimately triggering the snowball effect that characterises anti-corruption crusades.

Finally, Argentina is a case in which the main targets of the inquiry were no longer in power in December 2016 and were weaker than those in Mexico or Ecuador (at least initially). Despite this relatively generous window of opportunity, the judicial system failed to criminalise corruption. We attribute failure to the absence of meaningful reforms, including the non-implementation of the accusatorial system and the lack of bureaucratic differentiation conducive to prosecutorial specialisation in different types of white-collar crime. This makes for a Kafkian and highly inefficient criminal justice system. Argentina also allows us to show how the lack of coordination between prosecutors in charge of corruption inquiries, that is, the absence of a task force or analogous investigative arrangements, blocked the design of zealous prosecutorial strategies. In sharp contrast to the positive cases of Peru and Ecuador, where prosecutors operated as a team and quickly reached a cooperation agreement with Brazilian authorities that unlocked the case, Argentine prosecutors in charge of different legs of the inquiry never joined forces and failed to obtain high quality incriminatory evidence. In other words, institutions and poor case management blocked the "moment of agency."

ECUADOR

The Ecuadorian chapter of *Lava Jato* moved at a very fast pace since the investigation started in December 2016. Prosecutors secured high-profile convictions in a relatively short period of time against financial intermediaries, former government ministers, former president Rafael Correa, and former vice president Jorge Glas. As a "positive" case, Ecuador therefore allows us to trace the role of institutional change in setting the stage for successful prosecutions, as well as the importance of task force creation and the implementation of aggressive investigative protocols in triggering the snowball effect during the "moment of agency." More cynical interpretations of the outcome, namely that success boils down to changing political dynamics outside the courtroom, are not without merit. The imperatives of *realpolitik*, however, only tell a very shallow version of the story.

Shortly after President Correa was installed in 2007, he expelled Odebrecht from Ecuador and cancelled a series of contracts on the grounds that the company had failed to successfully complete a major hydroelectric power plant. According to US prosecutors, between 2007 and 2016 Odebrecht paid around

US$33.5 million in bribes presumably to mend fences with the government, gain permission to return to the country, and secure various projects. As part of this charm offensive, in 2010 the company publicly pledged to repair the faulty hydroelectric power plant. This prompted the Correa administration to lift all sanctions and prosecutors to shelve an investigation against Odebrecht.[1] By the time information about the bribes became public, President Correa was already reaching his final months in office and the race to succeed him was well under-way. The outcome of that election in early 2017 was a victory for Lenin Moreno, who shared the ticket with Correa's own vice president, Jorge Glas. Despite this continuity, and the fact that the Chief Prosecutor (Fiscal General de Estado) was a regime insider, the investigation quickly gained momentum. Why was this the case?

It certainly helped that after being sworn in, Moreno sought to distance himself from Correa to become his own man.[2] This realignment eased the political constraints on an inquiry that would inevitably have to train its eyes on prominent members of the previous administration. Prosecutors with close links to the establishment likely identified the benefits of adapting to the new balance of power within the ruling coalition by embracing Moreno's anti-corruption rhetoric. They may have even received informal encouragement from allies of the new president to weaponise the case, although nothing in the public record points in that direction. This perspective, however, can perhaps only explain why some within the prosecution services, namely those at the very top, were willing to take the allegations seriously. It does not explain how the prosecutorial machine was successfully mobilised to that end. A more comprehensive explanation is therefore one that also considers the impact of institutions, the legal framework, and prosecutorial skills on the outcome of the investigation. This is especially true because despite Moreno's best efforts, Correa and his inner circle never ceased to exert a strong gravitational pull over Ecuadorian politics.[3] As a result, going after this group always remained a risky strategy. It was never a foregone conclusion that investigators would be able to secure the necessary evidence to convict or amass enough political clout to avoid sanctions. As we shall see, following the "moment of serendipity" Ecuadorian prosecutors were able to do so because they leveraged improve-ments in investigative capacity and a recently reformed criminal code to devise a theory of the case that facilitated the flow of high-quality information via plea deals and international cooperation agreements. They also relied on the media to build defensive shields, often playing at the margins of the law.

---

[1] "Diez claves para entender el caso Odebrecht en Ecuador," *El Comercio* (2 June 2017).
[2] Correa initially wanted Glas to succeed him but in the end decided to support Moreno. Had Glas been the next president, as opposed to continuing in his vice presidential role, the Odebrecht case might have played out differently.
[3] To the point that the *correista* candidate nearly won the 2021 presidential race.

Like other countries in the region, Ecuador participated in the wave of reforms discussed in Chapter 2. Most notably, the 1998 constitution embraced the accusatorial model and established the autonomy and independence of the public prosecution services, which had hitherto operated under the orbit of the Executive branch. Congress subsequently passed a new Code of Criminal Procedure that operationalised the adoption of adversarial oral proceedings and the delegation of investigative prerogatives to prosecutors. Admittedly, the election of Rafael Correa in 2007 ushered in a period of profound constitutional reengineering and co-optation of horizontal accountability institutions that challenged this process and sought instead to concentrate power in the presidency (Basabe-Serrano 2009; Ortiz Ortiz 2018; Freeman 2020; Stoyan 2020). The main implication of these counter reforms for the prosecution services has been that the chief prosecutor is no longer chosen by qualified congressional majorities. Instead, he or she is now appointed by the newly created *Consejo de Participación Ciudadana y Control Social* on the basis of merit examinations and personal interviews. And yet, while in practice this meant that during the Correa years the president was able to regain control over this (and other) critical nominations, other features of the system remained unchanged. For example, the 2008 constitution preserved the functional administrative autonomy and organisational decentralisation of the prosecution services, and also kept the accusatorial system.

More importantly, prior to and during the Correa administration, there was progress in terms of building institutional capacity to tackle corruption. Inspired by the ratification of the Inter-American (1997), Palermo (2002), and UN (2005) conventions, Ecuador strengthened its anti-money laundering legislation. Major bills passed in 2005, 2010, and 2016 established a robust framework for the prevention, detection, and sanctioning of money laundering and the financing of illegal activities. One key innovation was the creation of an autonomous financial intelligence unit, today known as the *Unidad de Análisis Financiero y Económico* (UAFE), which together with the Office of the Comptroller General, rings alarm bells and provides critical assistance to investigators. In addition, a new criminal code approved in 2014 clearly specifies a variety of white-collar crimes, including graft (article 278), illicit enrichment (article 279), the acceptance and demand of bribes (articles 280 and 281, respectively), influence-peddling (article 285), the use of figureheads (article 289), and money laundering (articles 317–319). This sort of precision greatly facilitates prosecutorial efforts.

Reacting to these changes, and also in observance of international standards, starting in 2010 the prosecution services created a series of units tasked with the investigation of specific crimes singled out by the new legislation.[4] For instance,

---

[4] See for example, Resolución No. 0040FGE-2010. Two things are worth mentioning. First, article 283 of the new criminal code makes reference to "specialized prosecutorial units," providing a strong legal basis for a type of restructuring that seeks to build thematic expertise. Second, this and similar resolutions creating specialised units (see below) cite international anti-corruption instruments as a key inspiration.

in 2014 the chief prosecutor created a money laundering unit.[5] The new criminal code explicitly allows this and other units to rely on a variety of tools, including plea deals and international legal assistance, to investigative complex crimes (articles 491–497). Armed with such tools, the money laundering unit secured thirty-two convictions during its first two years of existence. It also made significant progress in cases such as *Petroecuador* (against high-ranking executives of the state-owned oil company) or *Ecuafutbol* (against former directors of the national football association). More broadly, based on more than 1,800 reports of suspicious activities published by the Comptroller General, prosecutors obtained 245 convictions in cases of white-collar crime. These successes were a sign of things to come. As Chief Prosecutor Galo Chiriboga put it in his annual report to Congress on 18 January 2017, "gone is the past that, like the old country, kept the Prosecutor's Office stagnant as a conservative, bureaucratic, and inefficient body in the fight against crimes and permissive with impunity."[6]

Institutional and legal change, as well as the development of investigative expertise, left the prosecution services surprisingly well-equipped to respond to the Odebrecht scandal. The case was initially assigned to Wilson Toainga, who had ample experience prosecuting white-collar crime. The day after the allegations were made public, he conducted a search in the company's Guayaquil headquarters. In the following weeks, Toainga put additional pressure on the company with a second search, this time in the Quito offices, and two court orders that banned Odebrecht from contracting with the state and its local clients from honouring debts worth US$40 million. More importantly, Toainga worked closely with Chief Prosecutor Chiriboga on a multi-pronged international cooperation strategy to complement a series of formal information requests wired in late December 2016 to the United States, Brazil, and Switzerland. Most notably, in February 2017 they travelled to Washington, DC with twenty-five other members of the Ecuadorian prosecution services to meet with their US counterparts. The meeting resulted in an agreement that would speed up the discovery phase. The following month Chiriboga also flew to Peru, where he met with Chief Prosecutor Pablo Sánchez (see Chapter 3) and started informal talks about a possible cooperation agreement with Odebrecht executives. Finally, in April Spanish authorities wired the transcript of an interview with a former Odebrecht lawyer containing details of the bribery

---

[5] Resolución No. 106-FGE-2014.

[6] Unless otherwise stated, all quotes and factual references about the *Lava Jato* investigation mentioned in this and subsequent paragraphs come from press briefings published by the Chief Prosecutor's Office. To facilitate our process tracing exercise, we arranged the press briefings in chronological order in a 63-page single-spaced document. The document is available in the Appendix, which can be found on http://www.narapavao.com/book.html

scheme. This led to the arrests of Alecksey Mosquera, former electricity minister under Correa, and his uncle, both charged with money laundering.[7]

Emboldened by this first victory, Ecuadorian investigators maintained a razor-sharp focus on securing further confessions via international cooperation agreements. This approach reflected their theory of the crimes in question. Because they were not dealing with ordinary criminals, an ordinary criminal investigation would not cut it. As the Chief Prosecutor's Office put it in a press release, it is a scheme "with illicit purposes, simulation mechanisms, structured procedures, and penetration at different public and private, national and international levels [with] behaviours typical of transnational organized crime. The investigation is therefore expected to be extensive and technically highly complex." The chief prosecutor also made it clear that this is "a highly complex transnational crime [. . .] Most of the money from Odebrecht bribes did not go through the Ecuadorian financial system." In this context, confessions played a key role: "without them it would have been almost impossible" to trace the money.

The international dimension of the investigative strategy became particularly central after Carlos Baca replaced Chiriboga as chief prosecutor in May 2017.[8] Baca took two important steps to boost and centralise investigative capacity. First, in May he created a unit specialised in "transparency and the fight against corruption" based in Quito and with national jurisdiction.[9] Under the leadership of Diana Salazar, another experienced prosecutor, the unit was a seventeen-strong task force in charge of all proceedings related to the *Lava Jato* case. Second, Baca put a pre-existing money laundering unit (see above) under the supervision of the new anti-corruption task force.[10] It is worth noting that these moves were possible thanks to the high levels of organisational autonomy and flexibility of the Ecuadorian prosecution services, which coupled with accusatorial rules enable the quick deployment of qualified investigators to specific cases.

Almost immediately following this tactical reorganisation, the team reached a far-reaching agreement with Brazilian authorities, which gave Ecuadorian prosecutors direct access to all the relevant evidence stored in Brazil and the ability to conduct interviews with Odebrecht executives in Brazilian territory.[11] The agreement also put into force a Memorandum of Understanding on Criminal Cooperation signed between the two countries in 2015, with the goal

---

[7] The bribery scheme was indeed quite convoluted. According to this witness testimony, Odebrecht paid Mosquera US$1 million in exchange for favours during negotiations over a hydroelectric power plant project. The money, initially wired through one of Odebrecht's offshore companies, eventually ended up in an Andorran bank.

[8] Chiriboga's six-year term should have ended in July, but he stepped down to allow a new chief prosecutor take charge in lockstep with the Moreno administration. Like Chiriboga, Baca had previously worked for President Correa.

[9] Resolución No. 002-FGE-2017.   [10] Resolución No. 025-FGE-2017.

[11] In March 2019, Ecuadorian authorities announced a second cooperation agreement with Brazil.

of facilitating the rapid flow of information. Days later, the task force reached a similar agreement with Odebrecht. While the exact terms of the deal are not public, we know that as a gesture of goodwill the company surrendered myriad written documents, as well as video and audio recordings, which would be the smoking guns used later on to go after high-profile defendants. The effects were almost immediate. While the task force was still in Brazil, the Ecuadorian police conducted searches in three different cities, leading to a series of crucial arrests, presumably based on information supplied by Brazilian authorities. The *Lava Jato* case had suddenly become a much more ambitious affair.

By June 2017, the task force had collected sixty-nine testimonies, secured twenty-six international information transfers, and carried out eighteen searches. Among the nine individuals serving time in pretrial detention there were former public officials, lawyers, and financial intermediaries. Ominously, the list included an uncle of the then vice president Jorge Glas. As the case continued to expand with additional arrests, prosecutors tried their luck in court, officially charging some of the defendants. Most notably, in August they successfully charged Carlos Polit, former comptroller general and part of Correa's inner circle, with extortion for demanding millions in bribes from Odebrecht in exchange for favourable oversight reports. Thanks to the cooperation agreement signed with the company, the prosecutors had obtained audio records of a private conversation between José Santos, a former executive in Odebrecht's Ecuadorian branch, and Polit. The recordings provided strong proof of intent. Twelve days later, investigators made even more headlines when they charged eleven individuals with criminal conspiracy, including vice president Glas. Most defendants were placed in custody, with the exception of Glas, who was only banned from leaving the country. Former Odebrecht executives who had assisted the investigation were spared punitive measures.[12] Importantly, thanks to this escalating pressure on the criminal network, some of the financial intermediaries charged with conspiracy entered plea deals in which they described the bribery scheme, corroborated the evidence obtained in Brazil, and implicated other public officials. The snowball effect continued in September when Jose Santos testified before a judge, detailing how the company had bribed its way to secure five major public works contracts.

The trial against Glas, Polit, and associates started in November 2017. The prosecution decided not to press charges against five defendants, mainly Odebrecht executives. Some had already been convicted for the same crimes in Brazil and the remaining ones did not play a central role in the bribery scheme. This decision likely honoured the agreements signed with Brazilian authorities and Odebrecht. One month later, a year after the start of *Lava Jato*,

---

[12] Because the crimes in question had taken place before the approval of the new criminal code, prosecutors could not charge defendants with "participation in a criminal conspiracy," a new and more serious crime. Doing so would have been in violation of the legality principle and therefore jeopardised the case put before the court.

a court convicted sitting vice president Glas and four associates to six years in prison (the maximum allowed by law). Three additional defendants only received a fourteen-months sentence on the grounds that they had helped the investigation. Because the rest of the accused, including Polit, were fugitives, they could not be tried successfully.[13] In any case, the ruling was a major achievement. The work of the prosecutorial team received praise, most notably from Cesar Montúfar, a professor at Universidad Andina who had joined the case as a private claimant and was at times very critical of the investigation. Quite understandably, Montúfar initially suspected that former chief prosecutor Chiriboga was determined to stall the local chapter of *Lava Jato* due to his close ties to Correa. Specifically, Montúfar accused him of splitting the case into several lines of inquiry to prevent any progress.[14] As we discussed previously, Chief Prosecutor Baca reversed that decision when he appointed a task force in May 2017 to oversee all aspects of the case. In an interview conducted after Glas's conviction in December 2017, Montúfar acknowledged that "the charges were solid and categorical. The Prosecutor's Office did a very good job preparing the evidence. This demonstrates professionalism."[15]

Following this daring conviction, the task force moved aggressively in January 2018 to bring additional charges against Polit and his son, this time for extortion, a crime that could be tried *in absentia*. Once again, the evidence supplied by Brazilian authorities and Odebrecht was crucial. The move, however, tested the tolerance limits of the establishment. In fact, it triggered the most significant "moment of backlash" of the Ecuadorian saga. After the court approved the charges, Chief Prosecutor Baca held a press conference to denounce that he and his family had received threats. He then played the recording of a conversation between José Serrano, member of the ruling party and president of Congress, and Polit, in which the two heavyweights discussed their plans to get rid of Baca and thus stop the investigation. It was clear that despite changing political dynamics following Moreno's election, there were still prominent figures determined to put an end to *Lava Jato*. This was hardly surprising if one considers that Moreno's party was full of individuals with links to the previous administration and whose loyalties had not necessarily changed overnight. Baca's actions were not strictly legal. The recordings had been collected as part of the inquiry and ought to have been presented in court, not during a press conference. It was therefore a high-risk strategy aimed at shielding the anti-corruption effort, one not entirely dissimilar to the ones pursued in Brazil, when Moro leaked the conversation between President Rousseff and Lula Da Silva (see Chapter 2), or in Peru, when the leaders of

---

[13] Polit had fled to the United States and others were in Venezuela. The ruling was appealed, but the courts upheld the decision at every stage.

[14] "Exfiscal Galo Chiriboga asegura que investigó los casos Odebrecht que le correspondieron," *El Universo* (16 November 2018).

[15] César Montúfar, "El fiscal Carlos Baca ha hecho lo que debía," *El Telégrafo* (17 December 2017).

the task force faced dismissal in late 2018 (see Chapter 3). Indeed, the breach of conduct eventually cost Baca his job. But "going public" in this dramatic way helped abort Polit and Serrano's plot. For example, President Moreno turned against Serrano and the National Assembly subsequently impeached him.

Once the turbulence subsided, the task force cracked on with several spin-offs of the main line of inquiry. In April 2018, for example, they secured a conviction for money laundering against former electricity minister Alecksey Mosquera and two of his associates. Similarly, in June a court convicted Polit and his son. And in July, another court found two former bankers guilty of serving as financial intermediaries for the bribery scheme. It wasn't until mid-2019, however, that the *Lava Jato* case would start the most ambitious and politically consequential episode of the saga.

In May 2019 the task force reacted quickly to media reports indicating that Odebrecht was also at the heart of an illegal campaign financing scheme that operated during the Correa years. The key to solve the case was the arrest of Pamela Martinez when she was about to board a plane in Guayaquil. Martinez, a former Constitutional Court judge and advisor to President Correa, was charged with criminal conspiracy, influence-peddling, and accepting bribes. She eventually confessed that between 2012 and 2016 she was instructed by the president and members of his cabinet to collect millions in bribes and then funnel the money to the coffers of the ruling party. One of Martinez's close aides, who was also arrested and charged, testified along similar lines. And José Santos, the aforementioned Odebrecht executive, corroborated both testimonies, explaining that his company was repeatedly asked to pay between 1.3 per cent and 1.5 per cent of the value of public works projects to Correa's party using an intricate network of offshore accounts. Armed with this information, the prosecutors moved on to charge a former minister of transportation and public works and a former secretary of legal affairs with the same crimes as Martinez. By August, Correa and other members of his administration, including former vice president Glas and two additional members of the cabinet, suffered the same fate. Correa, who was not present in Ecuador at the time, protested the move and organised marches to repudiate the work of the prosecutors.[16] The trial against him (in absentia) and twenty others started in February 2020, and ended two months later with eighteen 8-year convictions. Correa, Glas, three of their ministers, a former congressman, a former governor, and several businessmen were found guilty of setting up a criminal organisation that collected around US$8 million in bribes.[17] Martinez and her assistant received reduced sentences in recognition for their

---

[16] Two of the former ministers were also fugitives.

[17] This decision of course played into Moreno's hand. The president organised a referendum in 2018 with the goal of changing the Constitution. One of the proposed amendments, which was subsequently backed by 74 per cent of voters, banned those convicted for corruption from running for office or working for the state.

confessions. The ruling, which was upheld on appeal, had one crucial political implication: it made it impossible for Rafael Correa to return to the country and run for president in 2021, throwing the race wide open.

The trajectory of the Ecuadorian chapter of *Lava Jato* largely comports with the framework we proposed in Chapter 2. Following the "moment of serendipity," the success of the criminalisation effort can be attributed to a combination of institutional and legal re-engineering, and the creation of an experienced and shrewd task force that quickly understood the need to deploy investigative protocols attuned to the specifics of transnational white-collar crime. As in the case of Peru, the contributions of prosecutorial agency to the outcome cannot be fully understood without first taking into account changes to the institutional context. But also like in the Peruvian example, contingent choices and developments during the "moment of agency" played a role, especially when confronting backlash.[18]

The momentum behind the case was hard to stop. The timely avalanche of confessions and smoking guns strengthened the prosecutors' hand vis-à-vis those who preferred a narrower investigation, and likely fuelled a stronger commitment to the case among all officials involved. Indeed, the press briefings released by the Chief Prosecutor's Office suggest that securing convictions in the *Lava Jato* case progressively became an institutional priority, one they were not willing to surrender or water down. Moreover, on various occasions the chief prosecutor urged Congress to pass legislation that would help in the struggle against corruption. Prosecutors were not alone in this fight; they had the support of civil society actors, who unlike in other countries joined some of the cases as private claimants. This certainly helped, as did the fact that for the most part the prosecutors operated in a political context in which punishing past corruption helped the incumbent's agenda. Yet, the strategy was not without risks. Correismo was alive and well throughout. Crucially, the case gained momentum via key international cooperation agreements *before* Correa's departure from office and Moreno's "betrayal" of his former boss. Moreover, Correa and his remaining allies did not all of a sudden become marginal political actors. Their threats carried some weight. In fact, backlash could have become quite severe and effective had Correa's candidate won the run-off of the 2021 presidential race, after emerging victorious from the first round of the contest. Finally, even if we accept that the Moreno-Correa split gave *Lava Jato* decisive breathing space, institutional reforms and contingent investigative choices are still important to understand how the prosecutorial machine could be successfully mobilised in response to a more generous window of opportunity.

---

[18] For example, had Pamela Martinez boarded the plane in Guayaquil and left the country, it is possible that the prosecutors might not have been able to prove the illegal campaign financing scheme. And of course, the decision to put pressure on her, and later on reward her contributions, was also important in triggering a snowball effect.

ARGENTINA

US Department of Justice documentation revealed that between 2007 and 2015, Odebrecht used the infamous Division of Structured Operations to pay at least US$35 million in bribes to Argentine officials and thus secure a series of public works contracts. To many Argentines, this information did not necessarily come as a shock. President Néstor Kirchner (2003–2007) and his successor, President Cristina Fernández de Kirchner (2007–2015), increased levels of public spending in the economy, including through large infrastructure projects. There were hence multiple opportunities for corruption during this period, which many in government were ready to exploit. According to several media exposés and reports by opposition politicians published since 2003, the Ministry of Planning, which Kirchner created, was the focal point of a prolific operation in which top government officials systematically requested bribes from a variety of construction companies. They also awarded contracts at higher than market prices to a cartel of friendly businessmen, who returned the favour by funnelling money, in cash and through joint ventures, to the Kirchner family (Manzetti 2014; Volosin 2019; Figueroa 2021). The allegations reached the courts, but federal judges and prosecutors either dismissed them summarily or made little investigative progress.

In December 2015, however, the space for pursuing corruption accusations widened following the victory of Mauricio Macri (2015–2019), the opposition's presidential candidate. Importantly, the new president tasked the Anti-Corruption Office with closely monitoring judicial proceedings and intervening in them as a claimant.[19] Argentine federal judges have long been known to be politically savvy and quick to adapt when political winds change direction (Helmke 2005). The election of Macri therefore provided the thrust and incentives needed to reactivate some dormant cases against Kirchnerist officials. Given these developments, the prospects for the success of the local chapter of *Lava Jato* appeared more auspicious than in Ecuador, where Correa was still in control of the Executive when the investigation started. The information that surfaced in December 2016 not only resonated with ongoing investigations, but also emerged at a time when the conditions of political possibility for punishing corruption during the Kirchner years were riper. The case, however, failed to follow the trajectory we saw in Brazil, Peru, and Ecuador, where initial allegations snowballed, leading to multiple spin-offs and ever more ambitious prosecutorial efforts. In Argentina, by contrast, evidence to fully corroborate Odebrecht's intriguing confessions to US prosecutors failed to materialise and the inquiry stalled.

Taking a close look at the Argentine experience is instructive because it further sheds light on how the institutional context can determine anti-corruption

---

[19] The Anti-Corruption Agency was created in 1999 as part of the de la Rúa administration's (1999–2001) attempt to address rampant corruption during the Menem years. The agency, while nominally autonomous, was placed under the orbit of the presidency. It has ample prevention and investigation powers but is not politically independent.

capabilities, even when "political will" is not necessarily in short supply. More importantly, it also allows us to see that the absence of a centralised investigative effort, that is, the absence of a task force, blocks the synergies required for law enforcement officials to bring about the "moment of agency" and trigger productive evidentiary flows.

Before 1994, the place of the federal prosecution services in Argentina's constitutional order was ambiguous. Functionally, the body of prosecutors was dependant on the Executive branch, but the president did not unilaterally choose the chief prosecutor. The weakness of the legal framework governing the status of the *Ministerio Público*, however, allowed Carlos Menem (1989–1999) to break with tradition early on in his presidency and appoint an ally to the top prosecutorial job without Senate confirmation. Rattled by this and other moves that ostensibly undermined checks and balances, the opposition used the 1994 constitutional convention to strengthen horizontal accountability. The document that emerged from the reform process put Argentina in line with regional trends, finally stipulating the independence and autonomy of the prosecution service. The new constitutional provisions were still rather thin on the matter, so three years later Congress passed "organic" legislation that further clarified the main prerogatives of the *Ministerio Público* as well as the need for the Senate to confirm the president's nominee for chief prosecutor with a two-thirds majority.

This launched a process of organisational re-engineering that significantly expanded the size and internal complexity of the federal prosecution service. Under the new scheme, the chief prosecutor continued to litigate cases before the Supreme Court but gained autonomy to prioritise certain domains of criminal prosecution via the allocation of institutional resources. For example, starting in 1998, successive chief prosecutors used their new prerogatives to create specialised prosecutorial units. One important innovation on this front was the creation of the Prosecutor's Office for Administrative Investigations, which specialises in crimes against the federal administration (i.e., corruption). This was the only unit whose creation was explicitly mandated in the 1997 Organic Law of the *Ministerio Público*. Chief prosecutors promoted specialisation and greater investigative capacity in other areas too. This was especially true under Alejandra Gils Carbo (2012–2017), who took inspiration from elsewhere in the region to establish units dedicated to various forms of macro-criminality, including drug trafficking, money laundering, human trafficking, and crimes against humanity (Guthmann 2019: 70).[20] One factor that facilitated these long-term investments in bureaucratic differentiation and

---

[20] The creation of some of these units tracked legislative changes in the area of macro-criminality, which were also in line with the international reform templates discussed in Chapter 2. For example, Congress passed targeted laws on terrorism (Law 25.241, 2000) and money laundering (Law 25.246, 2000). The creation of a unit specialised in crimes against humanity responded to a broader push for transitional justice across all branches of government (Gonzalez-Ocantos 2016a).

capacity-building was the dramatic reduction in turnover at the top of the prosecution services, which was in turn a function of greater formal autonomy. For instance, between 1983 and 1997, chief prosecutors stayed in office for an average of 25.5 months, whereas between 1997 and 2017, the average duration was eighty months.

These changes, however, suffered from a series of key limitations that muted their impact on investigative capacity. One is that chief prosecutors after 1997 were not bureaucratic insiders, as was the case, for example, of Brazilian chief prosecutors since 1988. In fact, two of them, Righi (2004–2012) and Gils Carbó (2012–2017) were very close to the presidents that nominated them. This meant that when it came to strengthening anti-corruption capabilities, the results were ultimately disappointing. For example, as corruption allegations against the Kirchner administration gained salience in the mid-2000s, Manuel Garrido, a relatively independent Prosecutor for Administrative Investigations, clashed with Chief Prosecutor Righi. After being marginalised from important cases, Garrido resigned in March 2009 and was not replaced until 2015 (Manzetti 2014: 193). During this period, the specialised unit was virtually paralyzed. According to internal reports, rather than pursing independent investigations, the team instead focused on superfluous and largely innocuous administrative matters.[21] Not only was there a total absence of leadership; the unit also lacked basic personnel. In 2016, nine out of twelve prosecutorial positions remained vacant, and most employees were on the verge of retirement.

Another limitation is that specialisation at the top failed to filter down. This has less to do with leadership and political will, and more with institutional design. The new prosecutorial units, including the Prosecutor for Administrative Investigations, play a supporting role, with little direct involvement in actual judicial proceedings. For example, the units spend most of their time generating data about the incidence of certain forms of criminality, drafting legislative proposals, or organising meetings with federal prosecutors working on similar issues to consolidate professional networks. To the extent that the units have formal investigative powers, the reach of those prerogatives is highly contested and ambiguous. Some units do conduct their own preliminary investigations; they sometimes even "judicialise" cases. But when that happens, the case is transferred to autonomous rank-and-file prosecutors, who may or may not follow the elite unit's recommendations or seek its assistance. To understand why, it is necessary to briefly explain how the criminal justice system works.

Argentina is yet to adopt the accusatorial model at the federal level. Because judges still serve an investigative function, and cases are assigned to specific

---

[21] This emerges from various annual reports published annually since 2015. Available at www.mpf
.gob.ar/pia/

courts, the prosecution service is organised so that it mirrors the structure of the judicial branch in each jurisdiction. In other words, for each lower-level court there is a prosecutor (or a group of prosecutors in the case of appellate and trial courts with multiple chambers). These prosecutors, not those that are part of elite units, are the ones formally empowered to litigate cases and investigate alongside their respective judge.

This arrangement has implications that conspire against the development of the kind of technical finesse and zeal needed to make a success of white-collar crime cases. First, the *Ministerio Público* lacks the flexibility we find in Brazil, Peru, or Ecuador. In those countries, prosecutors are fully in control of the exercise of criminalisation prerogatives, so chief prosecutors can quickly deploy individuals or task forces to manage specific investigations.[22] In Argentina, by contrast, those who gain experience as part of specialised units are unable to use that expertise where it matters the most, even when they are responsible for initiating an inquiry. As a result, the rank-and-file prosecutors conducting the bulk of the investigative work are still generalists dealing with a vast and varied docket, and do so individually before an assigned judge, rather than as part of a team. Moreover, related cases can end up in different courts under the orbit of different prosecutors, who have no mandate or infrastructure to work together to generate evidentiary economies of scale or detect wider patterns of macro-criminality.[23]

Second, the legal process remains incredibly cumbersome. Even if prosecutors were to coordinate efforts during the investigative phase, they would still need to deal with their respective judges. The criteria applied by different judges in charge of similar cases can vary widely, rendering moot prosecutors' cooperative ventures. In addition, before a case is sent to trial, defendants can resort to a wide range of appeals to challenge decisions made during the investigation, including decisions on the admissibility of evidence or indictments. In so doing, they can try their luck at a federal Court of Appeals, the Court of Cassation, and the Supreme Court. These courts have their own prosecutors, so case files change hands several times, including at the trial stage. One of the difficulties with this structure is that the various prosecutors that intervene during the process can show different levels of interest in an investigation or apply diametric criteria when evaluating the evidence or the merits of interlocutory appeals. The non-implementation of the accusatorial model adds to the delays that inevitably ensue because the transition from written to oral

---

[22] To our knowledge, this has only happened once in the Asociación de Mutuales Israelitas Argentinas (AMIA) case, which investigates a terrorist attack that took place in Buenos Aires in 1994. Unlike the *Lava Jato* case, which was split across three different federal courts, the AMIA case fell under the remit of one judge. This made it possible to appoint a task force.

[23] For example, in the federal criminal courts based in the city of Buenos Aires, where most (if not all) high-profile corruption cases end up, cases are distributed using a lottery system.

proceedings is also pending.[24] Written proceedings obviously slow cases down. This is true even during oral trials, as the hearings still devote a lot of time to reading the documents that result from the investigative and appellate phases (Casares 2009).

The absence of prosecutorial flexibility and specialisation, coupled with the Kafkian nature of inquisitorial proceedings, undermine the effectiveness of corruption investigations. The prosecutors who are ultimately in charge never come to see themselves as "anti-corruption prosecutors" or allowed to refine their skills. Furthermore, the sluggish pace of most inquiries kills any investigative momentum. In the constant back and forth, prosecutors lose focus and any sense of urgency. And, of course, cases are normally devoid of any element of surprise. The kind of shock therapy approach deployed in Brazil's *Lava Jato* through the multiple, well-branded, and highly publicised "phases" of the investigation is unimaginable in Argentina. All of this affords defendants ample time to plan legal and extra-legal diversionary tactics. It also increases the likelihood that even the most serious allegations are quickly forgotten. In other words, Argentine prosecutors are structurally incapable of engineering the "moment of agency."

It is therefore little surprising that in Argentina one cannot find the kind of successful antecedents that prepared Peruvian, Brazilian, and Ecuadorian law enforcement agents for their respective chapters of *Lava Jato*. Indeed, a National Judicial Council report shows that impunity for corruption is rampant. In all cases initiated between 1996 and 2016, only 2 per cent of defendants got to the trial stage and less than 1 per cent were convicted. The average duration of all completed cases managed by the federal courts with a seat in the City of Buenos Aires, where most corruption cases involving the national government are investigated, was two years and nine months. But some high-profile ones took more than ten years! With regard to cases still ongoing when the report was published in 2016, their average duration was three years and six months. Of these cases, only 1.28 per cent had a defendant in pretrial detention. Moreover, the court had formalised the charges in a meagre 12.9 per cent, and interrogated suspects in just over a quarter.[25] It goes without saying that because the system is still inquisitorial, prosecutorial deficits are only part of the story behind these dismal figures. Federal judges exercise ample control over investigations and are usually the ones responsible for keeping cases dormant. This can be attributed to the size of the docket, but also to political motivations. Some "hot potatoes" no one wants to touch, and others have high transactional value precisely when they do not make much progress. Put bluntly, delays allow judges to defend themselves from political attacks: "at the moment your case is not moving, but if you provoke me that can change very quickly."

---

[24] The only exception is the trial phase. Since the early 1990s, trials take place in oral tribunals.
[25] The report is available online: www.cipce.org.ar/sites/default/files/2019/04/articulos2787.pdf

The Argentine chapter of *Lava Jato* offers a microcosm in which we can observe how many of these limitations play out in practice. After December 2016, the investigation was divided into three main parts. Each ended up in a different federal court in the City of Buenos Aires, and of course, in the hands of a different prosecutor. Federal Criminal Court No. 3 was tasked with investigating the payment of bribes during the execution phase of a large gas pipeline. Odebrecht had partnered with local companies to secure the project back in 2006. Irregularities with that contract had already been investigated in federal courts. The case started in 2007, got dismissed in 2011, and reactivated in early 2016 before *Lava Jato* took centre stage. The judge and the prosecutor were therefore now asked to look at both the contract and its implementation. Federal Criminal Court No. 7, in turn, looked at Odebrecht's dealings with a state-owned water company (AySA), and Federal Criminal Court No. 8 was assigned the line of inquiry related to the construction of an underground train line, by far the most significant of the three and the one most closely linked to the information released by US authorities.

Like in other countries, the key to finding incriminating evidence of both bribe paying and bribe receiving was a comprehensive information-sharing agreement with Brazilian authorities. While the Peruvian and Ecuadorian task forces secured one relatively quickly, Argentine investigators failed at almost every turn.[26] To be sure, some rank-and-file prosecutors joined forces with the new Prosecutor for Administrative Investigations – at the time trying to revitalise his office after five years of inactivity – to ensure some level of coordination during negotiations with Brazil. In the first half of 2017 there were some signs that the relationship would be a productive one. For example, the Prosecutor for Administrative Investigations managed to get hold of copies of a few witness testimonies and even speak to some of the witnesses in Brazil. But because the documentation was not received through formal international cooperation channels, and because the interrogations had not been conducted under oath, that evidence had little value and was immediately subject to procedural objections.

More worryingly, the prosecutors soon reached the conclusion that the requirements of the Brazilian *Ministério Público* would stand in the way of an agreement.[27] In their view, Argentine law made it impossible to offer immunity from prosecution to Odebrecht executives. For one, under the inquisitorial system, judges and prosecutors cannot make discretionary use of

---

[26] In what follows, we base our reconstruction of the negotiations with Brazil on newspaper reports and confidential interviews with key participants from all the agencies involved in the process between 2017 and 2018. During some of the interviews we were also allowed to read a few relevant documents that are still classified. For this reason, we do not specify the sources of the claims we make in the text.

[27] Hernán Capiello, "Las limitaciones jurídicas que frenan el trámite en la Argentina," *La Nación* (28 May 2017).

their criminalisation prerogatives.[28] Moreover, a new plea bargain law passed in 2016, which extended the use of this tool to corruption cases, only mentions the possibility of applying reduced sentences and provides that any agreement remains provisional until endorsed by a trial court. Recall that investigative prosecutors are not the same as those who argue the case during trial, so *Lava Jato* prosecutors could not guarantee that any deal would be honoured further down the line. Compounding things further, so argued the Argentines, a second piece of government-sponsored leniency legislation approved by Congress in 2017 did not allow the state to exchange corporate immunity for information about corruption.[29]

While there was some merit to this pessimism, the truth is that prosecutors in other countries found ways to circumvent similar procedural obstacles. For example, the Ecuadorian task force ultimately refrained from bringing charges against Odebrecht executives on the grounds that they could not be charged in two countries for the same crimes, something stipulated in international conventions. Citing these experiences, and determined to push for an information-sharing agreement, the Macri administration, via the Anti-Corruption Office, filed a brief in one of the three courts. Government lawyers argued that while it is true that Argentine law limits the applicability of the "opportunity principle" in criminal investigations, one could interpret Brazilian demands not as a request for unconditional immunity but as a request to limit the use of the evidence. In other words, all that local prosecutors had to do was to refrain from using the information coming from Brazil against Odebrecht and its executives, which did not preclude the possibility of going after these individuals on the basis of evidence gathered through other means. This way of looking at the conditions set by Brazilian authorities, government lawyers believed, was consistent with established principles of international anti-corruption law that limit the use of evidence obtained via international channels. Argentine prosecutors could not only sign the deal, but also had an obligation under various conventions to live up to those standards.

Jolted by this powerful new argument, but still doubtful and in need for reassurance, two of the *Lava Jato* prosecutors sent the government's brief to the chief prosecutor. To the objections raised previously, they added a few more. Two stand out. First, they argued that the draft of the agreement proposed by Brazil was still quite vague regarding the possibility of indicting Odebrecht executives on the basis of evidence obtained through alternative channels. Second, the prosecutors were not sure who had the authority to sign the deal (they believed their boss should sign it, not them). In order to study the issue, and try to get a deal that could satisfy everyone involved, in March 2018 the chief prosecutor created a working group that included the two prosecutors (although

[28] This objection had a basis in articles 41 and 71 of the Federal Criminal Code.
[29] The Kirchnerist opposition leveraged its still sizable congressional delegation to force the Macri administration to drop this crucial aspect of the anti-corruption reform package.

only one decided to take part); officials from the Ministry of Foreign Affairs (which would serve as intermediaries between the two nations); officials from the Anti-Corruption Office; the Prosecutor for Administrative Investigations; and the Ministerio Publico's Secretary for Institutional Cooperation and its Director of International Cooperation.

After ironing out internal disagreements and working for six months to regain the trust of Brazilian authorities, a deal was finally on the table.[30] As the Anti-Corruption Office had initially proposed, the deal was firmly anchored in well-established principles of international penal cooperation enshrined in treaties signed by both countries. Specifically, the agreement recognised states' obligation to find ways of making cooperation possible despite differences in domestic legislation, and endorsed the idea that states can indeed limit the use of the information they share with other jurisdictions. On this basis, Argentina accepted the terms required by Brazil, but in exchange secured greater clarity regarding the reach of those conditions. For instance, it would now be possible to indirectly use the evidence if the Argentine state decided to impose fines on the company. Moreover, it was explicitly stated that prosecutors and judges could go against Odebrecht executives on the basis of other evidence as long as the crimes in question had not already been punished in Brazil.

In August 2018 the press informed that a deal had been finally signed.[31] Unfortunately, however, the practical implications were rather limited. First, significant time had already passed since the start of the inquiry, and all momentum had naturally languished in the absence of incriminating evidence.[32] As a federal judge put it to a journalist back in June 2017,

> We had hoped that by a given date we would obtain the information [...] With that date gone, we know that the information never arrived, and we don't know if it will arrive. This generates the need to design another investigative template that will put us, perhaps, down a more difficult road.[33]

Second, the deal only established a general framework for inter-jurisdictional cooperation. Each prosecutor was free to use it or not. And if they did decide

---

[30] After the initial rebuke, Brazilians were not hopeful that a deal would be possible. There were also other signs that the Argentines could not be trusted. For example, someone leaked information regarding related talks between Argentine officials and the US Department of Justice, which prompted the Americans to abandon the negotiating table. Interestingly, our Argentine sources told us that part of the charm offensive to regain trust involved informal contacts with Brazilian authorities at events promoted by institutions of the international anti-corruption regime, including meetings of the OECD Bribery Convention and the EU's Eurojust initiative.

[31] Alberto Armendáriz, "*Lava Jato*: Se firmó el pacto con Brasil," *La Nación* (4 August 2018).

[32] It did not help that almost immediately after the deal was signed another major corruption scandal involving the Kirchner administration broke out. The so-called "notebooks scandal" was way more riveting than the local chapter of *Lava Jato* so it sucked up all media and public interest (Cabot 2018; Figueroa 2021). This added to the loss of momentum.

[33] Hernán Capiello, "Marcelo Martínez de Guorgi: 'Brasil trabaja como garante de la impunidad de Odebrecht'," *La Nación* (11 June 2017).

to use it, they then had to convince their respective federal judges to accept it too. In other words, while the agreement with Brazil was living proof of the importance of coordination in corruption investigations, coordination was still missing where it mattered the most. For instance, one of the prosecutors in charge of *Lava Jato* had decided to remain on the sidelines during the negotiations with Brazil, so it was not a given that he would work with his colleagues to operationalise the deal. As we shall see, all of this led to further delays.[34]

In the meantime, the investigation made little progress. One potentially promising development took place in October 2017, when Federal Criminal Court No. 3 agreed to send the part of the *Lava Jato* case concerning bribes paid during the execution phase of the pipeline project to Federal Criminal Court No. 8. As the Macri administration, via the Anti-Corruption Office, argued in a brief:

It is possible to assume that all the alleged bribes paid in Argentina have followed the same illegal procedure [...] All these issues are of difficult factual verification and for this reason we consider that the accumulation of the three investigations is the best way to guarantee a more effective prosecution of these conducts, saving scarce judicial resources and avoiding a possible overlap and obstruction of ongoing investigations [...] *In general terms, the effectiveness and progress made in the set of cases grouped under the name of "Lava Jato" in Brazil [...] is a function, among other things, [of putting the cases under the orbit of one judge] and of the creation of teams of prosecutors to deal with them as a unit.*[35]

The possibility of triggering evidentiary economies of scale and greater investigative coordination, however, would remain limited, not least because a few weeks later the Appeals Court denied a request to consolidate all three arms in the docket of Federal Criminal Court No. 8.[36]

The problem of not having access to Brazilian documentation became clear when federal judges issued the first set of indictments. In April 2018, Criminal Court No. 3, which by now only had the smaller portion of the pipeline case, charged three individuals, including former planning minister Julio de Vido, not with bribery but with a crime called "negotiations incompatible with the exercise of public duties." All the judge could reasonably prove was that the bidding process had been highly problematic, tilting the playing field in Odebrecht's favour. Without any confession on file, however, he could not prove that bribe money had changed hands. A month later, his colleague in Criminal Court No. 7, the one dealing with the water company case, reached a

---

[34] Hernán Capiello, "Odebrecht: Se frena la aplicación del acuerdo con Brasil," *La Nación* (26 December 2018).
[35] The brief is on file with the authors.
[36] "Mantienen separadas las causas por las coimas de Odebrecht," *La Nación* (10 November 2017).

similar conclusion.[37] Interestingly, some of the businessmen charged in this resolution had entered plea bargains in another corruption case, but refused to do so in this one.[38] This is because with no strong incriminating evidence coming from Brazil, no one felt the need to talk.

As for the largest line of inquiry, the one in Federal Criminal Court No. 8, indictments would have to wait even longer. In December 2018 the prosecutor asked the judge to endorse the agreement with Brazil but had to wait for a definitive answer. The defendants immediately challenged this possibility, taking the case to the Court of Appeals, which in March 2019 ruled the evidence that could stem from the agreement as potentially admissible.[39] It also urged the Federal Judge to approve the deal. The judge's reluctance to issue a speedy resolution regarding the legality of the agreement would in fact prove highly problematic.[40] For example, at some point the prosecutors managed to convince a member of the former planning minister's inner circle to confess, only to see the witness recant his testimony a few weeks later.[41] Again, in the absence of a deal with Brazil, no one was particularly worried about going to jail. Due to the continued absence of smoking guns, when Criminal Court No. 8 finally issued its first set of indictments, it therefore had to ascribe to the same theory of the case as the other two courts, that is, the judge did not charge the defendants with bribery. This decision was immediately appealed by the prosecutor and the Anti-Corruption Office, resulting in an annulment of all the proceedings.

While the two smaller legs of the investigation were eventually referred to trial courts,[42] the third and largest portion of the case is yet to yield significant results. At the time of writing, the fate of all cases remains highly uncertain.[43]

---

[37] Ivan Ruiz, "Confirman los procesamientos contra empresarios por el caso Odebrecht," *La Nación* (19 December 2018). This changed in February 2019, after the court obtained evidence of bribery thanks to an agreement with Uruguayan authorities. One of the financial intermediaries had used accounts in that country to receive the payments intended for Argentine officials. But because the documentation does not necessarily specify which projects the bribes were intended to secure, it is hard to use it as evidence if the different lines of inquiry are handled separately.

[38] This is known as the "notebooks" scandal. See fn. 165 and Diego Cabot, "El relato más brutal de la historia sobre cómo funciona la corrupción en la Argentina," *La Nación* (12 August 2018).

[39] Hernán Capiello, "Piden apurar definiciones en el caso Odebrecht," *La Nación* (7 March 2019).

[40] Hugo Alconada Mon, "Las coimas de Odebrecht: Dos años después, las pruebas y confesiones duermen en Brasil," *La Nación* (27 May 2019).

[41] Hugo Alconada Mon, "El testaferro de Jaime ahora se arrepintió de haberse arrepentido," *La Nación* (23 May 2019).

[42] The gas pipeline case was referred to the trial court in June 2019. Due the convoluted nature of the appeals process, it took time for the Federal Appeals Court in the City of Buenos Aires to confirm the referral. The water company case was also referred to a trial court in 2020 and that decision has also been confirmed, allowing the trial to go forward. At the time of writing, both trials are still pending.

[43] In March 2021, after the judge in charge of Federal Court No. 8 authorised the agreement with Brazil, the evidence started to arrive. See Hugo Alconada Mon, "Soterramiento del Sarmiento:

The Argentine chapter of *Lava Jato* missed the window of opportunity that opened with the change in government in 2015. Kirchnerism is now back in power following its victory in the 2019 presidential elections. Former president (and now Vice President) Cristina Fernandez de Kircher wasted no time to launch a full-frontal attack against the judicial system, accusing the courts and her political rivals of "lawfare" (Smulovitz 2022). Her supporters even refer to former government officials who are serving time in prison (due to the convictions and pretrial detention orders that resulted from other corruption cases) as "political prisoners." Furthermore, the new government is adamant to pass legislation to significantly curb the autonomy of the *Ministerio Público* and the power of federal judges with a seat in the City of Buenos Aires.[44] Emboldened by the demise of *Lava Jato* in Brazil, some government supporters also floated the idea of spearheading an international effort to criminalise "lawfare" and thus annul all corruption related convictions.[45]

The absence of a timely deal with Brazil that could supply the necessary incriminating evidence to corroborate the December 2016 allegations and incentivise local actors to enter plea deals destroyed any chances that the case had to gain momentum, let alone snowball into a much bigger anti-corruption crusade. Partly to blame are the organisational structure of the *Ministerio Público* and the inquisitorial nature of the judicial process. Institutions stifle the development of the kind of prosecutorial zeal and savoir faire required in white-collar crime investigations, and thus turn all judicial proceedings into a sluggish affair. But failure was not necessarily overdetermined by institutions; there was some room for agency. It is clear that prosecutors could have reached an agreement with Brazil early on had they coordinated better or had more ambitious legal imaginations. Moreover, the various pleas to ensure the maximum level of investigative coordination permissible under this framework were not taken on board.

That judges and prosecutors failed to unify all three lines of inquiry meant that the case was deprived of the kinds of synergies characteristic of task forces. We conceptualised those in Chapter 2 and described how they played out in various crusades. For instance, the reader will recall that in Peru the case was

---

Llegaron las evidencias desde Brasil sobre las coimas que involucran a Julio de Vido y 'Corcho' Rodríguez," *La Nación* (23 March 2021). In early 2022, however, Brazilian authorities suspended the deal. This is because Odebretch accused Argentine prosecutors of violating the confidentiality clause. See Hugo Alconada Mon, "Odebrecht logro paralizar la cooperacion desde Brasil y demanda a la Argentina por US\$50 millones," *La Nación* (17 April 2022).

[44] For instance, at the time of writing the governing coalition was seeking to change the organic law of the *Ministerio Público* to allow a simple majority in the Senate to appoint a new chief prosecutor. Pro-government legislators were also pushing for the early implementation of a select group of provisions included in the new Code of Criminal Procedure. If successful, this move could spare defendants convicted of corruption in lower courts from spending time in jail.

[45] Hernán Capiello, "El kirchnerismo buscan tipificar el 'lawfare' como un delito y anular condenas," *La Nación* (23 March 2021).

swiftly assigned to a specialised task force, itself made up of highly skilled prosecutors from existing units dedicated to white-collar crime. This task force was in full control of the investigation. Crucially, the team brought together prosecutors with the authority to litigate cases before different types of courts, facilitating coordination throughout the judicial process. Moreover, some defendants could only be tried in upper-level courts, so having senior and junior prosecutors working together to collect and analyse evidence about related cases, but ones that would need to follow different judicial trajectories, proved a smart decision. In Ecuador there was also a high degree of coordination between the task force and the chief prosecutor, who litigated different arms of the investigation before different courts.

MEXICO

In contrast to the other cases analysed thus far, the Mexican chapter of *Lava Jato* never really took off. The December 2016 revelations implicated the Fox (2000–2006) and Calderón (2006–2012) administrations but were particularly problematic for sitting President Peña Nieto (2012–2018) and his inner circle.[46] Towards the end of the Fox *sexenio*, Odebrecht signed two contracts with the state-owned oil giant PEMEX to modernise an oil refinery in Minantitlán. The project finished in 2013, costing 66 per cent more than originally expected. Furthermore, Odebrecht secured forty additional contracts without going through a public bidding process.[47] According to the documents released by US authorities, during this period the company admitted paying US$10.5 million in bribes to Mexican officials: US$4.5 million between 2010 and 2012, and an additional US$6 million between 2013 and 2014, when Peña Nieto was already in power. As a result, the incumbent, who at that stage had two more years left in office, found himself at the centre of the scandal. This is in many ways similar to what happened in Ecuador, where *Lava Jato* immediately trained its eyes on individuals close to the then president Correa, suggesting that the criminalisation of grand corruption is not necessarily doomed when the incumbent is the main target. But because Correa's administration ended soon after, and President Moreno subsequently broke ranks with his predecessor, the political space for a serious anti-corruption effort widened relatively quickly. That the inquiry touched people close to Peña Nieto therefore goes a long way to explain the absolute failure of the case. As we shall see below, however, attention to the institutional context, especially the lack of investigative capacity in the federal prosecution services, helps provide a more comprehensive explanation of the outcome. Our point is that due to the absence of

---

[46] Angelika Albaladejo, "Mexico's Odebrecht Investigations Stalled by Politicization," *InSight Crime* (13 June 2018).

[47] "Las oscuras ganancias de Odebrecht en Mexico suman 1,429mdd: Investigación," *Expansion* (2 February 2017).

the human and organisational resources required for "the moment of agency," success would have been highly unlikely even under a more favourable political environment.

The Mexican federal prosecution services, known until recently as the *Procuraduría General de la República* (PGR), are in essence an appendix of the Executive branch. In other words, Mexico is perhaps one of the most notorious Latin American exceptions to the trend towards greater prosecutorial autonomy we described in Chapter 2.[48] For example, the chief prosecutor or attorney general sits at the president's cabinet table and can be dismissed relatively easily (Aguiar Aguilar 2012; Michel 2018b). Because prosecutors have the exclusive prerogative to file criminal charges, this lack of functional autonomy means there is no independent actor capable of investigating the incumbent. The setup reflects the political logic of the *Partido Revolucionario Institucional*'s (PRI) single-party regime, which the new democracy inherited after the 2000 transition. Under authoritarianism, the complex of criminal justice institutions, including prosecutors and the courts, existed to control society and police dissent (Magaloni 2008). As Olvera Rivera (2019: 6; our translation) puts it, "its poor investigative capacity was used mainly to identify risks to political stability and not to punish criminals." Due to institutional continuity, Mexico therefore still has a prosecution service "whose institutional design and practices correspond to those of an authoritarian government" (Aguiar Aguilar 2015: 160; our translation).

The democratisation process was soon followed by the "war on drugs" and the concomitant surge in criminal and state-sponsored violence. This combination of conditions created incentives for criminal justice reform in 2008. The goal of President Calderon's legislative package was to boost the efficiency and transparency of the judicial process, and enhance respect for fundamental rights, including the presumption of innocence. To this end, the government promoted a gradual transition to an accusatorial system anchored in oral proceedings. Reform adoption, however, was territorially uneven and fraught with difficulties, and ultimately did little to change the opaque and sclerotic nature of key institutions. Crucially, instead of investing in retraining the police and the prosecutors to help them adjust to a new role and improve investigative capacity – both of which are essential for the success of adversarialism – reformers invested more time and resources, for example, in erecting new buildings to house oral trials (Olvera Rivera 2019: 16). As a result, the prosecution service is still scandalously deficient. There are no stable career paths, personnel turnover rates (including at the very top of the institution) are very high,[49] and political appointees abound (Aguiar Aguilar 2015: 165). In particular, the lack of clear professional horizons precludes the

[48] The judiciary did experience independence-enhancing reforms, most notably at the level of the Supreme Court (Magaloni 2003; Ríos-Figueroa 2007; Finkel 2008; Ansolabehere 2010).
[49] Since 2006 the country has had eight chief prosecutors.

professionalising dynamics we saw in the cases of Brazil, Peru, and Ecuador, where job stability and thematic specialisation contributed to building capacity to investigate macro-criminality. Instead, Mexico stands out for its prosecutors' dismal performance in this type of cases, including most tragically, those involving serious human rights violations (Gonzalez-Ocantos 2016a; Gallagher 2017; Contesse and Gallagher 2022). Professional futures are so uncertain that prosecutors simply have no incentive variously to learn, become zealous watchdogs, abandon routine tasks, or take risks. A recent internal evaluation even speaks of "administrative anarchy" within the PGR. There is no clarity as to who might be responsible for a particular case; rather, workloads are distributed irrationally among the rank-and-file. According to the same report, this organisational mess is responsible for a staggering 95 per cent of cases remaining unresolved, over 20,000 unexecuted arrest warrants, and numerous instances of administrative impropriety.[50]

Mexico has also been no stranger to anti-corruption reforms. Again, however, the results thus far leave a lot to be desired.[51] Most notably, in 2014 the Peña Nieto administration launched a reform programme that led to the creation of the National Anti-Corruption System (NACS) a year later. The president's initial move consisted of a series of decrees that promised an overhaul of the PGR, including a change of name to *Fiscalía General de la República* (FGR), greater political autonomy, and the appointment of a special prosecutor in charge of corruption crimes (Arellano-Gault 2020: 154). Following arduous negotiations, Congress eventually approved a constitutional amendment that created the NACS, a coordinating institution that brings together six agencies to make policy conducive to the prevention, detection, and punishment of corruption,[52] all overseen by a committee of independent experts. According to Arellano-Gault (2020: 160), the NACS "is obviously an innovation. Risky, complex and expensive, it has proved difficult to get off the ground." Indicative of this is the fact that three years after its creation, the system's steering committee had not yet been convened, the special anti-corruption prosecutor had not yet been nominated (the first special prosecutor eventually took office in March 2019), and the nominees for the new administrative justice courts were yet to receive Senate confirmation.

Thanks to these reforms there is now some potential for anti-corruption capacity building, but the innovations are too recent and too incomplete for

---

[50] Artuto Angel, "Diagnostican caos en la extinta PGR: 95% de impunidad, 21 mil órdenes sin cumplir, 300 mil casos rezagados," *Animal Político* (7 May 2019).

[51] It is worth mentioning that Mexico was an early ratifier of the Inter-American and UN anti-corruption conventions (in 1996 and 2004, respectively) and of the OECD bribery convention (1999).

[52] The six agencies that make up the system's steering committee are: the Department of Public Administration; the Office of the Auditor General; the National Transparency Institute; the Judicial Council; the Office of the Special Anti-Corruption Prosecutor; and the Federal Court for Administrative Justice.

them to have had any impact on the course of the *Lava Jato* investigation. The remainder of the case study must therefore logically turn to the details of the investigation to get a sense of what went wrong.

Long before the December 2016 revelations, the Auditor General's Office issued warnings to successive administrations about possible irregularities in Odebrecht contracts, but these warnings did not lead to serious investigations. Once the scandal broke out, however, inaction was no longer an option. In January 2017 the PGR opened a formal investigation.[53] This move proved to be more of a simulation that a genuine attempt to uncover the truth. For example, the authorities never created a special task force. According to the *New York Times*, the ruling party was adamant to avoid a still more serious scandal on the eve of the 2018 presidential race.[54] Further evidence of the presence of a political firewall around the president and his inner circle was the sacking of Santiago Nieto in October 2017. In his role as special prosecutor for electoral crimes, Nieto had opened an investigation that ran parallel to the PGR's main case. He believed that Emilio Lozoya, former PEMEX CEO, had taken bribes from Odebrecht to fund Peña Nieto's presidential campaign in 2012. This is because Lozoya was one of Peña Nieto's closest campaign advisers around the time that Odebrecht allegedly paid the bribes. When Nieto asked the PGR for the banking records gathered as part of the *Lava Jato* inquiry, the government ordered his removal.

Before leaving the PGR in October 2017, Chief Prosecutor Raúl Cervantes stated that the investigation had been completed. While neither him nor his successor ever agreed to discuss progress, everything indicates that the prosecutors failed to activate productive lines of inquiry, arrest suspects, extract confessions, or issue indictments. In other words, they never triggered the evidentiary cascade typical of the "moment of agency." It is interesting to note that the paucity of publicly available information about the progress of the case contrasts sharply with the other chapters of *Lava Jato*, during which investigators were eager to share their tactics with the press. This is in part because Brazilian, Peruvian, and Ecuadorian prosecutors had something to show. Moreover, because they were committed to go after powerful figures, the various task forces needed to shore up support for the anti-corruption effort by going public. In this sense, "missingness" in the Mexican case, that is, the lack of traceable information about the criminal proceedings, is very telling, both regarding the nature of the investigative effort and the reasons for its failure.[55] The opacity or lack of data about *Lava Jato* makes sense if we consider that the chief prosecutor was institutionally attached to the presidency,

---

[53] The government also tried to save face by banning Odebrecht from contracting with the state.

[54] Azam Ahmed, "Mexico Could Press Bribery Charge: It Just Hasn't," *New York Times* (11 June 2018).

[55] For a discussion of how "missing data" can aid inferences during process tracing, see Gonzalez-Ocantos and LaPorte (2021).

had no incentives to mount a campaign against his boss, and little to show for as a result. Opacity is also consistent with the country's record of rampant impunity in criminal cases against high-level state officials. For instance, reflecting on the impact of prosecutorial secrecy on the failure of human rights prosecutions in the early 2000s, Human Rights Watch (2006: 48) writes: "a culture of secrecy prevails, for the most part, in the work of Mexican judges." The problem is not just one of lack of political will, but also one of inadequate professional role conceptions: "many judges still believe that access to information and transparency belong to common law judicial systems and are incompatible with Mexico's legal system" (ibid.). As we know, this approach is particularly fatal when it comes to complex investigations against the establishment. In fact, asked to comment on the way Mexican investigators handled *Lava Jato*, Brazilian judge Sergio Moro attributed the lack of progress to a failed media strategy, contrasting it with his decision to make all information publicly available – even when doing so triggered accusations of activism. In his view, publicity offers "protection against any type of obstruction of justice."[56]

The PGR's mishandling of the investigation (deliberatively, due to incompetence or formalistic professional role conceptions) is even more apparent if we consider that Mexican civil society actors were able to obtain a number of "smoking guns" that implicated the suspects. For example, the NGO *Mexicanos contra la corrupción y la impunidad* (Mexicans against corruption and impunity) obtained a court document in Brazil in which an Odebrecht executive claimed that Lozoya had requested US$5 million in bribes in 2014.[57] Furthermore, the NGO gained access to the testimony of three additional sources, all of whom indicated that Lozoya had received at least US$10 million in bribes. Other documents uncovered by Mexican journalists point to an even higher figure. None of these revelations jolted prosecutors into action.

The investigation remained stagnant until 2019. At this point, Peña Nieto was already out of office and largely discredited. His successor, President López Obrador (2018–), ran for office on an anti-corruption, anti-establishment platform. On paper, at least, conditions were now ripe for a more zealous inquiry, especially given the usual political capture of the prosecution services in Mexico. In fact, the new chief prosecutor, who attributed the lack of progress under the previous administration to a "cover up,"[58] promised swift action. In July 2019, investigators issued an arrest warrant against Emilio Lozoya, who was eventually detained in Spain and extradited to Mexico. Upon arrival in July 2020, he applied to change his status to that of a "cooperating witness" and

[56] Angelika Albaladejo, "Mexico's Odebrecht Investigations Stalled by Politicization," *InSight Crime* (13 June 2018).

[57] See Mexicanos Contra la Corrupción, https://contralacorrupcion.mx/web/lanegrarelacion/la-negra-historia-de-odebrecht.html (accessed 19 April 2019).

[58] "Fiscal: Mexico no indagó caso Odebrecht por encubrimiento," *Los Angeles Times* (18 February 2020).

handed over evidence of the illegal campaign financing scheme. In his testimony, Lozoya accused Peña Nieto and former finance minister Luis Videgaray of ordering the use of Odebrecht money to pay the fees of ten advisors to the 2012 presidential campaign.[59] Lozoya also confessed that he created an offshore company in the British Virgin Islands to receive the bribes, and that he pocketed half of the funds. Finally, he also implicated other former presidents, two former presidential candidates, eleven legislators, PEMEX executives, and financial intermediaries. Among the claims made was the accusation that they all had received bribes in exchange for contracts with the state-owned oil company and support for Peña Nieto's controversial energy bill.

At the time of writing, however, this confession is yet to produce additional arrests. The investigation seems once again to have stalled. The prosecutors also remain keen to do all they can to curtail public scrutiny of their actions. One reason for this lack of progress is that unlike what happened in other Latin American cases, where spectacular confessions by key witnesses were quickly corroborated by other testimonies or documentary evidence supplied by Odebrecht, in Mexico this never happened. Quite the contrary: Luis Meneses Weyll, former director of Odebrecht's Mexican branch, challenged Lozoya's statements. He told the prosecutors that while the company does not deny paying millions to Lozoya, it rejects claims that Odebrecht funded Peña Nieto's campaign, bribed legislators who hesitated to lend support for the energy bill, or made illegal payments to secure public works contracts during the Calderón administration. Put another way, there seems to be an effort to scapegoat Lozoya, making sure the investigation maintains a narrow focus. Because Lozoya's confession was more wide-ranging than some initially hoped, he ended up implicating various political parties as well as individuals working for President Lopez Obrador. This means that investigators were probably wary of reaching the kind of cooperation agreement with Odebrecht to corroborate Lozoya's information and crack the case as it happened in Peru, Brazil, or Ecuador.[60] Odebrecht likely knew this, so remained reticent to assist the inquiry and hedged its bets on the case making little progress.

In sum, the Mexican story is one in which the institutional environment conspired against the emergence of the kind of skilled and committed prosecutors required to observe anti-corruption crusades. Under such conditions, "the moment of agency" never materialises because there are no investigators willing

---

[59] "Exdirectivo de Braskem vincula campaña presidencial de Peña Nieto con Odebrecht," *Forbes Mexico* (23 October 2017).

[60] Some believe that those implicated in the scandal made it clear to the Lopez Obrador administration that they would not tolerate further revelations. The president took note of these threats, ordering investigators to slow down the case. For example, the Lozoya affair quieted down after the release of a video that showed the president's brother accepting "off-the-books" campaign contributions. The message to the government seemed to be that its own skeletons in the closet could be easily exposed if it did not turn a blind eye on the past.

or able to accept risk, taking the fight to the establishment in defiance of their superiors. The space is therefore wide open for obstructionist shenanigans. Corruption investigations are left at the mercy of extra-legal political dynamics and fail to gain any degree of autonomy.

CONCLUSION

The three shadow case studies bring the first part of the book to a close. Table 4.1 summarises how the different national chapters of *Lava Jato* we examined in detail in this and the previous chapter "score" on key institutional, agentic, and political variables.

The analysis of the drivers of anti-corruption crusades confirms the explanatory importance of reforms that enhance prosecutorial autonomy and enable bureaucratic differentiation within the prosecution services. These changes make grand corruption more legible and punishable from a legal point of view, push the issue up the ladder of prosecutorial priorities, and boost investigative capacity. The analysis also reveals that the day-to-day of an investigation matters too. Without taking a closer look at the decisions that law enforcement actors make during the inquiry, it is hard to understand why the seemingly narrow (and often vague) corruption allegations that surface during the "moment of serendipity" sometimes snowball into a much bigger affair. The various cases discussed in Chapters 3 and 4 teach us one clear lesson in this regard: crusades are a function of the adoption of aggressive and unorthodox investigative strategies, and this is more likely when prosecutors form task forces. Small group dynamics facilitate coordination, spur innovation, and reinforce professional commitments.

We argued throughout that instead of reducing corruption investigations to "lawfare," we are better off seeing them as an open-ended battle between, on the one hand, a handful of zealous and autonomous rank-and-file investigators, and on the other, politicians and their allies in senior judicial and prosecutorial roles. In other words, the politics that unfold outside the courtroom do not fully drive the direction or speed of the inquiry. In all cases, prosecutors went after individuals with a non-trivial number of political resources and capacity to block anti-corruption efforts, yet investigations did not universally fail to gain momentum and investigators did not universally fail to undermine those powerful actors. If prosecutors are determined and skilful enough, they can make good progress, often against all odds. Politics is, of course, not irrelevant. For example, Correa's departure from office and Moreno's betrayal of his former boss certainly expanded the space for a successful chapter of *Lava Jato* in Ecuador. At the same time, it is fair to conclude that prosecutors were only able to move as quickly and effectively thanks to certain characteristics of the institutional environment. Similarly, the fact that in Mexico the main suspect was the sitting president made it highly unlikely that the investigation would gain momentum. The institutional infrastructure of the criminal justice system, however, suggests

TABLE 4.1 *Summary of explanatory variables and case outcomes*

Country	Favourable political conditions to investigate corrupt elites?	Prosecutorial empowerment via reforms?	Was a task force created to investigate *Lava Jato*?	Crusade?
Peru	Some defendants clearly weak, but key ones retained important institutional and political resources to obstruct the case.	Yes – formal prosecutorial autonomy, transition to accusatorial system, criminal code reforms, bureaucratic differentiation leading to specialisation in white-collar crime	Yes	Yes
Ecuador	Change in government at the start of *Lava Jato* favoured the investigation (Moreno admin.), but key defendants still retained important institutional and political resources to obstruct the case.	Yes – formal prosecutorial autonomy despite setbacks during the Correa admin., transition to accusatorial system, criminal code reforms, bureaucratic differentiation leading to specialisation in white-collar crime	Yes	YES
Argentina	Change in government at the start of *Lava Jato* favoured the investigation (Macri admin.), but key defendants still retained important institutional and political resources to obstruct the case.	No – formal prosecutorial autonomy but no transition to accusatorial system, limited criminal code reforms, limited bureaucratic differentiation leading to specialisation in white-collar crime	No	No
Mexico	Initially, defendants were linked to the incumbent (Peña Nieto admin.). Change in government (Lopez Obrador admin.) did not favour the investigation.	No – no prosecutorial autonomy, deficient transition to accusatorial system, limited criminal code reforms, no bureaucratic differentiation leading to specialisation in white-collar crime	No	No

that even under more auspicious political conditions prosecutors would have still struggled to display high levels of zeal and effectiveness.

Politics may not overdetermine the outcome of anti-corruption efforts, but it does complicate the trajectory of investigations. This is because corruption prosecutions generate high political costs and large political dividends. Powerful defendants do not just let zealous prosecutors collapse their parties or governments; they usually fight back. Our argument indicates that defendants have an easier time neutralising investigative efforts in the absence of institutional reforms, when prosecutors do not present a united front (e.g., because they do not operate under the umbrella of a task force), or when they fail to "go public." These conditions notwithstanding, the vengeful force of corrupt actors is always one to be reckoned with. In fact, the "moment of agency" tends to be followed by "moments of backlash." While the outcome of the clashes that unfold during the moment of backlash is uncertain, the case studies suggest that the more anti-corruption investigations increase in scope and tempo, the more space there is for effective retaliatory attempts or for contingent developments and mistakes that derail the inquiry. This might explain why Peruvian prosecutors had a harder time than their Ecuadorian peers. While the latter also had to deal with fierce backlash, the Ecuadorian chapter of *Lava Jato* was narrower and shorter. The case did not drag on for several years or radically alter its scope over time, thus limiting the number of "enemies" and reducing the likelihood of deadly setbacks.

One of the key paradoxes of anti-corruption crusades is therefore that the zeal that makes them possible is also prosecutors' biggest enemy. Zeal is threatening, especially when crusades never cease to expand in scope. Zeal is also extremely controversial from a rule of law standpoint; it strengthens the hand of critics and can put the champions of transparency in a difficult spot. In other words, zeal turns what is a noble cause that everyone should in principle welcome, into something incredibly contested.

Having dissected this core attribute of anti-corruption crusades, we are now in a good position to explore how the public reacts to unprecedented levels of prosecutorial zeal, in particular, whether crusades bring hope in the possibility of moral regeneration or simply reinforce cynicism about the corrupt nature of political institutions. Part II is devoted to this question, examining the obstacles that prosecutors face in turning their professional commitment into broader and stable anti-corruption coalitions that make the criminalisation effort sustainable and ultimately successful.

PART II

PUBLIC REACTIONS

In the first part of the book, we described how, armed with new prerogatives, role conceptions, and professional skills, prosecutorial task forces in several Latin American countries deployed an aggressive approach to criminalise corruption. The remaining chapters shift attention away from the institutional and agentic determinants of anti-corruption crusades to explore the impact of these sagas on public opinion.

When it comes to studying the consequences of anti-corruption crusades, we could have chosen to remain at the level of institutions and elites, looking, for instance, at how *Lava Jato* affected economic and party-political dynamics, or whether it indeed helped curb corruption. After all, many national chapters of the inquiry paralysed activities in the construction sector, contributing to a sharp slowdown in economic growth. Furthermore, zealous prosecutorial campaigns damaged the reputation of major parties and banned leading candidates from participating in elections, thus throwing key races wide open and creating space for the rise of political outsiders. In other instances, *Lava Jato* triggered massive political earthquakes that culminated in the collapse of national governments. These are undoubtedly important consequences, but not the ones we study in Part II. Our focus is instead on how voters process these shocks, particularly whether and how crusades affect their attitudes towards politics and corruption.

There are several reasons why focusing on the impact of crusades on mass attitudes is a sound analytical choice. First, the structural effect of *Lava Jato* on levels of systemic corruption is something that cannot be assessed just yet. Investigations are ongoing in most countries, so it is too early to tell whether they will have an impact of this kind. Other elite-level consequences have already been felt and are quite apparent. Indeed, one can readily observe candidates going to prison, outsiders rising from obscurity, governments becoming embroiled in scandals they cannot survive, economic indicators plummeting, and so on. In our view, however, because these effects are so apparent, they are not as interesting as an object of study. By contrast, what voters make of all of this is much more elusive, requiring detailed empirical work. Little surprising, then, that public reactions to *Lava Jato* (or other anti-corruption crusades for that matter) are yet to receive systematic scholarly attention. It is therefore in this area where we can make a more significant contribution to the literature and public debate.

Second, many of these elite-level consequences depend on how citizens react to the crusade. Are voters energised by the anti-corruption drive, providing a platform for anti-establishment or anti-corruption candidates? Do they turn against corrupt elites, potentially altering the basis of support for existing governments, parties, and leaders? And do crusades change voters' expectations about what politics should look like going forward, or what politicians should and should not do, thus also altering the incentives that elites face when they enter politics? To be sure, the experience of a crusade may turn law enforcement institutions into a serious threat for corrupt elites, forcing them to think twice before engaging in future corruption. But if this kind of empowerment of watch-dog agencies is not accompanied by a change in voters' expectations and the emergence of a strong consensus around the merits of anti-corruption, prosecutors will remain fleeting threats rather than become a long-term, systemic engine of transparency.

Third, this is a book about anti-corruption crusades. Like all crusaders, our prosecutors are campaigners that seek to cultivate a following. Their mission is unprecedented and fraught, which is why, as discussed in Chapter 2, one of the elements in the toolkit that investigators deploy during the "moment of agency" are public outreach efforts. The goal is to amass public support and diffuse threats. Ensuring that the public stays loyal is important because of its defensive properties. But it is also critical because crusaders justify their zeal – and the unorthodox tactics that come with it – with reference to citizens' dissatisfaction with systemic wrongdoing and self-serving elites. In other words, prosecutors explicitly or implicitly claim to be fulfilling a societal mandate, one that validates their choice to redefine the boundaries of legality so that anti-corruption efforts actually bite. Without a robust base of support, unorthodoxy is much less defensible and sustainable. It is therefore pertinent to explore the conditions under which prosecutorial behaviour during a crusade resonates with the electorate. This is a key pathway to building broad anti-corruption coalitions that back the accountability project and help maintain the momentum that is required if the prosecutorial campaign is to leave a long-lasting mark on politics. In this sense, the preceding chapters feature examples of judges and prosecutors trying hard to nurture public support, as well as instances in which popular mobilisation played a critical role in the survival of crusades. But they also feature examples of innovative investigative choices and trade-offs that complicated the relationship between prosecutors and their audiences.

Part I thus sets the ground for our analysis in Part II. To think systematically about why crusades may be received or assessed differently by different electorates or groups within the electorate, making them more controversial in practice than they are in principle, one first needs to understand what triggers the phenomenon and what it looks like. Put differently, an account of the public reception of crusades must be anchored in an account of the legal and political dynamics of these investigations. It is only after identifying what a resolute anti-corruption push entails, particularly in terms of prosecutors' unorthodox tactics, and how such pushes tend to unfold, mainly the dialectic between prosecutorial zeal and elite backlash, that we can begin to understand why it is not obvious that the public will universally welcome and support what is in principle a noble cause.

Part II explores the challenges that law enforcement agents face when trying to build these broad anti-corruption coalitions. Does the fact that prosecutors champion a cause that is in principle incontrovertible, namely, fighting corruption, translate into unwavering public support? If one reads the public statements that *Lava Jato* prosecutors regularly made to the press, they certainly seemed to think so. Is this expectation realistic or ever met? More broadly, does the enthusiasm and promise of renewal that inspires the prosecutors spread easily to voters? Do crusades thus begin to augur to voters a future in which politics gets cleaner and redeems itself? Or do crusades have diametric effects? For example, does the revelation of pervasive criminal activity and the concomitant demonisation of politics dampen hope in a different kind of politics? In addition, do high levels of prosecutorial zeal ultimately turn anti-corruption from a valence issue into something that is hotly contested and therefore divisive? In other words, does the nature of crusades, particularly the tensions identified in Part I between fairness and zeal, alienate supporters? And what happens when anti-corruption efforts generate political costs for voters? Are they willing to accept those costs, for example, the demise of leaders they hitherto supported, or do they turn against the prosecutorial effort?

In promising redemption and seeking to cultivate a following, crusaders touch very intimate fibres. Part II probes competing stories about voters' likely (emotional) reactions to anti-corruption efforts, investigating whether prosecutors indeed inspire hope and enthusiasm, or more negative feelings about politics that exacerbate cynicism, disaffection, and/or division. We also rely on a variety of methodological tools to explore how voters' priors (e.g., their partisan affiliations and trust in the courts), as well as their evaluations of the tactics responsible for a crusade's momentum, condition whether responses to the criminalisation of corruption exude optimism about the system's ability to produce a new form of politics or harden pessimism.

Anticipating our findings, the main lesson we derive from Part II is that building broad, durable, and hopeful anti-corruption coalitions that can sustain crusades in the short run and change politicians' incentives in the long run, is quite difficult when anti-corruption ceases to be an aspiration and is operationalised in the form of unusually zealous prosecutorial campaigns. The zeal necessary for the emergence and momentum behind the crusade sometimes fatally complicates prosecutors-cum-crusaders' ability to secure a consensus around the methods and outcomes of anti-corruption. Prosecutors ought to carefully nurture the "myth of legality," that is, an image of impartiality/non-partisanship. But this is hard to do when the very nature of the enterprise is to launch relentless attacks against political figures. In contexts where voters are highly polarised and these figures are popular (e.g., Brazil), it is particularly difficult to bridge partisan divides when pursuing high-profile lines of inquiry. And in those places where political cynicism is pervasive (e.g., Peru), resolute anti-corruption efforts led by compelling prosecutors can struggle to persuade hopeless citizens to feel inspired by the crusade.

The empirical analysis takes snapshots of popular reactions to the Brazilian and Peruvian crusades at different points in time. This exercise and its findings largely track the "moments" in the framework we develop in Part I. Initially, as the moments of "serendipity" and "agency" give the crusade much needed momentum, hope is more pervasive among voters. As the investigation moves forward, widening the range of political targets and relying on unorthodox tactics – and thus becoming more controversial – hope struggles to take root. At this point, division and disenchantment take centre stage. This shift in attitudes accompanies the clashes documented during the "moment of backlash," and exacerbates the precarity of the crusade and its snowball effect in the face of elite counterattacks.

All in all, combining a study of the causes of *Lava Jato* with one of its public receptions helps us make what we see as our main normative or policy contribution, namely, to show that there is no silver bullet when it comes to anti-corruption. Even after resolute crusades of historic proportions, societies are bound to continue disagreeing about the best route away from ethical particularism.

5

Fighting Corruption, Curbing Cynicism?

Crusades, Emotions, and the Future of Politics

INTRODUCTION

Part II is about public reactions to *Lava Jato*. We explore how far-reaching investigations shape voters' attitudes and emotions towards politics, corruption, and anti-corruption. This allows us to think about the possible shifts in public opinion that may follow a crusade, and whether those shifts could affect structures of political representation going forward. Tracing reactions to *Lava Jato* is also important to understand the fate of these initiatives, especially why they often lose momentum during the moment of backlash. Given the precarity of crusades, building broad coalitions that support unusual severity in the face of wrongdoing, and that are willing to stand behind controversial efforts to clean politics, is critical for their survival. But achieving this goal is no small feat.

The key assumption guiding our inquiry is that anti-corruption crusades are "eventful" (Sewell 1996) in ways that conventional corruption cases are not, and therefore have the potential to strongly influence public opinion. We rely on Meierhenrich and Pendas's work to characterise our crusades as a type of "political trial":

[I]nstances in which at least one government is a claimant, an object of claims, or otherwise associated with the proceedings; the outcome of the proceedings crystallizes or communicates a political conflict [...]; *or* courtroom proceedings are directed at the defeat of a political enemy, real or imagined. We are in agreement with Leon Friedman, who, in a little-known contribution more than forty years ago, argued that the concept of political trials encompassed three varieties of proceedings, namely 'cases which are politically *motivated*, those that are politically *determined*, and those which in turn have substantial political *consequences*' (Meierhenrich and Pendas 2017: 48–49; emphasis in the original).

When it comes to the public opinion consequences of anti-corruption crusades, it is useful to place them under one of the three categories of political
trials in Meierhenrich and Pendas's typology: "didactic" trials. These are trials
that "seek, first and foremost, to spread a political message" (ibid.: 53). Jeremy
Bentham highlighted the didactic qualities of trials when he advocated for the
publicity of judicial proceedings in nineteenth-century England:

> By publicity, the temple of justice is converted into a school of the first order, where the
> most important branches of morality are enforced, by the most important means; into a
> theatre, where the sports of the imagination give place to the more interesting exhibitions
> of real life (Bentham 1983: 317).

Didactic political trials always communicate something. Some tell moral tales
of right and wrong, of appropriate and inappropriate behaviour. In so doing,
these trials signal noble aspirations about what politics and society should be
like in the future. A contemporary example is the recent wave of human rights
prosecutions in Latin America. As Kim and Sikkink (2010: 940) put it, human
rights trials are "high profile symbolic events that communicate and dramatize"
the international anti-impunity norm, thus cementing a democratic consensus
and deterring future state crimes. But not all political trials are didactic in this
way. For instance, the trial against oligarch Mikhail Khodorkovski in Russia
during the early 2000s was a "signal that the era of the power of independent
tycoons was over, and henceforth big business could make money but only on
condition that it made no overt political demands, and thus accepted its subal-
tern place" in Putin's new order (Sakwa 2017: 374). Put another way, the trial
served as a warning.

As we saw in the discussion of the "moment of agency" in Part I, anti-
corruption crusades include public campaigns that stage a struggle between
what politics is and what it should be. Prosecutors put political and business
establishments on the stand, portraying corruption as an elusive yet ubiquitous
enemy of the public good, one which ought to be swiftly eradicated via the
deployment of unusually zealous tactics. In so doing, these didactic trials
communicate a political message about what kind of future is within society's
grasp. But the exact content of that message, namely the exact trajectory of
politics the crusade foreshadows, is rather ambiguous.

On the one hand, crusades could signal the end of impunity. An optimist
might suggest that citizens are likely to perceive these developments as a sign of
the nascent capacity of their political systems to disrupt "business as usual."
Prosecutorial displays of institutional virtuosity may thus lead citizens to
experience feelings of system satisfaction that undermine cynical attitudes
towards politics, re-engage them with the political process, and reduce tolerance for graft. This virtuous cycle is expected to halt the reproduction of
cultures of impunity, facilitating the consistent activation of horizontal and
electoral accountability mechanisms and the progressive weeding out of corrupt
politicians. Yet, crusades could also have a diametric effect. By disclosing

authoritative evidence of wrongdoing on a grand scale, and painting politics in such a negative light, prosecutors may reinforce political cynicism, further undermine trust, and persuade voters to accept endemic corruption as inevitable. The crusade may also disappoint, either because it generates unrealistic expectations or incurs in procedural failures, including the (ab)use of tactics that defy traditional understandings of the rule of law. This can polarise views about the merits of anti-corruption, and even push some citizens away from politics, leading them to abdicate their role in the chain of accountability.

The job of this chapter is to present a framework that conceptualises these opposite stylised outcomes and identifies the mechanisms that could drive publics to interpret anti-corruption crusades like *Lava Jato* in an optimistic or pessimistic way. We ask: what messages do prosecutors communicate during anti-corruption crusades? How do citizens decode these messages? And what are the effects on mass attitudes towards politics, corruption, and anti-corruption? One body of research suggests that voters tend to be put off by information about corruption. Another indicates that voters are at best inconsistent when it comes to punishing corruption. But could the scope and salience of anti-corruption crusades alter the accountability equation? Is there something about crusades that affects more fundamental attitudes such as political cynicism or tolerance for corruption? After reviewing some of the common themes in the literature, we present the main contours of the pessimistic and optimistic narratives, which provide different answers to these questions. We pay special attention to the role that emotions play in shaping the attitudes and behaviours that are likely to result from these shocks. Finally, we discuss the narrow set of conditions under which the optimistic narrative stands a chance, with emphasis on the moderating effect of perceptions of prosecutorial performance and individuals' pre-judicialisation attitudes. When trying to build broad and stable coalitions in support of anti-corruption efforts, crusades face an uphill battle despite pursuing what is in principle a noble goal.

VOTERS, CORRUPTION, AND POLITICAL CYNICISM

One key and disheartening insight from research on corruption is that it is easy for societies to fall into accountability traps. As Fisman and Golden (2017: 4–6) explain, corruption can be thought of as an equilibrium from which not everyone benefits, but "no one person can make herself better off by choosing" a course of action that defies the status quo:

> Not only would denunciations lead to social disapproval and perhaps even physical danger, they don't do much good unless others join in. That is, you need a critical mass of disapproval to be effective. Similarly, if everyone you know pays a bribe to get a doctor's appointment, you conclude that if you want to see a doctor, you had better save up your bribe money. In both cases, deciding whether to pay a bribe or denounce them hinges on how many others participate in or speak out against corruption.

In addition to these perverse incentives, the equilibrium likely nurtures permissive social norms that help perpetuate corruption. If the punishment of corruption faces so many hurdles, and levels of corruption remain high as a result, citizens come to normalise illegal behaviour by themselves, fellow citizens, and politicians, and acquiesce (Andvig and Moene 1990; Rothstein 2011; Simpser 2013; Klašnja et al. 2016; Corbacho et al. 2016; Pavão 2018).[1]

Indeed, corrupt ecosystems tend to thrive when they manage to mould foundational attitudes towards politics. Chief among these foundational attitudes is political cynicism, the core "dependent variable" in our analysis. The concept of "political cynicism" became popular among students of American politics in the 1960s and 1970s, when surveys and prolonged protest cycles showed deep discontent with the status quo (Citrin 1974; Miller 1974). A cynic is someone who has no faith or hope in others, whom s/he perceives as innately driven by crass motives. In the realm of politics, "healthy scepticism" about the good nature of politicians and government institutions may thus give wave to "corrosive cynicism" (Capella and Jamieson 1996). When this happens, citizens come to see politicians as a class of self-serving individuals and develop an aversion to institutionalised politics. In other words, political cynicism refers to the generalised absence of trust in politics (Agger et al. 1961; Easton 1975). The opposite of a political cynic is a trusting citizen, one who thinks "the government is producing outcomes consistent with their expectations" (Hetherington 1998: 9).

Cynicism and trust are central to the processes that help maintain or disrupt corrupt political ecosystems. Exposure to, and awareness of corruption, especially systemic corruption, may turn voters into political cynics, and by implication lead them to conclude that engaging in "normal" politics to change the status quo, for example, by punishing corrupt candidates on election day, is futile. As Miller (1974: 951) puts it, cynicism is associated with a sense of

futility in bringing about desired social change or control through political efforts [...] Such feelings of powerlessness and normlessness are very likely to be accompanied by hostility toward political and social leaders, the institutions of government, and the regime as a whole.

In light of this, some cynical voters may helplessly withdraw from political life. Others, by contrast, may come to tolerate politicians' wrongdoing as endemic and inevitable.[2] Tolerance naturally pushes corruption down the list of voters' priorities, and in so doing, lowers the likelihood of social or electoral opprobrium (Pavão 2018). Voters sometimes tolerate corruption begrudgingly, but a true sign of cynicism and of the normalisation of corruption is when they do so quite flippantly, with a laugh.

[1] For a contrasting finding, see Klašnja et al. (2020).
[2] Tolerance implies the "willingness to put up with something one rejects" (Sullivan et al. 1979: 784) and captures individuals' willingness to accept corrupt practices in politics.

While not always acknowledged, the spectre of political cynicism haunts research on corruption, especially work that focuses on electoral responses. Democratic theory expects that where elections are free and fair, voters will be willing and able to weed out corrupt politicians. Citizens care about their general welfare, which should lead them to punish poor performance (Fearon 1999). The findings of numerous cutting-edge articles and books, however, stubbornly defy this mantra. Voters are rather inconsistent when it comes to punishing corruption. In fact, scholars have shown that corrupt politicians often get re-elected in both developing and developed democracies. Put differently, the activation of electoral accountability mechanisms is hardly a foregone conclusion (Fisman and Golden 2017). One possible reason is that exposure to or information about corruption turns voters into political cynics, and by implication, leads them to conclude that the electoral punishment of corruption is futile, should not be prioritised, or is likely to depress rather than boost the utility they derive from politics. In this sense, de Vries and Solaz (2017) remind us that accountability chains involve many complicated steps: acquiring information about corruption, attributing blame, and responding electorally by considering viable alternatives and prioritising corruption over other concerns. Failures at any of these stages "can result in corruption not being punished at the ballot box" (ibid.: 393; Hellwig and Samuels 2007).

Over the last decade or so, political scientists have used a variety of research designs, but notably, lab, field, and survey experiments, to explore such failures, and thus understand why the electoral punishment of corruption is so inconsistent (Dunning et al. 2019). These studies also seek to identify the conditions under which punishment is more or less likely. Many focus on the role of information. Because corruption usually happens under the radar, voters do not have the knowledge they require to effectively punish it. Ferraz and Finan (2008) leverage the quasi-random nature of municipal audits in Brazil to show that the release of negative reports hurts incumbents' re-election prospects. This effect is stronger when incumbents are reportedly more corrupt than voters anticipated. Chang et al.'s (2010) work on Italy during the years of Mani Pulite similarly shows that information activates accountability. They demonstrate that the widespread availability of news stories about corruption allowed voters to coordinate responses against those implicated in the scandal. Too much information, however, can be problematic. For instance, Klašnja and Tucker (2013) find that corruption information activates accountability only in low-corruption contexts. In high-corruption contexts, where yet another set of allegations is unlikely to shock voters, punishment is more conditional (see also Vera 2020). Pavão's (2018) work on Brazil points in a similar direction: if corruption is perceived as widespread, new information about corruption tends not to activate electoral accountability. Under these conditions, voters cannot expect alternative candidates to practice clean government, or reliably use corruption information to distinguish between good and bad politicians.

Group norms also contribute to accountability failures. The identity of those implicated in corruption is especially important to understand the activation of electoral accountability. Empathy operates differently in different circles of closeness (Singer 2011). We know that groups that are perceived to be more similar to oneself are judged by different rules than those applied to groups that are perceived to be distant. As a result, proximity to and affinity with elites directly implicated in corruption makes individuals more tolerant of it. In this sense, several scholars focus on how partisanship affects responses to corruption. For example, Anduiza et al. (2013) find that Spanish partisans are less likely to characterise questionable behaviour by their in-group politicians as an instance of corruption. Solaz et al. (2019) use survey and laboratory data to show that reactions to a corruption scandal in Spain are also highly conditioned by partisanship.

Finally, voters may be well informed or able to overcome partisan biases, but still choose not to punish corruption. One possibility is that they do not think corruption is a serious issue, or one that should take primacy. The economic performance of the incumbent, for instance, is often a more salient concern, leading voters to ignore corruption during "good times" (Klašnja and Tucker 2013; Zechmeister and Zizumbo-Colunga 2013). Similarly, when voters benefit directly from corruption, they are less likely to stigmatise or punish it (Gonzalez Ocantos et al. 2014; Fernández-Vazquez et al. 2016; Klašnja et al. 2021). Boas et al. (2019: 386) find that Brazilian voters punish corruption when presented with hypothetical instances of wrongdoing in a survey experiment, but when it comes to actual voting, behaviour "is constrained by [...] personal attitudes toward local political dynasties and trade-offs with government performance in more tangible areas such as job creation and health." Another possibility is that voters care about corruption and disapprove of it but choose "exit" over "voice." Chong et al.'s (2015) field experiment in Mexico shows that corruption information depresses turnout instead of damaging an incumbent's electoral fortunes.

How to break this vicious cycle, whereby corruption breeds indifference, acquiescence, and more corruption, remains a puzzle. Matthew Taylor (2018) insightfully distinguishes between two viewpoints. On one camp are those who believe that disrupting a vicious cycle in which incentives and mass attitudes conspire against clean politics "requires a 'big bang,' a critical juncture, or a historical turning point momentous enough to pull a country off its current path," for example, wars or economic shocks that increase incentives to improve the efficiency of public bureaucracies or lead to elite replacement (ibid.: 63). The problem is that these structural shocks are rare and costly, and when they materialise, they only bear fruit in the long run. On another camp are those who believe in the power of institutional re-engineering and propose "a laundry list of one-size-fits-all remedies," but "without much guidance for implementation, sequencing, or concern for the systemic whole," these remedies "at best will correct topical maladies" (ibid.: 64).

As we discussed in Chapter 1, one could think of anti-corruption crusades as falling somewhere between these two models, and therefore feel more optimistic about their potential to change politics. They are short-term events rather than long-term processes, but they still have shock-like qualities. Moreover, their very nature may lead to elite replacement, raise perceptions about the expected cost of engaging in corruption among surviving elites, promote institutional reforms, and galvanise society behind the anti-corruption cause. In this sense, it is worth noting that one thing studies drawing pessimistic conclusions about the effectiveness of electoral accountability have in common, is that they either look at the impact of abstract perceptions of corruption or of isolated (and hypothetical, in the case of vignette experiments) revelations of corruption. By contrast, the shock and processes set in motion by anti-corruption crusades may dramatically alter the equation: the scale and concreteness of the information provided is much higher, information tends to be accompanied by some form of punishment, and the crusade often acquires movement-like qualities. Consequently, exposure to this kind of exceptional prosecutorial zeal could be the missing link that puts in play foundational political attitudes and beliefs, including political cynicism, leading to more satisfactory outcomes. As we discuss in the next section, however, the process leading to these satisfactory outcomes is far from straightforward.

BREAKING OR REINFORCING THE CYCLE OF CYNICISM?

In a departure from most existing studies, our focus is less on the relationship between information about corruption and electoral accountability. We are instead interested in studying more general dispositions at the heart of accountability choices, including political cynicism and tolerance for corruption. How do anti-corruption crusades affect levels of political cynicism? Anti-corruption crusades produce focused and extended commentary on the problem of corruption in politics, cutting across informational echo chambers and reaching wider audiences. The drama that accompanies these events is therefore uniquely positioned to shock and capture the public's imagination. But are the events associated with these rare investigations likely to exacerbate or halt the reproduction of cynicism? Do they have the potential to build broad, stable, and engaged coalitions that consistently champion severity in the face of wrongdoing?

The message of anti-corruption crusades *qua* didactic political trials is far from clear. There are two possible stories, one pessimistic and the other optimistic. On the one hand, citizens can plausibly interpret the large-scale criminalisation of corruption as a sign of the system's ability to disrupt "business as usual." As Fisman and Golden (2017: 1) put it, "[o]rdinary citizens are often well aware that they are the victims of corruption, but feel powerless to do anything about it." Prosecutors can step in to give people a renewed sense of agency and efficacy, and thus combat the defeatism at the heart of cynical

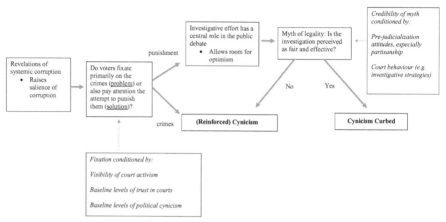

FIGURE 5.1 Summary of the public opinion argument

orientations towards politics. On the other hand, by disclosing authoritative evidence of wrongdoing on a grand scale, prosecutors may reinforce political cynicism, undermine trust in politics, and persuade voters to accept corruption as endemic and inevitable. In this section we conceptualise these two stylised expectations. We pay special attention to the kinds of emotional reactions that pave the road to more (or less) cynicism.

Our point of departure is that the effect of anti-corruption crusades is the result of complex interactions between what transpires in the legal realm and how citizens process what is going on there. In other words, the message regarding the likely trajectory of politics is at the mercy of people's interpretations of the work done by law enforcement agents. Even when courts and prosecutors are above good and evil, and even when they are fighting something that is not controversial (no one likes corruption), citizens can interpret these institutional efforts in different ways. Compounding things further, courts and prosecutors are not always above good and evil and what they are fighting for is in fact more controversial than many observers assume.

The argument begins with the observation that crusades make spectacular revelations that raise the salience of systemic corruption. (For a summary, see Figure 5.1.) If this negative information about politics is what dominates the narrative, as pessimist observers and many scholars of corruption tend to believe, voters are likely to become (more) cynical. But given the unique qualities of courts and the prosecution services as anti-corruption crusaders, their protagonist role in these sagas introduces other possibilities. If the public conversation pays attention to their legal and probatory efforts to combat corruption, that is, if both the problem *and* the apparent solution are debated, we argue, there is room for optimism. Whether or not cynicism is curbed, however, ultimately depends on the type of public discussion that emerges about those efforts. Voters need to buy into the "myth of legality," that is, the idea that courts and prosecutors behave in line with their role – fairly and effectively. Projecting a credible myth of legality is no small feat, and ultimately depends on voters' pre-judicialisation attitudes, including partisan ties to defendants, as well as the day-to-day behaviour of judges and prosecutors during the crusade, which often proves quite divisive. This means that pessimistic expectations can materialise both due to the public's fixation with the crimes revealed during the process, or actual and perceived legal failures. It also means that as the crusade expands and accumulates controversies, hope will struggle to take root. In other words, optimists are only bound to be right under a rather limited set of conditions in which citizens focus on the courts and prosecutors, not just the crimes, and evaluate their behaviour positively. Let us unpack these claims.

On Pessimism

One straightforward possibility is that crusades overwhelm the electorate with negative information about politics, and thus reinforce cynicism. In this sense, several studies find that corruption perceptions undermine political trust. For example, Mishler and Rose (2001) show that in Central and Eastern Europe, high corruption levels are associated with lower levels of trust. Similarly, using a sample of old and new democracies, Andersen and Tverdova (2003) find that citizens in high corruption countries are much less trusting of civil servants. van der Meer (2010) partly attributes differences in trust in European parliaments to varying levels of corruption. In line with these findings, scholars have also shown that perceptions of corruption erode the positive effects of education on political efficacy and trust. Agerberg (2019) finds that educated citizens in high corruption contexts are not different from their less educated counterparts when it comes to feelings of system satisfaction. According to Hakhverdian and Mayne (2012), education leads citizens to be more aware of corruption, which helps explain why education and political sophistication negatively affect political trust in certain contexts. Seligson (2002) reaches a similar conclusion for Latin America: "highly educated individuals are likely to know more about the political system [...] and, consequently, are more likely to be in a position to be critical of it" (Seligson 2002: 423).

If voters see their representatives behaving in ways that are morally reprehensible or plainly illegal, they are likely to lose confidence in the system (Wang 2016; Whiteley et al. 2016). Warren (2004: 328) summarises what is at stake in the relationship between corruption and trust:

Corruption reduces the effective domain of public action, and thus the reach of democracy, by reducing public agencies of collective action to instruments of private benefit [...] When people lose confidence that public decisions are taken for reasons that are publicly available and justifiable, they often become cynical about public speech and deliberation.

It is therefore not surprising that the futility engendered by perceptions and awareness of corruption often depress turnout and other forms of institutionalised political participation (Gamson 1968; McCann and Domínguez 1998; Machado et al. 2011; Scartascini and Tommasi 2012; Stockemer et al. 2012; Chong et al. 2015; Agerberg 2019).

Now imagine a situation in which prosecutors bombard the citizenry on a daily basis, and for months on end, with authoritative information about grand corruption. Backed by research on corruption and trust, the pessimistic prediction is that in these circumstances the most likely consequence will be disillusionment and disgust. By turning against the political class, sparing few political actors of corruption charges, and producing troves of evidence of *systemic* wrongdoing, anti-corruption crusades merely serve to amplify the sense of futility at the heart of cynical orientations towards politics.

Take, for example, the following statement by one of the prosecutors involved in Brazil's *Lava Jato*:

Each accusation is like a small piece of a huge puzzle, and we need to fit a sufficient number of pieces of this puzzle so that everyone who looks at this set can know how it would look, if complete. Only then can the population spear the wheat from the chaff (cited in Moreira Leite 2015: 35–36; our translation).

Pessimists disagree with this prediction. When authorities manage comprehensively to reconstruct the puzzle of systemic corruption, they create space for generalisations about the crass nature of politics, not for the careful discernment that the prosecutor expects. This is because anti-corruption crusades portray corruption as constitutive of political activity, rather than the product of circumstantial individual greed or moral failure. It is only natural that the sheer scale of the revelations leads some voters to wonder why they should ever trust politicians again or get involved in politics at all, and others to wonder why they should prioritise corruption when deciding whom to support (instead of just tolerating or taking it for granted). How can the problem of corruption possibly get better if politics has been shown to be fundamentally rotten?

Reflecting on Italy's post-Mani Pulite era, Luigi Ferrajoli (2013: 60) laments the depoliticisation and indifference of the electorate, its "growing antipolitical aversion [...] in relation to the political class in its entirety, which is perceived as an abusive and parasitic caste." This is the kind of resignation that Bauhr and Grimes (2014) document among well-informed voters in contexts of high corruption, where the prospects for changing deeply flawed and broken institutions are indeed grim. What makes anti-corruption crusades particularly problematic *qua* source of information, so the pessimistic argument goes, is that they almost always rely on large amounts of evidence to paint a picture that is direr than the one voters could have imagined, and accompany the production of evidence with caustic anti-political rhetoric. We know that when information about corruption surpasses expectations, its corrosive effects on trust worsen (Ferraz and Finan 2008; Arias et al. 2019).

In the pessimistic account, the road to cynicism is paved by the emotions triggered during multiple rounds of scandalous revelations. Emotions are "internal, mental states representing evaluative, valenced reactions to events, agents, or objects [...] They are generally short lived, intense, and directed at some external stimuli" (Nabi 1999: 295). Political psychologists have recently rediscovered the role of emotions in shaping attitudes and behaviour. Emotions matter in politics in addition to resources because they structure the way people process new information and often urge individuals to find coping mechanisms that ultimately influence how they act (Ottati et al. 1997; Isbell et al. 2006; Groenendyk 2011; Petersen 2011; Valentino et al. 2011; Webster 2020). Given the shock value of anti-corruption crusades, they likely trigger politically consequential emotions. In the pessimistic account, cynicism is the outcome of a series of negative emotions elicited by the spectacle of elites of all stripes parading through the courts.

Emotions such as shame, disgust, sadness, worry, fear, or anxiety are likely conducive to cynicism because they are a sign of growing political alienation. In the pessimistic account, individuals experience such emotions because they interpret crusades as a bad omen. Voters come to think of political activity as threatening or unpleasant. Corruption is so entrenched that politics is unlikely to change for the better. Psychologists have shown that people tend to avoid situations that are threatening or difficult to cope with, so political withdrawal, paralysis, or surrender are likely when these emotions are pervasive. For instance, shame "motivates individuals to hide" rather than take things into their own hands (Albertson and Kushner Gadarian 2015: 8). Similarly, sadness "comes from an inability to achieve goals" and causes attention to information, but "this attention is backward looking and reflective rather than directed at ameliorating future threats" (ibid.: 8). Finally, threats often cause anxiety or fear, putting individuals on high alert. But when the threat feels overwhelming, the response tends to be exit rather than voice (Lerner and Keltner 2001; Valentino et al. 2009; Moons et al. 2010; Petersen 2011; Valentino et al. 2011).

To be sure, some scholars find that anxiety caused by certain events (e.g., climate change, terrorism, epidemics) re-engages people with politics. Under such circumstances anxiety encourages learning and attention to information, makes citizens more trusting of government, and creates support for protective policies (Albertson and Kushner Gadarian 2015). An epidemic or a terrorist attack, however, is different from revelations of grand corruption, where the threat that looms large is politics itself. In other words, politics is not the solution but the problem, and a seemingly unsolvable one. As a result, the response to anxiety is to trust less and withdraw support from the system.

In the pessimistic story, anger is another negative emotion that paves the road to cynicism. Scholars tend to treat anger as an emotional reaction to threats, one which arises when individuals feel in control. Individuals are frustrated and actively seek to right wrongs perpetrated against them or their group. For instance, Brader et al. (2010) argue that voters become angry when they can attribute blame for a political failure. Similarly, Goldberg et al. (1999) show that angry individuals become "intuitive prosecutors" because their desire for punishment increases (see also Petersen 2011). This is why anger is often associated with political mobilisation (Valentino et al. 2009; Aytaç and Stokes 2019). One could therefore argue that angry citizens are likely to find some satisfaction in crusades and join the anti-corruption effort, as it were. If this happens, then anger may not after all be a sign of cynicism or foreshadow disengagement. According to the pessimistic story, however, this satisfaction is unlikely to prevent the development or deepening of political cynicism.

First, given that crusades are often protracted, as well as uncertain and non-linear, angry individuals are unlikely to have the necessary patience to avoid frustration with the system. Second, and relatedly, anger is often associated with extra-systemic mobilisation, rather than forms of institutional participation that affirm and validate the system. For example, Banks et al. (2019: 918) find that when black Americans "are made to feel angry about race, they will gravitate toward political solutions that center on expeditiously empowering the racial group by bypassing universalistic forms of political engagement." In the case of corruption prosecutions, the mobilisation of angry voters through conventional institutional channels (as opposed to abstention, protests, or protest voting) may therefore depend heavily on the presence of certain supply conditions, for instance, the emergence of attractive and credible anti-corruption candidates. As Aytaç and Stokes (2019: 106) put it, the effects of emotions like anger are the result of effective elite politicisation, of the "narratives of attribution constructed around [adverse events]." Third, anger is known to deplete trust. Carnevale and Isen (1986) find that negative moods are associated with a lower propensity to engage in cooperative behaviour with others. More specifically, Webster (2017: 2) shows that anger correlates with cynicism: "a greater belief that people have no say about what the government does, that public officials do not care what people think, and that government is run by crooked individuals."

In sum, according to the pessimistic account, the message of anti-corruption crusades is one that pushes voters further away from politics because prosecutions *signal decay, not regeneration*. Voters experience predominantly negative emotions that nurture alienation rather than encourage engagement with the political system in its own terms. In this pessimistic story the crusade is primarily associated with the crimes it uncovers, not with the actions being taken to address the problem of corruption. This is what voters "see," or at least what they focus on. And because citizens fixate on the crimes, they will interpret the crusade as anticipating further political degeneration. The inevitable conclusion is that politics is broken and cannot get better, so why bother with corruption (higher tolerance) or with politics (higher cynicism)?

There is, however, an alternative story. Anti-corruption crusades may be capable of defying the pessimistic conventional wisdom about the relationship between corruption and trust/cynicism if voters do not just fixate on the crimes, but also take a close look at the unprecedented legal and probatory effort to punish wrongdoing. This is because attention to the judicial element of the story introduces promising, albeit highly conditional, possibilities.

On (Conditional) Optimism

In a statement released in 2016 in the wake of massive anti-corruption protests, Judge Sergio Moro claimed: "There is no future with systemic corruption that destroys our democracy, our economic wellbeing, and our dignity." A year later, as he convicted a former senator to nineteen years in prison, Moro took that opportunity to quote Theodore Roosevelt: "The exposure and punishment of corruption is an honour to the nation, not a disgrace." Like Moro, optimists argue that anti-corruption crusades are a display of institutional virtuosity, a sign that the system, while broken, has the necessary antibodies to heal itself. There is no reason to feel sadness, shame, or anxiety; after all, through exemplary decisions, prosecutors and the courts demonstrate that political regeneration is achievable. Importantly, the message conveyed by the investigation is that politics need not be equated with corruption. That kind of cynicism is misplaced because what crusades show is that it is possible to separate the bad apples, and that politics is redeemable as a result. In his seminal essay on horizontal accountability, Guillermo O'Donnell made a similar argument:

> As for social demands and media coverage [of corruption], *in the absence of duly authorized state agencies of investigation and oversight capable of parcelling out responsibility and sanctions*, they are extremely important, but sometimes they risk merely creating a climate of public disaffection with the government or even the regime itself (O'Donnell 1998: 113; our emphasis).

In other words, the effective and even-handed intervention of horizontal accountability actors such as judges and prosecutors can prevent anti-corruption efforts from exacerbating disaffection, and thus turn crusades into a positive force for change.

The optimistic account expects emotions such as hope or enthusiasm to dominate the narrative surrounding anti-corruption crusades, potentially undermining defeatist and cynical beliefs about politics. Corruption is not inevitable; citizens are not condemned to either having to tolerate it or to give up on politics altogether. Crucially, optimists believe this because they do not expect citizens will fixate on the crimes uncovered by the investigation, as pessimists do. Instead, optimists anticipate the focus will also be on the investigation itself, an orientation that makes it possible to develop feelings of system satisfaction that rally citizens behind a cause. This is exactly what Judge Moro was inviting Brazilians to do in the statements cited previously.

According to psychologists, enthusiasm results when a person feels their goals are being met (Marcus et al. 2000). The behavioural response to hope or enthusiasm is usually participation rather than withdrawal or retreat

(Brader 2005, 2006). Enthusiasm gives people confidence in establishment institutions, actors, and processes. In fact, because positive emotions do not indicate a need to change course, when someone is enthusiastic, they instinctively resort to routine behaviour and existing heuristics to navigate social reality (Albertson and Kushner Gadarian 2015: 6). Unlike negative emotions, which open a wedge between voters and politics, positive emotions thus induce support for, and engagement with, the system. This of course does not mean giving corrupt politicians a pass; quite the contrary. But it does mean that the kind of political engagement that is expected from enthusiastic or hopeful individuals is generally one that embraces the system as *perfectible*, and thus leads to a constructive form of accountability. Instead of revolting against the system, or abandoning politics, the response is to strengthen surveillance mechanisms to remain alert. Politics is not necessarily the enemy, only some politicians are, and political activity is not necessarily threatening or defined by corruption.[3]

There are reasons to have faith in this optimistic prognosis. As we saw in the first part of the book, anti-corruption crusades require the creation of zealous task forces that elevate the salience of individual prosecutors. It is therefore possible that citizens will not fixate on the crimes revealed during the process but also pay attention to those working hard within the system to clean it up. In other words, the task forces created to criminalise corruption have the potential to become visible and respected, especially when they go public during the "moment of agency," and thus turn into a source of system satisfaction. Crucially, so the optimistic account goes, these actors are better positioned to trigger positive changes in public attitudes towards corruption and politics than other anti-corruption agents (e.g., investigative reporters, NGOs, etc.). When judges and prosecutors are the ones driving the narrative centre stage, the message they convey benefits from two key qualities of the messenger, making it possible to curb cynicism and build broad, stable, and engaged anti-corruption coalitions.

First, judges and prosecutors communicate via rituals inherent to the legal field. In so doing, they project a "myth of legality" (Scheb and Lyons 2000), or the belief that a "neutral process of legal reasoning" (ibid.: 929) structures their judgment. This in turn legitimises what they do and sets them apart from other institutions or actors (Gibson et al. 2003). To be sure, judges and prosecutors can be deeply "political," but the language they use, the clothes they wear, the buildings they inhabit, or the adversarial methods they use to draw conclusions nurture a special aura that taints perceptions (Gibson et al. 1998; Gibson and

---

[3] Pessimists could of course respond by pointing out that optimism, while welcome, could be fleeting, and most importantly, have uncertain consequences for democratic quality. For example, it is not entirely clear whether the optimism experienced by some voters translates into a productive engagement with the political system or throws voters avid for change into the arms of populist politicians, with potentially destructive implications for democracy.

Caldeira 2009; Bybee 2010). In fact, the myth of legality conditions public discourse about judicial behaviour (Casey 1974). For many citizens who observe judicial behaviour, it probably feels inaccurate to refer to judges simply as politicians in robes because the optics are markedly different. Whereas politicians operate in contexts where self-interest, opportunism, or crass motives prevail in the open (Hibbing and Theiss-Morse 1995), judicial words and deeds have an additional layer of ceremony and complexity. As a result, what judges and prosecutors say or do carries special weight in processes of opinion formation. Indeed, scholars have shown that when courts uphold a policy they can increase its popularity, more so than other endorsers (Mondak 1990). For example, the myth of legality is associated with a favourable predisposition towards decisions rendered by the US Supreme Court (Gibson and Caldeira 2009). Legalisms or legalese, irrespective of whether they are genuine or mere pretence (Bybee 2010), act as shields, ensuring that even highly polarising rulings fail to undermine citizens' "basic commitment to support the institution" (Nicholson and Howard 2003; Gibson et al. 2005: 189; Hetherington and Smith 2007).

Reflecting on the trials against opposition figures in Weimar Germany, Kirchheimer (1961) concluded that proceedings imbued with legalistic rigour allowed the regime to legitimise the elimination of its rivals. Similarly, in the case of anti-corruption crusades, the rituals of legalism allow judges and prosecutors to produce authoritative narratives of guilt. For instance, citizens may reasonably suspect businessmen who chronicle their corrupt dealings with public officials to a journalist but are likely to see prosecutors and courts as more genuine anti-corruption agents. After all, they follow pre-established procedures, gather evidence from multiple sources, and are not themselves directly implicated in corruption. Similarly, citizens should not be blamed for being sceptical about politicians' intentions to effectively curb corrupt practices from which many parties obtain benefits. In their role as anti-corruption agents, by contrast, courts and prosecutors are less likely to be seen facing such conflicts of interest. Overall, because citizens tend to assign more weight to corruption accusations that come from trusted sources, the ability of prosecutorial task forces and judges to project the "myth of legality" should endow them with greater potential to legitimise anti-corruption campaigns. As a result, on average, when the narrative is driven by the actions of zealous judges and prosecutors, the anti-corruption effort and its implications for politics should be perceived in a more positive light. Citizens should experience mobilising emotions such as hope or enthusiasm, as there is finally a credible alternative to impunity within the system. This excitement should re-engage them with politics; political regeneration is now possible.

There is a second feature of anti-corruption crusades that reinforces this advantage. Unlike other actors who disclose or attack corruption, judges and prosecutors deliver the results people expect from anti-corruption efforts. They go beyond the public shaming that comes with journalistic investigations, or the uncertain promises of new transparency laws championed by legislators. When judges and prosecutors launch corruption cases in waves, results appear almost immediately, and are by no means restricted to convictions, which obviously remain the ultimate prize. Other important results include the questioning of suspects, arrests, indictments, or the recovery of stolen assets. Crusades thus force the powerful to appear in front of a court, sending a strong message of legal equality. This greater capacity to deliver is likely to trigger feelings of satisfaction that undermine cynicism. Indeed, scholars suggest that re-engaging and mobilising emotions such as enthusiasm arise "when goals are being met" (Valentino et al. 2011: 158). This disrupts the cynical belief that nothing of consequence can be done to combat malfeasance, leading the average citizen to toughen their attitudes towards corruption in line with (or imitating) court behaviour. In fact, because of the scale of these investigations, crusades can undermine generalised feelings of futility and powerlessness, and help coordinate effective (electoral) responses to the problem of corruption (Chang et al. 2010).

Having said this, the virtuous cycle of trust and constructive political engage-ment faces serious obstacles. To begin with, if feelings of system satisfaction are to stand a chance, the judicial process, not simply the information about the crimes it reveals, must be central to the public debate surrounding the investi-gation. *Prosecutorial task forces' media strategy, and the ways in which the media itself chooses to tell the story of the crusade* play a key role in determin-ing whether this is the case. The more visible and media savvy task force members are relative to the crimes they uncover, the greater the chances that the public spotlight will shine on them, and their rituals and actions.

Baseline levels of trust in the integrity and institutional capacity of the courts and prosecution services before the start of the judicialisation process also matter. Positive attitudes are usually derived from prior positive experiences with the judiciary, and greater attention to, and knowledge of, judicial insti-tutions (Gibson and Caldeira 2009). In societies where individuals already hold these institutions in high regard, for example because they have a proven anti-corruption record or citizens know more about them, the sudden experi-ence of large-scale criminalisation efforts may draw more attention to the work of judicial actors rather than produce a perverse fixation with the rotten side of politics that is revealed during the process. When citizens already trust courts and prosecutors, they are perhaps more likely to think that something good can come out of judicialisation, inviting them to take a second look. Finally, baseline levels of trust in judges and prosecutors likely determine the ease with which this attention to the courts translates into acceptance of the myth of legality. The reason is fairly obvious: communicating credible messages of neutrality, legal equality, and system effectiveness is easier if citizens already evaluate law enforcement institutions positively. When citizens already trust these actors, they do not have to make up their minds from scratch during highly controversial and divisive proceedings.

Baseline levels of cynicism further determine the extent to which the investigation will attract attention relative to the crimes. As Blais et al. (2010) show, pre-existing levels of cynicism condition perceptions of and responses to corruption scandals, with the most cynical reacting "more harshly in nearly every way." In this sense, if citizens are already deeply alienated from the political process, task forces might struggle to get voters to focus on their attempts to clean up, which is the key source of system satisfaction in the optimistic story. Cynical voters have a hard time believing in anything, and as a result will have little time for the new anti-corruption promise. In other words, cynicism may automatically direct the public's attention to the crimes revealed during the investigation rather than the prosecutorial effort, because those revelations are all too consistent with their priors about the crass nature of politics.

If these obstacles were not enough, even when the public trains its eyes on the judicial effort, the outcomes predicted by the optimistic narrative are highly conditional on an effective projection of the myth of legality. This process is also shaped both by pre-existing attitudes and the decisions that judges and prosecutors make during the investigation. Despite the comparative advantage of anti-corruption prosecutorial task forces in communicating credible messages of legal equality and system effectiveness, shifts in public attitudes that halt the reproduction of cynicism are unlikely to be straightforward. For example, studies show that even when courts enjoy high levels of public legitimacy, the way their behaviour in specific cases is framed during public debates determines the impact of judicialisation on public opinion (Grosskopf and Mondak 1998; Hoekstra 2003; Gonzalez-Ocantos and Dinas 2019). Indeed, the ability of the US Supreme Court to deploy its comparative advantage to command acceptance of rulings and bolster approval for their policy implications is not constant (Mondak 1990). When rulings look like the outcome of partisan, as opposed to legalistic decision-making procedures, they fail to command widespread acceptance (Nicholson and Howard 2003; Zink et al. 2009; Nicholson and Hansford 2014).

Observing the outcomes predicted by the optimists therefore depends on whether the public interprets judicial/prosecutorial behaviour during anti-corruption crusades in ways that reinforce the unique qualities of the messenger outlined previously. This has two implications.

First, judges and prosecutors must proceed carefully to bolster the myth of legality and their reputation as effective crusaders. This is crucial to avoid politicisation and disrepute, which can diminish their ability to boost confidence in the system or inspire hope. The positive effects predicted by the optimistic account will obtain only when fairness, impartiality, objectivity, professionalism, and effectiveness are not mere pretence, but are dramatised in credible ways. This, however, is difficult. As we saw in Part I when we discussed the challenges posed by the investigative tools prosecutors rely on to go after corrupt politicians, striking a balance between zeal and prudence, unorthodoxy and due process, or prosecutorial selectivity and punitivism is no small feat. Second, while valuable, these efforts to induce the public to see the investigation in a positive light might sometimes be in vain. Voters are unlikely to interpret events uniformly. Crucially, some voters are not predisposed to believing in the myth of legality or in the goals of the investigation, for example, due to their partisan allegiances. Let us unpack these two implications.

Following Tyler (2004), *perceptions of procedural fairness or impartiality* refer to views about the extent to which judicial authorities respect the rights of the parties in a dispute, and generally care about their well-being. These perceptions play a crucial role in conditioning the positive impact of anti-corruption crusades because procedural fairness is a key standard of behavioural appropriateness that anyone who exercises a judicial function must adhere to. If judicial or prosecutorial decisions are not perceived as grounded on technical, legal, and objective considerations, the relative advantage of courts and prosecutors, and their symbolic capital, quickly disappears because judicial actors are not acting in accordance with what their role prescribes (Ferejohn 2002). Perceptions of failure, especially with regard to fairness, not only will prevent political cynicism from being curbed, but are also likely to reinforce generalised feelings of institutional mistrust and disappointment.

This is likely to happen, for example, if while claiming that corruption is systemic, investigators disproportionately target certain parties or politicians while sparing the rest. Impartiality is critical to diffuse rejection and feelings of victimisation among partisans of the accused, and to avoid disappointment among non-partisans who care about due process. If the charge that the investigation is being instrumentalised, that it is partial and amounts to "politics by other means," is a credible one, the view that the crusade represents the dawn of an era of political regeneration is unlikely to gain traction. Crusaders cease to be an exception in an otherwise rotten system and become part of the problem. More worrying is the fact that sometimes courts cannot avoid this kind of criticism, even when they behave impartially. This is because *partisan attachments*, where strong, almost always guarantee that sooner or later there will be conflicting interpretations of the motives and merits of corruption probes. And if the investigation fuels divisions along partisan lines, that is, between those who attack judicial actors for their lack of professionalism and impartiality and those who praise and defend them, hope and system satisfaction among the latter will come at a high cost, both for judges and prosecutors, whose reputation will suffer among portions of the population, and the democratic system, which will have to endure polarisation.

Anti-corruption crusades make the task of preserving the myth of legality and bolstering an image of effectiveness, particularly challenging. First, corruption prosecutions are the ultimate form of judicial intervention in political affairs, and as such can quickly become deeply divisive. Willingly or not, judges and prosecutors are bound to exacerbate the latent tension between two key elements of the rule of law: the activation of accountability mechanisms when it is necessary to do so, and the openness of the processes that regulate access to power in a democracy. Della Porta and Vannucci (2007: 846) refer to this as the divide between "'judicialists' and 'guarantors' of the political system." Take the conviction of former president Lula Da Silva. Whereas for some the ruling was inappropriate and disrupted democracy by excluding the most popular candidate from the 2018 presidential race, others maintain that Lula's status as a candidate, let alone the most popular one, should not exempt him from having to respond to corruption charges. Judges and prosecutors can therefore be seen as introducing anti-majoritarian distortions to the democratic process. This is likely even in less extreme instances, for example, when their decisions do not fundamentally alter the dynamics of a presidential race, but simply sully the reputation of parties or governments. *Partisan attachments and deep rifts in the electorate obviously exacerbate the problem because they taint perceptions of the motives behind judicial decisions.*

Second, demonstrating effectiveness is also hard. Only when courts and prosecutors clearly show that their efforts are not yet another straw in the wind that politicians can easily dodge, but actions of great consequence, are voters likely to experience enthusiasm and see political regeneration within reach. As we showed in Part I, the evidentiary and political challenges that characterise corruption investigations, as well as the convoluted structure of the appeals process, conspire against this. For instance, taking stock of the Mani Pulite operation, Della Porta and Vannucci (2007: 844) conclude that "the main lines of inquiry have been exhausted with few confirmed sentences; the decrease in the number of confessions has made new inquiries increasingly difficult; and a combination of slow judicial machinery and the success of obstructionist political tactics has caused many cases to collapse." In other words, anti-corruption task forces often struggle to satisfy the public's punitivist desires.

Third, and perhaps most importantly, it is not always possible to simultaneously project an image of effectiveness and one of fairness and impartiality. As we also argued in the preceding chapters, the prosecutorial tools that make these investigations possible are quite controversial. For example, pretrial detentions and some innovative criminal definitions have a complicated relationship with due process and the rule of law. This tends to open the door to accusations of vindictiveness and "lawfare," even among those who do not have partisan stakes in the game. But not using these tools in the information-poor and politically hostile environments that characterise corruption prosecutions can lead to prosecutorial failure. Similarly, reliance on plea bargain agreements and other forms of selectivity can quickly create the perception that investigators are being too soft and ineffective, even though it is usually necessary to turn a blind eye on certain crimes to obtain confessions and go after the "big fish." To accept these trade-offs and cut investigators some slack, citizens therefore require patience and a sophisticated understanding of the evidentiary and procedural hurdles that prosecutorial task forces must overcome.

In sum, while a public narrative that takes an intense look at the judicialisation effort *qua* purported solution to the problem of corruption makes the optimistic prognosis possible, things can still go horribly wrong. Partisanship, the trade-offs between legality and effectiveness at the heart of prosecutorial success, media coverage of the anti-corruption effort, and general levels of trust in judicial institutions, all conspire against the goal of curbing political cynicism. Crucially, while at their onset anti-corruption crusades might be broadly welcome, they are bound to generate multiple controversies and disappointments as the snowball effect gains traction. This means any hope that results from the initial promise to redeem politics will likely be precarious.

At this stage we can list our main propositions about the public opinion effects of anti-corruption crusades:

- Negative emotional reactions to crusades (e.g., anxiety, worry, shame, anger) reflect greater cynicism and feelings of helplessness vis-à-vis corruption. They are a sign of a deepening wedge between voters and the political system, which is increasingly seen as irredeemably corrupt. The response could be political withdrawal or greater tolerance of corruption. By contrast, positive emotional reactions (e.g., hope, enthusiasm) are a sign that voters are willing to embrace the system as perfectible and re-engage with it. This should correlate with lower levels of cynicism and tolerance for corruption, as redemption is now seen as a possibility.
- Curbing cynicism and eliciting positive emotional reactions is dependent upon the extent to which citizens focus on the investigative effort at the heart of anti-corruption crusades, not just the crimes, and find this effort a plausible and serious attempt to fight corruption.
- More visible investigative teams or task forces are more likely to attract attention to the legal and probatory effort and avoid a fixation with the crimes. The relative visibility of this effort vis-à-vis the crimes can be a function of the type of media coverage and the media savviness of judges and prosecutors.
- Higher baseline levels of trust in courts and prosecution services are likely to induce greater attention to the investigative effort as opposed to a fixation with the crimes.
- Higher baseline levels of cynicism are likely to result in more attention to the crimes than the investigative effort because revelations of criminal activity are all too consistent with entrenched priors about the crass nature of politics.
- Attention to the investigative effort is likely to curb cynicism and elicit hope/enthusiasm when citizens accept the "myth of legality," that is, when citizens evaluate the investigation as fair and effective, and are satisfied with the work of those involved.
- Evaluations of fairness and effectiveness are shaped by
  ○ Judicial and prosecutorial behaviour, that is, whether or not investigations are even-handed and not biased, and whether or not they deliver concrete results. In particular, investigative strategies that appear to breach due

process or seem to follow a very selective approach (e.g., via leniency agreements) complicate the public's relationship with the crusade;
○ Partisan feuds in the electorate. Partisans of the accused are more likely to feel aggrieved and therefore reject the myth of legality. Rival partisans, by contrast, are more likely to derive satisfaction from the crusade.
• Perceptions of fairness and effectiveness are likely to suffer as the crusade expands its remit, widening its pool of targets and deploying unorthodox tools in a sustained fashion. As a result, while enthusiasm is sometimes pervasive at the onset of the crusade, it eventually gives way to pessimism.

THE ROAD AHEAD

Crusades are an anti-corruption strategy that can in principle curb cynicism and push societies out of the accountability trap. The likelihood of this happening, however, is rather slim. It is easier for crusades to decant into generalised cynicism than to inspire widespread hope and system satisfaction. Given the stringent set of conditions under which the outcomes optimists expect are likely to materialize, if they do materialize, citizens with a renewed sense of hope will likely still coexist, often in very unfriendly terms, alongside a large group of cynics and also groups of partisans that feel victimised by the inquiry. All of this means it is hard for crusaders to successfully build the broad and stable coalitions required to sustain the momentum behind the investigation. At the heart of this lies a tragedy: the zeal that propels investigations forward is also what complicates prosecutors' ability to nurture a widespread following and thus overcome the inherent political precarity of their project.

Crusades are complex and protracted, so it is difficult to isolate their effects on public opinion. Moreover, the competing narratives about what is likely to happen when voters are exposed to these shocks predict a bundle of outcomes conditional on a variety of contextual and individual-level factors. This means that we do not have a single smoking gun that is able to tell us whether pessimists stand on firmer grounds than optimists. Instead, what we do in the following chapters is present empirical approximations to different elements of the story. Taken together, our focus groups and (observational and experimental) survey data suggest that while there are reasons for hope, the potential for crusades to delegitimise political systems, fuel polarisation, and undermine democratic processes is very real.

In Chapter 6 we begin to adjudicate the debate between pessimists and optimists relying on focus groups (and descriptive survey statistics) to dissect the main contours of the public conversation elicited by *Lava Jato* in Brazil and Peru. Since one of the preconditions for the activation of the optimistic narrative is that citizens pay attention to the judicial effort rather than fixate on the crimes, we first investigate whether the conversation is dominated by a discussion of wrongdoing, or also features a discussion of the legal process and its protagonists. If the crimes are more salient than the investigation, it is harder for courts and prosecutors to put their symbolic capital to good use, and these episodes become negative information shocks. A narrative that is crime-focused is a breeding ground for cynicism.

We find that while Peruvians focus almost exclusively on the crimes, Brazilians are divided between those who do the same and those whose discourse is dominated by references to judicial actors. This is reflected in similarly contrasting emotional responses: whereas Peruvians express overwhelmingly negative emotions and are deeply cynical, attitudes among Brazilian participants are more mixed, with some voters signalling re-engagement and system satisfaction. We argue that these differences make sense from the point of view of the framework developed in this chapter. For example, we show that the media environment is much more crime-focused in Peru. In addition, given the longer duration of the Brazilian chapter of *Lava Jato*, judges and prosecutors became more visible and central to the public debate. Finally, pre-*Lava Jato* levels of cynicism were higher in Peru, whereas pre-*Lava Jato* levels of trust in courts were higher in Brazil, leading to greater attention to the judicial effort in the latter case.

Chapter 6 also relies on focus groups to explore how voters evaluate the fairness and effectiveness of *Lava Jato*, and whether these evaluations mediate how voters feel about the future of politics. The cases are interesting because Brazil offers a context of deeper partisan polarisation than Peru. This has implications for what we find. When it comes to performance evaluations, Brazilians are divided (mostly along partisan lines) and engage in lively debates about the merits of the investigation. Dissatisfaction is particularly prevalent among supporters of the PT, who feel victimised by a "partial" investigation. Those who do not sympathise with the left defend the integrity of the inquiry and express confidence in its ability to redeem politics. Optimism in Brazil therefore comes at a cost because it is fuelled by (and fuels) polarisation. Peruvians, on the other hand, do not talk much about the investigative effort. When prompted to do so, they do not see it through partisan lenses. This is because they inhabit an environment where parties are discredited and trust in politics is extremely low. The problem, however, is that high baseline levels of cynicism leave little room for positive evaluations of the work of the prosecutorial task force. For example, voters are deeply critical of the trade-offs investigators had to make to crack the case. They look at these with suspicion, especially when it comes to plea bargains. As a result, they are doubtful the effort will amount to much in terms of regenerating politics and prefer to stick to their pessimistic priors.

We start Chapter 7 with an analysis of surveys conducted in Brazil both during the apogee of the crusade and when objections became more serious and salient. Trends at the aggregate level show that opinions about *Lava Jato* became more divided (and more negative) over time, pointing to the precarity of hope. We then study the determinants of perceptions of fairness and effectiveness, finding that partisanship, in particular support for the PT, is associated with lower levels of satisfaction with the crusade on both dimensions. Taken together, these results indicate that prosecutorial zeal can quickly become controversial and backfire, with voters' priors and crusaders' own tactical decisions playing a role in how criminalisation is ultimately perceived. Second, we present the results of an experiment conducted in Brazil in April 2021, when *Lava Jato* was already languishing following a series of setbacks. The experiment was designed to prime participants to think about either the problem of widespread corruption or *Lava Jato*'s anti-corruption effort. After making these two central considerations accessible to voters in a controlled manner, we assess whether they lead to different emotional reactions and levels of cynicism. We find that a narrative that focuses on the judicial effort, as opposed to a narrative of Brazilian corruption that looks exclusively at the crimes, reduces negative feelings about politics but also reduces voter's sense of external political efficacy. This suggests that pessimists might be right in warning that the anti-political message that crusaders espouse does more harm than good to the view that politics is perfectible.

Finally, Chapter 8 turns to original survey data from Peru. We show that satisfaction with the *Lava Jato* task force correlates with more positive emotions as well as with more optimistic prognoses about the future of politics. Positive emotions are also associated with a lower propensity to tolerate corruption. A conjoint experiment confirms that the *Lava Jato* task force, by virtue of its reputation, induces voters to impose greater penalties on politicians than other sources of corruption allegations. But another conjoint and additional descriptive survey data show that prosecutorial trade-offs and mistakes can easily destroy optimism. Together with findings in Chapter 6, these results remind us of how hard it is for prosecutors to effectively dramatise the "myth of legality," and of the precarity of any sense of hope crusaders may have originally instigated.

6

Of Cockroaches and Superheroes
Talking about *Lava Jato* in Brazil and Peru

INTRODUCTION

This chapter analyses public reactions to *Lava Jato* using focus group data from Brazil and Peru. Anti-corruption crusades can fundamentally disrupt political life in a democracy because they disclose and punish grand corruption by multiple political parties, business conglomerates, and bureaucrats, rather than isolated or minor instances of corruption. Moreover, the judicial actors at the forefront of these inquiries often mount campaigns that portray corruption as systemic and pathological, and thus trigger sustained informational shocks that raise the salience of corruption among voters. For some, citizens should see in this a sign of political regeneration and march in lockstep with judges and prosecutors, re-engaging with politics to severely repudiate corruption. It is also possible, however, that by increasing the salience of systemic corruption, crusades serve merely to re-enforce an environment of cynicism that demoralises voters. And, of course, crusades' controversial methods may lead voters to question the merits of anti-corruption, and therefore fail to join the support coalition that law enforcement actors so adamantly try to build.

We know little about how voters feel or respond when exposed to sustained informational shocks that portray corruption as a serious systemic problem. This chapter begins to address this gap. It is very hard to isolate the effect of protracted and messy anti-corruption sagas on citizens' political behaviour or attitudes. The findings we report here therefore do not have that kind of "causal" interpretation. Rather than estimating the precise impact of *Lava Jato*, we explore how the public decodes these informational shocks and talks about them. In so doing, we evaluate some of the propositions advanced in Chapter 5. What kind of emotions and attitudes towards corruption and politics do voters report when asked to reflect upon *Lava Jato*? Are voters put off by these investigations or do they display greater political engagement?

Are they cynical or hopeful about the possibility of changing politics? Are all *Lava Jatos* created equal, or does the way in which different investigations unfold, and the political environment in which they take place, shape emotional and attitudinal responses?

Documenting voters' reactions – and establishing whether they are more in line with the optimistic or pessimistic narratives – is important to have a better sense of what kind of political and electoral consequences we might expect from these shocks. On the one hand, citizens can plausibly interpret the large-scale criminalisation of corruption as a sign of the system's ability to disrupt "business as usual" from within. These "big bangs" dramatise a country's potential for political regeneration. Courts and prosecutors, we argued, are well positioned to convey a message of regeneration because their rituals and procedures endow them with symbolic capital, what some call "the myth of legality." Furthermore, courts and prosecutors can combine revelations of corruption with concrete, and in some cases, relatively swift forms of punishment. This can elicit feelings of system satisfaction that undermine cynical attitudes towards politics and reduce tolerance for graft. The message is simple: "corruption doesn't have to be inherent to politics; something can be done to address the problem." Such feelings of system satisfaction may be accompanied by mobilising emotions like hope or enthusiasm, leading to a virtuous cycle of critical engagement with institutionalised politics.

But there is another, more pessimistic possibility. The optimistic narrative requires citizens to buy into the "myth of legality," which is no small feat given the unorthodox and aggressive nature of the prosecutorial tactics at the heart of crusades. In addition, we know that as perceived levels of corruption go up, voters tend to normalise illegal behaviour. By disclosing authoritative evidence of wrongdoing on a grand scale, judges and prosecutors may thus reinforce political cynicism, undermine trust in politics, and persuade voters to accept corruption as endemic and inevitable. A system shown to be rotten could also inspire paralysing emotions such as fear, anxiety, or worry, and the generalised feeling that there is little that can be done to change reality. This cynicism could ultimately lead the public to abdicate its accountability functions, abstain in large numbers, or withdraw support from all establishment actors and institutions.

The process whereby citizens decode and ascribe meaning to large-scale criminalisation efforts is inherently discursive and dialogical. We argued in Chapter 5 that two dimensions of the public conversation elicited by cases like *Lava Jato* are especially important in this process of meaning construction. First, whether the conversation is dominated by a discussion of the judicial effort, or whether it is dominated by a discussion of what judicial authorities uncover about politics. In other words, what is more salient in the minds of voters, the investigation or the crimes it reveals? If the crimes are more salient, it is harder for courts and prosecutors to put their symbolic capital to good use, and these episodes become primarily negative information shocks. A narrative that is crime-focused is a breeding ground for cynicism, despair, and hopelessness. By contrast, a public that focuses on the institutional response creates space for a debate about process and the role of courts and prosecutors, which in turn makes it possible to activate the mechanisms driving the optimistic narrative. Second, when citizens focus on the investigative effort, how do they evaluate it in terms of its fairness and effectiveness? The optimistic narrative crucially depends on the credibility of the "myth of legality," but this myth is not something courts and prosecutors automatically project and citizens buy into. Perceptions of fairness matter because they lead voters to think the system is rising to the occasion, and that judicial actors are not acting inappropriately or out of character. In other words, the criminalisation process is not "corrupt politics by other means," but a credible intervention to sanitise politics. Perceptions of effectiveness also matter because they lead voters to believe the system is indeed disrupting business as usual, thus pre-empting disillusionment. In short, if during discussions of the investigative effort voters conclude that judicial actors are neither fair nor effective, the space for optimism narrows.

To unpack meaning construction along these two dimensions, we need an approach that captures the discursive and dialogical nature of the process. Focus groups are particularly well-suited for this purpose. Focus groups have recently re-emerged as a popular research method in political science (Cyr 2019). They are an efficient way to establish what people think about specific issues and why. As Denzin and Ryan (2007: 585) put it, "focus groups can be used to examine the meanings and group processes involved in participants' experiences and what is being studied." First, focus groups generate data about how people talk about issues and what they "think from," namely the concepts, analogies, and assumptions that underpin processes of attitude construction and articulation. Second, focus groups allow us to make inferences "simultaneously at the individual, group, and interactive level" (Cyr 2016: 232). Since perceptions of, and attitudes towards corruption, politics, and judicial actors are collectively constructed overtime, it is key for us to explore how citizens discuss their views with their peers. In addition to gauging participants' individual opinions, we must be able to understand how voters use cues and information from others to communicate, reinforce, and update their own attitudes. As Cyr notes (2016: 250) "researchers who measure socially produced and reproduced phenomena should seriously consider undertaking focus groups as part of their research design." This is because focus groups provide a window into collective processes of opinion formation.

This chapter analyses fourteen focus groups we conducted in Brazil and Peru in 2019. We also use survey data (collected by us and others) to contextualise the findings. We begin with a brief overview of the fieldwork. We then explore how focus group participants in both countries think about *Lava Jato*, that is, whether they primarily associate the brand with an investigation or with the crimes it uncovers. In so doing, we pay attention to emotional reactions. The analysis then turns to how participants evaluate the investigative effort in terms of its fairness and effectiveness, and how this shapes attitudes towards politics and corruption. On both dimensions we find important differences between the focus groups in Peru and Brazil.

For Peruvians, talking about *Lava Jato* is synonymous to talking about the crimes, not the judicial or prosecutorial effort. In the process, they express highly cynical political attitudes and negative emotions. Many Brazilians, by contrast, tend to think of *Lava Jato* as an investigation. This court or prosecutor-centric narrative, in turn, is accompanied by a mix of cynical and hopeful reactions. Put differently, while Peruvians are crime-focused and only see "cockroaches," some Brazilians see judicial "superheroes." Regarding the second dimension, the discussion in Chapter 5 indicates that constructing the myth of legality is very hard. The kind of judicial and prosecutorial behaviour that makes crusades, as well as pre-judicialisation attitudes, can both derail the process. The focus groups suggest that much. When it comes to evaluations of fairness and effectiveness, Brazilians are quite divided and engage in lively debates about the merits and demerits of the investigation. This debate, which is primarily driven by conflict between partisan groups, allows a portion of participants to air optimistic views and provide rationalisations when their more sceptical peers highlight the shortcomings of the investigation. But this optimism comes at the expense of polarisation (primarily along the cleavage dividing supporters and opponents of the Workers' Party). Peruvians, on the other hand, live in an environment where political disaffection and fragmentation rather than polarisation are the norm. As a result, in addition to spending less time discussing the investigative effort, evaluations of fairness and effectiveness do not divide participants along partisan lines. In fact, when prompted to discuss the investigation, there is a general sense of disappointment. Participants are deeply unhappy about the trade-offs prosecutors had to make to obtain evidence, and are not at all hopeful about the effectiveness of criminalisation. The overall tone of the debate is therefore quite gloomy. *Lava Jato* seems to have merely reinforced priors about the crass nature of politics.

Taken together, the two sets of focus groups indicate that optimism is unlikely to ever dominate the discussion of anti-corruption crusades. Yet both optimistic and pessimistic narratives can develop in reaction to large-scale criminalisation efforts, with contextual factors determining whether there is some room left for feelings of enthusiasm. As we present the results, we discuss the factors that might explain differences between the two countries, and how these conjectures relate to the framework proposed in Chapter 5.

THE FOCUS GROUPS

This chapter looks at *Lava Jato* from the point of view of Brazilian and Peruvian citizens. The bulk of the data comes from fourteen focus groups conducted in the cities of Recife, Brazil, in February 2019, and Lima, Peru, in July 2019. As we showed in the first part of the book, Brazilian and Peruvian

TABLE 6.1 *Focus groups: Recife, Brazil (February 2019)*

Social grade[a]	Focus group no.	Gender		Duration
		Male	*Female*	
A	1	5	5	2:33:12
	2	5	5	2:32:58
B	3	5	5	2:00:54
	4	5	5	2:30:37
C/D	5	0	10	2:02:01
	6	10	0	2:03:19
	Total	30	30	

[a] A is the highest.

judicial actors launched the most far-reaching and ambitious national chapters of *Lava Jato* in Latin America, with both inquiries stretching their tentacles across the political and business establishments. As a result, anti-corruption efforts have gained unprecedented salience, dominating the agenda. The question we ask is how that salience translates into mass attitudes and emotions towards politics and corruption. At the time we conducted our research, the Brazilian and Peruvian chapters of *Lava Jato* still enjoyed momentum, and while controversies were beginning to emerge around certain investigative decisions, they were yet to be tarnished by major scandals. However, the two countries featured very different political contexts: polarisation between *petistas* and *anti-petistas* (supporters and opponents of the Workers' Party, or PT following its initials in Portuguese) in Brazil, and acute party weakness, political fragmentation, and disaffection in Peru. This contrast has important implications for our findings, suggesting that the impact of anti-corruption crusades is context dependent.

Tables 6.1 and 6.2 show the composition and duration of our fourteen focus groups.[1] Following best practices, we segmented participants by socio-economic status, or social grade, and in the case of Peru, also by age. This is thought to level the discursive playing field, for example, by preventing age or status-differentials from intimidating certain participants. It also improves communication, ensuring most participants understand each other. In addition, socio-demographic homogeneity within groups creates conversational environments that more closely resemble those citizens encounter in their everyday lives. The prompts and questions we used to guide the discussion were not exactly the same in both countries because we wanted to make sure the protocols were sensitive to context, and also because we learnt new techniques

---

[1] We initially aimed for six focus groups in each country, two per socio-economic groups. However, in Peru we ended up with eight. This is because more participants than expected showed up for two of the sessions. Instead of turning them away, we organised parallel sessions.

TABLE 6.2 *Focus groups: Lima, Peru (July 2019)*

Social grade[a]	Focus group no.	Age group	Gender		Duration
			Male	*Female*	
A/B	1	18–25	4	4	1:48:20
	2	26–60	4	4	1:36:19
	3	18–25	1	2	1:29:35
	4	26–60	2	3	1:08:37
C	5	18–25	3	4	1:33:28
	6	26–60	5	3	1:47:57
D/E	7	18–25	4	3	1:35:56
	8	26–60	4	4	1:54:20
		Total	27	27	

[a] A is the highest.

between the first and second wave of focus groups.[2] We did, however, replicate the broad contours of the conversation. The focus groups started with a general discussion about how participants felt vis-à-vis their country's political situation. We then moved on to talk about *Lava Jato*, trying to get a sense of how knowledgeable participants were about the case; their thoughts about the political implications of *Lava Jato*, both in general and with respect to different parties and politicians; what they had learnt from the investigation; and how they felt about it. The conversation then turned to questions of fairness and effectiveness. We asked whether participants thought the investigation was politically motivated or impartial, and whether they thought it had been effective, taking special care to emphasise that we wanted to know their views about the strengths and weaknesses of the crusade. At this stage we also asked them to evaluate key aspects of the prosecutorial strategy, including the use of plea bargains, leniency agreements, and pretrial detentions. The discussion ended with questions about the future of politics and of *Lava Jato*.[3]

Located in the North East of the country, Recife is Brazil's ninth largest city and home to 1.6 million people. Lima is the capital city of Peru, concentrating nearly a third of the country's population. Recife and Lima are of course not representative of Brazil and Peru. We chose these field sites mainly due to convince and familiarity with the context. Given the small number of participants in each focus group, our samples are also not representative. But these are not shortcomings we necessarily worry about. Our goal is not to estimate average attitudes or opinions; to achieve that, here and in subsequent chapters we rely on nationally representative surveys. Instead, we use focus groups to

---

[2] For example, in Peru we used a map of emotions and personification/animalisation games.
[3] See the Appendix for information about the focus groups protocols we applied in both countries. The Appendix can be found on http://www.narapavao.com/book.html

describe how voters articulate their opinions about *Lava Jato*. These opinions are likely underpinned by complex thought processes because the phenomenon of interest is itself very complex. We suspect that while standard survey techniques can support generalisations, they cannot fully capture this richness. Furthermore, we are interested in how citizens discuss and form their opinions during interactions with their peers, which is also something that cannot be easily done with a survey. Focus groups are better suited for these purposes. Given the relatively intimate setting and homogenous socio-demographic make-up of each focus group; the extended discussions that took place during our sessions, which allowed participants to build rapport with each other and the moderator; and the ample variation in the "experiences and perspectives" (Morgan 1996: 134) of participants across groups, it is possible to imagine that conversations similar to the ones we witnessed and report here take place when citizens talk about politics in their everyday lives.[4]

WHAT *IS LAVA JATO* AND HOW DO VOTERS *FEEL* ABOUT IT?

We begin to dissect the conversation about the criminalisation of corruption in Brazil and Peru by looking at participants' emotional reactions to *Lava Jato*. We also identify which references to actors, events, and facts associated with *Lava Jato* dominate public discourse. We are interested in understanding popular representations of *Lava Jato*, what participants think about when they think of the scandal, and whether the salience of certain representations is associated with positive or negative feelings about politics. This is a key first step in the analysis because the framework we introduced in Chapter 5 indicates that representations of *Lava Jato* that focus on the crimes, not the investigative effort, are likely to be accompanied by negative emotions as well as cynical conclusions about the nature and future of politics.

In Peru we asked participants to examine a "map of emotions"[5] and privately write down the emotions that best described how they felt about *Lava Jato*. They each then shared their list with the group. As shown in Table 6.3, emotions were overwhelmingly negative, with four sets of emotions standing out: ashamed, unhappy/displeased, indignant/hurt, and angry/furious. In terms of unequivocally positive emotional reactions, only one participant felt happy and another reported feeling inspired/optimistic. The emphasis on negative

---

[4] Of course, because of the rapidly changing dynamics of anti-corruption crusades and the fact that focus groups only capture views at a particular moment in time, the tone and content of those conversations in periods before and after our fieldwork could be quite different. This is something we reflect upon in the analysis, especially with regard to Brazil due to high-profile revelations in July 2019 that likely altered perceptions about the fairness and impartiality of *Lava Jato*. See Chapter 2 for an account of the *Vaza Jato* scandal and Chapter 7 for a quantitative perspective on how it impacted public opinion.

[5] See the focus group protocols in the Appendix for a copy of the "map of emotions." The Appendix can be found on http://www.narapavao.com/book.html

TABLE 6.3 *Reported feelings about Lava Jato in Peru (focus groups)*

Emotion	Young male (A/B)	Young female (A/B)	Adult male (A/B)	Adult female (A/B)	Young male (C)	Young female (C)	Adult male (C)	Adult female (C)	Young male (D/E)	Young female (D/E)	Adult male (D/E)	Adult female (D/E)	Total
NEGATIVE													
Sad, Depressed							1						1
Unhappy, Displeased	1	3	1				2	1	2	2			12
Indignant, Hurt		2		2			4			1	1		10
Incredulous, Skeptical	1				2	2		1					6
Bored	1	1		1						1			5
Guilty, Remorseful													0
Disappointed, Disillusioned	1				1		1	1			2	1	7
Ashamed	1	1	2	1			2	2					9
Confused	1					2			1			2	6
Worried, Anguished	1												1
Angry, Furious	1	1	2	2			3	1	3	1			14
Shy, Intimidated													0
POSITIVE													
Surprised	1				1	2			1				5
Thankful													0
Interested, Curious	1				2	3		1					7
Seduced													0
Peaceful, Relieved					1								1
Enthusiastic													0
Amused													0
Happy									1				1
Identified											1		1
Amazed					1				1			1	3
Inspired, Optimistic					1								1
Tenderness													0
Proud													0

185

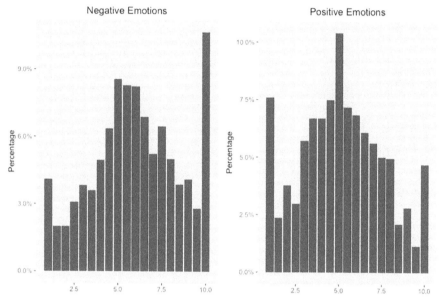

FIGURE 6.1 Emotional reactions to *Lava Jato* in Peru (survey).
Source: Authors' face-to-face, nationally representative survey fielded in November 2019 in
partnership with *Proetica*. Question: "Thinking about the Odebrecht case (also known as the *Lava
Jato* case), how does it make you feel? Using a scale from 1 to 10, where 1 means 'nothing' and
10 means a lot, do you feel [angry, worried, enthusiastic, hopeful]?" Each graph shows the average
for the two negative and positive emotions, respectively.

rather than positive emotions is consistent with the results of a survey we
conducted in November 2019, jointly with Proetica, the Peruvian chapter of
Transparency International. Figure 6.1 shows the results of four questions that
asked respondents to rate their levels of anger, worry, enthusiasm, and hope
vis-à-vis politics in the age of *Lava Jato*. Like in the focus groups, the average
intensity of negative emotions is higher.[6] These initial pieces of evidence suggest
that the public conversation in Peru is more aligned with the pessimistic
narrative about the likely public opinion consequences of large-scale criminalisation efforts.

One possible reason why in the Peruvian focus groups emotions are overwhelmingly – and more intensely – negative is that the social imaginary
constructed around *Lava Jato* is one that emphasises the crimes and not the
judicial/prosecutorial effort to punish corruption. A crime-focused narrative is
a breeding ground for despair and cynicism. Indeed, when explaining their
choice of emotions, participants started to reveal the events and actors they

---

[6] See Chapter 8 for a more detailed analysis of this data.

associate with *Lava Jato*; in other words, what *Lava Jato* represents or *is*. The only participant who felt optimistic highlights the judicial effort: "I put down 'inspired/optimistic' because of the two prosecutors and the judge who could shed light on this" (Male, Young, C). Focusing on the institutional response is a source of hope. But for the majority of participants, *Lava Jato* is not an institutional solution to the problem of corruption; *Lava Jato represents corruption.* They justify negative emotions with reference to the crimes revealed by the inquiry as well as the perpetrators, and all seem to share a general sense of hopelessness. The message they receive is that corruption is pervasive, deeply entrenched, and difficult to eradicate:

They are painting for us a worrying picture of all that is wrong with politics [...] They never show the good side of politics (FG7, Male, Young, D/E)

Unhappy. It's not just one politician or two; not even one political party. It's practically all political parties. That reflects Peruvian reality (FG1, Male, Young, A/B)

I'm ashamed and worried about the democratic system. These are leaders we elected! I'm ashamed because the people we elected do not represent us well [...] Who are we going to choose if they are all the same? (FG2, Male, Adult, A/B)

I wrote down indignant, hurt, bored. Indignant and hurt because of the level of selfishness of the people involved in *Lava Jato*. They [the politicians] all say they care about the country. They promise things and all of that, but in the end, everything is about amassing power for themselves [...] And bored because each day we see that more people were involved. I get bored seeing that new people keep showing up (FG1, Female, Young, A/B)

Angry, furious because every time I hear about them [the politicians] I get in a bad mood. I'm also bored because I want to hear about something else [...] They are stuck on this topic; they don't know how to solve it (FG2, Male, Adult, A/B)

Incredulous and sceptical because one doesn't really know what to expect [...] Ashamed because Peru is rich in many things and is well regarded internationally. It will be a shame if this stains [that image] and people stop wanting to invest or visit (FG6, Female, Adult, C)

The association of the *Lava Jato* brand with corruption crimes rather than with an institutional effort to curb corruption also dominated the discussion when we asked participants to brainstorm words, names, or ideas that came to mind when thinking about *Lava Jato*. Figure 6.2 shows word clouds broken

Social Grade A/B   Social Grade C   Social Grade D/E

FIGURE 6.2 Terms associated with *Lava Jato* in Peru (focus groups)

down by social grade. While the range of vocabulary varies significantly across socio-economic groups, the most salient words are the names of politicians (e.g., Keiko Fujimori, Alan García, Alejandro Toledo) or companies and company cartels (e.g., Odebrecht, Club de la Construcción) implicated in the scandal, and, of course, the word "corruption." The names of the leaders of the prosecutorial task force in charge of the case (Rafael Vela, Jose Domingo Perez) or the word "prosecutors" (*fiscales*), for instance, are not central to the discussion. In fact, in the case of lower socio-economic status groups, these terms do not feature at all. This suggests that when asked to think about *Lava Jato*, participants focus on the problem (i.e., corruption), not the solution (i.e., the judicial effort to address it), possibly because as some of the above quotes indicate, it is unclear to them that there is a real solution in sight. Compounding things further, some participants have very limited knowledge of the judicial effort. For instance, in all focus groups the moderator asked them to identify the prosecutors. Whereas higher socio-economic status participants had some success in naming the relevant actors, lower status participants consistently failed to do so. Take the following exchange among our young, low socio-economic status participants when they were trying to come up with the correct names of the relevant prosecutors:

FEMALE: There was another one . . . [Pauses to think]. I can't remember.
MALE: Of course! His lawyer. . .
MALE: Domingo Santos? I can't remember.
MALE: The one that litigates against Keiko. . .
MALE: Ah, the one with the glasses!
MALE: I don't remember his name. . .
MALE: Me neither. I have it on the tip of my tongue, but I don't remember his name.
   (FG7, Young, D/E)

The fact that the *Lava Jato* brand is associated with the crimes and not the investigation became even more apparent when we asked participants to play a "personification" game, which involved imagining what would "*Lava Jato*" look like if he or she suddenly walked into the room. This exercise saw the participants collectively construct a human identity that in all focus groups, that is, across age and socio-economic status groups, converged in a person with the following characteristics: male, middle aged, married, living in a posh part of Lima, and a shady businessman with excellent social skills, which he uses to advance his position. Some even joked that *Lava Jato* would probably have a lover. Below is an example of the kind of collective identity construction we witnessed during the focus groups:

MODERATOR: How do you imagine *Lava Jato*? As a man or a woman?
FEMALE: A man.
MALE: A man.

MODERATOR: **What age?**
FEMALE: In his fifties.
FEMALE: Mature.
MALE: Sixty.
MODERATOR: **Socio-economic status?**
MALE: High.
FEMALE: High.
MODERATOR: **What are his virtues?**
FEMALE: He is intelligent.
MALE: Very cool.
FEMALE: Very capable.
FEMALE: Very able.
FEMALE: Astute.
MODERATOR: **And his weaknesses?**
FEMALE: He offers bribes.
MALE: Arrogant.
FEMALE: A person with very few values, principles.
MODERATOR: **Is he single, married, a widower, divorced?**
FEMALE: Married.
MALE: Divorced.
FEMALE: Divorced.
MALE: Second marriage.
FEMALE: Or if he is married, he cheats on his wife.
FEMALE: I see a picture-perfect family, but with a lover.
FEMALE: Exactly!
FEMALE: Yes!
MODERATOR: **Where does he live?**
FEMALE: In San Isidro, Miraflores.
MALE: Miraflores.
MALE: La Planicie
MODERATOR: **How would this person be as a friend?**
FEMALE: Very sociable.
FEMALE: A party animal.
MALE: He has a yacht, a sports vehicle.
FEMALE: He pays for everything.
MALE: He also likes casinos (FG2, Adults, A/B)

A few participants dissented, saying, for example, that *Lava Jato* would actually be a woman because "when women are bad, they are worse than men, and more intelligent than the most intelligent man" (FG8, Female, Adult, D/E). This personification, however, fits with the general pattern of associating *Lava Jato* with corruption, greed, and evil, rather than with the possibility of ending this calamitous state of affairs with a thorough investigation. The "animalisation" exercise revealed a similar way of thinking: *Lava Jato* would be an animal typically associated with dirt (a rat or a cockroach) or with danger, duplicity, and treachery (a snake, a wolf, a fox, or a tiger). One participant, for example, joked that *Lava Jato* is the "cockroach that you find in your bathroom at three in the morning" (FG1, Male, Young, A/B). For a handful of participants, *Lava Jato* would in fact be a friendly animal such as a dolphin, but this is because "it presents itself as noble. It won't present itself as a fierce wolf. It is camouflaged" (FG2, Male, Adult, A/B).

If this is how Peruvians imagine *Lava Jato*, it is possible that the whole judicial saga amounts to a negative information shock that serves merely to disclose the darkest side of politics, undermining trust, and nurturing a kind of cynicism and despair that pushes citizens away from politics. In other words, the Peruvian case seems to follow the path predicted by the pessimistic narrative, with political disenchantment winning the day. Later on, we will discuss how such attitudes are related to depoliticisation and withdrawal, but for now it is instructive to compare these representations of *Lava Jato* with those we heard about in the Brazilian focus groups.

The story in Brazil is quite different. We also started the focus groups with a discussion of participants' feelings towards *Lava Jato*. This discussion revealed a broader range of positive *and* negative feelings, with the former being much more prevalent than in Peru. There is also some indication that *Lava Jato* may have produced a politicising impact, leading to greater sense of political efficacy among some participants. These individuals report being more interested in, and engaged with, political affairs because *Lava Jato* has shown that there are meaningful ways of changing politics. Not all is lost: *Lava Jato* is not just revealing or confirming the prevalence of corruption; it is also offering a solution. Unfortunately, because we did not provide participants with a map of emotions, we cannot present a breakdown similar to the one in Table 6.3. Instead, we report quotes that are illustrative of the two streams of opinion that emerged during the conversations.

As expected, many participants across focus groups expressed despair and hopelessness, and like in Peru, they justified these emotions with reference to the crimes uncovered by the investigation. These revelations confirm participants' priors about the irredeemably corrupt nature of Brazilian politics. One, for instance, made it clear that they did not harbour any sense of hope about the possibility of political change: "since the time of my grandfather, great-grandfather, it's the same thing; corruption is always there" (FG2, A). The following exchange between two participants also exemplifies the kind of negative feelings we documented during the focus groups. These individuals see corruption as pathological and impossible to eradicate because it is part of human nature:

PARTICIPANT 1: To be honest, I think it will never end.
PARTICIPANT 2: Where there are people, there will always be corruption
PARTICIPANT 1: It's like a cancer; there will always be a metastasis (FG4, B).

Another group of Brazilian participants, however, expressed more hope. Interestingly, when these participants are asked to think about *Lava Jato*, they instinctively talk about the judicial process, not the crimes it uncovers. This is very different from what we found in Peru, where the general conversation instantly veered towards a discussion of the crimes. One participant in Brazil, for example, made the contrast between these two "faces" of *Lava Jato* explicit, and highlighted the promise of greater accountability:

I have friends who say they don't believe in anything anymore because of the number of corruption cases. But there is another side to it. Now there is accountability, there is hope that there will be accountability and that people will be more afraid to [engage in corruption] (FG5, C/D)

Hope is justified because *Lava Jato* is "a game changer" in terms of criminal accountability: "people can see that not only the poor go to jail; white-collar criminals can also go to jail. It's harder, but they also go to jail" (FG2, A). Corruption does not seem to pay off anymore: "The president of a global construction company fell, renowned politicians fell, people of great import-ance fell. People fell in all spheres. The message is that crime does not pay" (FG2, A). And this is all thanks to the judges and prosecutors. For example, one participant associated *Lava Jato* not with the cockroaches it reveals, but with a "moralising force": "I'm starting to feel hopeful. I'm not saying that everyone will become a saint [...] but a process of moralization has started" (FG5, C/D). As we saw in Chapter 2, Brazilian judges and prosecutors tried to transform the judicial inquiry into a broader anti-corruption effort, for example, by making strategic use of the media or tabling legislative initiatives. This seems to have resonated with some citizens, who highlight the movement-like qualities of the crusade. They find pleasure in watching the spectacle unfold. It is like seeing an "avenger" or superhero coming to the rescue: *Lava Jato* "gives you a sense of satisfaction [...] A movement that shows us that it is possible, that these people won't go unpunished as it has always been [...] You feel avenged" (FG2, A).

When Brazilians explained their emotions, they also made references to the impact of *Lava Jato* on their political attitudes and behaviour. Here too, we observe a divide between those who emphasise the crimes and describe a personal process of political withdrawal, and those who emphasise the judicial effort and describe a personal journey towards greater engagement. Among the pessimists it was common to see an association between the generalised nature of the accusations (i.e., no one was spared) and feelings of political disorien-tation. This was particularly true among former PT supporters, arguably the party that has suffered the most as a result of *Lava Jato*:

Lava Jato put a villain's hat on some parties; it suggests that no party is any good, everyone is bad. Before, I only voted for the PT; now no party is any good (FG4, B)

I always thought the PT stood for [good] things [...] Now that what happened [when the PT was in power] is clear to all of us, and also how it happened, I don't think the end justifies the means. I was greatly disappointed in the PT (FG5, C/D)

This sense of loss and betrayal leaves voters with few options, and some decide to stop participating in politics: "I swear that in these past elections I was neutral; I didn't want to participate because there was no one I could vote for. My relationship with politics got worse" (FG1, A). More worrying is the perception among some that the corruption revealed by *Lava Jato* does not only undermine trust in (specific) parties but reflects the generally crass nature of politics. This kind of conclusion is the hallmark of political cynicism:

Lava Jato made the circus worse; I think Brazilian politics is a joke (FG3, B)

Corruption is not about a party; it has to do with politics itself. But it is clear that in recent years it has increased (FG3, B)

At the other end of the spectrum are those who see in *Lava Jato* a reason to become more politically engaged and alert. Here the emphasis is, for example, on the high informational value of what the prosecutors and the courts are doing. *Lava Jato* is an eye-opener. Crucially, the behaviour of judicial actors sets an example that citizens should follow by becoming anti-corruption watch-dogs themselves. One participant, for example, explained: "I started to do my own investigation. I downloaded an app that detects corruption, so every time I see a candidate, I investigate their life [...] Had it not been for *Lava Jato*, I wouldn't have tried to find out more" (FG4, B). Similarly, others told us that they plan to put the information coming from the courts to good use. Unlike the cynics, they are not inclined to withdraw from politics, but think of *Lava Jato* as proof that something can be done to address the problem of corruption:

[*Lava Jato*] showed me who is involved in corruption, even people that I trusted [...] You become interested in finding out more [...] I think that in the next elections I will investigate more and think twice before voting for someone whose party is involved in *Lava Jato* (FG3, B)

I must confess that in the past I didn't really try to find out, but I think that after this I started reading more. I am more interested in knowing what's going on (FG6, C/D)

This sense of efficacy is accompanied by greater interest in politics. Politics may be in a sorry state, it may even be repellent. After *Lava Jato*, however, one cannot simply ignore corruption or withdraw from politics. *Lava Jato* is a call for action:

People started to see the mechanisms behind [corruption] and started to be interested in politics (FG1, A)

I think people started to hate politics but like to talk more about politics. I like to talk, everyone talks. On a bus, at a bar, wherever they are, people talk (FG4, B)

Between 2014 and 2018 I matured, and I think that it's practically impossible for someone not to position themselves politically. That didn't happen before (FG1, A)

The focus group data presented thus far suggests that citizens can indeed experience both positive and negative emotions, and respond accordingly, by becoming more or less cynical about politics. But the focus groups tell us little about why some citizens experience positive or negative emotions during anti-corruption crusades. They also tell us nothing about why, when they think about *Lava Jato*, the investigation takes centre stage in the minds of some citizens whereas others fixate on the crimes. What the data does suggest, however, is that, in line with the framework introduced in Chapter 5, the prevalence of more or less cynical attitudes, and the expression of negative or positive emotions associated with those attitudes, goes hand in hand with the prevalence of representations of *Lava Jato* either as the crimes it reveals or as an institutional anti-corruption effort centred around courts and prosecutors. In the Peruvian focus groups, the *Lava Jato* brand is a synonym of corruption and greed, emotions are overwhelmingly negative, and cynicism is pervasive. In Brazil, by contrast, perceptions are more divided, with some participants focusing on corruption and reporting hopelessness and despair, and others deriving a sense of hope and efficacy from the judicial effort. Activating the mechanisms associated with the optimistic narrative therefore does seem to depend on the extent to which the investigators are salient actors in the narrative the public constructs around the case.

The contrast between Peru and Brazil allows us to speculate about why the investigation may attract comparatively more attention in Brazil, and by implication say something about the conditions that may prevent cynicism from taking over the electorate, thus favouring the partial activation of the kind of system satisfaction associated with the optimistic narrative.

First, baseline attitudes towards judicial institutions, that is, levels of trust in the integrity and institutional capacity of courts before *Lava Jato*, likely play a role. Positive attitudes towards courts are derived from positive experiences with the judiciary, and greater attention to and knowledge of judicial institutions (Gibson and Caldeira 2009). In societies where citizens already hold these institutions in high regard (e.g., because they have a proven anti-corruption record), and know more about them, the sudden experience of large-scale criminalisation efforts may draw more attention to the work of judicial actors rather than produce a fixation with the rotten side of politics that is revealed during the process. Moreover, when citizens already trust the courts, they are perhaps more likely to think that something good can come out of the criminalisation effort and therefore focus more on that aspect of the crusade.

Available survey data points in this direction (Figure 6.3). Brazilians consistently reported much higher levels of trust in judicial institutions than Peruvians prior to *Lava Jato* (pre-2014 in Brazil and pre-2016 in Peru). For example, in 2013, the year before *Lava Jato* took the Brazilian political system by storm, over 40 per cent of respondents expressed a lot of or some trust in the judiciary. The comparable figure for Peru is under 20 per cent. This is perhaps not surprising given that Brazilians had recently been exposed to the *Mensalão* trial at the Supreme Court. This was a criminal case involving forty defendants, including prominent politicians from the PT and its coalition partners. The term

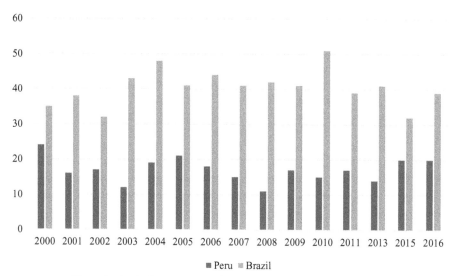

FIGURE 6.3 Trust in the judiciary in Brazil and Peru (% "a lot" or "some" trust).
Source: Latinobarometer

Mensalão refers to the monthly payments by the PT to President Da Silva's congressional allies in return for parliamentary support. The case received intense media coverage, likely increasing awareness of, and confidence in, the judiciary's anti-corruption credentials (Paiva 2019). In fact, according to Ortellado and Solano (2016) the case inspired large anti-corruption protests and represented a turning point in the relationship between middle-class voters and the PT. While Peru also experienced high-profile corruption trials against former president Fujimori and his cronies, these took place many years before *Lava Jato*. In this sense, studies show that their impact on judicial legitimacy was rather short-lived (Gonzalez-Ocantos 2016b).

Second, the centrality of the prosecutorial and judicial effort in the public narrative about *Lava Jato* may be a function of the type of media coverage. To assess the informational environment in Brazil and Peru, we selected four leading newspapers (*O Globo* and *Fohla de São Paulo* for Brazil and *El Comercio* and *La República* for Peru), and retrieved all headlines that included the words "*Lava Jato*" or "*Odebrecht*" between January 2015 and January 2021. We then coded the words that appear more than five times according to whether they are neutral terms, or terms associated either with the investigation and the judicial process or with the crimes, including, for example, the names of defendants, companies, and public works projects. The results show that Peruvian journalists, like our focus group participants, pay a lot more attention to the crimes than their Brazilian colleagues (Figure 6.4). We also conducted a lexicon-driven sentiment analysis of all headlines to establish what proportion

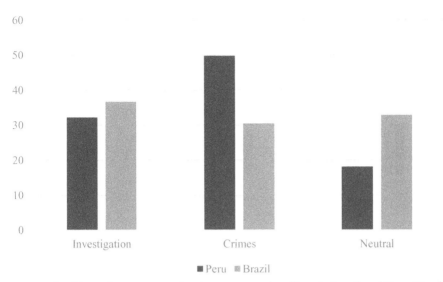

FIGURE 6.4 Type of terms appearing in newspaper headlines in Brazil and Peru (% of terms by category).
Source: Fohla de São Paulo, O Globo, El Comercio, La República (2015–2021)

has positive, negative, and neutral connotations.[7] The findings suggest that while headlines with a positive connotation are in the minority across the four newspapers, the proportion of negative "sentiments" is higher in Peru. This too is consistent with the differences we found between the two sets of focus groups (Figure 6.5).

The relative (media) salience of the investigative effort vis-à-vis the crimes, and voters' concomitant knowledge of – and attention to – judicial and prosecutorial actors, could also be a function of the characteristics of the crusade. For example, the time judges and prosecutors dedicated to the case prior to the focus groups could matter. A longer investigation may not only impact the extent to which citizens get to know individual judicial personalities and the work they do, but also allows judicial actors to show more results in the form of new evidence, testimonies, indictments, and trials, and thus nurture optimism. In this sense, it is important to note that Peru's *Lava Jato* started two years after Brazil's. Moreover, as we saw in Chapter 2, *Lava Jato* task forces in Brazil were extremely active and media savvy from the get-go. By contrast, as the case study in Chapter 3 revealed, it was only when prosecutor Vela took charge of the case in July 2018 that the Peruvian inquiry really "went public" and gained

---

[7] See the Appendix for a description of the media content analysis. The Appendix can be found on http://www.narapavao.com/book.html

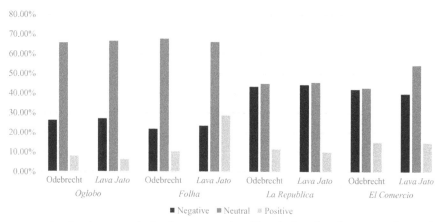

FIGURE 6.5 Sentiment analysis of newspaper headlines in Brazil and Peru (% of terms by type of "sentiment").
Source: *Fohla de São Paulo, O Globo, El Comercio, La República* (2015–2021)

visibility. Consequently, the salience of Peruvian judicial actors pales in comparison to, say, Brazilian Judge Sergio Moro.

These are, of course, mere conjectures, ones we cannot properly test with our focus group data. They do, however, have some basis in the framework outlined in Chapter 5. Importantly, the possible roles of pre-*Lava Jato* levels of trust in judicial institutions and task force visibility both point to the difficulties in projecting a credible "myth of legality." On this crucial point, the focus groups do allow us to take a closer look at whether or not voters indeed perceive the judicial effort as fair and effective, and how that may condition feelings of system satisfaction. This exercise will help us better understand the differences in the prevalence of cynicism as a response to *Lava Jato* in Peru and Brazil.

The reader will recall that one of our key propositions is that even when voters pay attention to the work of the courts (in addition to the crimes), perceptions of fairness and impartiality determine if that attention leads to optimism or reinforces cynicism. Perceptions of fairness condition the credibility of the judicial effort as a genuine attempt to improve politics. Similarly, perceptions of effectiveness condition levels of disillusionment. It is therefore possible that when our Brazilian participants debate the judicial process, contrasting evaluations of court performance produce a divide between those who find reasons for hope and others who see no solution in sight, reverting to a crime-focused narrative. By contrast, Peruvians may find fewer reasons for system satisfaction, opting to emphasise the crimes and developing a generally cynical or pessimistic outlook. Focus group discussions of fairness and impartiality reveal exactly this contrast. We also show that due to higher levels of political polarisation in Brazil, the debate about fairness and impartiality is more intense. This leads us to speculate, in line with our argument, that the salience of the judicial effort vis-à-vis the crimes it uncovers could also be driven by partisan interpretations of judicial behaviour. Finally, because the absence of polarisation in Peru is a function of extremely low levels of partisanship and widespread distrust in politics, we also suggest that baseline levels of cynicism matter for the kind of conclusions voters are likely to draw from the crusade. A citizenry that is hopelessly cynical to begin with may not be prone to focusing on the judicial effort and its promise, and instead fixate on criminal revelations that are all too consistent with their priors about the crass nature of politics.

PERCEPTIONS OF FAIRNESS AND EFFECTIVENESS

Process evaluations are the second dimension of the public conversation that we think helps shape the type of narrative that voters construct around crusades. In Chapter 5 we argued that in addition to paying attention to the work of the courts, the activation of the mechanisms associated with the optimistic story, including system satisfaction, the perception that the investigation has seriousness of purpose, and so on, depends on the credibility of the "myth of legality." Two aspects are particularly important in this regard: perceptions of fairness/impartiality and perceptions of effectiveness. Unfortunately, this myth is not something courts or prosecutors automatically project; it is something they need to nurture. Moreover, it is not something the public automatically buys into, but it is mediated by pre-judicialisation attitudes. In particular, partisanship and the prosecutorial toolkit used in anti-corruption crusades often conspire against the credibility of the myth of legality, and in so doing, create barriers for the optimistic narrative.

Political allegiances and partisanship are of course important in shaping discussions about fairness and impartiality. Even if the investigation is widespread, targeting multiple partisan groups, partisan affinity with some of the accused may still bias how citizens perceive the affair, determining whether they see justice in the making or political persecution. But performance evaluations are not simply a function of partisan attitudes. Investigators face an uphill battle when it comes to projecting an image of fairness and effectiveness, even among more neutral observers. As we showed in the first part of the book, the success of these criminalisation efforts is largely a function of the adoption of aggressive and selective prosecutorial strategies, often ones that redefine standards of legality. For example, judicial authorities sometimes lower evidentiary thresholds or order pretrial detentions for some of the accused but not others. The use of these tools can prove highly controversial and strengthen the "lawfare" narrative that delegitimises the investigation. Investigators are also in a bind when it comes to projecting an image of effectiveness. These are cases that are extremely hard to investigate; there are few smoking guns and discovery takes time. Moreover, prosecutorial selectivity, or reliance on plea bargains, which are often key to secure evidence in information-poor environments, can give the impression of a soft approach. Public disappointment and disillusionment are therefore always a latent possibility.

Brazil

One of the most striking features of the focus groups we conducted in Brazil is the time participants spent debating process.[8] We witnessed extremely lively and often heated discussions about whether *Lava Jato* is indeed fair and effective. One reason for this are the partisan rivalries that characterise Brazilian politics. According to Samuels and Zucco (2018: 27), during the 1990s and 2000s the PT nurtured a strong base (about a third of Brazilians). Simultaneously, and partly in reaction to the consolidation of *petismo*, other voters developed a strong anti-*petista* identity. Samuels and Zucco (2018: 7) describe these voters as anti-partisans or negative partisans: they have a weak identification with an in-group, but "strong antipathy" for an out-group. When *Lava Jato* took off in 2014, anti-partisans constituted around 22 per cent of the electorate. At the aggregate level, and in the focus groups, the presence of strong partisans of high-profile defendants, in this case PT leaders, means there is a critical mass that questions the credibility of the judicial process.[9] But the presence of anti-*petistas* means that there is another group that derives pleasure from seeing the courts imprison their figures of hate and is therefore willing to defend the inquiry. This was especially true in February 2019: Bolsonaro had only just won the presidency riding the coattails of the anti-*petista* sentiments that *Lava Jato* exacerbated. The back and forth between these two camps raised the salience of the courts and prosecutors in the focus group conversations. In other words, having strong partisan rivals in the room triggered a more thorough evaluation of process, highlighting both strengths and weaknesses, rather than simply one that revolved around the despair produced by the disclosure of evidence of systemic corruption.[10] While this allowed for the activation of system satisfaction, the feelings of hope experienced by some voters came at the expense of greater polarisation and judicial discredit among others.

The results of a 2018 nationally representative survey offer interesting contextual information about the role of partisan rivalries in discussions about *Lava Jato*. Below we report the answers to a question that asked respondents to indicate whether *Lava Jato* investigates all parties equally or investigates specific parties more than others. Figure 6.6(a) shows a divided public. While few think the main targets of the investigation are parties of the center or the center-right, around 30 per cent of respondents think the PT is the main target and nearly

[8] Interestingly, these intense debates about process increased the average duration of our Brazilian focus groups. See Tables 6.1 and 6.2.
[9] While identification with the PT suffered initially, it eventually recovered.
[10] Which is what we see in Peru. See the next subsection.

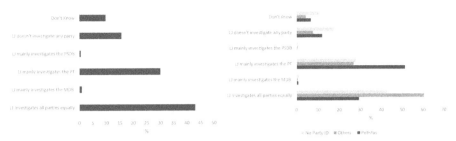

FIGURE 6.6 Perceptions of *Lava Jato*'s impartiality in Brazil. (a) Overall views on impartiality; (b) Views on impartiality by party ID.
Source: ESEB 2018. Question: "Operation *Lava Jato* is an operation to fight against corruption in politics. Regarding Operation *Lava Jato*, do you think it investigates all political parties equally, it mainly investigates the MDB (formerly, PMDB), it mainly investigates the PT, it mainly investigates the PSDB, or it doesn't investigate any party?"

45 per cent think *Lava Jato* investigates all parties in equal measure. Turning to Figure 6.6(b), which breaks down responses by whether respondents identify as PT supporters, supporters of other parties, or express no party identification, it is clear that *petistas* feel victimised by *Lava Jato*. By contrast, those who do not identify with the PT overwhelmingly see the investigation as impartial.[11]

We see a similar divide in the focus groups. When asked to consider whether the investigation has been fair and impartial, many instinctively offered praise for the judges and prosecutors. To justify this view, participants pointed to the symbolic value of high-profile detentions, which signal legal equality and the end of privileges:

Lava Jato, in particular the imprisonment of Lula, is highly symbolic. We always heard that the law applied equally to everyone, but we never saw someone so important, so influential, so rich, going to jail [...] *Lava Jato* has a great symbolic power in terms of the fight against corruption in Brazil." (FG4, B)

Others pointed out that the investigators have cast a wide net, demonstrating they are indeed impartial and guided by the evidence:

The same *Lava Jato* investigators are accusing Bolsonaro's son, so if it was only against the left, well, now they are on top of the current president [...] They are thinking of cleaning up, of making a sweep (FG1, A)

Lava Jato [...] has no [political] flag. It goes after the corrupt. It just pulled a little thread and the ball started to roll, revealing one name after another (FG2, A)

These assessments were often accompanied by positive evaluations of Judge Moro. Survey data from 2016, for example, indicates that he was quite popular

---

[11] See Chapter 7 for further quantitative analysis of the relationship between partisanship and perceptions of fairness in Brazil.

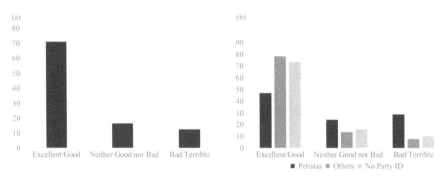

FIGURE 6.7 Evaluation of Judge Sergio Moro. (a) General approval/disapproval; (b) Approval/disapproval by party ID.
Source: DATAFOLHA 2016. Question: "How do you evaluate the job of Judge Sergio Moro during *Lava Jato*: excellent, good, neither good nor bad ('regular'), bad or terrible?"

among Brazilians, even among PT supporters (Figure 6.7). Some of our focus group participants shared this sentiment. In fact, many of those who praised the investigation did so with reference to Moro's exceptional personal qualities. Moro's "selflessness" turned him into a hero:

I really don't know if there is another judge with the same courage as him [...] He deserves a round of applause (FG4, B)

He will have my eternal admiration [...] The only thing I talk about is *Lava Jato*, which ended up having Moro's face (FG5, C/D)

He no longer lives in society [...] He has five or six bodyguards; he doesn't remember the last time he went to the cinema [...] He gave up his social life for something much bigger. And he didn't do it just for himself; he really believes in fighting corruption (FG5, C/D)

Interestingly, for some of these participants, the fact that Moro took up a new position as minister of justice under Bolsonaro in January 2019 is not problematic. Far from thinking this appointment revealed Moro's true partisan, biased motives, they celebrate the move: "he will be able to do more" (FG1, A); "it's his obligation. He has to do that. He is there to put his finger on the wounds of those who steal" (FG4, B).

At this stage of the discussion, some, in particular PT supporters, stepped in to correct the record and question the impartiality of the investigation. For them it is obvious that the prosecutors and judges disproportionately targeted the left. This amounts to a "lack of respect for the population" (FG2, A). It seems as though "the only one who pays the price in Brazil is Lula" (FG3, B). *Lava Jato* was definitely "created to arrest people on the left, it was politically motivated" (FG1, A). In most focus groups there were participants who referenced the situation of Aecio Neves, former Partido da Social Democracia Brasileira (PSDB) presidential candidate and governor of Minas Gerais, as strong proof of this lack of impartiality. Neves was indicted but invoked his parliamentary privileges to escape prosecution. One participant explained that Aecio's good fortunes, coupled with Moro's decision to join the Bolsonaro administration, triggered his instant indignation:

Lava Jato started as a big project to fight corruption, it started with hope, but it has gradually become a disappointment. I saw they ended the case against Aecio because he has *foro privilegiado*. And then he was re-elected and will continue having *foro privilegiado* [...] And Moro now enters politics ..." (FG2, A)

These developments reveal that there are indeed special interests behind *Lava Jato*. They are evidence that the way judges and prosecutors conduct their duties is not appropriate. Citizens should remain sceptical:

You see the judges and the prosecutors talking to each other, having coffee, being friends, and on the other side you have defense attorneys. It's a strange relationship. One is there to accuse, the other is there to defend, and the other is there to judge. If the person who judges is close to the person that makes the accusation, he will end up being partial (FG2, A)

The prosecutors are very ideological, mainly in Curitiba [...] They focus on cases that give them more visibility. And the case with greatest visibility for *Lava Jato* is the case against Lula (FG6, C/D)

[*Lava Jato*] is a means to sell people a story. People are buying into something that doesn't exist (FG2, A)

Not all criticisms took the form of partisan quibbles. When discussing the prosecutorial strategies characteristic of large-scale criminalisation efforts, many non-*petistas* could also see problems. It is worth noting that we conducted the focus groups before the infamous Intercept scandal of July 2019, also known as *Vaza Jato*. Leaked WhatsApp messages revealed an inappropriate relationship between Judge Moro and the prosecutors (similar to the one described in the above quote!), as well as their animosity against the left. In March 2021, the Supremo Tribunal Federal (STF) ruled that Moro's behaviour had indeed been partial and ordered a retrial in Lula's case. This means that the focus groups likely underestimate non-partisan, procedural critiques. These voices would most certainly be louder were we to conduct additional focus groups today. To plug in the evidentiary gap, in Chapter 7 we rely on a survey experiment conducted immediately after the STF's decision to directly explore the impact of *Vaza Jato*. For now, let us look at the flaws that some participants already saw in February 2019, which suggest that even back then, prosecutorial and judicial behaviour introduced tensions that made it harder for the criminalisation of grand corruption to trigger widespread system satisfaction.

For instance, a few participants expressed a strong dislike for plea bargains. They are unfair: "the law should be for everyone" (FG2, A); "the scale is always going to tilt to one side [...] but they should strive for a better balance" (FG2, A). Others were more forceful: "I don't believe in plea bargains. You steal millions, you report your partner in crime and you get away with it!" (FG4, B).

The dynamics of plea bargains also make it clear that "there are some who manipulate others from behind" (FG3, B). And in addition to being unfair, they are not effective:

Take, for example, Léo Pinheiro. Léo Pinheiro was the person that reported Lula, but they really didn't manage to collect any evidence [on the basis of his testimony]. Everything was extremely circumstantial [...] I am not saying Lula is innocent, but this Leo Pinheiro arrived and talked, he spent a year denying everything, and after a year in jail he changed his story completely. Now Lula goes to jail (FG2, A)

Similar criticisms were levelled against pretrial detentions and police raids. Many viewed them as excessive, even when the defendants were politicians they did not necessarily support:

A typical example is Lula. I am not a *lulista;* I don't defend him. But he never refused to cooperate with the investigation. People set up a circus to get him. It wasn't necessary (FG1, A)

They went, arrested a person, took a vehicle, did not warn anyone. It was excessive. Many people criticized this; jurists criticized it. They really crossed a line (FG5, C/D)

The conversations about impartiality, however, never ended on this critical note. Partisan and non-partisan questioning triggered passionate counterarguments in support of the investigation. Such responses reinforced the court or prosecutor-centric narrative that highlights hope, system satisfaction, and a sense of renewed efficacy in the struggle against corruption. Interestingly, some of the counterarguments consisted in efforts to explain away or rationalise the evidence of partiality brought up by other participants. For example, while supporters of the investigation acknowledge that *Lava Jato* may have originally targeted the left, they do not think this is true anymore. And in any case, corruption by the left is real and is being dealt with even-handedly:

Lava Jato doesn't have a political motivation; it investigates people from all parties. People are being arrested because there is evidence against them. Maybe the initial spark was political; maybe they wanted to find something out about a specific politician. But later on, they discovered other things, so it stopped being political. The final balance is positive (FG4, B)

Others argued that it was only natural for the PT to be the main target. After all, the PT was in power for four consecutive presidential terms. Here we see arguments that highlight the success of *Lava Jato* in taking on "real" corruption:

It's important to clarify that *Lava Jato* dismantled a business, a business set up in the public sphere in order to protect a political project. That is why you see more people from the PT [under investigation] (FG2, A)

[The prosecutors] didn't say "let's investigate the PT." It just happens that the majority of congressmen were from the PT (FG3, B)

And yet another group, mainly among higher socio-economic status participants, warned that citizens should be careful when criticising *Lava Jato*. In the
case of Aecio Neves, for example, the failure to punish him had nothing to do
with the *Lava Jato* task force. It was all down to the STF, which had original
jurisdiction over the case:

People have to be careful because sometimes they criticize certain aspects or suspect the
system. For example: Aecio is a crook, he should be in jail. But his *foro privilegiado* gives
him the right to be tried by the STF. Lula went to jail because he no longer had *foro
privilegiado* (FG4, B)

In addition to reminding their peers of these technicalities, participants also
pointed out that prosecutors are up against powerful people who obviously
have the means to escape the tentacles of justice. Some politicians are simply
more skillful than others when it comes to resisting the investigative effort:
"Perhaps the PT couldn't get away with it. Aecio managed to out-maneuver
them politically; he managed to dodge *Lava Jato*" (FG2, A). In any case, it is
too early to jump to conclusions: "It's all too recent. People know that it takes
time for things to happen" (FG2, A); "the investigation has a maturation
period" (FG5, C/D).

Opinions were also divided when it came to debating effectiveness, but this
division was less driven by partisanship. What we saw instead was a return to
the themes of optimism and pessimism, hope and cynicism, that dominated the
initial conversation about representations of *Lava Jato*. Opposing views about
the effectiveness of *Lava Jato* among focus group participants mirror those
among the general population, which is split between hope and resignation
regarding *Lava Jato*'s impact on the country's level of corruption (Figure 6.8).
On the one hand, pessimists do not think it is going to work: "LJ is not 100%
effective. It will continue being partial, it will continue being ineffective." (FG2,
A). Others are more categorial: "*Vai acabar em pizza e isso*" (FG4, B).[12] This is
in part because the investigation is too slow: "Unfortunately our justice system
is a tortoise" (FG1, A). Politicians will most certainly find ways to take advantage of the slow pace of the inquiry, and stage comebacks: "Those politicians
will come back [...] Why then do this whole thing [*Lava Jato*] if we then get
slapped in the face when we see everyone there again?" (FG3, B).[13] Comebacks
will be possible because punishment has not been as severe as it should
have been. And even if corruption is effectively punished, the authorities have
not put enough effort into trying to compensate for the economic costs of
corruption:

---

[12] This is a common Brazilian expression to indicate futility ("it will end in pizza").
[13] Recent developments, in particular Bolsonaro's announcement of the "death" of *Lava Jato* and
STF decisions calling into question the impartiality of Moro's actions against Lula, likely
exacerbated this sense of futility. See Chapter 2.

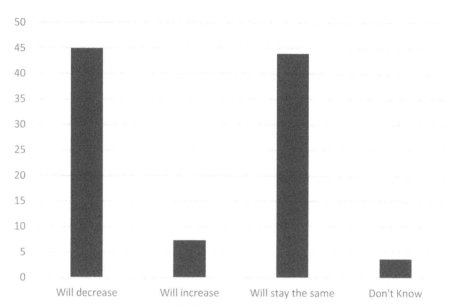

FIGURE 6.8 Expectations about the future of corruption in Brazil.
Source: ESEB 2018. Question: "In your opinion, after Operation *Lava Jato*, will corruption in Brazil decrease, increase, or stay the same?"

Who has the money? Imagine all the things we could do with that money! Take these goods and put them up for auction; take that money, take care of hospitals, schools (FG3, B)

What you really need is a more severe form of punishment. They have to pay [...] They have to return the money (FG3, B)

For some, at the end of the day the problem lies in the judiciary. Judges and prosecutors are part of the elite, so one cannot expect much from them in terms of an effort to clean up politics:

Lava Jato is seen like a gentleman in a white horse; a hero that comes to save the world. But that doesn't happen, it doesn't exist. [The people behind *Lava Jato*] grew up in that same political environment. If you want to go after the truth of politics, you can't put politics in charge. You have to get people who are qualified to go after it, to be able to challenge corporatism. If you are part of it, you won't go after your friend (FG2, A)

The previous testimonies suggest that even a relatively effective investigation like Brazil's *Lava Jato* finds it hard to project an image of effectiveness. When corruption is perceived to be widespread, and cynicism is deeply entrenched, the satisfaction bar is set too high. Other participants, however, exude optimism and highlight the various ways in which *Lava Jato* has already been effective. For example, these participants point to the unusually wide scope of the inquiry, the fact that high-profile politicians went to jail, and that *Lava Jato* has reignited debates about institutional reforms that could help curb corruption. These optimists are of course not naïve about the prospects of ending corruption and redeeming politics, but they are nevertheless hopeful. In this sense, one recurrent theme was the view that *Lava Jato* was not simply an investigation, but has become (or should become) a permanent feature of Brazilian politics, almost like an additional branch of government:

Let's have a *Lava Jato* in each state, in each city (FG6, C/D)

It should exist forever (FG1, A)

It will end up becoming an institution (FG2, A)

People want more; people are happy because of *Lava Jato*. They never had anything of this quality. But people want more. They want continuity (FG3, B)

These quotes take us back to a theme we discussed earlier in the chapter. Representations of *Lava Jato* in Brazil are not exclusively dominated by the crimes; for many participants what is most salient about the saga is the judicial effort to address corruption. While citizens understand it may not be a silver bullet, *Lava Jato* is a source of satisfaction with, and faith in, the system. Calls to institutionalise *Lava Jato* are in this sense a far cry from the feelings of political disorientation, and the tendency towards withdrawal and cynicism we saw in Peru.

Overall, in Brazil we witnessed lively debates about process, with highly divided opinions. The debate between partisan rivals certainly directed the conversation towards a thorough examination of the judicial effort. Despite scathing criticisms by PT supporters, and also by non-partisans who find some prosecutorial strategies objectionable, the conversation opened a window for others to sing their praises and thus construct a partial narrative of hope anchored in the "myth of legality." The Brazilian focus group data therefore shows that system satisfaction and an associated sense of optimism can indeed materialise among some voters. But the data also suggests that these are unlikely to be the dominant responses to the criminalisation of grand corruption, especially in divided societies. This type of attitudinal reaction simply faces too many obstacles, and often comes at the expense of greater political polarisation and diminished judicial legitimacy.

Peru

Optimism was conspicuously absent in the Peruvian focus groups. In a previous section we saw that representations of *Lava Jato* in Peru are strongly dominated by corruption crimes, providing a breeding ground for despair and cynicism. In what follows we look at how this finds echo in the way Peruvians discussed the judicial process. Scepticism and a sense of futility also dominated this second dimension of the conversation.

In sharp contrast to the extended examination of process in Brazil, Peruvians had less to say about fairness and effectiveness. When not prompted to discuss these issues, the dominant narrative was crime-focused, one of deep worry and disgust at the corruption revealed during *Lava Jato*. One reason for the lack of attention to the judicial effort could be the absence of the partisan exchanges we saw in the Brazilian focus groups. Following Samuels and Zucco's (2018) definition, a significant number of Peruvians can be characterised as negative or anti-partisans. For example, using representative surveys, Meléndez (2019) finds large groups of anti-Fujimoristas and anti-Apristas, that is, citizens who would never consider voting for candidates representing these parties. Unlike in Brazil, however, in Peru there are very few partisans. In fact, Peruvians are generally non-partisans, and Peru approximates the ideal type of what Levitsky and Cameron (2003) call "a democracy without parties." This means that few Peruvians are likely to feel victimised or aggrieved by efforts to incarcerate specific politicians, which in turn reduces the chances of seeing clashes about impartiality like the ones we witnessed in Brazil relative to Lula's situation. Moreover, party weakness is a symptom of the generalised lack of trust in political institutions prevalent since the collapse of the party system in the 1990s (Muñoz 2019). Given these high baseline levels of cynicism, it is perhaps not very surprising that even an event of the magnitude of *Lava Jato* fails to inspire hope.

In order to elicit a discussion of fairness and effectiveness, we had to bring up these issues ourselves. To be sure, when Peruvian participants were prompted to talk about the investigation, they had some positive things to say. This is consistent with the results of the survey we conducted in November 2019 where we asked respondents to indicate their level of satisfaction with the performance of the *Lava Jato* task force, with lower values representing more negative evaluations. As Figure 6.9 shows, voters seem satisfied with the work of the prosecutors, although less than 50 per cent are either satisfied or very satisfied.[14] Peruvians may be cynics, but they still enjoy the look of handcuffs on politicians.[15] In other words, cynicism does not prevent voters from deriving pleasure from punitive measures directed at the political establishment, which they despise. But this pleasure does not translate into enthusiasm. This is because cynicism is so pervasive that Peruvians have a hard time trusting anyone or anything, including the judicial actors in charge of the crusade.

---

[14] For a more thorough analysis of how satisfaction with the task force and with pretrial detentions shape emotional reactions and cynicism, see Chapter 8.

[15] For example, Vera's (2020) experimental work on Peru shows that "while [Peruvian] voters punish corruption more leniently when a candidate is competent, they respond negatively to corruption regardless of the prevalence of corruption, which casts doubt on the idea that voters in highly corrupt environments are acceptant of corruption."

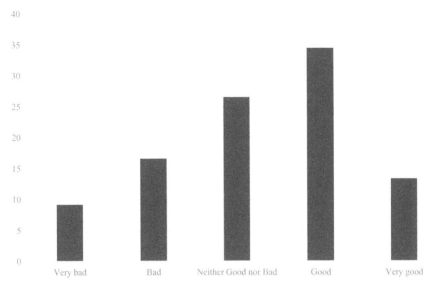

FIGURE 6.9 Evaluations of the *Lava Jato* task force in Peru.
Source: Authors' face-to-face, nationally representative survey fielded in November 2019 in
partnership with *Proetica*. Question*:* "How would you rate the performance of the *Lava Jato* Task
Force in the fight against corruption? Very bad, bad, neither good nor bad, good, very good?"

When it comes to satisfaction with the prosecutors or hope in the outcome of
their efforts, the focus groups paint a negative picture. Scepticism about the
overall prosecutorial strategy surfaced quickly. In other words, when voters
were invited to elaborate on issues of process, the prosecutors did not get a free
pass. To begin with, participants reached the conclusion that the inquiry is less
than transparent. Power and resource differentials among defendants determine
how prosecutors proceed. Even if they could not come up with specific
examples to support this assessment, for them it was inconceivable not to
assume that some shady business is unfolding behind the scenes. They are,
after all, highly cynical. Take, for example, this exchange between high socio-
economic status adults:

MODERATOR: **Do you think that the investigation has been impartial or politically
motivated?**
FEMALE: It definitely has [a political motivation].
MALE: It's impossible to separate the politics because [the judiciary] is another branch
of the state. It has a boss, interests, enemies, friends; it's hard.
FEMALE: And they surely must be hiding stuff; they must be protecting people involved
in things. It's not convenient [for the prosecutors] because these people come
from politics.
MODERATOR: **And why are they being protected?**
MALE: Because they know too much.

FEMALE: [If they were to fall], several others would follow.

MALE: For example, if [former president] Toledo were to fall, his ministers, his aides would also fall (FG2, Adults, A/B)

The focus group of adults from the lower socio-economic status cohort reached a similar conclusion:

MODERATOR: **We have seen a lot of people involved in the case. Do you think that all of them are treated in the same way?**

FEMALE: No.

MODERATOR: **Is someone treated better? Or is it impartial?**

FEMALE: No, there are favourites.

FEMALE: There are favourites because there are people who know more than others.

FEMALE: But they are trying to follow the same approach with everyone.

FEMALE: *Por el dinero baila el mono* [Money makes the world go around].

MODERATOR: **But they all seem to have money, or not?**

FEMALE: Yes, but some have more and others have less.

FEMALE: As you said, some know more (FG8, Adults, D/E)

Discussions of pretrial detentions, for which there is widespread support among the general population (see Chapter 8), also revealed a high dose of scepticism. To be sure, several focus group participants supported these measures. While pretrial detentions may not be ideal (e.g., they are not definitive and may be legally questionable), justice needs to be achieved by any means available:

If they have done something improper, well, they have to be behind bars whatever the circumstance and for whatever reason; they have to pay for what they did wrong (FG4, Female, Adult, A/B)

But many participants brought up issues of fairness and legality to express their disapproval of pretrial detentions:

I used to agree. But pre-trial detentions are supposedly an exceptional measure that isn't used all the time. Now the prosecutors are using them left, right and center! (FG1, Male, Young, A/B)

It's abusive, I mean, pre-trial detentions are abusive. This can be used but only when you have the necessary evidence. But if you don't have the evidence and only have clues, why are you ordering a pre-trial detention? For example, [former president] Kuczynski is now under house arrest, or the other guy [former president Garcia] had to kill himself out of pride (FG4, Male, Adult, A/B)

MALE: Like they say (well, I don't know if it's a saying or a law): "everyone is innocent until proven guilty."

FEMALE: That's the principle "*In dubio pro reo.*" Doubt favors the defendant (FG5, Young, C)

I don't think it's OK because there are people who are in jail (and I'm not only referring to Keiko [Fujimori] [...]) for years and years and never go to trial (FG7, Male, Young, D/E)

Interestingly, not all criticisms raised issues of legality. For some of the lower socio-economic status participants, the use and abuse of pretrial detentions sets a bad precedent for the poor: "those who have money to pay a good lawyer can turn things around at any time; they are cool. But normal people like us could be caught up in a situation where they order a pre-trial detention, and, well, in that case we would be screwed" (FG5, Female, Young, C). Finally, pretrial detentions are also unfair, but not because they violate principles of legality; they are unfair because they cost taxpayer money: "They should do pre-trial detention at home because if someone goes to jail, they have to be fed [...] These people have money" (FG8, Female, Adult, D/E).

On the issue of plea bargains, there were no divisions: Peruvian participants unanimously hated them. As we saw in Chapter 3, the Peruvian chapter of *Lava Jato* is highly reliant on a cooperation agreement prosecutors signed with Odebrecht and its executives. The task force understood that no deal meant no evidence and therefore no case, so they were willing to make concessions. Voters who want punishment should support this move given the high informational constraints. But our focus group participants did not seem to share this view, partly because it implies selectivity and it is not punitive enough.

The list of complaints was long. Plea bargains are ineffective: "[defendants] only give limited information; only what benefits them" (FG6, Female, Adult, C). They are also unjust: "only because the guy provided information they let him go" (FG4, Male, Adult, A/B). The fundamental problem for some is that plea bargains are incompatible with prosecutors' institutional mission: "It should not be like this. I think that the duty of the police, the prosecutors, here or in any other country, is to show that someone is guilty, not to wait and base a case exclusively on what someone tells them" (FG3, Male, Young, A/B). Others do recognise plea bargains can be useful, but because they are so unfair, they should be reserved for minor criminals: "if you are not powerful, then you can benefit from this. How else do I get the evidence against the people who masterminded these crimes? If you only played a minor role, then you can help me out in this case. You can help me get to the bigger guys" (FG2, Female, Adult, A/B). Even if some agree with this, they still think that in all instances defendants should spend some time in prison: "They should only reduce the punishment. They must go to jail" (FG7, Male, Young, D/E). And if possible, prosecutors should trick defendants: "It would be wonderful if they [signed a deal] and once they've investigated everyone and cracked the case, they told them: [...] You are not getting anything. You'll be in jail for 50 years. Goodbye!" (FG1, Male, Young, A/B).

The concessions built into plea bargain agreements feel like betrayals and reinforce cynical priors about the dubious nature of the whole affair. In Chapter 8 we present the results of a conjoint experiment, which we use to investigate the trade-offs citizens are willing to accept in more detail. For now, it suffices to say that the results are in line with the focus groups: Peruvians do not like to compromise with the "corruptors." This kind of prosecutorial

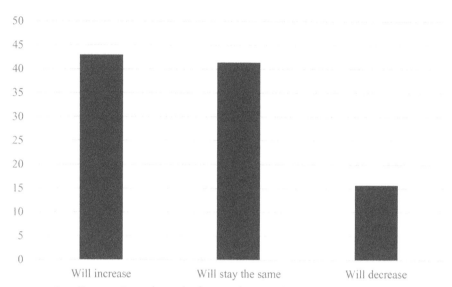

FIGURE 6.10 Expectations about the future of corruption in Peru.
Source: Authors' face-to-face, nationally representative survey fielded in November 2019 in partnership with *Proética*. Question: "Do you think that in five years' time, corruption in Peru will have increased, decreased, or stayed the same?"

selectivity, coupled with other criticisms voiced against the process, may explain why participants were also generally pessimistic about the effectiveness of *Lava Jato*, especially in the longer term. In many ways, this level of pessimism about the effectiveness of the investigation is not that surprising because Peruvian judicial authorities are yet to show results beyond a few pretrial detentions and high-profile revelations.

On effectiveness, Peruvians are also less divided than Brazilians. Focus group participants thought corruption would remain rampant. This is consistent with the results of our November 2019 survey, where less than 20 per cent of respondents believed corruption would decrease in the next five years (Figure 6.10). In the focus groups we only heard optimistic assessments among younger citizens, the emphasis being on the deterrent effect of the investigation and the fact that it could make it possible for new politicians to emerge. In other words, for some the future looks slightly brighter than before:

Since the political dinosaurs, the better-known politicians, have all fallen, maybe there will be an opportunity for other candidates to appear. Younger candidates, with better ideas and the determination to do things the right way (FG5, Female, Young, C)

But overall, pessimism wins the day. Precisely because after the wave of revelations, indictments, and pretrial detentions politics looks like a clean slate, voters wonder what they will do in an election:

What's going to happen now? Who do we trust and who do we not trust? [...] They've all fallen and continue to fall. We are running out of politicians! (FG4, Male, Adult, A/B).

More worrying is the feeling that a process of natural selection will ensue, whereby politicians will get better at the game of corruption and the savviest ones will prevail: "You finish these politicians, you literally finish them, but behind them there are others who think 'why could the others steal but not me'" (FG4, Male, Adult, A/B). Even if *Lava Jato* does make it harder to launder money via public works projects, for example, politicians "will develop better techniques to steal" (FG1, Female, Young, A/B). Corruption will be transformed "into something more subtle" (FG2, Male, Adult, A/B); "they will find a name different from Odebrecht, and problem solved!" (FG7, Male, Adult, D/E). In the end, we will find out that everything has been a sham: the prosecutors "are negotiating, but we have no idea what lies behind [the negotiations]. The money keeps rolling so that [the politicians] can be released from prison, and we have no idea" (FG4, Male, Adult, A/B). Finally, beyond the issue of corruption, some voters worry about the economic consequences of *Lava Jato*. For instance, one of them articulated the concern as follows: "We already have three generations of presidents that were involved in corruption. This probably intimidates foreign investors, or maybe it encourages them. Who knows! But I think this [political mess] will affect foreign investment" (FG5, Female, Young, C).

CONCLUSION

The way Brazilians talked about *Lava Jato* during our focus groups shows a strong divide between optimists and pessimists. For optimists, the investigation is a reason to remain involved and enthusiastic about the possibility of changing politics. Among the pessimists are those who think, by contrast, that politics is so irredeemable that the only option is withdrawal, as well as those for whom the investigation is deeply flawed. This divide emerged clearly when participants discussed their representations of *Lava Jato* and related emotional reactions. Negative emotions were justified with representations of *Lava Jato* that emphasised criminal activity, whereas positive ones arose from more court or prosecutor-centric narratives. These different visions of what the *Lava Jato* brand is – or represents – suggest that, at least in the focus groups, the spectre of cynicism has not fully overtaken the citizenry. The discussions in Brazil were also marked by strong partisan counterpoints, which led participants to intensely debate the fairness and effectiveness of the judicial process. We speculated that in addition to partisan fault lines, other drivers of this debate may include the controversial nature of the prosecutorial strategy as well as the high salience of judicial personalities, both of which draw attention to process rather than just the crimes revealed. It is this focus on process which we think opened a space for the activation of mechanisms associated with the optimistic narrative in some quarters, but also for polarisation around anti-corruption.

The tone of the conversation in the Peruvian focus groups, by contrast, reflects deep cynicism about politics. The *Lava Jato* brand is intimately associated with corruption crimes, with little emphasis on the actual judicial process. The emotions that transpire are overwhelmingly negative. Few see a way out of the mess. Moreover, there is little evidence that *Lava Jato* has mobilised Peruvians in a constructive way. This is consistent, for example, with voting behaviour in the 2020 legislative elections and the first round of the 2021 presidential elections, which were marked by high abstention rates, protest voting, and historic fragmentation. Peruvians have a hard time trusting and believing in anything, let alone in the possibility of change. For example, participants in all focus groups half-joked that they did not even buy the idea that Alan García had killed himself. For them, García is probably still alive, enjoying a cosy exile in a Caribbean beach. In this climate of generalised distrust, it is only natural for *Lava Jato* to merely reinforce priors about the crass nature of politics rather than favour an optimistic updating. Finally, in the absence of partisan clashes over process, the space for airing passionate defences of the investigation narrows, effectively blocking optimistic voices.

Taken together, the focus groups indicate that large-scale criminalisation efforts have the capacity to take voters down the paths anticipated by both our pessimistic and optimistic narratives. But the discussions also reveal that widespread optimism is highly unlikely. First, partisan ties, where strong, colour perceptions of accountability efforts. Second, investigations are themselves controversial. Prosecutors have to accept trade-offs between strictly adhering to fairness criteria and obtaining results, and between strong punitivism and selectivity. Voters are not always ready to accept these choices. Third, the nature and scope of the corruption crimes uncovered by *Lava Jato* are such that it is almost impossible for some voters not to fall into a state of anxiety and despair. Finally, fulfilling punitive expectations in the long run is hard. Investigations take time and nothing guarantees that a case built by diligent prosecutors will stand the scrutiny and the politics of appellate stages.

All of this implies that if some citizens become hopeful at the start of the process, this optimism is likely to be short-lived due to disappointment in prosecutorial methods and outcomes. Disappointment might then reinforce the idea that being cynical is always the right approach: do not be fooled by the occasional accountability mirage. And even if optimism does partially flourish, the focus group data suggests it comes at the expense of severe political polarisation. Moreover, it is unclear whether the hope experienced by some voters translates into a productive engagement with the political system, or instead throws voters into the arms of Bolsonaro-type politicians, who promise radical forms of redemption with potentially destructive implications for democracy.

The focus group data supports a broader point we made in Chapter 5, namely that even if in principle crusades mount a fight against a phenomenon that no one really likes and most would like eradicated, citizens interpret these institutional efforts in different ways. The effect on mass attitudes is therefore not straightforwardly positive; it is the outcome of complex interactions between what transpires in the courts and the priors citizens rely on to assess what goes on there. Crucially, courts and prosecutors are not always perceived as being above good and evil, so their mission eventually becomes much more controversial and problematic than naïve observers initially expected.

7

Is Prosecutorial Zeal What Partisans Make of It?

Survey Evidence from Brazil

INTRODUCTION

In the previous chapter, we showed that Brazilians are divided when it comes to *Lava Jato*. Whereas some saw in this unprecedented anti-corruption probe a reason for hope and enthusiasm about the future of politics, others remained staunchly cynical. This division is partly due to contrasting interpretations of the merits of *Lava Jato*. Such interpretations are in turn driven by partisan rivalries, with PT supporters being in general more critical than the rest, but also by the crusade's own procedural failures or excesses. Overall, these findings point to the limits of the optimistic narrative outlined in Chapter 5: while corruption is something most voters would in principle like to see combated and eradicated, real-world attempts to do so are prone to elicit controversy rather than universal praise, and to disappoint many observers as the inquiry progresses. This is because of the unorthodox and aggressive nature of the prosecutorial zeal that makes crusades possible, and because criminalisation creates tensions between the desire for accountability and other values close to citizens' hearts, including their partisan affiliations.

Our goal in this chapter is twofold. First, we take a more systematic look at Brazilians' evaluations of *Lava Jato*, leveraging nationally representative surveys conducted since 2016. This data allows us to paint a more dynamic picture of how evaluations of fairness and effectiveness changed as the crusade moved forward. Specifically, we show that consensus about the merits of *Lava Jato* gradually deteriorated, with the crusade eventually becoming a hotly contested process. As the reader may recall, our argument in Chapter 5 was that anti-corruption crusades can restore citizens' relationship with politics only if they are successful at consistently projecting the myth of legality. This, however, becomes harder as the inquiry widens and gains momentum. In fact, the decline in support we document here is most likely a result of the controversies that *Lava Jato* triggered since it started in 2014, including its role in the downfall of Dilma Rousseff's administration in 2016, the aggressive approach adopted during proceedings against Lula (and the impact of this strategy on the 2018 presidential election), the 2019 *Vaza Jato* scandal mentioned in Chapter 2, and finally, the STF's decision in 2021 that ruled Moro was "partial." These episodes created the perception that crusaders had overplayed their hand. In this regard, the survey data strongly confirms that positive affect for the PT is a key factor shaping fairness and effectiveness evaluations, and therefore one that complicates the public's relationship with the crusade. In so doing, partisanship undermines the capacity of anticorruption efforts to produce the outcomes predicted by the optimistic story. Our analysis further shows that while partisan divides make the projection of the myth of legality harder, the judiciary's reservoir of goodwill among portions of the public, measured as individuals' level of trust in the courts (Gibson and Caldeira 2009), can help protect the legitimacy of the crusade amidst controversy.

Second, the chapter reports the results of a priming experiment designed to assess the public opinion consequences of *Lava Jato* more directly. This takes us back to another part of the argument presented in Chapter 5, namely the proposition that different types of narratives about corruption and anticorruption matter for how crusades affect citizens' relationship with politics. We argued that narratives that focus on the problem of corruption as opposed to the judicial effort to address it are more likely to trigger negative emotions, deepen cynicism, and increase disaffection. We also argued that narratives that focus on the judicial effort, but in which courts fail to clearly project and dramatise the myth of legality, lose their potential to restore trust in politics. Chapter 6 already showed that whether citizens think about *Lava Jato* in terms of the corruption it uncovers or adopt a more investigation-centric perspective that highlights a possible solution to the problem matters a great deal. The experimental evidence we present below is partly in line with that finding, but also suggests that the benefits and shortcomings of corruption-centric and investigation-centric narratives are not clear cut.

PARTISANSHIP AND EVALUATIONS OF *LAVA JATO*

The data we present in this section reveals clear divisions in attitudes towards *Lava Jato* and shows that these divisions became more pronounced as the inquiry gained momentum and accumulated controversies. Divisions are present both in opinions regarding *Lava Jato*'s impartiality and its expected effectiveness in curbing corruption.

Figure 7.1 provides a picture of citizens' changing prognoses about the likely impact of *Lava Jato* on the incidence of corruption in Brazil. The data comes from a question asked by DATAFOLHA in nationally representative surveys conducted at three points in time (April 2017, August 2017, and April 2018),

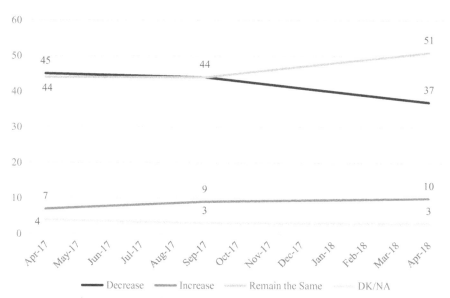

FIGURE 7.1 Changing views about the future of corruption in Brazil (April 2017–April 2018).
Source: DATAFOLHA. Question: "In your opinion, will corruption in Brazil decrease, increase, or remain the same after *Lava Jato*?"

and captures whether respondents believe that levels of corruption will decrease, increase, or remain the same after *Lava Jato*. The trend indicates that, far from being unanimous, opinions were split during this period, with pessimism gaining the upper hand towards the end. Initially, about 45 per cent of respondents believed that *Lava Jato* would reduce corruption in the country, but this proportion decreased over time. The remainder of the sample believed that corruption would remain the same after *Lava Jato*, with this group gradually growing in numbers, and a small proportion expected corruption to increase as a result of the operation.

Figure 7.2, in turn, reports changing perceptions of *Lava Jato*'s fairness or impartiality. Here we report answers to a survey question that asks whether respondents believe *Lava Jato* is investigating all political parties equally. This question was included in seventeen different nationally representative surveys conducted between April 2016 and August 2018. As in the case of effectiveness evaluations, perceptions of investigative bias are divided, with divisions becoming starker as the series progresses. This suggests that *Lava Jato* lost credibility over time. Whereas initially nearly 70 per cent of Brazilians deemed the effort impartial, by August 2018 less than half shared that view. By contrast, the proportion of respondents that thought of *Lava Jato* as partial increased dramatically. The perceived politicisation of *Lava Jato* likely hindered the ability of

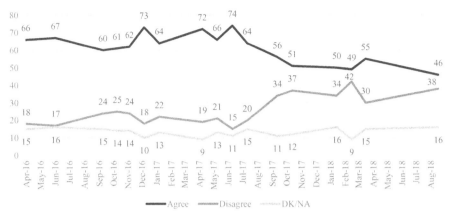

FIGURE 7.2 Changing views about *Lava Jato*'s impartiality in Brazil (April 2016–August 2018).
Source: IPSOS. Question: "Is *Lava Jato* investigating all political parties?"

crusaders to communicate a message that led to attitudinal changes in an optimistic direction.

What explains these divisions in attitudes towards *Lava Jato*? To investigate the correlates of opinions about *Lava Jato* we rely on surveys conducted in Brazil at two points in time, November 2018 and June 2019. These surveys asked respondents to express their views about different dimensions of *Lava Jato*, including perceptions of impartiality and effectiveness, general approval of the operation, and judgments about Judge Sergio Moro's behaviour.

We begin by looking at the determinants of perceptions of effectiveness and impartiality. These procedural evaluations condition the construction and projection of the myth of legality, and therefore affect the capacity of anti-corruption crusades to break vicious cycles of cynicism and reconcile voters with politics. The survey that contains the most complete set of questions and is more suitable for our purposes is a post-election survey conducted by the Brazilian Electoral Study project in November 2018.[1] Interestingly, this was a point in time by which *Lava Jato* had already shown its potential not only to prosecute grand corruption, but also to disrupt the normal course of democratic politics in ways that many surely found controversial or undesirable. Specifically, the survey was fielded in the aftermath of the campaign that led to the election of Jair Bolsonaro as president. Months earlier, *Lava Jato* had upended the contest, banning former president Lula from running for office. This forced the PT to find an alternative candidate. Bolsonaro exploited this

[1] The data can be downloaded here: www.cesop.unicamp.br/eng/eseb

TABLE 7.1 *Breakdown of attitudes towards Lava Jato (November 2018)*

Impartiality		Effectiveness	
Investigates all parties equally	49.91%	*Lava Jato* fights corruption	62.49%
Investigates mostly the PMDB	1.04%	*Lava Jato* does not fight corruption	30.13%
Investigates mostly the PT	34.73%	Don't Know/No Answer	7.39%
Investigates mostly the PSDB	0.61%		
Don't Know/No Answer	13.72%		

Source: Brazilian Electoral Study, November 2018. Questions: "Operation *Lava Jato* is an operation to fight against corruption in politics. Regarding Operation *Lava Jato*, do you think it investigates all political parties equally, it mainly investigates the MDB (formerly, PMDB), it mainly investigates the PT, it mainly investigates the PSDB, or it doesn't investigate any party?" and "In your opinion, does *Lava Jato* fight corruption or does it not fight corruption?"

drama, constructing a strong anti-corruption, anti-politics, and anti-left message that further polarised Brazilian democracy.

To measure perceptions of impartiality, we use a question that asks whether respondents believe *Lava Jato* is investigating all political parties equally, investigating mostly the PMDB (Partido do Movimento Democrático Brasiliero), the PT, or the PSDB, or not investigating any political party at all. Table 7.1 presents the original distribution of answers, which we recoded into a binary measure in which 1 means that *Lava Jato* investigates all parties equally, and is therefore perceived as impartial, and 0 means that investigations are biased against a specific political party (either the PT, PMDB, or PSDB). To measure perceptions of effectiveness, we rely on a question that asks whether *Lava Jato* fights corruption. Summary statistics are also reported in Table 7.1. The distribution of the answers to these two questions indicate that evaluations of *Lava Jato* continued to be quite divisive in Brazil beyond the period covered in Figures 7.1 and 7.2. While the impartiality of *Lava Jato* seems to be more controversial than its effectiveness, opinions regarding the investigation are far from unanimous. The data also shows that most respondents who perceived the operation as politically motivated believed that the investigation was biased against the PT, which suggests that opinions about *Lava Jato* are likely structured by attitudes towards this party.

To investigate the correlates of perceptions of *Lava Jato*'s effectiveness and impartiality, we include two main independent variables in the models. First, and most obviously, we investigate the impact of respondents' partisan allegiances using a question that measures affect towards the PT, the main political party in the country. The PT is also perceived by many as the main target of *Lava Jato*. This variable ranges from 0 to 10 and represents ascending levels of affect towards the PT. In line with the data reported in Chapter 6, we expect that support for the PT will correlate negatively with perceptions of impartiality and effectiveness. Second, we also explore whether attitudes towards courts may function as a buffer that mitigates the impact of *Lava Jato's* multiple controversies on its overall levels of legitimacy. As we argued in Chapter 5, and hinted at in Chapter 6, trust in the judicial system may make it easier for voters to buy into the myth of legality, especially when confronted with the most unorthodox, contentious, and politically consequential criminal investigation in history. In this regard, the literature on the US Supreme Court suggests that the institution's "reservoir of goodwill" among the mass public protects it from backlash in the aftermath of controversial decisions. As a measure of this reservoir, we use a standard question that asks respondents to declare how much they trust judicial institutions in Brazil. This variable has four categories and was recoded to represent ascending levels of trust in courts.[2]

In addition to these two main independent variables, the models include important controls. Political sophistication is measured as an index that combines three variables directly related to the concept: interest in politics,[3] attentiveness to political news on TV, radio, newspapers, or the internet,[4] and internal efficacy.[5] The models also include a control that taps the intensity of individuals' punitive attitudes[6] and their levels of tolerance for corruption.[7] This is because punitivism and lower tolerance for corruption may lead individuals to derive instant satisfaction from the crusade or overlook its failures. Finally, the models control for standard sociodemographic variables like age, sex, income, and education.

Given the binary nature of the two dependent variables, we estimate logistic regression models. The main results are presented in Table 7.2. We estimate

---

[2] Question: "Generally speaking, would you say that you have a lot of trust, some trust, little trust or no trust in Brazil's judicial institutions?"

[3] Question: "How interested are you in politics? Not interested at all, a little interested, interested, or very interested?"

[4] Question: "With what intensity do you follow politics on TV, radio, newspapers or on the internet? A lot of intensity, some intensity, little intensity, or do not follow politics at all?"

[5] Question: "Using a scale that ranges from totally agree to strongly disagree, how much do you agree with the following statement: 'I understand the most important political problems in the country?'"

[6] Question: "Using scale that ranges from totally agree to strongly disagree, how much do you agree with the following statement: 'Ensuring that corrupt politicians are convicted is more important than preserving their rights to defend themselves?'"

[7] This variable is an additive index that combines respondents' levels of agreement with the following five statements: "It does not matter if a politician steals or not. What is important is that he does what the population needs"; "A politician who does a lot and steals a little deserves the vote of the population"; "A politician who does a lot and steals a little does not deserve to be convicted by justice"; "A politician who governs well must be able to divert public money to finance his electoral campaign"; and "The best politician is someone who is efficient and delivers public goods, even if he steals a little."

TABLE 7.2 *Determinants of impartiality and effectiveness evaluations*

	Impartiality			Effectiveness		
	(1)	(2)	(3)	(4)	(5)	(6)
Affect PT	-0.170***		-0.181***	-0.0879***		-0.0972***
	(0.015)		(0.017)	(0.013)		(0.015)
Trust in courts		0.123***	0.141***		0.152***	0.148***
		(0.019)	(0.022)		(0.018)	(0.020)
Political sophistication			0.00714			0.0410
			(0.023)			(0.022)
Punitivism			0.0279			0.108**
			(0.036)			(0.033)
Tolerance corruption			-0.00351			-0.00531
			(0.012)			(0.011)
Age	0.0996*	0.0871*	0.0569	-0.00899	-0.0271	-0.0358
	(0.039)	(0.038)	(0.043)	(0.035)	(0.036)	(0.040)
Male	0.645***	0.626***	0.513***	0.734***	0.702***	0.635***
	(0.110)	(0.106)	(0.120)	(0.103)	(0.103)	(0.114)
Income	0.00438	0.150**	0.0240	0.0866	0.220***	0.124*
	(0.056)	(0.055)	(0.062)	(0.054)	(0.054)	(0.060)
Education	-0.00896	0.0382	0.00174	0.0265	0.0534*	0.0243
	(0.029)	(0.028)	(0.033)	(0.026)	(0.026)	(0.030)
Constant	0.411	-2.162***	-0.913*	0.554*	-1.713***	-1.353***
	(0.305)	(0.327)	(0.431)	(0.278)	(0.299)	(0.397)
N	1,605	1,613	1,425	1,988	2,007	1,735

Note: Logistic regressions. Standard errors in parentheses; *$p < 0.05$, **$p < 0.01$, ***$p < 0.001$.

three types of models for each dependent variable. Models 1 and 4 include *Affect PT* as the main independent variable, controlling for standard socio-demographic variables. Models 2 and 5 include *Trust in Courts* as the main predictor as well as standard sociodemographic controls. Models 3 and 6 include both independent variables as well as a more complete set of controls (political sophistication, punitivism, and tolerance for corruption).

The results confirm our expectations. As Models 1 and 4 indicate, the perception that *Lava Jato* is impartial or effective is predicted by affect towards the PT. In other words, evaluations about the anti-corruption crusade in Brazil are divided along partisan lines. More specifically, those who like the PT are less likely to declare that *Lava Jato* is neutral or effective. These coefficients are always statistically significant at the $p < 0.000$ level. With regard to trust in the judiciary, Models 2 and 5 also confirm our expectations: respondents who display higher levels of trust in Brazilian courts are more likely to hold positive views about *Lava Jato* as an impartial and effective anti-corruption effort. Since we do not measure trust before *Lava Jato* started, we of course cannot rule out endogeneity. The crusade's procedural failures could in principle undermine the legitimacy of the entire judicial system. This, however, seems unlikely, given that not all courts adopted the same aggressive and unorthodox approach to the prosecution and judgment of grand corruption. Most notably, as we discussed in Chapter 2, the STF was more lenient (for some, more orthodox and rule abiding) throughout.

Models 3 and 6 include both independent variables as well as additional controls. They show that the association between affect towards the PT and perceiving *Lava Jato* as both impartial and effective against corruption remains strong and statistically significant even when we include both independent variables in the model and a longer list of controls. Furthermore, the results suggest that higher levels of punitivism are associated with the perception that *Lava Jato* is effective at reducing corruption. Additionally, those more prone to tolerating corruption are more likely to think that *Lava Jato* is politically motivated. This, however, could also be a product of endogeneity: experiencing procedural and other failures might persuade citizens that attacking corruption is futile or does more harm than good, and by implication, that there is no other choice than to tolerate corruption as something inherent to politics. Finally, whereas positive views about *Lava Jato* are more prevalent among male and wealthier respondents, the models suggest no clear association between respondents' age or levels of education and attitudes towards *Lava Jato*.

So far, we have reported the evolution and determinants of attitudes towards *Lava Jato* in the period *before* the most salient and harmful controversy triggered by the crusade: the 2019 *Vaza Jato* scandal. The reader may recall that *Vaza Jato* started when the news portal *The Intercept* published evidence that Judge Sergio Moro had engaged in unethical and potentially illegal coordination efforts with the prosecutorial task force to go after former president Lula. The leaks also revealed animosity on their part against the PT and the left.

TABLE 7.3 *Breakdown of attitudes towards* Lava Jato *and Moro's behaviour*
(June 2019)

Evaluation of *Lava Jato*		Moro's irregularities		Moro's conduct	
Very bad	12.53%	Serious	65.52%	Appropriate	34.79%
Bad	5.53%	Irrelevant	34.48%	Inappropriate	65.21%
Regular	24.86%				
Good	24.72%				
Very good	32.36%				

It is possible that given the salience and impact of this exposé, more citizens turned against *Lava Jato*, washing away the partisan divide in attitudes we reported thus far.

To assess this possibility and further study the correlates of attitudes towards the anti-corruption crusade, we turn to a different nationally representative survey conducted in June 2019.[8] This survey includes a set of questions that tap important opinions about *Lava Jato* and *Vaza Jato*. The first question of interest asks respondents to evaluate the *Lava Jato* operation in general terms.[9] Answers to this question were collected using five categories (very bad, bad, neither good nor bad – "regular" –, good, or very good). The second dependent variable captures respondents' attitudes towards the accusation against Judge Moro.[10] This binary variable takes a value of 1 when respondents deem the potential irregularities as irrelevant and 0 when they consider them to be serious and think they should be subject to further judicial scrutiny. Finally, the third dependent variable asks whether respondents think that Moro's conduct, as revealed by the *Vaza Jato* scandal, was appropriate or not.[11] This binary variable takes a value of 1 when respondents are sympathetic towards Moro and 0 when respondents disapprove of his actions. All three dependent variables were coded to represent ascending levels of support for *Lava Jato*.

Table 7.3 shows the distribution of responses for the three measures of support. Interestingly, the public held very mixed views. Overall support for the operation remained relatively high. Moro's behaviour in the case against Lula, however, was generally considered inappropriate and serious enough to merit further scrutiny. In fact, this emerging scepticism about Moro and the motives driving his zealous approach to anti-corruption did not go away. For

---

[8] This is a study conducted by Instituto Datafolha.

[9] Question: "The *Lava Jato* investigation has completed 5 years. In your opinion, *Lava Jato* is doing a very good, good, neither good nor bad, bad or a very bad job?"

[10] Question: "In your opinion, any irregularities incurred by Judge Sérgio Moro during the *Lava Jato* operation are 1) irrelevant given the results of *Lava Jato* in fighting corruption or 2) serious and should be reviewed?"

[11] Question: "From what you know or have heard, Sergio Moro's conduct in the context of private conversations with Lula's accusers was appropriate or inappropriate?"

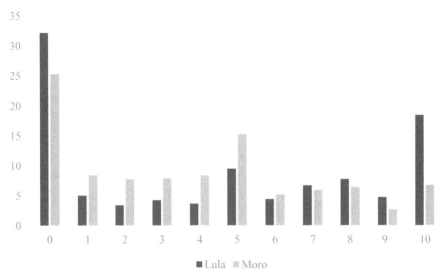

FIGURE 7.3 Affect towards Moro and Lula (April 2021).
Source: Authors' online, nationally representative survey. Question: "On a scale from 0 to 10, where 0 means 'I do not like him at all' and 10 means 'I like him a lot,' how much would you say you like Moro/Lula?"

example, in a survey we conducted in April 2021 (after *The Intercept* had intensified its campaign against Moro, Moro's tenure as Bolsonaro's minister of justice had come to an ignominious end, and the STF had handed down its harsh indictment of Moro's behaviour in the case against Lula), we found that opinions about Moro were quite unfavourable.[12] We asked respondents to indicate how much they liked both Lula and Moro, using a 0–10 scale in which 0 means "I do not like him at all" and 10 means "I like him a lot." Figure 7.3 compares the distribution of answers and shows that affect towards Lula is considerably higher than affect towards Moro. The former judge consistently received more negative ratings than the leader of the PT.

Once again, we explore whether partisan attitudes and trust in the judiciary are important correlates of our three dependent variables. To measure the former, we rely on a question that asks respondents to name their preferred political party. The variable *PT Partisan* takes a value of 1 when respondents identify the PT as their preferred political party, and 0 when respondents name either another political party or no political party when answering this question. The variable *Trust in courts* is measured with three categories representing ascending levels of trust: no trust, a little trust, and a lot of trust. Because this

---

[12] See next section for details about this survey.

TABLE 7.4 *Determinants of attitudes towards* Lava Jato *and Moro's behaviour*

	Evaluation of Lava Jato (1)	Moro's irregularities (2)	Moro's conduct (3)
PT partisan	−0.572***	−1.727***	−1.326***
	(0.072)	(0.196)	(0.170)
Trust in courts	0.481***	0.479***	0.493***
	(0.039)	(0.077)	(0.075)
Age	0.0415*	0.200***	0.323***
	(0.020)	(0.041)	(0.040)
Male	0.507***	0.648***	0.674***
	(0.055)	(0.109)	(0.107)
Income	0.0156	0.144***	0.0678*
	(0.017)	(0.035)	(0.033)
Education	0.0928***	0.198***	0.0934**
	(0.015)	(0.031)	(0.029)
Constant	1.931***	−3.565***	−3.338***
	(0.132)	(0.281)	(0.273)
N	1,989	1,826	1,825

Note: Model 1 is a linear regression. Models 2 and 3 are logistic regressions. Standard errors in parentheses; $*p < 0.05$, $**p < 0.01$, $***p < 0.001$.

survey has a more limited number of questions than the Brazilian Electoral Study survey we used before, the statistical models feature a reduced set of controls: age, sex, income, and education.

The results presented in Table 7.4 suggest continuity rather than change in the determinants of attitudes towards *Lava Jato* after *Vaza Jato*. Evaluations of *Lava Jato* and of its main icon, Sergio Moro, are still strongly associated with partisan allegiances. Models 1, 2, and 3 show that sympathising with the PT is negatively associated with approval of *Lava Jato's* work and of Sergio Moro's conduct. On the other hand, trust in courts is associated with positive views about *Lava Jato* and Moro's behaviour: those who display higher levels of trust in judicial institutions are also more likely to evaluate *Lava Jato* positively, to disregard Moro's irregularities as irrelevant, and to perceive Moro's behaviour as appropriate. Finally, unlike the previous set of models, virtually all control variables cross traditional levels of statistical significance. Positive views about *Lava Jato* are more prevalent among men and older, wealthier, and more educated respondents.

In sum, as the crusade made progress thanks to unusual displays of prosecutorial zeal in the form of aggressive and unorthodox investigative tactics, it triggered controversies that complicated its relationship with the public. Indeed, the Brazilian data shows that *Lava Jato* gradually haemorrhaged support. In Chapter 8 we identify a similar pattern in Peru, albeit for different reasons.

In the case of Brazil, statistical models suggest that *Lava Jato's* deteriorating legitimacy is primarily a function of reactions by PT supporters, who felt victimised and unfairly treated by an anti-corruption effort of dubious credentials and uncertain effectiveness. In a context where citizens feel relatively strong sympathies for certain parties, anti-corruption efforts are not universally praised because they have negative implications for the politicians some voters are keen to support. As a result, attitudes towards different aspects of *Lava Jato* ended up divided along partisan lines. This goes to show that in addition to prosecutorial unorthodoxy, political loyalties further condition the ability of crusades to construct broad support coalitions via the projection of the myth of legality, a myth that according to the optimistic story outlined in Chapter 5 could in principle induce citizens to develop more hopeful prognoses about the future of politics. Optimism is therefore highly unlikely to be universal. If it takes root, it will do so among those portions of the electorate that derive pleasure from seeing their rivals suffer the consequences of unrelenting anti-corruption efforts.

THE EFFECTS OF ANTI-CORRUPTION CRUSADES ON PUBLIC OPINION: EXPERIMENTAL DATA

Having explored how partisanship complicates or conditions the construction of an image of fairness and effectiveness using observational data, we now turn to a survey experiment that allows us to test how different narratives of corruption and anti-corruption shape mass attitudes towards politics, all other things being equal. The literature reviewed in Chapter 5 finds a strong negative correlation between perceptions of corruption and institutional trust, and a positive correlation between perceptions of corruption and the feeling that political involvement is a futile endeavour. But can the visible and decisive intervention of judges and prosecutors disrupt, on average, the cynicism and hopelessness engendered by systemic corruption? In tackling this question, the chapter returns to a theme we already addressed in Chapter 6, namely, whether public discussions of *Lava Jato* that focus on the judicial/prosecutorial effort to address corruption, as opposed to ones that only look at the corruption uncovered during the process, produce attitudinal shifts that are more in line with the optimistic story. The focus group data suggested that when the public imagination associates *Lava Jato* with criminal activity, and not with the judicial actors and procedures that uncover and punish it, the outcome was a gloomy and defeatist prognosis about the future of politics. Conversely, and this was especially true among Brazilian participants, when voters paid attention to judicial activity, and did not fixate narrowly on the crimes, they were capable of voicing cautious optimism and felt more politically efficacious.

To assess the possible effects of different corruption and anti-corruption narratives in a more rigorous way, we embedded a priming experiment in an online survey conducted in Brazil in April 2021. This study was implemented seven years after the start of *Lava Jato*, at a time when the major developments and consequences brought about by this anti-corruption crusade had already been felt and the contours of the operation, as well as the major controversies surrounding it, were clearly defined. Because of the timing of our study, we believe it is well positioned to identify some possible effects that *Lava Jato* may have had on the political attitudes of Brazilian citizens.

Priming experiments are frequently used to understand the effects of certain considerations on attitude formation and on the evaluation of political actors and institutions. These types of experiments rely on the idea that, when prompted to make a political choice or judgement, individuals do not take into account all plausible considerations that could inform their choices or judgements. Instead, they adopt time and effort saving strategies by using the most accessible pieces of information available in their memory (Krosnick and Kinder 1990). Individuals rely on these most accessible pieces of information in a spontaneous and effortless manner to form attitudes (Tversky and Kahneman 1981). Like many other experimental studies, ours is therefore designed to manipulate what considerations are most accessible to participants precisely when they are prompted to form and offer opinions about politics.

The experiment was embedded in an online survey of 3,000 respondents fielded between 1 April and 12 April 2021 by the company Netquest.[13] The main goal of the study was to prime participants in a controlled way to think about specific aspects of the crusade in Brazil. We accomplished this by randomly assigning participants to view a series of information posts (combining text and images) that mimic the format of information people often encounter in online social media environments. We adopted this format because we believe that it enhances the study's experimental realism and is an effective way of conveying messages.

The study consisted of three main parts. In the first part, all participants answered questions about their attitudes towards politics and the political system, levels of political interest, feelings towards Lula and Moro, trust in courts, and vote in the last presidential election. Our goal was to measure pretreatment levels of important attitudes that could shape participants' responses to the experimental manipulation.

The second part of the study consisted of experimental manipulations that primed participants to think about, and to focus on, different aspects of the fight against corruption in Brazil. We expect that the different pieces of information/images we manipulate make specific considerations – about either the problem of corruption, the anti-corruption effort promoted by *Lava Jato*, and the shortcomings of the operation – more accessible to participants when they answer questions about their political opinions and attitudes. Respondents

---

[13] The sample is representative of the population with access to the Internet in Brazil.

Corruption Condition: In 2011, a series of popular demonstrations against corruption broke out. In one of them, the participants occupied and "swept" the ramp of the National Congress to protest against corruption. Each year, approximately R$ 70 billion is diverted from public coffers in Brazil. It is estimated that for every R$1 that is misappropriated, society loses approximately R$3. The consequences are felt in areas such as health, education and infrastructure. There are constant scandals in the country. In 2012, for example, four Brazilians – including politicians and businessmen – were cited in a World Bank report that presented emblematic cases of money laundering and corruption around the world. In 2013, the country fell 3 positions in a ranking that measures perceptions of corruption and lagged behind countries like Ghana, Malaysia and Cuba, occupying the 72nd position among 177 countries.

LAVA JATO Condition: The *Lava Jato* operation was one of the largest anti-corruption efforts in the world. It started in 2014, when a Federal Court in Curitiba started investigating four criminal organizations that included public agents, businessmen and foreign exchange brokers. The *Lava Jato* operation carried out more than a thousand search and seizure warrants, temporary arrests, preventive detentions and coercive questionings, aiming at investigating a money laundering scheme that paid billions of reais in bribes. *Lava Jato* had 80 authorized operational phases that arrested and convicted more than one hundred people. *Lava Jato* investigated crimes of active and passive corruption, fraudulent management, money laundering, criminal conspiracy, obstruction of justice, fraudulent foreign exchange operations and influence peddling.

VAZA JATO Condition: Starting in June 2019, conversations were leaked that raised suspicions about the behaviour and the real intentions of judges and prosecutors directly involved in the *Lava Jato* investigation. Huge files containing private messages, audios, photos, court documents and other items were leaked by an anonymous source. The conversations disclosed by the American journalist Glenn Greenwald, in the online newspaper *The Intercept*, showed that there was collaboration and exchange of information between judge Sergio Moro and the prosecution services. This is considered unethical. Conversations between Judge Sergio Moro and Prosecutor Deltan Dallagnol show that Moro issued a series of guidelines and instructions to Dallagnol in relation to the investigation against former President Lula. Documents released by the newspaper also showed that *Lava Jato* leaked classified information to media outlets.

STF Condition: Recently, the Supremo Tribunal Federal (STF) tried to correct some of the excesses of *Lava Jato*. STF Justice Edson Fachin, annulled the convictions issued against former President Lula as part of *Lava Jato*, and ruled that all proceedings should be now handled by federal courts in Brasilia. He did so on the basis that the 13 Vara de Curitiba, where Judge Sergio Moro used to work, did not have jurisdiction to judge events that took place in other parts of the country. Following a request by former President Lula's lawyers, STF justices also analysed Sergio Moro's behaviour in the case and noted that his behaviour was politically motivated. Some of the arguments put forward by the justices include the "spectacularization" of Lula's coercive questioning and the release of recorded conversations between Lula and Dilma Rousseff.

FIGURE 7.4 Experimental conditions

were presented with a "slide show" consisting of five slides, each featuring a portion of the text of the experimental vignette superimposed on an image (see Figure 7.4). They had about 15 seconds to read the text on each slide, with the following slide appearing automatically afterwards.

We included five experimental conditions. The first condition is a pure control (*control condition*), in which participants did not receive any type of information. This condition allows us to estimate the baseline levels of the attitudes we are interested in. The second experimental condition (*corruption condition*) contained information and images that called attention to the problem of corruption in Brazil, the one forcefully exposed by *Lava Jato*, without making any sort of reference to anti-corruption initiatives. This condition allows us to identify the types of political attitudes that arise when considerations regarding the pervasiveness of corruption are activated. The third experimental condition (*Lava Jato condition*) offered participants information and images that primed them to think about the fight against corruption promoted by *Lava Jato*. In other words, we provided a narrative of anti-corruption efforts with judicial actors and their efforts taking centre stage, with the expectation that it will move attitudes in an optimistic direction. The fourth and fifth conditions (*Vaza Jato and STF conditions, respectively*) offered participants information and images that highlighted the failures of *Lava Jato*. This allows us to see whether an investigation- or court-centric narrative, but one that highlights bias and procedural shortcomings inimical to the construction of the myth of legality, preclude the outcomes predicted by the optimistic story.

Randomisation ensures that all treatment groups in the sample are equivalent, on average, in terms of both observable and unobservable characteristics. Any systematic difference in the answers to each of the post-treatment questions across experimental conditions should therefore serve as an estimate of the impact of the different pieces of information we offer. The sample of 3,000 survey participants was divided into 5 randomly assigned groups of roughly 600 individuals, which appear balanced across observed covariates.[14]

Finally, following the experimental manipulation respondents answered questions that tap key dimensions of our outcomes of interest. First, participants indicated how much *hope, enthusiasm, anger,* and *worry* they feel when they think about politics in Brazil. Next, respondents offered their level of agreement with three items designed to capture respondents' levels of *political cynicism*.[15] Subsequently, respondents were offered three types of candidate profiles – a politician from a traditional party, an outsider that is willing to govern with traditional parties, or a populist outsider – and asked to choose the one they believe would be best suited to run the country. This variable, which is coded to represent ascending levels of support for *outsider* politicians, helps us understand the degree to which voters think of the system as perfectible or in

---

[14] See the Appendix for balance tests. The Appendix can be found on http://www.narapavao.com/book.html

[15] This variable is an index that combines answers to the following questions: "Corruption is a fact of life; there is little that anyone can do about it"; "It doesn't matter if a politician is corrupt or not, what matters is that he/she delivers what citizens need"; and "Under certain circumstances corruption is acceptable."

need of radical adjustment.[16] Finally, we also included questions that measure respondents' evaluations of the country's *political situation*,[17] levels of political engagement (measured in terms of *external*[18] and *internal political efficacy*[19]), and *satisfaction with democracy*.[20] All three of these variables could be thought of as capturing the extent to which citizens feel pessimistic about politics and think of political participation as a futile endeavour.

Our five conditions allow us to make the exact types of comparisons we need to empirically test key aspects of the argument. More specifically, we use the experimental data to accomplish three goals. Our first goal is to understand the consequences of corruption for political attitudes. The idea here is to understand the negative implications of perceptions of widespread corruption for political attitudes, or of narratives of the crusade that fixate exclusively on the crimes it uncovers. We therefore compare the attitudes of participants assigned to the control and to the corruption conditions (corruption condition vs pure control).

The second goal of the analysis is to understand whether *Lava Jato* changed the political attitudes of Brazilians in a context plagued with corruption. Do the judicial actors, actions, and symbols associated with *Lava Jato* help mobilise people against corruption and restore citizens' relationship with politics? To answer this question, we compare attitudes of participants randomly assigned to the *Lava Jato* and corruption conditions (*Lava Jato* condition vs corruption condition). If the optimistic story about the likely impact of narratives that focus on the anti-corruption potential of courts and prosecutors is plausible, we should observe that, compared to the treatment that puts corruption crimes at the top of voters' minds, the treatment that puts *Lava Jato's* efforts to combat graft centre stage exacerbates positive emotions and dampens negative ones; undermines political cynicism and a preference for outsiders while boosting internal/external efficacy; and improves views about the country's political situation and satisfaction with its democratic system of government.

Finally, our third goal is to investigate the implications of the failures of *Lava Jato*. Do these failures overshadow the positive effects we expect *Lava Jato* to have on the public's relationship with politics? Can *Lava Jato's* excesses

---

[16] Question: "Who do you think would do a better job running the country? a) A reputable politician from a traditional party, b) Someone reputable from outside of politics who knows how to govern with traditional parties, or c) Someone reputable from outside of politics who fights traditional parties?"

[17] Question: "Do you consider that the political situation in the country is worse, the same, or better than ten years ago?"

[18] Question: "Some people say that it makes a big difference who governs Brazil. Others say it makes no difference who governs Brazil. What do you think?"

[19] Question: "Some people say that our vote greatly influences what happens in Brazil; others say that our vote does not influence anything that happens in Brazil. What do you think?"

[20] Question: "In general, how satisfied are you with the functioning of democracy in Brazil? Not satisfied at all, a little satisfied, satisfied, very satisfied."

and partiality undermine the benefits of anti-corruption? To answer these questions, we compare the post-treatment attitudes of participants in the *Vaza Jato* and STF conditions against those of participants assigned to the *Lava Jato* condition (*Vaza Jato* condition vs *Lava Jato* condition, and STF condition vs *Lava Jato* condition).[21]

The Effects of Corruption-Centric Narratives: Does Corruption Boost Pessimism about Politics?

To assess whether and how *Lava Jato* has changed the landscape of political attitudes in Brazil, it is important to first understand how Brazilians feel in the face of perceived widespread corruption. We can estimate these effects by comparing the post-treatment attitudes of those randomly assigned to be primed about endemic corruption with those randomly assigned to the pure control condition (in which no priming information was provided). This could also be viewed as a test of the effects of narratives of *Lava Jato* that fixate on the crimes revealed during the crusade, that is, on the dark side of politics.

The results of this comparison are presented in Figure 7.5 They indicate that being primed to think about corruption crimes makes respondents angrier and more worried about the state of Brazilian politics. As in the focus groups, when participants fixate on the crimes, they experience emotions that could lead to less favourable appraisals of politics or to more pessimistic prognoses about the future. Conversely, thinking about corruption decreases positive attitudes like hope and enthusiasm, but these effects are not statistically significant. Furthermore, we find that participants primed to consider widespread corruption display lower levels of satisfaction with democracy. Interestingly, however, they report higher levels of external political efficacy, namely, they agree more with the view that not all politicians are the same and that who exactly is elected to office matters a great deal. This suggests that while corruption-centric narratives do produce some of the corrosive effects associated with the pessimistic story outlined in Chapter 5, they do not fully pull people away from the political system. In this sense, the positive impact on external efficacy could be interpreted as indicating that information about systemic corruption makes voters more vigilant and discerning. The negative effect that being primed about corruption has on the political cynicism index, although not fully crossing traditional thresholds of statistical significance, reinforces this point.

These results serve as an illustration of the political implications of corruption in the absence of anti-corruption efforts, and pave the way for the central part of the analysis, which focuses on the public opinion effects of anti-corruption crusades. As Judge Sergio Moro and Prosecutor Dallagnol tried to convince

---

[21] To assess the extent to which the specific issues primed became more salient in participants' minds after each treatment, the Appendix features a series of manipulation checks. The Appendix can be found on http://www.narapavao.com/book.html

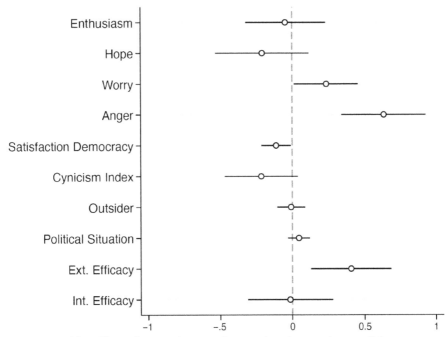

FIGURE 7.5 The effects of corruption-centric narratives (corruption condition vs pure control)
Note: Coefficients represent average treatment effects. Whiskers represent 95 per cent confidence intervals.

the public in their various media appearances, a key motivation behind *Lava Jato* was to restore the damage caused by perceptions of endemic corruption in Brazil. The next section presents experimental evidence that allows us to empirically assess the extent to which this promise was in fact fulfilled.

The Effects of Crusade-Centric Narratives: Does *Lava Jato* Inspire Hope?

To understand the effects of narratives that put crusades and crusaders centre stage, we compare post-treatment attitudes reported by participants randomly assigned to the *Lava Jato* and *Corruption* experimental conditions. This comparison allows us to evaluate whether *Lava Jato*, especially a relatively favourable depiction of it, significantly changed how Brazilians feel about politics despite widespread corruption.

The results reported in Figure 7.6 partially support the insights derived from our theoretical framework in Chapter 5 and the focus group data in Chapter 6: when citizens are primed to think about *Lava Jato* as a serious effort to punish corruption, some of the negative effects reported above for the corruption

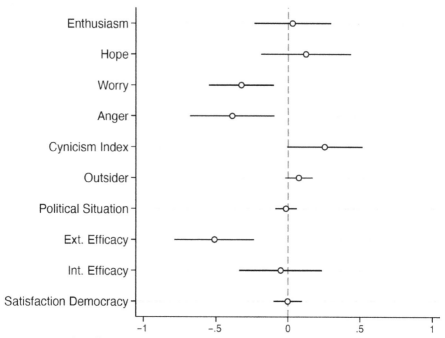

FIGURE 7.6 The effects of crusade-centric narratives (*Lava Jato* vs corruption conditions)
Note: Coefficients represent average treatment effects. Whiskers represent 95 per cent confidence intervals.

condition disappear. Specifically, the data indicate that when compared to participants who were primed to think about the problem of corruption, those who were primed to think about *Lava Jato* displayed significantly lower levels of negative emotions such as worry and anger. In other words, while thinking about the problem of corruption made participants more worried and angrier about politics, thinking about the anti-corruption effort reverted these negative effects. Conversely, information about *Lava Jato* slightly increased positive emotions such as enthusiasm and hope, but these coefficients are statistically indistinguishable from zero. The results suggest that anti-corruption crusades, by offering a response to the problem of corruption, are capable of triggering emotions that could eventually lead to more optimistic prognoses about the future and nature of political activity.

Despite reducing negative emotional reactions, the results also show that the effects of *Lava Jato* do not go as far as to restore more deep-rooted political attitudes. First, the results indicate that being primed to think about *Lava Jato* led participants to report higher levels of cynicism when compared to the group that received information about corruption. Second, being primed about *Lava*

Jato decreased participants' external efficacy. These two statistically significant results show that rather than having a positive and restorative effect on attitudes towards politics in Brazil, the ambitious anti-corruption probe may have exacerbated political cynicism and disengagement.

When taken together, our main findings thus far point to three interesting conclusions. First, being primed to think about corruption in politics does not necessarily lead to political disengagement or to perceptions that the system is unresponsive. In fact, the results suggest an opposite trend: being primed to think about the anti-corruption crusade is what seems to be disengaging people from politics. This could be because of the anti-politics messages that crusades send to citizens, a point that is at the heart of the pessimistic story outlined in Chapter 5. While the crusade-centric narrative does not lead voters to fixate on the crimes or the dark side of politics, it still pits nominally non-political actors and institutions against the political class. If citizens side with the crusaders and come to see politics as the enemy, they may conclude that reform is pointless and reject any call for being optimistic about the possibility of changing politics. This could explain why, for instance, while not statistically significant, the effect of the *Lava Jato* condition on preferences for outsiders is positive. In other words, while some people can experience hope (or less worry/anger) after seeing judicial actors attack the establishment and try to correct its abuses, that very same hope could throw them into the arms of candidates that promise dangerous forms of revenge and do not embrace the system as perfectible or redeemable.

Second, the results complicate the picture we have painted thus far regarding the connection between emotions and attitudes towards politics. While the link between negative emotions and political cynicism was clear and strong in the focus groups (and is also clear in the Peruvian survey data we report in Chapter 8), here the story seems to be different. Most notably, negative emotions and external political inefficacy, which signals a sense of "futility in bringing about desired social change or control through political efforts" (Miller 1974: 951), and is therefore one of the hallmarks of cynicism, consistently move in diametric directions. Citizens who become more (or less) worried and angry as a result of corruption-centric narratives (or crusade-centric narratives), also express more (or less) external political efficacy.

Finally, the results do not seem to be driven by relevant subgroups responding differently to the *Corruption* or *Lava Jato* treatments. For example, we estimated heterogenous effects using pre-treatment questions such as vote choice in 2018, support for Lula or Moro, and trust in the courts, finding no differences. This suggests that while evaluations of *Lava Jato's* effectiveness and impartiality are indeed a function of citizens' political loyalties and attitudes towards the justice system, the effects of exposure to narratives of *Lava Jato* that emphasize either the corruption it uncovers or the seriousness of the anti-corruption effort cut across these partisan and attitudinal divides.

The Effects of Crusade-Centric Narratives That Challenge the Myth of Legality

The data from the experiment in principle allows us to also assess whether increasing the salience of *Lava Jato's* failures, which were made apparent to the public both during the 2019 *Vaza Jato* scandal and in the 2021 STF decision overturning Moro's conviction against Lula, has any noticeable effects on political attitudes. Because both *Vaza Jato* and the STF's ruling cast a shadow over the legacy of *Lava Jato*, it is important to see the extent to which respondents primed to think about these events display different attitudes than those primed to think about *Lava Jato* as a serious attempt to fight corruption. In other words, what happens to cynicism when the myth of legality is shattered?

Unfortunately, however, the manipulation checks available in the Appendix reveal that the two strategies we employed to induce participants to think about partiality and unfairness were not effective. Specifically, participants assigned to both the *Vaza Jato* and the STF conditions were not more likely than participants in the other experimental groups to identify the failures of *Lava Jato* as the most important event in recent Brazilian politics. Consequently, we anticipate finding weak or null results from comparisons that rely on the attitudes of participants in either the *Vaza Jato* or the STF condition because our messages were not internalised as intended.

The results in Figure 7.7 confirm this. Priming participants to think about *Lava Jato's* failures did not generate discernible effects on the four types of emotions we measure in the study or on participants' political attitudes. The only exceptions are external political efficacy and preference for an outsider politician, which were affected by the *Vaza Jato* priming: thinking about the *Vaza Jato* scandal increases participants' external efficacy and reduces their

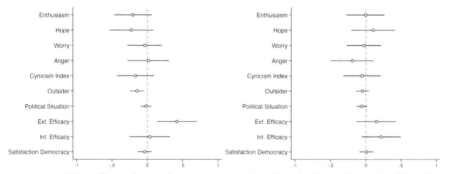

FIGURE 7.7 The effects of crusade-centric narratives that challenge the myth of legality (failure vs *Lava Jato* conditions): (a) *Vaza Jato* versus *Lava Jato*; (b) STF versus *Lava Jato*
Note: Coefficients represent average treatment effects. Whiskers represent 95 per cent confidence intervals.

preference for outsiders. This is an interesting finding. As we saw above, being primed to think about *Lava Jato* as a serious and resolute attempt to curb corruption reduced external efficacy and increased support for outsiders in politics (though this latter effect did not reach conventional levels of statistical significance). These new results suggest that being primed to consider the partiality and lack of procedural fairness of *Lava Jato* counterbalances those effects. In other words, this might be a sign that the damage that *Lava Jato* inflicted on citizens' relationship with politics can be repaired with information showing that the crusade's depiction of the political class (or prominent members of it) as evil or unredeemable is actually not to be fully believed. For example, one could imagine someone who abandoned the left appalled by what *Lava Jato* revealed about Lula, finding in *Vaza Jato* some solace or a reason for revisiting their decision.

CONCLUSION

This chapter highlighted two challenges facing the optimistic story linking anti-corruption crusades to the possible restoration of citizens' relationship with politics. First, we showed that while the positive reputation of judicial insti-tutions helps crusaders project the myth of legality and enhances perceptions of fairness and effectiveness, partisan loyalties complicate things. Specifically, we found that support for the PT is consistently and negatively associated with satisfaction with the crusade's methods and contributions to the fight against corruption. This likely explains why *Lava Jato* in Brazil suffered a gradual loss of support among the public: as it became increasingly evident that the anti-corruption probe disproportionately affected the PT, those who sympathised with this party turned away from Moro and the prosecutors. This seems to be true both before and after *Vaza Jato*, arguably the most serious controversy elicited by *Lava Jato*, suggesting that partisanship is a serious obstacle for crusaders keen on (and often in need of) widespread popular backing *even* when they do not make serious mistakes or engage in blatant forms of miscon-duct. In this sense, because crusades that take place in countries where partisan sympathies (and antipathies) are relatively strong put in tension citizens' desire for accountability with their political loyalties, the criminalisation of corruption is prone to dividing rather than uniting the citizenry. This is the case even when criminalisation is in principle a noble enterprise long awaited by many. The result is that optimism, if it takes root, will only be present among those who derive satisfaction from seeing their figures of hate parading through the courts.

The second challenge facing the optimistic story is perhaps more serious, and relates to the actual message that, partisan preferences aside, courts and pros-ecutors convey to the public. In this regard, our survey experiment showed that when compared to narratives of Brazilian politics that fixate on corruption, including the corruption revealed by *Lava Jato*, narratives that put resolute anti-corruption efforts at the top of voters' minds make citizens less angry and worried about politics. This much is in line with what optimists expect, and what the focus groups in Chapter 6 indicated. But the experiment also revealed that when it comes to more deep-rooted attitudes like political cynicism or external efficacy, the effect is in the opposite direction. In other words, less intense negative emotions are not accompanied by a more favourable assessment of the state or nature of political activity. This could be attributed to the fact that the *Lava Jato* project, especially in its most credible formulation, stigmatises politics to a degree that makes it hard for citizens to believe in the possibility of change. While Moro might have thought of prosecuting corruption as "an honour to the nation, not a disgrace" (see Chapter 5), portraying politicians and major political parties as disgraceful enemies does more harm than good to the view that politics is redeemable. The outcome in the end is a deeper sense of futility.

In the next chapter we further probe the impact of crusades on public opinion with observational and experimental evidence from Peru. We show that in a context of weaker or non-existent partisan loyalties, hope and optimism are equally precarious.

8

Prosecutorial Trade-Offs and the Precarity of Hope

Survey Evidence from Peru

INTRODUCTION

The focus group data discussed in Chapter 6 painted with a broad brush a picture of how Peruvians felt about politics during the largest and most disruptive anti-corruption probe in history. We uncovered high levels of political cynicism, accompanied by overwhelmingly negative emotions and the absence of hope. Moreover, we showed that while reluctant to say much about the prosecutorial effort, when pushed, participants had a long list of complaints, dusted with a strong dose of scepticism about the merits and potential of the tactics and trade-offs involved. Because of the nature of focus group data, this analysis is not only non-representative, but also likely obscures variation in attitudes. Public opinion is hardly ever this monolithic. The present chapter therefore leverages original survey data collected in November 2019 to explore possible nuances in Peruvians' attitudes towards *Lava Jato* and its impact on politics.[1]

A first indicium that *Lava Jato* may have instilled more hope than the focus groups indicated comes from comparing one of the items in our survey over time. We can do this because our instrument was embedded in the 2019 edition of a study of attitudes towards corruption that Proetica, the local affiliate of Transparency International, commissions every two years. To be sure, the 2019 survey shows that 62 per cent of respondents considered corruption to be one of the three main problems facing the country, the highest percentage

---

[1] Apart from limited representativeness, the attitudinal homogeneity we found in the Peruvian focus groups could be the result of group dynamics. For example, in a context of widespread cynicism, less cynical participants may feel uncomfortable voicing hope when most of their peers express strongly pessimistic views. This could be due to shame or fear of being accused of naïveté.

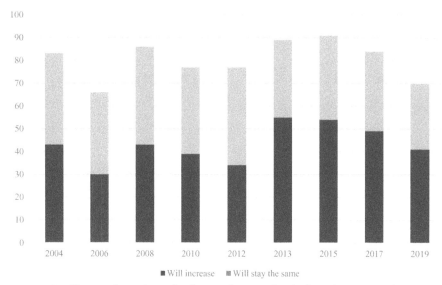

FIGURE 8.1 Expectations about the future of corruption in Peru (2004–2019).
Source: Proetica. Question: "Do you believe that in the next five years corruption in Peru will increase, decrease, or stay the same?"

since the series began in 2002.[2] This is most likely due to the salience of *Lava Jato* at the time when the data was collected,[3] and is consistent with the sense of worry expressed by focus group participants. Most 2019 respondents also considered that corruption was going to increase or stay the same in the next five years. Looking at the long-term trend, however, what is interesting is that respondents in 2019 were somewhat more optimistic than those who answered this question in waves prior to *Lava Jato* (Figure 8.1).

Armed with this intuition, this chapter first probes whether variation in satisfaction with the *Lava Jato* task force correlates with more intense positive/negative emotions as well as with more or less optimistic prognoses about the future of corruption, as our argument in Chapter 5 would predict. In other words, could this increase in optimism be due to the crusade? We also study if emotional reactions to politics in the age of *Lava Jato* are associated with voters' varying propensities to tolerate corruption, assessing whether positive emotions are indeed linked to greater severity, and negative ones to greater cynicism in the form of leniency or resignation. A conjoint experiment then

---

[2] In the 2017 wave the percentage was 52 per cent, and in the first wave of 2002 the percentage was just 29 per cent.

[3] We fielded the face-to-face survey between 31 October and 1 November 2019. This was shortly after the dissolution of parliament on 3 September over a conflict regarding nominations to the Constitutional Court. See Chapter 3.

allows us to directly assess whether the task force, by virtue of its reputation, induces voters to impose higher penalties on politicians in a hypothetical election than other sources of corruption allegations. Optimists maintain that crusaders have special qualities that impact voters in ways that other anti-corruption agents cannot. If optimists are right in thinking that large-scale criminalisation efforts undermine cynicism or lead voters to engage proactively to clean up the system, feeling hopeful about politics should reduce tolerance for graft. Similarly, accusations that benefit from the *Lava Jato* "brand" should elicit tougher sanctions. The results are in line with both expectations.

As the focus groups suggest, however, this optimism is unlikely to be pervasive or entrenched in what is otherwise a sea of cynical voters. In particular, no matter how satisfied or immediately hopeful some may feel thanks to *Lava Jato*, prosecutorial efforts are too controversial to leave no scars on the legitimacy of the inquiry and its positive effects on attitudes towards politics and corruption. If the key issue in Brazil was a fierce debate about the fairness of *Lava Jato* driven primarily by partisan feuds (see Chapters 6 and 7), the Achilles' heel of the case in Peru was prosecutorial selectivity. As we know from Chapter 3, the inquiry gained momentum precisely when prosecutors negotiated an information-sharing agreement with Odebrecht. But the deal came at a high cost: immunity for executives, a cap on the fines imposed on the company, and the green light to continue contracting with the state. This chapter shows how problematic these concessions are from voters' perspective. Citizens are not as ready as the prosecutors to accept trade-offs between "truth" and "justice." To this end, in the second part we leverage another conjoint experiment that studies how voters evaluate the deal to better understand why this kind of investigative choices eventually complicate citizens' relationship with crusades. The results reveal that Peruvians are reluctant to give away any of the truth or any of the justice; they want it all. We also discuss public reactions to other controversial prosecutorial choices, which further underscores the precarity of satisfaction with the task force and of any short-term hope that may have initially stemmed from it.

The findings in this chapter are therefore ultimately in line with those in Chapter 6. They both show how hard it is for prosecutors to effectively dramatise the "myth of legality." In other words, as our argument indicates, it proves very difficult to maintain any semblance of optimism as the crusade moves forward because the room for (perceived) prosecutorial failings never goes away. What happens in the courts on a day-to-day basis matters a great deal in determining the impact of crusades on public attitudes towards politics.

TASK FORCE SATISFACTION, EMOTIONS, AND TOLERANCE FOR CORRUPTION

According to the optimistic narrative, crusades signal that the system, while broken, can still work, generating the necessary antibodies to heal itself. When citizens see this kind of institutional virtuosity on display, they will experience positive emotions and begin to expect political regeneration rather than further decay. Importantly, since the judicial system now shows corruption can indeed be detected and punished, citizens should no longer feel they are condemned to either having to tolerate it or give up on politics altogether. We argued that while this optimistic prognosis is plausible, it hinges on how people evaluate the work of the judges and prosecutors. The perception that the intervention of horizontal accountability actors is effective and even-handed can prevent anti-corruption efforts from exacerbating disaffection or cynicism; conversely, real or perceived judicial and prosecutorial failures take voters back to a more pessimistic worldview.

From this it follows that approval of the investigation should elicit hope and enthusiasm about the future. To evaluate this observable implication, our survey measured general levels of satisfaction with the work of the Peruvian *Lava Jato* task force, and also support for one of its signature – and most talked about – methods: pretrial detentions. To measure the former, we asked: "How would you evaluate the performance of the *Lava Jato* Team in the fight against corruption?" Respondents selected an answer from an ordinal 5-point scale, ranging from "very bad" to "very good." Approximately 48 per cent of respondents thought the prosecutors were doing either a good or a very good job. To measure support for pretrial detentions, we asked: "The authorities determined that some politicians must spend time in prison while the Odebrecht inquiry is ongoing. Using a scale from 1 to 10, where 1 represents 'strongly disagree' and 10 'strongly agree,' how much do you agree with these measures?" Respondents very much supported the use of this kind of punitive measures: the average level of agreement with the statement is 7.6.

In the regression models (Table 8.1), we assess the relationship between these attitudes and two dependent variables. First, we look at respondents' emotions vis-à-vis politics in the age of *Lava Jato*. Respondents used a 10-point scale to express, separately, their levels of hope, enthusiasm, anger, and worry. In the analysis, we group emotional reactions into two categories (positive – hope and enthusiasm, and negative – anger and worry). The average level of positive emotions is 5.2, and of negative emotions, 6.0. Second, we asked participants to tell us their prediction about the future of corruption in Peru using the question we reported in Figure 8.1. The models also include a battery of controls, namely, age, gender, education, socio-economic status, level of information about politics, and whether respondents live in the capital city.

The results suggest that approval of the *Lava Jato* team is positively and significantly associated with feeling enthusiastic/hopeful about politics (Model 3), and negatively and significantly associated with feeling angry/worried (Model 1). This finding is in line with the focus group data. The reader will recall that when thinking about "*Lava Jato*," focus group participants associated it with the crimes, not the investigation. The result was a deep sense of disgust and worry in the face of the spectacle of corruption unfolding before

TABLE 8.1 *Emotions and the future of corruption*

| | Dependent variable | | | | | |
| | Angry/Worried | | Enthusiastic/Hopeful | | Corruption in the Next Five Years | |
	(1)	(2)	(3)	(4)	(5)	(6)
Approval of LJ team in the fight against corruption	-0.198***		0.504***		0.127***	
	(0.059)		(0.056)		(0.016)	
Approval of the use of Pretrial detentions		0.112***		0.257***		0.016**
		(0.027)		(0.023)		(0.007)
Female	0.289**	0.328**	-0.218*	-0.330***	-0.030	-0.058
	(0.132)	(0.129)	(0.122)	(0.117)	(0.038)	(0.038)
Age	0.013***	0.015***	-0.001	0.003	0.001	0.001
	(0.005)	(0.005)	(0.005)	(0.004)	(0.001)	(0.001)
Education	-0.076	-0.083	0.026	0.052	0.016	0.017
	(0.065)	(0.064)	(0.058)	(0.058)	(0.018)	(0.019)
Socio-economic status (8 levels)	-0.037	-0.034	-0.141***	-0.136***	0.001	-0.002
	(0.049)	(0.048)	(0.045)	(0.044)	(0.014)	(0.014)
Informed about politics	0.200**	0.160*	0.297***	0.322***	0.049*	0.069***
	(0.094)	(0.091)	(0.089)	(0.086)	(0.027)	(0.026)
Not from Lima	-0.360**	-0.346**	0.070	0.072	-0.023	-0.027
	(0.141)	(0.137)	(0.131)	(0.126)	(0.041)	(0.040)
Constant	6.270***	4.781***	3.651***	3.003***	1.151***	1.422***
	(0.573)	(0.568)	(0.527)	(0.516)	(0.160)	(0.161)
Observations	1,775	1,846	1,775	1,846	1,693	1,754
Log likelihood	-4,261.816	-4,418.246	-4,123.051	-4,265.717	-1,927.516	-2,018.082
Akaike Inf. Crit.	8,539.633	8,852.492	8,262.103	8,547.435	3,871.032	4,052.163

Note: Survey-weighted generalised linear models *$p < 0.1$; **$p < 0.05$; ***$p < 0.01$.

their eyes. But one participant did express hope. They did so with reference to the investigative effort: "I put down 'inspired/optimistic' because of the two prosecutors and the judge who could shed light on this" (Male, Young, C). In other words, a positive focus on the investigation can inspire hope. The relationship is less clear-cut when it comes to approval for the use of pretrial detentions (Models 2 and 4). This variable is significantly and positively associated with both negative and positive emotional reactions. One possible explanation is that what we are capturing here is not just the role of punitive measures in placating concerns about systemic malfunction and boosting hope in the possibility of political redemption, but also their role in channelling, and exacerbating, voters' anger vis-à-vis corrupt politicians.

Earlier we showed that at least since 2002, Peruvians tended to be quite pessimistic about the future of corruption. This reflects the deep roots of political cynicism in the country. In line with the conditional version of the optimistic narrative, regression analyses in Table 8.1 also show that crusades can potentially alter this gloomy outlook. A positive evaluation of the investigation can curb defeatist or cynical views. General satisfaction with the *Lava Jato* task force is associated with the view that corruption will get better over the next five years (Model 5).[4] Approval of pretrial detentions yields the same outcome (Model 6), providing evidence that the perceived effectiveness of the prosecutorial effort against corruption can contribute to curbing cynicism even in contexts with high baseline levels of political mistrust.

As we argued in Chapter 5, emotions such as hope or enthusiasm reflect and reinforce people's confidence in establishment institutions, actors, and processes. Unlike negative emotions, which open a wedge between voters and politics, positive emotions induce support for, and engagement with, a system that now seems perfectible rather than incorrigible. When faith is partially or temporarily restored, voters become more open to the possibility of giving accountability a chance. In other words, rather than withdrawing from politics or tolerating it as it is (corrupt), the response is to strengthen surveillance mechanisms and adopt tougher standards. After all, the judicial system is showing that checks and balances are not always futile; something of consequence can be done to combat malfeasance.

In a second set of models, we explore this possibility, that is, that renewed hope in politics reduces tolerance for corruption, using two alternative measures. Tolerance implies the "willingness to put up with something one rejects" (Sullivan et al. 1979: 784) and captures individuals' tendency to accept corruption as a fact of life and move on. Our first proxy comes from a question that asked respondents, "What would you be willing to do to fight against corruption?" and offered multiple response options. One of these was "Not vote for

---

[4] We coded the responses so that higher values indicate greater optimism: 1 = Increase, 2 = Stay the Same, 3 = Decrease. The results hold when we transform the variable into two dummies (Increase and Same/Decrease, Increase/Decrease and Same).

TABLE 8.2 *Emotions and tolerance for corruption*

	Dependent variable	
	Not vote for corrupt politicians	Better to keep quiet when encountering corruption
	(1)	(2)
Hopeful/enthusiastic	0.014***	−0.023**
	(0.005)	(0.009)
Angry/worried	−0.009*	−0.006
	(0.005)	(0.009)
Female	−0.010	−0.063
	(0.026)	(0.044)
Age	−0.0002	0.003
	(0.001)	(0.002)
Education	−0.009	−0.012
	(0.012)	(0.021)
Socio-economic status (8 levels)	0.013	−0.006
	(0.009)	(0.016)
Informed about politics	0.036**	−0.067**
	(0.017)	(0.031)
Not from Lima	0.023	0.090**
	(0.027)	(0.045)
Constant	0.393***	2.354***
	(0.112)	(0.193)
Observations	1,846	1,832
Log likelihood	−1,451.724	−2,418.721
Akaike Inf. Crit.	2,921.447	4,855.442

Note: Survey-weighted generalised linear models $^*p < 0.1$; $^{**}p < 0.05$; $^{***}p < 0.01$.

candidates or parties with a record of corruption." We used this to create a dichotomous variable in which a value of 1 indicates severity vis-à-vis corrupt politicians, and a value of 0 greater leniency or resignation. This measure is interesting because it captures tolerance in relation to voters' sense of efficacy. This is exactly how the optimistic narrative sees the relationship operating: a reduction in tolerance due to greater hope is a function of the fresh belief that it is indeed possible to do something about the problem. The second proxy we use is an ordinal variable that captures respondents' level of agreement with the following statement: "It is better to keep quiet when encountering corruption."

The results shown in Table 8.2 suggest our conjecture is at least plausible.[5] There is a substantively small but significant association between positive

[5] We find similar results if we replace emotions with satisfaction with the task force or support for pretrial detentions as the main independent variables. We think, however, that the specification in Table 8.2 is more in line with the implications derived from the argument in Chapter 5.

emotions about politics and tolerance for corruption. Specifically, those respondents that reported feeling more hopeful and/or enthusiastic tend to be, on average, less willing to vote for corrupt politicians and to keep quiet about corruption. When it comes to negative emotions, however, the results are less clear. There is a weak relationship (significant only at p-value < 0.1) between higher levels of anger and worry and expressing more tolerance for corruption, and there is no significant relationship between levels of negative emotions and the tendency to keep quiet.

Another way of exploring the relationship between crusades and tolerance for corruption is to see how *Lava Jato* impacts electoral choices in hypothetical races. As we argued in Chapter 5, political cynicism, which is often associated with higher tolerance for corruption, pushes corruption down the list of voters' priorities and makes it less likely that citizens will punish corrupt officials on the ballot (Fisman and Golden 2017; Pavão 2018). Optimists believe that by virtue of their visibility and zealous anti-corruption approach, the information released by prosecutorial task forces carries special weight at the polling station and disrupts this vicious cycle. Voters will no longer simply discount corruption out of cynicism (Pavão 2018) or assign less importance to it due to their many other policy and non-policy concerns. Quite the contrary – task forces make corruption a salient issue. Moreover, what prosecutors say is particularly credible. The result is that when a politician is handed an indictment, voters shift their preferences and electoral behaviour in a less lenient or acquiescent direction. And they do so to a greater extent than when they encounter similar information from other sources.

Our 2019 Peru survey included a conjoint experiment that among other things, varied the source of corruption allegations to evaluate how the *Lava Jato* task force impacts electoral choices. Conjoint experiments are a technique "for handling situations in which a decision maker has to deal with options that simultaneously vary across two or more attributes" (Green et al. 2001). They have become popular among political scientists[6] because they are useful to study multidimensional phenomena (e.g., voters' decision-making functions) or evaluate different hypotheses related to specific components of a treatment. Compared to other experimental designs, conjoints also have an advantage regarding the potential for social desirability bias (Wallander 2009). For instance, when making electoral decisions on the basis of stigmatised criteria, the presence of various attributes in a particular candidate profile gives respondents some degree of perceived anonymity and allows for multiple self-justifications, both of which lead to greater sincerity.

There are three main types of conjoint experiments: choice-based, rating-based, and ranking-based conjoints. Here we use a choice-based design. Respondents

---

[6] See, for example, Hainmueller and Hopkins (2015); Hainmueller et al. (2014); Carnes and Lupu (2016); Oliveros and Schuster (2018).

TABLE 8.3 *Attributes and levels for candidate conjoint*

Imagine that tomorrow there is a presidential election. We will show you the profiles of two hypothetical candidates, which we ask you to read carefully and then indicate which one you would vote for.

Age	35 years old
	45 years old
	65 years old
Gender	Male
	Female
Previous experience	None
	Was previously a mayor, but performance was poor
	Was previously a mayor, and performance was good
Where is the candidate from?	Lima
	Provinces
Candidate's stance on the role of the state in the economy	Believes that the state should have a bigger role in the economy
	Believes that the state should have a smaller role in the economy
Is there any accusation of corruption against the candidate?	There is no accusation of corruption against the candidate
	Has been accused of receiving S/. 20 million in exchange for public contracts
	Has been accused of receiving S/. 20 million (the equivalent to the annual salary of all the teachers in the country) in exchange for public contracts
	Has been accused of receiving S/. 20 million (the equivalent to three private planes) in exchange for public contracts
Source of the Accusation	The Prosecution
	The *Lava Jato* Team
	The Media
	*Does not apply (when the "accusation" attribute is set at the level of "There is no accusation against them")

were presented with a pair of candidate profiles and then asked to pick one. This was repeated several times so that by the end of the experiment each respondent had "voted" four times. For each profile in each round, we randomly varied candidate characteristics across seven dimensions or attributes (Table 8.3). In the analysis that follows we are interested in how two of these dimensions shape voting decisions: corruption accusation and the source of the accusation. While there are different types of accusations, we are only interested in whether the candidate was accused, and by whom.[7] The source of the accusation can be the

---

[7] We varied the type of accusation, that is, whether it is generic or points to more concrete costs of corruption, for another project (see Baraybar-Hidalgo 2020). The hypotheses that inspired this attribute are completely orthogonal to the argument developed in this book.

media, a generic prosecutor, or the *Lava Jato* team. This allows us to evaluate the added value of crusaders in shaping political behaviour.

There are both causal and descriptive interpretations of a conjoint experiment, which depend on the distribution of preferences across attributes and the difference in preferences across attribute combinations. Most analyses rely on either the Average Marginal Component Effect (AMCE) or Marginal Means (MM). The MM reflect the level of favourability towards a profile that has a particular attribute level, marginalising across all others. The AMCE is based on MM: it "is equivalent to the average marginal effect of each feature level for a model where each feature is converted into a matrix of indicator variables with one level left out as a reference category" (Leeper et al. 2020: 210). When profiles are randomised, the AMCE has causal interpretation, but it presents a problem for interpretation in subgroup analyses when "preferences between subgroups diverge in the reference category" (ibid.: 4). Though the AMCE is sometimes used to determine this kind of preference heterogeneity, it is not ideal for two main reasons. First, we cannot interpret causality in non-randomised features. Second, because the AMCE is highly dependent on the baseline/reference level used for each attribute, using it for subgroup analysis carries the risk of a certain subgroup having a particularly high or low preference for the reference category, which could skew the analysis. Consequently, when analysing our experiment, we use both the AMCE and MM, but for the subgroup analysis (especially in the second experiment – see next section) we rely exclusively on the MM. Importantly, because our two dimensions of interest in the candidate conjoint are mutually constrained in that there cannot be a source when there is no accusation, it is harder to interpret the AMCEs. This, however, can be easily solved if we look both at the MM and the AMCE of the attribute "Source."

Studies have shown that the source of corruption accusations can affect individuals' propensity to punish a politician (Botero et al. 2015; Breitenstein 2019). But do corruption accusations launched specifically by the *Lava Jato* task force reduce the likelihood that respondents will "vote" for a candidate? As we can see in Figure 8.2, the results show that when the accusation comes from this source, respondents are more likely to punish the fictional candidate by not voting for them. In this regard, it is worth noting that when the accusation comes from the "Media," this results in a marginal mean not statistically different from the grand mean. By contrast, being accused by the "*Lava Jato* team" leads to less favourability. It is also interesting that there is a difference between the favourability given to profiles in which the accusation comes from the "*Lava Jato* team" and those in which the accusation comes from a generic prosecutor. The difference is statistically significant at the 95 per cent level. Even though these are in essence accusations coming from the same institution, what the *Lava Jato* team says or does seems to carry more weight, perhaps making corruption more salient or the information more credible. We reach the same conclusion when looking at the AMCE of the attribute of "Source" in Figure 8.3. Here we use

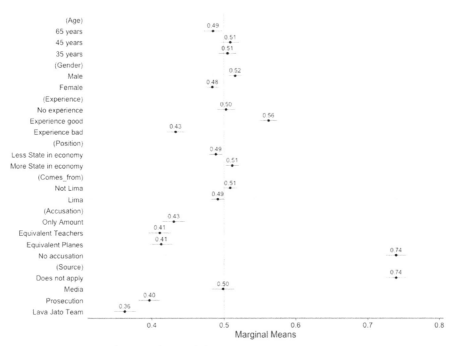

FIGURE 8.2 Marginal means for candidate conjoint
Note: Markers show marginal means – the average probability of a respondent choosing the candidate, averaged over all other treatment conditions. Whiskers represent 95 per cent confidence intervals.

"*Lava Jato* Team" as the baseline category to see whether an accusation coming from the "*Lava Jato* Team" leads respondents to punish a candidate more or less than when the accusation comes from the "Media" or the "Prosecution."

These results are interesting because they may in fact reflect voting behaviour in real world elections. For example, the legislative elections of January 2020, which summoned Peruvians to the polls to elect a new Congress following the inter-branch crisis described in Chapter 3, resulted in the unequivocal repudiation of all parties whose leaders were implicated in *Lava Jato*, including extreme fragmentation and historic abstention rates. Similar levels of anti-establishment voting and fragmentation were observed during the first round of the presidential election of April 2021. In fact, no candidate obtained more than 19 per cent of the valid votes. This meant the top two contenders, Pedro Castillo and Keiko Fujimori, had to compete in a run-off several weeks later, which Fujimori lost by a narrow margin.[8] Both candidates elicited high levels of

---

[8] Castillo is a leftist populist and outsider who comes from the interior of the country and who promised to overhaul Peru's market-friendly model of economic development.

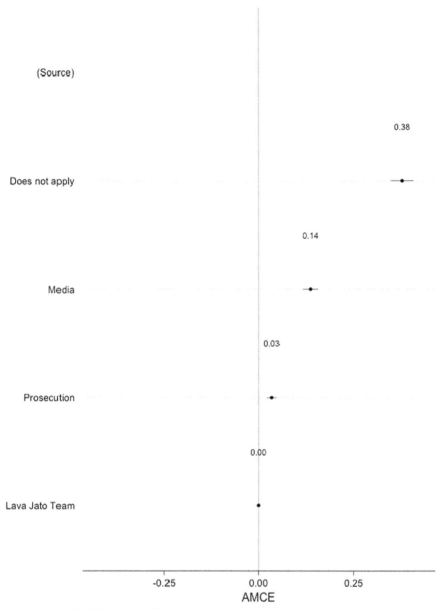

FIGURE 8.3 AMCEs for candidate conjoint, attribute "source of the accusation"
Note: Plot shows estimates of the effects of randomly assigned attribute "Source" values
on the probability that respondents choose a candidate with those characteristics.
Estimates are based on a benchmark OLS model and whiskers represent 95 per cent
confidence intervals. The absence of confidence intervals around an estimate indicates
that the attribute value is the reference category.

antipathy. Surveys suggest that *Lava Jato*, and corruption accusations more generally, may have been the single most important obstacle standing between Fujimori and the presidency. In May 2021, a survey company asked those who did not plan to vote for her (47 per cent of respondents), why they would never pick Fujimori. The vast majority, 62 per cent, cited the fact that "Fujimorismo represents corruption." When it came to Castillo, someone who was not implicated in *Lava Jato*, corruption did not feature among the key concerns cited by his detractors (35 per cent of respondents).[9]

Corruption undermines regime legitimacy (Rose-Ackerman 1999; Seligson 2002; Gingerich 2009) and erodes trust in institutions (Andersen and Tverdova 2003; Bowler and Karp 2004; Chang and Chu 2006; Morris and Klesner 2010). Due to their shock-like qualities, anti-corruption crusaders can come to the rescue, disrupting cynical equilibria, and changing behaviour and atti-tudes. The observational and experimental survey evidence presented thus far suggests that large-scale criminalisation efforts can indeed renew faith, even in contexts like Peru, where the reputation of political activity is dismal and voters exhibit very low levels of trust in their representatives and institutions. This disruptive potential is, of course, conditional on the degree of satisfaction that the prosecutorial effort induces in the electorate. Because of this, however, the disruption of the vicious cycle of cynicism can be quite precarious and short-lived. The prosecutorial methods that make crusades sooner or later prove controversial, scarring the legitimacy of the inquiry and its potential for build-ing broad support coalitions that transform attitudes towards politics in an optimistic direction. The next section provides more evidence of this precarity.

THE PRECARITY OF HOPE

Whereas voters' own biases and baseline attitudes towards politics, corruption, and institutions mediate their interpretations of anti-corruption crusades, and thus steer the narrative in more or less optimistic directions, contingent devel-opments also affect whether and how criminalisation efforts reinforce or curb cynicism. In particular, certain judicial and prosecutorial decisions taken during the course of the inquiry can complicate the relationship between crusaders and voters. As we discussed in Part I of the book, and again in Chapter 7 with reference to the *Vaza Jato* scandal in Brazil, prosecutors often gamble to push the investigation forward, redefining or defying the limits of what is strictly legal. For example, they sometimes filter information to the media to pre-empt attacks from powerful defendants or toy with unorthodox interpretations of criminal definitions that lower the burden of proof. They often also make extensive use of aggressive strategies like pretrial detentions, which make

---

[9] David Pereda, "Castillo incrementa su respaldo y Fujimori no consigue superarlo," *La Republica* (23 May 2021).

instant headlines and can incentivise defendants to cooperate. But gambling is dangerous. When legal imaginations run amok, controversial decisions are rejected on appeal, or high-profile media strategies are not perceived to be in line with the judicial role, prosecutors can easily haemorrhage the public support they need to keep going amidst numerous political constraints. If this happens, and voters lose faith in their putative saviours, the road back to cynicism is always around the corner.

When we conducted our survey in 2019, the *Lava Jato* task force was on a high, enjoying relatively high levels of support and inducing those who approved of the job it was doing to feel hopeful and enthusiastic. Fast forward a few months, and the situation had changed quite dramatically. To quote a former UK prime minister, "events, dear boy, events."

For instance, a public keen on revenge against a corrupt political class welcomed the flurry of pretrial detentions that characterised the Peruvian chapter of *Lava Jato* between 2016 and 2019. But the satisfaction derived from these measures was always bound to be short-lived. First, some pretrial detention orders quickly became embroiled in byzantine legal battles. This is because in some cases, prosecutors asked the courts to authorise daringly long prison terms (up to thirty-six months), arguing that the crimes in question required lengthy investigations and that defendants could engage in obstructionist shenanigans if set free. Appeals courts overturned or shortened a few of these, making it harder for the task force to quench the public's punitive thirst. Second, when the Covid-19 pandemic hit, some defendants successfully asked to be taken out of prison on health grounds and placed under house arrest. Among those released were César Villanueva (former mayor of San Martín and former prime minister, accused of having favoured Odebrecht in public tenders), Susana Villarán (former mayor of Lima, who confessed receiving campaign money from Odebrecht), Keiko Fujimori (investigated for money laundering and organised crime), Jaime Yoshiyama (Fujimori's aide and also investigated for money laundering), Rómulo Peñerada (investigated for receiving bribes to accelerate the construction of the Interoceanic Highway), and José Miguel Castro (Villarán's former aide). What proved particularly damaging was that many of these defendants were involved in the most publicly salient lines of inquiry. Compounding things further for the prosecution, these individuals were soon joined by others whose pretrial detention terms expired before the task force was able to send their cases to trial. The prosecutors requested extensions to keep them in jail, but they were not always successful. Most of the pretrial detention orders that are still in force at the time of writing are due to expire, meaning that if the investigative phase does not end in time, there could soon be very few allegedly corrupt politicians in prison.

Although the use of pretrial detentions was probably what most contributed to the image of *Lava Jato* as an effective tool against systemic corruption, it can also be what ends up re-enforcing pre-existing levels of cynicism. Pretrial detentions gave prosecutors unprecedented salience, helped engineer momentum by neutralising obstructionist moves, and allowed them to extract a few valuable confessions. The strategy thus helped curb the widespread view that nothing of consequence can be done to rein in politicians' worst instincts. But as voters watch the spectacle in reverse, seeing politicians leave the prisons en masse, they are likely to scent once again the smell of betrayal and futility. This kind of developments are in many ways part and parcel of any criminal investigation. It is therefore hard to fault the task force for inflating expectations excessively. Other developments, however, could have probably been avoided as they dealt equally serious blows to the tenuously optimistic narrative that was emerging around the investigation.

Most notably, on 10 November 2020, Congress removed President Martin Vizcarra from office. As we discussed in Chapter 3, parliamentarians did so based on rather dubious arguments, invoking the notion of "permanent moral incapacity." This happened after journalists published information about an ongoing plea bargain negotiation that had the potential to implicate the president in *Lava Jato*. For most observers it was clear that the leak came from the task force. After Vizcarra left office, Manuel Merino, leader of Congress, took over but not without controversy. Both the impeachment and Merino's promotion triggered huge demonstrations under the motto "it wasn't an impeachment; it was a coup!" The excessive use of force against the protestors left two dead and thousands injured, forcing Merino to resign on 15 November. Because the rumours that gave Congress the excuse to get rid of Vizcarra had allegedly come from the *Lava Jato* task force, the prosecutors had a lot to answer for. They had suddenly become an accessory not only to the impeachment of a president, but also to what was widely seen as a violent power grab. In fact, most Peruvians believed that the prosecutors acted wrongly when they filtered classified information to the press. In a survey conducted by IPSOS in November 2020, 70 per cent of respondents believed that the prosecutors were at fault.[10] This naturally led to a decline in overall levels of support for the task force. In December of 2020, another IPSOS poll found that 39 per cent of respondents were satisfied with the *Lava Jato* team, while 49 per cent disapproved.[11] This must have come as a shock to the prosecutors, who just one year earlier enjoyed sky-high approval ratings (72 per cent according to IPSOS).[12] In other words, in twelve months the task force's approval went down 33 percentage points among the same citizenry that, as we saw in Chapter 3, came out strongly to support them in January 2019 when the powers that be tried to remove the leaders of the task force. Prosecutors clearly overplayed their hand.

All of this points to how fragile the optimism surrounding crusades can be. Political cynicism is hard to curb, and pessimism can quickly resurface as soon

---

[10] See www.ipsos.com/sites/default/files/ct/news/documents/2020-11/od_noviembre_2020.pdf
[11] See www.ipsos.com/sites/default/files/ct/news/documents/2021-01/6981220inf_v1_16dic20.pdf
[12] "Según IPSOS, el 72% de peruanos aprueba el desempeño del equipo especial *Lava Jato*," *Caretas* (16 October 2019).

as the prosecution makes any real or perceived mistake. Social psychology tells us that predispositions affect how people respond to new stimuli, since people usually "arrive at those conclusions they want to arrive at" (Kunda 1990: 495). People are also more likely to recall information when it confirms their preconceptions (Taber and Lodge 2006). In this sense, previous studies have found that prior levels of cynicism affect how individuals interpret information (Blais et al. 2010). It is therefore very likely that in places like Peru, where voters' priors strongly suggest that politics is irredeemably corrupt, the pitfalls of prosecutorial zeal quickly reinforce the default position that nothing of consequence can be done to curb corruption, that one should not be fooled by the occasional accountability mirage. This return to cynicism can be the result of unmet expectations. Indeed, the public can derive unrealistically high expectations, for example, from pretrial detentions. But it can also be the result of high stakes gambles that backfire.

There is another aspect of the Peruvian inquiry that also proved highly controversial and likely did not help the construction of a robust and enduring sense of satisfaction with the task force. The local chapter of *Lava Jato* was highly dependent on a corporate leniency agreement with Odebrecht. This formalised an unprecedented information-sharing mechanism that allowed the task force to obtain the incriminating evidence it needed to move forward with various lines of inquiry. In exchange, the prosecutors granted impunity to Odebrecht executives, allowed the company to continue contracting the state, and imposed a large fine, but one due in relatively generous instalments. Importantly, should prosecutors discover that the company did not confess everything, the deal does not automatically become void but can be reopened to incorporate new crimes. As we discussed in Chapter 3, these concessions triggered criticisms from jurists and politicians. In fact, during the first round of the 2021 presidential race, some of the candidates questioned the constitutionality of the deal.[13] Immediately after the election, Congress announced an investigation to determine the legality of the agreement.

The focus group data discussed in Chapter 6 showed that this type of deal can prove unpopular with the public. Participants were not at all happy with trade-off between "truth and justice," whereby prosecutors refrain from criminalising certain individuals to collect the evidence they need to go after others. In voters' eyes, this amounts to condoning corruption and confirms their cynical view that the privileged and powerful can get away with the most serious forms of wrongdoing. Peruvians' unwillingness to compromise, especially when leniency became a key pillar of the prosecutorial strategy, most certainly added to the precarity of any goodwill the task force was able to generate during the first three years of the crusade.

---

[13] See, for example, "Justicia y corrupción: Compromiso electoral," *La República* (17 March 2021).

To further investigative citizens' willingness to compromise to obtain the evidence that can fuel the anti-corruption crusade, we turn to a second conjoint experiment. Precisely because the deal with Odebrecht included compromises on a variety of fronts or dimensions, this technique allows us to dive deeper into the types of concessions voters are happy to accept. Put differently, we can get a good sense of whether some areas of the deal prove more or less controversial, giving prosecutors the opportunity to protect the legitimacy of their actions, for example, by emphasising those aspects of the deal in the press and downplaying the others. Our use of conjoint analysis to explore preferences for different kinds of deals closely resembles the longstanding use of these experiments in marketing research, where the goal is to explore how product characteristics affect consumer choices.

We presented respondents with four pairs of hypothetical cooperation agreements and asked them to select the one they preferred the most. In each round of "voting," we randomly varied the characteristics of the competing deals across five dimensions (Table 8.4): the amount of the fine imposed on the company; the payment scheme; the amount of jail time for Odebrecht

TABLE 8.4 *Attributes and levels for cooperation agreement conjoint*

In order to investigate corruption cases that implicate political leaders, authorities sometimes sign cooperation agreements with the companies responsible for paying bribes. The authorities agree to a series of benefits in exchange for information. The company also pays a fine as a form of reparation. Imagine you have to decide between the following deals with a company that paid bribes that cost Peru around S/600 million. Which one would you prefer? The agreements have the following characteristics:	
Jail Time	No jail time
	Only 1 year
	Only 3 years
Fine	S./ 400 million
	S./ 600 million
	S./ 800 million
Payment Scheme	In instalments until 2028 so that the company does not go bankrupt and can continue providing information
	In instalments until 2023 so that the company does not go bankrupt and can continue providing information
	In one instalment in 2019, even if the company goes bankrupt and stops providing information.
Is the company allowed to continue contracting with the state?	Yes
	No
What happens if new crimes are discovered to which the company did not originally confess?	The company does not lose the benefits and cooperation continues
	The company loses the benefits and cooperation ends.

executives; whether or not the company will be allowed to continue bidding for public works contracts; and the provisions indicating what will happen if prosecutors subsequently discover that the company withheld information. Attribute levels vary the degree of severity of the deal, ranging from very permissive to very punitive agreements. To avoid bias in favour of punitivism, we made clear the trade-offs involved in choosing some deals over others. We chose the attributes on the basis of a review of the aspects of the deal most discussed in the press, as well as the testimonies gathered during elite interviews and focus groups.

The first step to evaluate voters' willingness to compromise was to calculate the AMCE for each level of the attributes of hypothetical cooperation agreements. Recall the AMCE represents the effect of a single attribute level compared to the baseline of that attribute while averaging over the possible combinations of the remaining attributes, or "the marginal effect of attribute X averaged over the joint distribution of the remaining attributes" (Hainmueller et al. 2014). For example, in our conjoint, the AMCEs for the levels of the attribute "Payment Scheme" represent the average effect of each attribute level on the probability that respondents prefer that agreement, taking "in instalments until 2028" as the baseline. The average is defined by the distribution of preferences over other attributes (except for the attribute level in question) across repeated samples. As mentioned before, the AMCE is highly dependent on the baseline category used for each attribute. In the case of "Payment Scheme" the AMCE of the level "one instalment in 2019" is calculated relative to the baseline of "in instalments until 2028," and so on. For ease of interpretation, our baselines are at the least punitive levels: no jail time, a 400 million fine, payment in instalments until 2028, authorisation to continue contracting with the state, no consequences if new crimes are discovered. If the different levels of an attribute do not produce differences in the probability of the agreement being chosen relative to the baseline, it can be interpreted as indicative of voter indifference vis-à-vis concessions on that dimension.

The results in Figure 8.4 suggest that respondents are very demanding and not willing to compromise. The most favoured agreement is one in which the fine is the highest (S./800 million); the company is forbidden from participating in future public tenders; and the executives spend the longest time in prison. While voters are willing to accept a delay in the payment (2028 vs 2019), they strongly favour recovering the money (with an extra S./ 200 million thrown in). When it comes to the attribute "Jail Time," deals with one or three years in jail are more popular than deals that spare the executives of time in prison (the baseline category). Finally, in terms of allowing the company to continue doing business in the country, voters strongly prefer a deal in which Odebrecht packs its bags and leaves. It is worth noting the most favoured deal in the conjoint is a very different deal from the one that was actually signed: S./610 million in fines, payment in instalments until 2034, no jail time, and green light to contract with

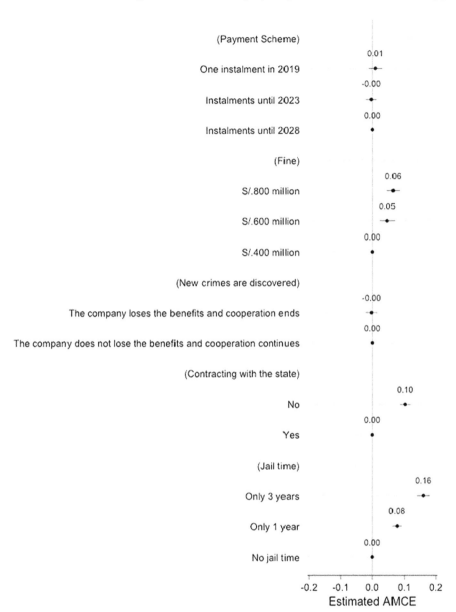

FIGURE 8.4 AMCEs for cooperation agreement conjoint
Note: Plot shows estimates of the effects of randomly assigned attribute values on the probability that respondents choose a cooperation agreement with those characteristics. Estimates are based on a benchmark OLS model and whiskers represent 95 per cent confidence intervals. The absence of confidence intervals around an estimate indicates that the attribute value is the reference category.

the state in the future. If voters had been put in charge of the negotiations, the agreement would not exist (at least not in its current form) and Peru's *Lava Jato* would look very different.

There is, however, one dimension of the hypothetical agreement that generates relative indifference: whether the deal is allowed to stand in the event that the prosecutors discover the company withheld information. This could be due to the framing of the two attribute levels: we indicated quite clearly what the consequences of the more severe option would be for the investigation (i.e., no more cooperation). We did this for "Payment Scheme" too, noting the implications of bankruptcy, and this also seems to have elicited acceptance of trade-offs on that dimension. Indifference regarding what should happen in the event of new information is also likely a function of the relative importance respondents gave to that aspect of the deal. In the Peruvian context, this is good news for the prosecutors because immediately after the deal was signed, evidence surfaced that the company had in fact not told everything it knew about the bribery scheme. This led to fierce criticisms of the agreement at a time when it was still being scrutinised by the courts and was not yet official. The prosecutors were therefore forced to publicly explain why it was important that the information-sharing framework had some in-built flexibility to deal with the snowball effect that characterises crusades. These explanations may have carried some weight.[14]

Our analysis in this section shows how hard it can be for anti-corruption crusaders to keep the public on their side. On the one hand, voters want everyone to pay and are quite unwilling to accept compromises when it comes to crucial negotiations with Odebrecht. Because the prosecution has to grant these concessions to make progress, concessions for which the public seems to have little tolerance, prosecutorial success via punitive selectivity can generate more problems than it solves in terms of legitimacy. This preference for punitivism means that voters were also likely to feel disappointment when one pretrial detention order after another started to expire. That too poses problems for the prosecutors. On the other hand, voters are not willing to accept every prosecutorial move that leads to punitive outcomes. The task force's loss of support in the weeks following Vizcarra's impeachment suggests that much. In other words, crusaders face a tough balancing act as they can be doomed if they do and doomed if they don't.

---

[14] In the Appendix we explore whether levels of approval for the *Lava Jato* task force, as well as beliefs about which actors (politicians or businessmen) are more responsible for corruption, condition support for these trade-offs. We find that these underlying attitudes introduce little heterogeneity in deal preferences. This reinforces our argument that prosecutors indeed faced an uphill battle. The Appendix can be found on http://www.narapavao.com/book.html

CONCLUSION

Systemic corruption and impunity nurture political cynicism, which can feed on itself, deepening tolerance for corruption, disengagement from public life, and a deep sense of futility. In this chapter we showed that a more optimistic outlook is possible as a result of anti-corruption crusades, even in a context like Peru, where this is in principle a very unlikely outcome given the extremely high baseline levels of mistrust in politics and institutions. Our analysis of observational survey data suggests that satisfaction with crusaders is related to optimism about the future. What people seem to like about these processes is not just that they execute a vengeance with a focus on the past, but also that they can do something quite concrete to change reality going forward. Task force satisfaction is also associated with stronger positive (and weaker negative) emotions, which in turn seem to be associated with a tougher stance vis-à-vis corruption. Through these emotion-driven cognitive processes, we argued, task forces can awaken the promise of accountability through elections.

But the chapter also highlighted the precarity of these trends. In particular, we offered additional support for the idea that the nature of these crusades often conceals the seeds of their own destruction. This is the key paradox at the heart of the book. There is a constant dialectic between the positive and negative implications of prosecutorial zeal that makes outcomes extremely uncertain and jeopardises the pro-social effects of criminalisation. Crusades trigger snowball effects that reveal systemic corruption, but this makes the process extremely protracted, which opens room for error and for unexpected events to derail the process. Crusaders also face difficult choices, which they often solve with great ingenuity, but creativity can open the door for severe criticisms that compromise the construction of the myth of legality. The latter, as we know, depends on the credible projection of the values of fairness and effectiveness. This dialectic leaves the message of anti-corruption crusades regarding the likely trajectory of politics at the mercy of people's divergent interpretations. At the end of the day, prosecutors are forced to accept a rather bleak fate, one in which they can hardly please anyone, not even their most obvious supporters, and in which they are bound to make one fatal mistake that puts an end to the impetus for change.

PART III

CONCLUSIONS

9

Theoretical Lessons and a Normative Assessment

INTRODUCTION

As we wrote this final chapter it was becoming increasingly clear that *Lava Jato*, the most ambitious attempt to criminalise corruption in the history of Latin America, stood on shaky grounds. In countries like Mexico and Argentina, where the inquiry never really took off, there were no signs of a change in direction. In more successful Peru, the Covid-19 pandemic put a break on prosecutorial efforts, slowing down the progress of what was already a rather embattled investigation. While prosecutors did manage to wrap up important streams of the inquiry, most notably those against Keiko Fujimori and Ollanta Humala, their zeal appeared more subdued after becoming embroiled in the scandals described in Chapters 3 and 8. In addition, despite important changes in the make-up of Congress following the 2021 elections and ongoing political instability, politicians continued with their attempts to weaken the prosecution services.[1] Similarly, Brazil's STF little by little dismantled the investigation conducted in Curitiba. Most notably, in March 2021 it declared that Judge Moro had not acted impartially and annulled the case against former president Lula Da Silva. Lula subsequently decided to mount a comeback by running for president in 2022. With Dallagnol's departure from the prosecutorial task force and Moro's decision to enter politics, first as minister of justice under Bolsonaro and then as a failed presidential candidate, there was little left of the team that managed to transform the initial allegations into a crusade.

---

[1] For instance, in February 2022 legislators in the Justice and Human Rights Committee gave green light to a bill intended to weaken incentives for witnesses to enter plea bargains. At the time of writing, the bill had not yet been voted on. See "Colaboración eficaz: Todo sobre los cambios planteados por el Congreso," *Agencia Andina* (23 February 2022).

These developments notwithstanding, the scars left by *Lava Jato* in both politics and society will be felt for a long time across the region: the case paralysed economies, destroyed presidencies, and changed the course of key elections. It also spurred important debates about what the boundaries of legal possibility ought to be when it comes to attacking corruption, and by implication, how much corruption we are willing to tolerate in the name of democracy, stability, and the rule of law. Our book offers insights to better understand why such an unprecedented anti-corruption drive was possible in the first place, and why both the inquiry and the institutions responsible for it became the subject and object of intense political battles. This chapter takes stock of our analysis of the causes and public opinion consequences of *Lava Jato*. It also evaluates crusades as an anti-corruption approach considering the evidence presented thus far.

To anticipate our normative conclusions, we disagree with those who see crusades as inherently bad for democracy because they destabilise politics and tend to fall short of uprooting corruption. Democracy cannot function properly when corruption is systemic. Something needs to be done and crusades do offer some promise. They may not fully eliminate corruption (how could they?), but they do have the potential to change the structure of incentives that political elites face and help identify what reforms are more urgent. We particularly disagree with those who see crusades as inherently bad for democracy on the basis that they are the product of the weaponisation of law enforcement by politicians. As we showed in Part I, this is not what produced our crusades, or at least not the only variable at play. Investigators were for the most part autonomous actors. Finally, crusades are not inherently bad for democracy in that they sometimes do instil hope in the electorate, as some of the evidence in Part II suggests, thus fulfilling the laudable accountability preferences of many voters. The fact that "coalitions of the hopeful" are usually precarious and short-lived should encourage us to think hard about how to improve criminalisation as an anti-corruption tool rather than do away with it altogether.

Having said this, we also disagree with those who see crusades as inherently good for democracy. Crusades are not always perfectly aligned with all the values needed to uphold and fortify democracy. For example, when trying to gain momentum and fend off attacks, prosecutors often cross certain lines and develop animosity against specific defendants. Furthermore, apart from offering no guarantees that the crusade will turn out to be a bona fide accountability effort, prosecutors also trigger unintended consequences. It is especially true that if not managed properly, snowballing investigations trigger problematic dynamics at the level of public opinion, leading to division and/or disenchantment with the methods and outputs of anti-corruption. In this sense, one key lesson is that prosecutorial zeal is not enough for crusaders to make productive contributions to democratic politics. They obviously need to show determination to fight corruption and mobilise much needed support, but prosecutors also need to make sure their zeal does not antagonise key constituencies, that is, that it does not appear as excessive or out of line with what is expected from them as professionals of the law. For this reason, we end the chapter with a call to "norm" the kind of zeal at the heart of anti-corruption crusades so that it may not produce these negative externalities.

MAIN FINDINGS AND LESSONS

In Part I we explored the conditions that explain why and how seemingly minor corruption revelations sometimes become crusades. We argued against Manichaean and voluntaristic interpretations. Rather than reducing cases like *Lava Jato* to a naked clash between partisan factions in a polity, or to a weapon manipulated by spurious interest groups against their rivals, we ought to take the autonomous dynamics of the legal process seriously. In particular, it is necessary to understand how the prosecutorial zeal and savoir faire that is on display in these unusual episodes of corruption criminalisation come to exist and are activated. How does a group of rank-and-file prosecutors (and occasionally judges) gain the space, motivation, and tools to defy powerful voices in the political and criminal justice establishments?

Our argument is that crusades are anchored in long-term processes of institutional and organisational change that affect primarily the prosecution services, producing greater levels of political insulation and specialisation via bureaucratic differentiation, as well as more robust legal frameworks to tackle white-collar criminality. But we also draw attention to more short-term factors that we referred to as "moments" during an inquiry: the moments of serendipity, agency, and backlash. These "moments" underscore how difficult it is to investigate corruption from an evidentiary and political perspective, even under the right institutional conditions, and the contingency that characterises the process. The story of our "moments" also points to the role of more tactical (rather than structural) organisational factors, namely the creation of dedicated task forces, in unleashing the forces of innovation and mutual protection that propel investigations forward and make them so controversial.

This argument contains a few lessons that travel beyond anti-corruption crusades. The main theoretical implication relates to how we think about the processes whereby robust institutions, that is, ones that do what they are designed to do, come about. We know that Latin America and other developing regions are characterised, simultaneously, by grand promises of institutional overhaul (Botero et al. 2022) and by acute institutional weakness in the form of deficient enforcement and low durability (Levitsky and Murillo 2005, 2009; Brinks et al. 2019, 2020). This generates myriad problems for effective policy-making, economic development, and democratic quality (O'Donnell 1993; Helmke and Levitsky 2006; Spiller and Tommasi 2007; Bersch 2019; Brinks et al. 2019, 2020). But we also know that most state apparatuses are rarely monolithically Weberian, irredeemably politicised, or utterly ineffective (Metz-McDonnell 2017). In this sense, our book joins a body of scholarship that is more preoccupied with understanding the drivers of this heterogeneity or how to improve institutional landscapes, than with identifying failure (Dargent 2014; Praça and Taylor 2014; Michel 2018a; Bersch 2019; Mayka 2019; Rich 2019).

Like some colleagues, for instance, we showed that gains in institutional strength can be achieved incrementally through various waves of reform, rather than through radical change, or what Bersch (2019) calls "powering." In so doing, we explored endogenous determinants of interstices of bureaucratic autonomy in Latin American prosecution services (Dargent 2014; Praça and Taylor 2014; Rich 2019). To be sure, the construction of pockets of institutional strength for policymaking and implementation (in our case, for the investigation of white-collar criminality) is sometimes aided by macro-political conditions as well as by inputs from international and domestic civil society (Michel 2018a; Mayka 2019). In this book, however, we emphasised internal processes of organisational differentiation within relevant units of the state as a possible complementary route to institutional strength.

In line with DiMaggio and Powell (1983), we looked at the role of ideas and models within an organisational field in determining the outputs of public administration. At a point of critical intervention (Domhoff 1979), for example, when prosecutorial reforms are first implemented, certain models of organisation and policymaking are introduced. With time, these models become institutional templates that constrain the range of available or appropriate choices for actors within the organisation when they confront new challenges (DiMaggio and Powell 1983). Crucial from our point of view was the adoption of models of bureaucratic specialisation and teamwork to tackle certain types of criminal behaviour. This was important for two reasons. First, the kind of specialisation we documented in Brazil, Peru, and Ecuador favoured the professionalisation of cohorts within the prosecution services, modifying their skills and commitment to certain causes, and creating professional networks across which models, ideas, and values diffused rapidly. Second, when the moment of serendipity in the *Lava Jato* case came about, in those countries where these practices had taken root prosecutors adopted a previously legitimated institutional form to rise to the challenge: the task force model. This model was an extension of the type of bureaucratic differentiation some among the rank and file had become attached to and from which they now derived their professional identity. We then showed that the tactical decision to work in small groups allowed prosecutors to engineer the moment of agency and sometimes navigate the moment of backlash.

A key conclusion in this regard is that what matters for the prosecution services to "bite" is not so much their formal independence from politics. Reality rarely approximates this ideal, even after serious reform efforts. For example, the connections between senior prosecutors and politicians are hard to sever in full (of course, doing so can be problematic in other ways). Moreover, incentives are never perfectly aligned to encourage productivity.

Instead, what can prove truly consequential is fostering specialisation because this modifies knowledge endowments, boosts the willingness and capacity to innovate, and enables mechanisms of boundary control that preserve interstices of autonomy (Metz-McDonnell 2017). In other words, organisational differentiation emerges as a plausible way of operationalising the kind of institutional strength promised "on the books."

Another mechanism supporting the effective operationalisation of formal institutional duties that we did not explore or theorise directly in this book, but which is implied throughout, is international diffusion. The book thus resembles work showing how state agents become better at enforcing their legally defined missions through transborder learning via professional networks and emulation (Bennett 1991; Weyland 2005, 2009; Braun and Gilardi 2006; Shipan and Volden 2008, 2012; Sugiyama 2012). In this sense, part of our story of institutional change revolved around the legal translation of fledging international anti-corruption norms. Although assessing the means via which this took place was not our goal, the case studies showed that domestic actors sometimes adopted legal templates attempting to gain international legitimacy (Meyer et al. 1997) or to demonstrate their adherence to emerging professional norms (Sugiyama 2012) in the judicial field. Imitation was also accompanied by pressures from international organisations (Simmons 2001), which conditioned access to exclusive clubs such as the OECD on reform implementation.

This transnational process sharpened the section of criminal codes dedicated to white-collar criminality, established clearer channels for penal cooperation, and legitimised the use of prosecutorial selectivity via leniency agreements. These changes helped catalyse anti-corruption crusades. But when it came to putting new missions into practice, there was another, perhaps more relevant diffusion channel. Anti-corruption crusades had a way of influencing each other. One way was through information-sharing agreements, which we showed were critical for the (positive *and* negative) fates of *Lava Jato* outside Brazil. In addition, because some crusades were so "eventful" (Sewell 1996) in the countries where they took place, they gained nothing short of iconic status, serving as models for others to emulate elsewhere. Put differently, they became vivid examples of how to deploy the anti-corruption toolkit available "on the books," carving out clear paths to success in what are otherwise complex, indeterminate, and risky investigations. For instance, Moro told the world in no uncertain terms that he had studied and learnt from Mani Pulite (Moro 2004, 2018). Peruvian prosecutors in the early 2000s also based legal and organisational innovations that enabled the criminalisation of Fujimori's corruption on lessons they took from the Italian case (Dargent 2005). Similarly, when *Lava Jato* landed on their dockets a decade and a half later, they emulated the Brazilians. In short, institutions bite, that is, they gain strength, when there are readily available actionable templates that articulate what strength means in practice. Those templates may be home grown, but they often travel across frontiers.

Our analysis of the sources of prosecutorial effectiveness has one further implication for contemporary debates about institutions in comparative politics. Institution building can fail because what is promised in law does not correlate with what happens in reality. This is the problem that concerns scholars of Latin America the most (Brinks et al. 2020). But problems can also arise when institutional strength goes into overdrive. In some cases, this triggers questions about democratic legitimacy, especially if it facilitates rule by insulated technocrats (Caramani 2017) or if the rigidity and stability of certain institutional arrangements obstructs adaptation to new citizen demands.[2] In others, like during the debates around *Lava Jato*, institutional strength made apparent the trade-offs between competing societal goals: how much accountability via stronger prosecutorial institutions is compatible with political stability, the rule of law, and competitive elections? During *Lava Jato* there were several "beware what you wish for" moments. These arose precisely because task forces were doing exactly what they had been empowered to do by long-term institution building and more immediate bureaucratic mandates. The issue here seems to be as follows. One thing is to empower accountability agencies in Denmark, where if they work well, they are not bound to ravage politics. Quite another is to build similar institutions in contexts of systemic corruption, where if they work half as well, they may end up crashing into reality in a spectacular and dangerous fashion. In this sense, our analysis of both the backlash that prosecutorial zeal invited and of the impact of crusades on voters suggests that there is more than one side to the noble aspiration of building robust institutions. And, by implication, that processes of institution building ought to carefully consider what kinds of improvements "really existing democracies" can support (see also Botero et al. 2022). In the final section of this chapter, we take on this question in more detail, thinking about how it might be possible to balance prosecutorial effectiveness in pursuing serious crimes that damage societies in incalculable ways, with those other competing goals.

In Part II of the book, we shifted gears to study how the public reacts to anti-corruption. Voters' attitudes towards large-scale criminalisation condition the ultimate impact of crusades on politics, not least because prosecutors depend on citizens to build broad, engaged, and stable coalitions to maintain momentum and resist backlash. We presented two stylised prognoses: an optimistic narrative that expects crusades to project a message of possible regeneration, and therefore instil hope in a new form of politics, and a pessimistic one in which crusades tell an all too familiar story of political decay that reinforces cynicism or creates deep fault lines around the merits of anti-corruption.

No one likes corruption, which is why most citizens welcome crusades, at least in principle. But when prosecutors make extensive use of criminalisation

---

[2] Murillo et al. (2021: 11–12) cite Chile's 1980 constitution as an example of a strong institution increasingly at odds with changing popular demands, and therefore one that exacerbates political conflict instead of helping to process it in an orderly manner.

prerogatives, their efforts do not guarantee the emergence of a strong consensus around anti-corruption. A number of factors shape public reactions. First, it matters whether citizens fixate on the crimes revealed during the process, and therefore experience a negative information shock, or also pay attention to the proposed judicial solution to the problem of corruption. We showed that the general orientation of the public narrative is possibly a function of the media environment, as well as of pre-existing levels of cynicism and trust in the judiciary's capacity as an anti-corruption agent. Second, evaluations of crusaders' fairness and effectiveness determine the credibility of the myth of legality upon which the activation of the mechanisms of system satisfaction associated with the optimistic story rests. Partisanship is one key correlate of these evaluations. But prosecutorial behaviour matters too because of the controversial nature of the investigative tactics deployed in these cases. For instance, selectivity disappoints those with more uncompromising views regarding punitive trade-offs. The inevitable tensions between prosecutorial zeal and due process are bound to sound similar alarm bells, including among non-partisan observers.

We started this project with strong optimistic priors, but gradually came to realise these crusades can be quite problematic. Indeed, our empirical analyses indicate that the outcomes anticipated by the optimistic story can only be obtained under a limited set of circumstances. And even if hope does materialise, it tends to be quite precarious and hardly ever majoritarian. This seems to be the case, first, because crusades almost always end up painting a picture of corruption that has the potential to alienate voters from politics. To restate a comparison used earlier, when you apply this kind of prosecutorial zeal in Peru or Brazil, the result is very different than when you do it Denmark or Sweden: prosecutors are bound to uncover a rotten political class rather than a few bad apples that voters can repudiate selectively. As a result, crusades ravage political systems leaving massive legitimacy voids, with voters perceiving a lack of credible options. This is, of course, more likely in contexts like Peru, where feelings of political alienation already run deep, and a crusade, no matter how effective or ambitious, is not enough to alter a generalised state of disaffection. While we did identify some signs of hope taking root in Peru, especially in the survey data explored in Chapter 8, in the end voters did not fundamentally update their pessimistic views about politics. Instead, the crusade seems to have hardened those priors, possibly due to perceived prosecutorial failures. The historic levels of abstention and fragmentation in the legislative and presidential elections of 2020 and 2021 are perhaps an indication that this is indeed what happened.

A second reason why hope is always precarious and never majoritarian is that the zeal that propels crusades forward, while initially hailed, eventually disappoints and divides. We saw this more clearly in Brazil, where politics is polarised to a greater extent than in Peru. As the inquiry progressed, it inevitably triggered controversies that split public opinion. In this kind of context, politicians who choose to cry foul or denounce "lawfare" as a defensive reaction do not struggle to find an audience ready to buy that argument. To be sure, other voters may still derive a lot of pleasure from seeing figures of hate parading through the courts and accept (or celebrate) audacious prosecutorial moves grounded in anti-political rhetoric. But this optimism or sense of satisfaction develops in the shadow of greater scepticism about institutions among rival groups. And because divides deepen, the response of those who find in the crusade a reason for hope may be to look for electoral options that hardly promise a constructive re-engagement with democratic politics, but a more radical, anti-system solution (think Jair Bolsonaro). Indeed, as Hagopian (2016) convincingly argues, the promise of greater accountability in Brazil, and the high expectations that came with it, increased the vulnerability of institutional channels of representation, especially established political parties.

Our findings add to the study of corruption and public opinion in three ways. First, we showed it is possible to explore the attitudinal impact of complex socio-legal phenomena if we accept that we will not ever find a silver bullet that definitively probes changes in mass attitudes, and instead rely on a combination of imperfect but complementary empirical approaches. In this regard, the study is quite unique in that it combined comparative evidence from focus groups, observational survey data, and experiments. Crucially, the results presented in each chapter became more interpretable when read in light of those reported in the others.

Second, the analysis recovered the concept of "political cynicism" and took seriously the role of emotions to understand how voters experience real world corruption and its antidotes. This allowed us to explore a more subterranean attitudinal layer that is overlooked when scholars focus exclusively on how corruption affects voting behaviour. In particular, we sought to describe how crusades shape voters' hope, enthusiasm, worry, or anger, and through these emotions, their visions about the future of politics. We paid particular attention to whether positive emotional reactions, and a concomitant renewed sense of possibility, trumped the feelings of futility and political inefficacy that are deeply ingrained in many Latin Americans. While we did find some evidence indicating that *Lava Jato*, in its most credible formulation, triggers positive emotions (or at least dampens negative ones), and thus induces lower levels of political cynicism and tolerance for corruption, this relationship is precarious and highly conditional. Our conclusion that cynicism most likely deepens when voters experience crusades, either because crusades eventually confirm individuals' negative priors about the nature of politics or because judicial efforts almost invariably prove to be unconvincing attempts to eradicate corruption, offers new perspectives on the vexing puzzle of why corruption considerations do not seem to carry much weight in voting decisions. In particular, if even these unprecedented shocks are unable to convince voters that a future in which politics is less corrupt is within the realm of possibility, that rule of law institutions are not bound to be weaponised for political gain, or that courts and prosecutors are not necessarily ineffective in their accountability mission, why should people bother with corruption?

Relatedly, a third contribution was to describe the complicated relationship that horizontal accountability efforts can have with public opinion. Ambitious corruption prosecutions need the public to succeed. Our crusaders were painfully aware of this and thought, perhaps naively, that the masses, which in poll after poll seem nominally concerned about corruption and demand a solution, would not hesitate to offer their backing. They soon found out that it would be very hard, if not impossible, to maintain this support. Even the most media savvy prosecutors eventually stumbled upon exacting publics. In particular, our various empirical probes suggest that far from galvanising the public against corruption, crusades turned corruption from a valence issue into something that is deeply politicised. This is intimately related to the nature of horizontal accountability via anti-corruption crusades, which introduces tensions between rule of law aspirations and rule of law methods, competes with voters' partisan loyalties, and ultimately yields uncertain results.

ASSESSING ANTI-CORRUPTION CRUSADES

This book intervenes in debates about best practices in the fight against corruption. As we noted in Chapter 1, scholars and practitioners are divided between those who champion prevention and those who favour enforcement. Anti-corruption crusades are, we argued, a type of enforcement "on steroids." After exploring the conditions that give rise to these efforts, as well as their broader societal reception, we are in a position to end the book with an evaluation of their merits and shortcomings, and to think of ways in which they could be improved in order to ensure more satisfactory outcomes. In particular, how can these efforts be "normed" so that they become less controversial and more compatible with a stable form of politics?

Enforcement anti-corruption approaches have been criticised from a variety of perspectives. Some scholars point out that corruption takes many forms, some of which are not, strictly speaking, in violation of legal norms. As a result, some highly harmful types of wrongdoing cannot be criminalised (Kaufmann and Vicente 2011). A particularly forceful version of this argument is the one recently put forward by political theorist Camila Vergara (2020). She recovers classic and early modern thinkers to posit that since the eighteenth century "corruption has been conveniently reduced to its most visible and clear expressions" (ibid.: 14). We should reject this trend and come to think of corruption like Aristotle or Machiavelli did, as a systemic problem of the political regime, one that goes beyond specific interactions between public and private agents. In particular, we ought to recognise that systemic corruption is underpinned by, and worsens, deep social and economic inequalities. These imbalances cannot be addressed through targeted enforcement:

[S]ystemic corruption in liberal democracies should be understood as a long-term, slow-moving process of oligarchization of society's political structure, and thus it should be analyzed at the macro level. Instead of looking at the inputs of political corruption (undue influence, which is hard to prove and thus prosecute), we should focus rather on its outputs, as anything pertaining to rules, procedures, and institutions that has the effect of benefitting the wealthy at the expense of the majority. We need to move away from intention and toward the consequences of political corruption to identify and measure its structural character. (Ibid.: 40)

Most scholars do not share this understanding of corruption as its societal consequences, instead ascribing to the narrower conceptualisation of "illegal" corruption that Vergara finds so inadequate. Some, however, are equally critical of the prioritisation of criminal enforcement. For example, Alina Mungiu-Pippidi highlights the importance of paying attention to context when determining what approach is bound to work better:

If indeed the norm is ethical universalism and corruption is a deviation (context A), it makes sense to build in a strategy for adequate control of corruption as something norm infringing (which indeed describes most of the current anticorruption industry's arsenal), based on suppression of corruption. If ethical universalism is not present and non-universal transactions of government are the most numerous (context B), the right strategy should be conceived instead along the lines of norm building, with suppression only complementing political reforms. (2015: 15)

Bo Rothstein's famous "indirect big bang approach" is in line with this view. With regard to Sweden's virtuous anti-corruption trajectory, he writes:

[W]hat this case reveals is that a more indirect approach was used which was directed not at corrupt practices in particular but at the general framework of what seems to be the full set of political institutions in the country. Instead of just attacking corruption and clientelism directly, this indirect approach served to change the political culture from a particularistic understanding of what politics is to a universalistic one. This has a clear parallel to Basil Liddell Hart's famous 'indirect approach' in military strategy. If the enemy was attacked directly, he would easily reinforce his strength at the position attacked and so be very difficult to defeat. (2011: 245)

In many ways, our book supports this scepticism. Institutional and legal reforms that strengthen enforcement superstructures can have serious shortcomings, including problematic unintended consequences. Where corruption is systemic, and the opportunity arises for some prosecutors to carry out new horizontal accountability missions, the results will be far from universally good and will most likely fail to attack the root causes of corruption.

First, crusades do shock, but far from upsetting the equilibrium of norms and behaviours that sustains corrupt ecosystems, they affect politics in pernicious ways. This is not just because crusades sometimes reinforce mass disaffection with the establishment and open the door to dangerous outsiders; they also exacerbate polarisation around the intrinsic merits of anti-corruption. In this sense, crusades prove destabilising for the very same judicial institutions that engineer them. As we saw, successful judges and prosecutorial task forces embrace investigative strategies that are controversial and test the limits of the law. Judicial legitimacy can be severely compromised in the process, eroding confidence in the instruments hailed as possible antidotes for corruption. At best, the controversies around such strategies further deepen political polarisation, drawing the courts into nasty feuds. At worst, at least from the point of view of judicial legitimacy, crusades can push more neutral observers into doubting prosecutors' and judges' true intentions and their ultimate value in the fight against corruption.

Second, as Rothstein's military analogy suggests, in contexts where corruption is systemic, the outcome of this kind of enforcement "on steroids" is that the establishment does not become cleaner but adapts, making corruption more elusive and therefore ubiquitous. Focus group participants seemed very alert to this possibility when they told us that they fully expected the political class to find ways around the new prosecutorial threat. Even more worrying is the prospect of a sort of "survival of the fittest" dynamic in which crusades only reach the low-hanging fruit and the most sophisticated members of corrupt establishments carry on with business as usual. Furthermore, as they try to adapt in the shadows, surviving elites can launch overt attempts to rein in judicial and prosecutorial power through reform efforts that counter decades of progress on the institutional front. Because this backlash is sometimes quite fierce, the results of ambitious anti-corruption probes always end up standing on extremely precarious grounds. In fact, crusades usually fade, with lines of inquiry coming to a halt or failing on appeal. In addition to potentially destroying judicial independence and emboldening rogue agents, effective backlash triggers feelings of disappointment among the many voters who watch this spectacle unfold, further fuelling political cynicism.

Third, irrespective of whether they effectively punish their targets, crusades produce a series of disruptions that can in fact make the pursuit of transparency less appealing, and thus discourage the formation of stable reform coalitions capable of attacking the root causes of corruption. In this regard, one important unintended consequence of *Lava Jato* was the blow it inflicted on key engines of economic growth in Latin America. That in the 2000s Odebrecht stretched its tentacles so prolifically beyond Brazil was of course a consequence of the commodity boom, which enabled countries to invest heavily on mass infrastructure.[3] *Lava Jato* irrupted as the export bonanza was coming to an end, and most certainly made things worse, precisely because it paralysed many of these strategic investment initiatives. Figure 9.1 shows the amount invested each year in public infrastructure projects with private sector participation in

---

[3] On the political economy of mass infrastructure in Latin America, see Holland (2021).

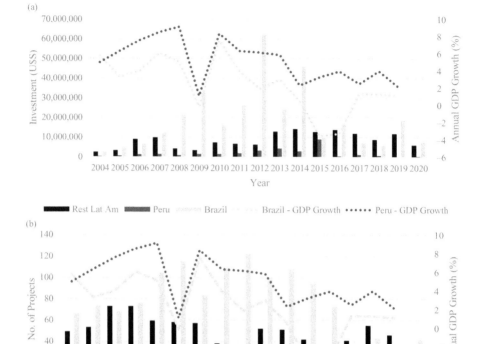

FIGURE 9.1 Public infrastructure projects with private participation (2004–2020). (a) Amount invested in public infrastructure projects with private participation (US$); (b) Number of projects.

Source: GDP Growth: World Bank's DataBank. Infrastructure Investments: World Bank's Private Participation in Infrastructure (PPI) Dataset. We thank Alisha Holland for alerting us to this data.

Brazil, Peru, and the rest of Latin America (Figure 9.1a), as well as the annual number of active projects (Figure 9.1b). To be sure, the sharp reduction we see in Brazil after 2014 is partly due to a worsening economy, but *Lava Jato* added to the vicious cycle. In fact, in both Peru and Brazil, this form of capital investment never recovered after the investigations started, whereas in the rest of Latin America the numbers were more stable.

One reason is that *Lava Jato* took big domestic and regional players in the construction sector out of the game of public contracting. The expectation that the crusade would not cease to snowball led banks to be extremely wary of financing the remaining players, further delaying infrastructure plans. All of this was not only problematic for the economy in the short term but complicated investment going forward. For example, the prospect of having to pay bribes or being accused of doing so by zealous prosecutors could reduce the pool of willing participants in public-private ventures to improve roads, dams, or telecommunications, effectively handing less scrupulous companies a larger portion of the pie. Additionally, the fear of more severe monitoring may decrease rather than increase the productivity of the bureaucrats in charge of allocating and managing these projects. It could even scare "the good types" away from entering the public administration, simply because of the expectation that they will likely have to acquiesce to corrupt agents or be perennially suspected of doing so. Rightly or not, criminalisation acts as a stigmatising force that not only casts a shadow over politicians, but also over the *res publica*. Little wonder then that considering these fears, some of the elites we interviewed for this project rehearsed arguments found in an older literature on corruption that described the benefits of bribery and impunity for developing countries. After all, bribes grease the wheels of government and help "get things done." Exploring how both private and public sector actors interpret the prosecutorial threat, and how it impacts their determination to be part of pro-transparency coalitions, is a possible avenue for future research, one with obvious implications for Latin America's development prospects.

The answer to these problems, however, cannot be to stay away from enforcement. First, corruption may grease the machinery of the state, but we know it produces myriad negative externalities. In this sense, one cannot but praise criminalisation for painting a timely picture of what Laurence Whitehead (2021) calls Latin America's "democratic delinquencies," that is, structural forms of malfeasance that reduce the quality of government. By singling out these underlying problems, *Lava Jato* may in fact contribute to efforts to address the root causes of corruption. The various national chapters of the inquiry made two of these delinquencies stand out, providing a clear focal point for reform initiatives. One is obviously the opaqueness of mega infrastructure projects, which clearly needs to be a priority for prevention-oriented transparency campaigners. The sheer size and duration of these initiatives, with several contractors and contractor consortiums participating at various stages, multiplies opportunities for extortion, inflating costs, or disguising malfeasance with accounting tricks. Moreover, such projects are highly strategic and in short offering, with benefits for all parties potentially huge. This naturally creates incentives for private sector actors to secure a portion of the pie via cartelisation, and for spurious gatekeeping by state officials. The other structural "delinquency" relates to how politicians finance electoral campaigns, especially when party organisations are not sufficiently rooted or strong to meet the rising costs of elections. This too emerges as a priority area for prevention-minded campaigners. New research persuasively traces the many ways in which money poisons politics (Figueroa 2021; Fouirnaies 2021; Gulzar et al. 2022). But the various chapters of *Lava Jato* have given us new insight into how exactly these transactions work. This information can help sharpen the focus of monitoring mechanisms going forward.

Second, from a more normative point of view, abandoning enforcement is simply an unacceptable path for any legal system that wishes to maintain a semblance of legitimacy. If an allegation merits an inquiry, and that inquiry stumbles upon more evidence and needs to grow in scope, that is exactly what should happen no matter how destabilising it may prove. The cost of not doing so can be equally problematic. For example, as we wrote these lines, a debate was starting to gain momentum in Argentina regarding the possible merits of pardoning high-profile politicians for their involvement in corruption during the Kirchner years. At the time, former president Cristina Kirchner was back in power, now as vice-president, and remained a defendant in several investigations and trials. For some, her attempts to stop or abort these proceedings via attacks on the judiciary and the prosecution services, including judicial reform proposals and scathing verbal diatribes, foreshadowed a period of institutional devastation and held politics hostage of a personal predicament. While Kirchner herself did not want a pardon (she much preferred absolution), a few observers began to think that the attempted cure (criminalisation) had been worse than the disease.[4] Amnesties or pardons in Argentina are highly unlikely, but the point is that if they were to materialise in any country, the message this would send would most certainly not be one that protects the integrity of judicial institutions or upholds the value of legal equality. Instead, the message would be that if you are sufficiently powerful to threaten a scorched earth response, you can get away with serious crimes.

In this sense, while our book offers a rich analysis of what happens to politics and mass attitudes when anti-corruption crusades take centre stage, and draws relatively pessimistic conclusions, it has less to say about the implications of impunity. We obviously chose to study cases of crusades in Brazil and Peru because we know little about the drivers and outcomes of this type of criminalisation processes. Under those knowledge conditions, positive cases are an excellent starting point for theory building. In addition, from an empirical perspective, it is easier to trace the consequences of dogs that bark than those of dogs that don't. But we suspect that if we were to conduct focus groups or surveys in places where *Lava Jato* did not amount to much, especially because it was grossly obstructed, we would not find a lot of optimism either. Even if prosecutors shy away from disrupting elections, collapsing governments, or generating unrealistic expectations among voters, and thus avoid some of the most destabilising features of criminalisation, inaction can be equally damaging. It may in fact fatally wound the credibility of judicial institutions and fuel cynical views about a political class that is effectively "untouchable."

---

[4] Carlos Pagni, "Ruidos que esconden una convivencia," *La Nacion* (4 March 2021).

Crises of representation can be strong under such circumstances because as much as citizens crave stability and find it hard to make up their minds about whether they actually like it when politicians are forced to answer for their actions (either because they like those politicians or find fault in some prosecutorial tactics), at the end of the day, they also crave accountability and a semblance of legal equality. Indeed, work on the collapse of Venezuela's party system in the 1990s (Coppedge 2005; Lupu 2016) and on Chile's most recent protest cycles (Luna and Altman 2011; Rhodes-Purdy and Rosenblatt 2021) demonstrates the perils of a political class that is perceived as a detached and self-serving oligarchy.

"NORMING" PROSECUTORIAL ZEAL AS A WAY FORWARD

This discussion of the pros and cons of *Lava Jato* highlights a dilemma: both prosecutorial action and inaction pose dangers to the rule of law, political stability, and democratic integrity. What is to be done? Prevention is obviously key to complement enforcement and make it less necessary in the future, or at least reduce the likelihood that minor investigations will snowball into full-blown crusades. But preventing corruption by attacking its root causes is a long-term project. In the meantime, enforcement will continue playing a role. So how do we make it better, even when operating "on steroids"?

We ought to accept, of course, that corruption prosecutions are always going to be disruptive and divisive. In particular, there are always going to be some who overplay their hand as they wave the transparency flag, and others who denounce political persecution and aggressively lash back against accountability efforts. This *is* the nature of the beast. However, we ought to begin to think of ways in which "lawfare," with its Manichaean and authoritarian legality connotations, does not come to dominate the narrative. In this way, criminalisation can go back to being just good old "judicialisation," which may prove controversial at times, but is not perceived by interested and neutral parties alike as a potential threat to the Republic. The challenge is to set standards that lower the voltage of corruption prosecutions so that the game becomes something most actors are willing or compelled to accept. It is worth remembering in this regard that what legitimises backlash, or the lawfare narrative, is the fine line that exists between prosecutorial zeal and sheer illegality. It is therefore important to "norm" that zeal so that faults in the judicial process do not become the main focus of debate. If the process is not credible or lacks integrity, and therefore polarises or disappoints, outcomes will not stand on firm grounds, either because citizens will not believe in what the courts say, because victories will be quickly overturned on appeal, or because criminals will claim victim status.

A few caveats are in order before we proceed. First, one can obviously understand why it is important to take seriously those who denounce due process violations and authoritarian legality. Everyone deserves equal treatment under law. Moreover, from a more consequentialist perspective, these aggrieved defendants often represent millions who can feel similarly wronged and unfairly excluded from the political process as a result of criminalisation. And even when defendants are not "representative," criminalising them can destabilize politics and economies in ways that also affect millions. So far so good. We should not, however, lose sight of the fact that these are still privileged individuals, whose grievances gain traction precisely because of their power. In fact, "lawfare" accusations are often political ploys to avoid jail. Moreover, these actors have access to high-flying lawyers and media platforms that allow them to activate multiple pressure points on the criminal justice system. This, in turn, helps them safeguard their rights. Recent developments in Brazil, with the STF annulling all proceedings against Lula, is a case in point. Lay citizens who are victims of similar, if not more serious due process breaches, are not so lucky. As a result, concerns about "lawfare" rarely extend to them. We think it is important to keep this in mind to put this alleged "problem" of criminalisation in perspective.

Second, prosecutorial zeal and unorthodoxy are in part the outcome of the realisation that standard investigative practices, including formalistic readings of the law and prosecutorial duties, are not fit for purpose when it comes to grand corruption. If law enforcement officials do not innovate, they might as well go home. What a zealous modus operandi does is precisely what some critics of enforcement approaches would like to see: it adopts a systemic conceptualisation of the problem of corruption and tries to extend the tentacles of the law to forms of wrongdoing that were hitherto immune from criminalisation. For this, prosecutors should be commended, as they are making the law bite in those places where it is needed the most. A critique of the methods they use to achieve this should therefore not throw the baby out with the bathwater.

With this in mind, "norming" zeal and bounding innovation so that prosecutorial practices are more readily accepted, and thus appear less sui generis and opportunistic, is potentially valuable. But it is also no small feat. A comparison with human rights prosecutions is in this sense quite telling. It is well established that the so-called justice cascade (Sikkink 2011) of trials and convictions against military and civilian officials responsible for the most egregious human rights violations perpetrated during dictatorships and armed conflicts stands on the shoulders of a long, arduous, and contested process of legal innovation (Sikkink 1993; Gonzalez-Ocantos 2016a; Zunino 2019). In Latin America, the constitutional and penal doctrines we now consider standard practice when it comes to (a) ignoring statutory limitations for horrendous crimes perpetrated in the distant past, (b) disapplying amnesty provisions, (c) importing extemporaneous criminal definitions from international law, and (d) increasing the weight of highly circumstantial evidence for criminal activity that had the backing of state power, were all once considered heretical even among some of those who wanted to see these criminals pay

(Roht-Arriaza 2015; Gonzalez-Ocantos 2020). Indeed, as Ruti Teitel (2003: 76) succinctly puts it, "the attempt to impose accountability through criminal law often raised rule of law dilemmas, including retroactivity in the law [and] tampering with existing laws," thus defying core tenets of political liberalism and triggering legal as well as political battles.

Critics of these innovations have, of course, not disappeared, with some still denouncing persecution and others adopting a more academic tone (e.g., Malarino 2010). But in many Latin American countries, acrimonious debates around these vexing legal questions are a thing of the past, even where prosecutions are still ongoing. This suggests that setting standards for unorthodox juridical practices in some of the most politically salient and divisive court cases imaginable is possible. The key to this was a long process of socio-legal mobilisation that built, legitimised, and diffused an alternative "legal" common sense applicable to human rights prosecutions and trials. Civil society actors, in alliance with academics and politicians, did so gradually and not without difficulties. But they eventually expanded highly formalistic horizons of legal imagination, finding ways to reconcile core imperatives of liberalism with the realisation that the international community cares just as much about justice for systematic affronts to human life and dignity. In this way, innovations that were necessary to bring to fruition criminal cases of incalculable constitutional, evidentiary, and procedural complexity, but that were initially considered at odds with due process and good judging, were regulated and legitimised.

This fraught but ultimately successful venture serves as a reminder that what the law says, or what it allows, is by no means determined objectively. It is rather the product of coalition building in politics and society, with some coalitions becoming salient and influential enough to define what is and what is not the legal "common sense." A similar standard-setting and consensus-generating process could take place in the realm of anti-corruption. This, however, is likely to face serious obstacles. First, corruption crimes are less serious than genocide or crimes against humanity, so it is harder to justify *sui generis* interpretations of existing criminal law standards. Second, corruption crimes invariably involve current not past actors, so passions are more likely to run wild, making consensus building much harder. And the passage of time, which may temper passions, works differently too: in the case of human rights trials, it almost always weakens the violators, and the presence of victims means there is always someone who will make sure the atrocities are never forgotten and remain in the docket, allowing judicial action when the air clears. With corruption cases, this is not necessarily the case. Third, it is immediately unclear who would benefit from a "norming" or standard-setting process, especially given that the controversy around corruption cases, the victimisation of some and the rhetoric of unyielding virtue of others, seems more politically profitable in the short run. In this regard, the absence of narrowly defined corruption "victims" is possibly fatal: the forward-looking, long-term societal push required for the norming process to take hold is likely to be absent.[5]

Despite important differences, the blueprint offered by human rights prosecutions is still a valid one. There are obvious stakeholders in domestic and international society who can take on the task of "norming" best practices for corruption prosecutions in an organic fashion. In fact, the international community has come a long way since the "corruption eruption" of the 1990s (Naim 1995). So far, however, the actors orbiting around the international anti-corruption regime, what Mungiu-Pippidi (2015) calls the "anti-corruption industry," have been more focused on equipping states with a better arsenal to attack corruption than on considering how this may sometimes clash with other values or aspirations. The "how to" kind of advice coming out of these circles is limited to technical issues such as criminal law reform, penal cooperation, or forensic accounting. In other words, the operating assumption is that states are underperforming and need better tools to punish corruption; not that they are "overperforming" and need standards to regulate zeal.

For example, the very recent Global Kleptocracy Initiative – spearheaded by the chairmen of the foreign relations committees in the US Senate, the UK House of Commons, and the European Parliament – is based on the premise that current efforts "have fallen short in addressing sophisticated practices of kleptocratic regimes and their private sector enablers. Going forward, a far more promising avenue would be more aggressive and better-coordinated action by the relatively few geopolitical actors that act as gatekeepers to the global financial system." The initiative thus seeks to elevate the status of kleptocracy to that of a national security threat in order to promote the "1) harmonization of regulatory standards; 2) strengthening of institutions with equities in the anti-kleptocracy fight; 3) more robust and coordinated use of existing anti-corruption and AML authorities; 4) lowered barriers to information exchange and joint law enforcement efforts; and 5) better integration of anti-corruption and anti-kleptocracy initiatives into national and regional-level security strategies."[6] Robert Rotberg's call for the creation of an International Anti-Corruption Court, similarly starts from the assumption that impunity is the norm, that countries cannot police themselves, and that we need more punitivism (Rotberg 2017: 95–97).

Few have considered a different kind of performance malfunction, one associated with instances in which state actors uncover and punish corruption too well but, in so doing, compromise due process or political stability. The reader will probably find it painfully unsatisfying that we will not offer here a list of standards to regulate, for instance, pretrial detentions when used to

---

[5] We thank Marcelo Leiras for alerting us to this difference between corruption and human rights prosecutions.
[6] Trevor Sutton and Ben Judah, "Turning the Tide on Dirty Money: Why the World's Democracies Need a Global Kleptocracy Initiative," *Center for American Progress* (26 February 2021).

neutralise obstruction or entice confessions, the treatment of circumstantial evidence, prosecutorial selectivity via plea-bargains and leniency agreements, relations between prosecutors and the media, or how long these proceedings should last. All we can do is suggest that these issues ought to be taken seriously, creating fora where relevant stakeholders can debate them in earnest without the usual fixation on remedying punitive deficits. In other words, the strategies that put punitivism on overdrive should also make it on to the agenda.

In many ways, this standard-setting exercise is already happening within national jurisdictions. For example, high courts in some of the countries affected by *Lava Jato* have dealt with vexing due process questions related to pretrial detentions or the use of extemporaneous criminal definitions in corruption prosecutions. In some instances, appellate judges have found fault in the approach adopted by rank-and-file prosecutors or lower courts, ordering retrials, shortening defendants' stints in jail, or invalidating incriminating evidence obtained through unorthodox channels. These tribunals have also exercised legality control of some innovative frameworks for international penal cooperation, norming what is and is not admissible in court, or what kinds of prosecutorial selectivity have a basis in law. As this body of jurisprudence grows, it can become the starting point of a broader, transnational effort to norm the criminalisation of corruption.

Unfortunately, the neutrality of these interventions can be called into question, failing to placate conflict. International institutions such as those of the Inter-American System of Human Rights may therefore be in a better position to norm such a contested legal field. In fact, this is exactly what they did with controversial issues such as human rights prosecutions following dictatorships and armed conflicts. Interestingly, both the Inter-American Court and Commission on Human Rights are already intervening to norm corruption investigations, producing promising jurisprudential developments. For example, in a standard-setting report published in 2019, the commission hinted at the tension between effectiveness and respect for due process at the heart of crusades, emphasising that both are necessary:

States have a duty to be effective in the face of a complex phenomenon where traditional investigation techniques seem insufficient. The Inter-American Commission reaffirms the full validity of the human rights of the accused in matters of corruption. Likewise, it reiterates that it is the duty of the State to seriously investigate corruption cases, establish the truth, and punish those responsible. This means that States have the obligation to respect the full enjoyment and exercise of all rights, particularly those that do not admit restrictions, such as the prohibition of torture.[7]

---

[7] "Corrupción y derechos humanos: Estándares Interamericanos," OEA/Ser.L/V/II. Doc. 236, 6 December 2019, p. 142.

In terms of the duty to investigate corruption, the commission has further highlighted the importance of safeguarding freedom of expression to protect journalists and whistle-blowers and issued precautionary measures in favour of prosecutors facing personal and professional threats.[8] It has also proclaimed states' responsibility to contribute to international penal cooperation, going quite far in defining what those efforts should look like in practice:

> The [Commission] highlights the importance of cooperation between justice systems, with a view to tackling a transnational phenomenon, such as the exchange of information, the creation of multilateral investigation units that could facilitate [...] a coordinated policy of identification of asset flows destined for corruption.[9]

The Inter-American Court has similarly trained its eyes on corruption investigations. In 2020, for the first time in its history, the court ruled that the arbitrary removal of prosecutors is illegal under the American Convention on Human Rights. It thus extended well-established jurisprudence on judicial independence to prosecutors, stating that they enjoy equivalent protections regardless of institutional design. This could imply that untenured prosecutors as well as those assigned to a case on an ad hoc basis (e.g., *Lava Jato* task forces) cannot be removed on a whim. But the court, perhaps more so than the commission, also puts a lot of emphasis on the limits of prosecutorial zeal and defendants' rights. In this sense, it has variously ruled that proceedings must be overseen by impartial courts and that their duration ought to be "reasonable" to prevent investigations from being deployed to neutralise political opponents;[10] that prosecutors should pursue various lines of inquiry to avoid investigations that are biased against specific individuals;[11] that regardless of the challenges involved in obtaining incriminating evidence investigators must not behave contrary to due process and that evidence-gathering decisions ought to be fully justified;[12] and that pretrial detentions are only admissible when there is strong evidence that defendants perpetrated the crime, and that even in those cases investigators must show that defendants are in a position to evade or obstruct justice.[13]

To be sure, the standards proposed by these regional institutions are still quite vague, further demonstrating that striking a balance between anti-corruption and respect for civil/politics rights is challenging and requires further thinking.

---

[8] E.g., Resolución 55/2021, Medida cautelar No. 576-21, José Domingo Pérez Gómez y su núcleo familiar respecto de Perú, 25 July 2021.

[9] Resolución 1/18, Corrupcion y Derechos Humanos, 2 March 2018, p. 7.

[10] *Zegarra* v. *Peru*, Ruling of 15 February 2017; *Andrade* v. *Bolivia*, Ruling of 1 December 2016.

[11] *Acosta y otros* v. *Nicaragua*, Ruling of 25 March 2017.

[12] *López-Mendoza* v. *Venezuela*, Ruling of 1 September 2011; *Acosta y otros* v. *Nicaragua*, Ruling of 25 March 2017.

[13] *Barreto-Leiva* v. *Venezuela*, Ruling of 28 January 2009.

But given what is at stake in corruption prosecutions, and how contemporary criminalisation efforts have played out in practice, dividing publics, alienating citizens, and jeopardising judicial integrity, continuing in this journey of norm construction is essential if we are to ensure that prosecutions make a productive and sustainable contribution to the quest for ethical universalism.

Bibliography

van Aaken, Anne, Eli Salzberger, and Stefan Voigt. 2004. "The Prosecution of Public Figures and the Separation of Powers: Confusion within the Executive Branch – A Conceptual Framework." *Constitutional Political Economy* 15(3): 261–280.

Abers, Rebecca Neaera. 2019. "Bureaucratic Activism: Pursuing Environmentalism Inside the Brazilian State." *Latin American Politics and Society* 61(2): 21–44.

Adebanwi, Wale, and Ebenezer Obadare. 2011. "When Corruption Fights Back: Democracy and Elite Interest in Nigeria's Anti-corruption War." *Journal of Modern African Studies* 49(2): 185–213.

Agerberg, Mattias. 2019. "The Curse of Knowledge? Education, Corruption, and Politics." *Political Behavior* 41(2): 369–399.

Agger, Robert E., Marshall N. Goldstein, and Stanley A. Pearl. 1961. "Political Cynicism: Measurement and Meaning." *Journal of Politics* 23(3): 477–506.

Aguiar Aguilar, Azul. 2012. "Institutional Changes in the Public Prosecutor's Office: The Cases of Mexico, Chile and Brazil." *Mexican Law Review* 4(2): 261–289.

2015. "The Public Prosecutor: The Achilles' Heel of the Rule of Law in Mexico." *Revista Mexicana de Análisis Politico y Administración Pública* 4(1): 159–172.

2019. "Reforms of the Public Prosecutor's Office in Brazil, Chile and Mexico: The Role of Justice Sector Interest Groups." In *Beyond High Courts: The Justice Complex in Latin America*, eds. Matthew Ingram and Diana Kapiszewski. Notre Dame: University of Notre Dame Press.

Albertson, Bethany, and Shana Kushner Gadarian. 2015. *Anxious Politics: Democratic Citizenship in a Threatening World*. Cambridge: Cambridge University Press.

Alonso, Angela, and Ann Mische. 2017. "Changing Repertoires and Partisan Ambivalence in the New Brazilian Protests." *Bulletin of Latin American Research* 36(2): 144–159.

Andersen, Christopher J., and Yuliya V. Tverdova. 2003. "Corruption, Political Allegiances, and Attitudes toward Government in Contemporary Democracies." *American Journal of Political Science* 47(1): 91–109.

Anduiza, Eva, Aina Gallego, and Jordi Muñoz. 2013. "Turning a Blind Eye." *Comparative Political Studies* 46(12): 1664–1692.

Andvig, Jens, and Karl Ove Moene. 1990. "How Corruption May Corrupt." *Journal of Economic Behavior & Organization* 13(1): 63–76.

Ansolabehere, Karina. 2010. "More Power, More Rights? The Supreme Court and Society in Mexico." In *Cultures of Legality*, eds. Javier Couso, Alexandra Huneeus, and Rachel Sieder. Cambridge: Cambridge University Press.

Anti-corruption Center. 2009. *Tracking Progress of Grand Corruption Cases*. U4 Expert Answers Series.

Arantes, Rogério. 2011. "The Federal Police and the Ministério Público." In *Corruption and Democracy in Brazil: The Struggle for Accountability*, eds. Timothy Power and Matthew Taylor. Notre Dame: University of Notre Dame Press.

Arellano-Gault, David. 2020. *Corruption in Latin America*. London: Routledge.

Arias, Eric et al. 2019. "Information Provision, Voter Coordination, and Electoral Accountability: Evidence from Mexican Social Networks." *American Political Science Review* 113(2): 475–498.

Aytaç, S. Erdem, and Susan C. Stokes. 2019. *Why Bother? Rethinking Participation in Elections and Protests*. Cambridge: Cambridge University Press.

Bakiner, Onur. 2020. "Endogenous Sources of Judicial Power: Parapolitics and the Supreme Court of Colombia." *Comparative Politics* 52(4): 603–624.

Banks, Antoine J., Ismail K. White, and Brian D. McKenzie. 2019. "Black Politics: How Anger Influences the Political Actions Blacks Pursue to Reduce Racial Inequality." *Political Behavior* 41(4): 917–943.

Banuri, Sheheryar, and Philip Keefer. 2013. *Intrinsic Motivation, Effort and the Call to Public Service*. Washington: World Bank.

Baraybar-Hidalgo, Viviana. 2020. "When and Why Do Voters Punish Corruption? The Role of Perceptions of Negative Externalities in Electoral Accountability." Unpublished MPhil dissertation, University of Oxford.

Barbacetto, Gianni, Peter Gomez, Marco Travaglio, and Piercamillo Davigo. 2012. *Mani Pulite*. Milan: Chiarelettere.

Basabe-Serrano, Santiago. 2009. "Ecuador: Reforma constitucional, nuevos actores políticos y viejas prácticas partidistas." *Revista de Ciencia Política* 29(2): 381–406.

Bauhr, Monika, and Marcia Grimes. 2014. "Indignation or Resignation: The Implications of Transparency for Societal Accountability." *Governance* 27(2): 291–320.

Bennett, Colin J. 1991. "What Is Policy Convergence and What Causes It?" *British Journal of Political Science* 21(2): 215–233.

Bentham, Jeremy. 1983. *The Collected Works of Jeremy Bentham: Deontology. Together with a Table of the Springs of Action and the Article on Utilitarianism*. Oxford: Clarendon Press.

Berghoff, Hartmut. 2018. "'Organised Irresponsibility'? The Siemens Corruption Scandal of the 1990s and 2000s." *Business History* 60(3): 423–445.

Bersch, Katherine. 2019. *When Democracies Deliver*. Cambridge: Cambridge University Press.

Bertossa, Carlo. 2003. "Difficulties Encountered by the Judiciary: A Summary of Key Issues." In *Effective Prosecution of Corruption*, ed. Asian Development Bank. Manila: Asian Development Bank.

Binder, Alberto. 2000. *Ideas y materiales para la reforma de la justicia penal*. Buenos Aires: Ad Hoc.

Bischoff, James L. 2003. "Reforming the Criminal Procedure System in Latin America." *Texas Hispanic Journal of Law & Policy* 9: 27–54.

Blais, André et al. 2010. "Political Judgments, Perceptions of Facts, and Partisan Effects." *Electoral Studies* 29(1): 1–12.

Boas, Taylor C., F. Daniel Hidalgo, and Marcus André Melo. 2019. "Norms versus Action: Why Voters Fail to Sanction Malfeasance in Brazil." *American Journal of Political Science* 63(2): 385–400.

Botero, Sandra et al. 2015. "Says Who? An Experiment on Allegations of Corruption and Credibility of Sources." *Political Research Quarterly* 68(3): 493–504.

Botero, Sandra, Daniel Brinks, and Ezequiel Gonzalez-Ocantos, eds. 2022. *The Limits of Judicialization: From Progress to Backlash in Latin America*. Cambridge: Cambridge University Press.

Bowler, Shaun, and Jeffrey A. Karp. 2004. "Politicians, Scandals, and Trust in Government." *Political Behavior* 26(3): 271–287.

Boyd, Christina, Michael Nelson, Ian Ostrander, and Ethan Boldt. 2021. *The Politics of Federal Prosecution*. Oxford: Oxford University Press.

Brader, Ted. 2005. "Striking a Responsive Chord: How Political Ads Motivate and Persuade Voters by Appealing to Emotions." *American Journal of Political Science* 49(2): 388–405.

2006. *Campaigns for Hearts and Minds: How Emotional Appeals in Political Ads Work*. Chicago: Chicago University Press.

Brader, Ted, Eric W. Groendendyk, and Nicholas A. Valentino. 2010. "Fight or Flight? When Politics Threats Arouse Public Anger and Fear." Paper presented at the Annual Meeting of the Midwest Political Science Association.

Braun, Dietmar, and Fabrizio Gilardi. 2006. "Taking 'Galton's Problem' Seriously." *Journal of Theoretical Politics* 18(3): 298–322.

Breitenstein, Sofia. 2019. "Choosing the Crook: A Conjoint Experiment on Voting for Corrupt Politicians." *Research & Politics* 6(1).

Brett, Roddy. 2016. "Peace without Social Reconciliation? Understanding the Trial of Generals Ríos Montt and Rodriguez Sánchez in the Wake of Guatemala's Genocide." *Journal of Genocide Research* 18(2–3): 285–303.

Brinks, Daniel. 2008. *The Judicial Response to Police Killings in Latin America*. Cambridge: Cambridge University Press.

Brinks, Daniel, Steven Levitsky, and María Victoria Murillo eds. 2020. *The Politics of Institutional Weakness in Latin America*. Cambridge: Cambridge University Press.

Brinks, Daniel M., Steven Levitsky, and María Victoria Murillo. 2019. *Understanding Institutional Weakness*. Cambridge: Cambridge University Press.

Buciuni, Giulio, and Vladi Finotto. 2016. "Innovation in Global Value Chains: Co-Location of Production and Development in Italian Low-Tech Industries." *Regional Studies* 50(12): 1–14.

Bueno de Mesquita, Bruce, and Alastair Smith. 2011. *The Dictator's Handbook: Why Bad Behavior Is Almost Always Good Politics*. New York: PublicAffairs.

Burt, Jo-Marie. 2016. "From Heaven to Hell in Ten Days: The Genocide Trial in Guatemala." *Journal of Genocide Research* 18(2–3): 143–169.

Bybee, Keith J. 2010. *All Judges Are Political, Except When They Are Not*. Palo Alto: Stanford University Press.

Cabot, Diego. 2018. *Los cuadernos. Cómo fue la investigación secreta del caso de corrupción más importante de la historia argentina.* Buenos Aires: Sudamericana.

Cappella, Joseph, and Kathleen Jamieson. 1996. "News Frames, Political Cynicism, and Media Cynicism." *The ANNALS of the American Academy of Political and Social Science* 546(1): 71–84.

Caramani, Daniele. 2017. "Will vs. Reason: The Populist and Technocratic Forms of Political Representation and Their Critique to Party Government." *American Political Science Review* 111(1): 54–67.

de Carli, Carla et al. 2011. *Lavagem de dinheiro: Prevenção e controle penal.* Porto Alegre: Verbo Juridico.

Carnes, Nicholas, and Noam Lupu. 2016. "Do Voters Dislike Working-Class Candidates? Voter Biases and the Descriptive Underrepresentation of the Working Class." *American Political Science Review* 110(4): 832–844.

Carnevale, Peter J. D., and Alice Isen. 1986. "The Influence of Positive Affect and Visual Access on the Discovery of Integrative Solutions in Bilateral Negotiation." *Organizational Behavior and Human Decision Processes* 37(1): 1–13.

Carothers, Christopher. 2022. *Corruption Control in Authoritarian Regimes: Lessons from East Asia.* New York: Cambridge University Press.

Carr, Indira, and Opi Outhwaite. 2008. "The OECD Anti-Bribery Convention 10 Years On." *Manchester Journal of International Law* 5(1): 3–35.

Casares, Martín. 2009. *El Ministerio Público Fiscal ante la Reforma.* Mimeo.

Casey, Gregory. 1974. "The Supreme Court and Myth: An Empirical Investigation." *Law & Society Review* 8(3): 385–420.

Cavise, Leonard L. 2007. "The Transition from the Inquisitorial to the Accusatorial System of Trial Procedure: Why Some Latin American Lawyers Hesitate." *Wayne Law Review* 53(2): 785–816.

Chang, Eric C. C., and Yun-han Chu. 2006. "Corruption and Trust: Exceptionalism in Asian Democracies?" *The Journal of Politics* 68(2): 259–271.

Chang, Eric C. C., Miriam A. Golden, and Seth J. Hill. 2010. "Legislative Malfeasance and Political Accountability." *World Politics* 62(2): 177–220.

Chemin, Rodrigo. 2017. *Mãos Limpas e Lava Jato: A corrupção se olha no espelho.* Porto Alegre: CDG.

Chong, Alberto, Ana L. de La O, Dean Karlan, and Leonard Wantchekon. 2015. "Does Corruption Information Inspire the Fight or Quash the Hope? A Field Experiment in Mexico on Voter Turnout, Choice, and Party Identification." *Journal of Politics* 77(1): 55–71.

Citrin, Jack. 1974. "Comment: The Political Relevance of Trust in Government." *American Political Science Review* 68(3): 973–988.

Comaroff, Jean, and John L. Comaroff. 2006. *Law and Disorder in the Postcolony.* Chicago: Chicago University Press.

Comisión Andina de Juristas. 2003. *El Debido Proceso en las decisiones de la Corte Interamericana de Derechos Humanos.* Lima: CAJ.

Conaghan, Catherine M. 2012. "Prosecuting Presidents: The Politics within Ecuador's Corruption Cases." *Journal of Latin American Studies* 44(4): 649–678.

Contesse, Jorge, and Janice Gallagher. 2022. "Critical Disconnects: Progressive Jurisprudence and Tenacious Impunity in Mexico." In *The Limits of Judicialization:*

From Progress to Backlash in Latin America, eds. Daniel M. Brinks, Sandra Botero, and Ezequiel Gonzalez-Ocantos. Cambridge: Cambridge University Press.

Coppedge, Michael. 2005. "Examining Democratic Deterioration in Venezuela Through Nested Inference." In *The Third Wave of Democratization in Latin America: Advances and Setbacks*, eds. Frances Hagopian and Scott Mainwaring. Cambridge: Cambridge University Press.

   2012. *Democratization and Research Methods*. Cambridge: Cambridge University Press.

Corbacho, Ana, Daniel W. Gingerich, Virginia Oliveros, and Mauricio Ruiz-Vega. 2016. "Corruption as a Self-Fulfilling Prophecy: Evidence from a Survey Experiment in Costa Rica." *American Journal of Political Science* 60(4): 1077–1092.

Coslovsky, Salo. 2011. "Relational Regulation in the Brazilian Ministério Publico: The Organizational Basis of Regulatory Responsiveness." *Regulation and Governance* 5(1): 70–89.

Couso, Javier. 2010. "The Transformation of Constitutional Discourse and the Judicialization of Politics in Latin America." In *Cultures of Legality*, eds. Javier Couso, Alexandra Huneeus, and Rachel Sieder. Cambridge: Cambridge University Press.

Cubas, Víctor. 2003. *El nuevo proceso penal peruano: Teoría y práctica de su implementación*. Lima: Palestra Editores.

Cuéllar, Mariano F., and Matthew Stephenson. 2020. "Taming Systemic Corruption: The American Experience and Its Implications for Contemporary Debates." Unpublished Manuscript.

Cyr, Jennifer. 2016. "The Pitfalls and Promise of Focus Groups as a Data Collection Method." *Sociological Methods & Research* 45(2): 231–259.

   2019. *Focus Groups for the Social Science Researcher*. Cambridge: Cambridge University Press.

Dargent, Eduardo. 2005. "Juzgando a los señores: Reflexiones sobre los procesos anticorrupción en el Perú." In *El Pacto Infame*. Lima: Red para el desarollo de las ciencias sociales en el Perú.

   2014. *Technocracy and Democracy in Latin America*. Cambridge: Cambridge University Press.

Dargent, Eduardo, and Paula Muñoz. 2016. "Peru: A Close Win for Continuity." *Journal of Democracy* 27(4): 145–158.

Dargent, Eduardo, and Stephanie Rousseau. 2021. "Peru 2020: El quiebre de la continuidad?" *Revista de Ciencia Política* 41(2): 377–400.

Da Ros, Luciano. 2014. *Mayors in the Dock: Judicial Responses to Local Corruption in Brazil*. Unpublished PhD Dissertation, University of Illinois at Chicago.

Da Ros, Luciano, and Matthew Taylor. 2022a. *Brazilian Politics on Trial: Corruption and Reform under Democracy*. Boulder: Lynne Rienner Publishers.

   2022b. "Kickbacks, Crackdown and Backlash: Legal Accountability in the Lava Jato Investigation." In *The Limits of Judicialization: From Progress to Backlash in Latin America*, eds. Daniel M. Brinks, Sandra Botero, and Ezequiel Gonzalez-Ocantos. Cambridge: Cambridge University Press.

Defensoría del Pueblo. 2008. *Decimosegundo Informe Anual de la Defensoría del Pueblo*. Lima: Defensoría del Pueblo.

2017. *Informe Anual 2017. Actividades y actuaciones llevadas a cabo a lo largo del año 2017.* Lima: Defensoría del Pueblo.

Denzin, Norma, and Katherine Ryan. 2007. "Qualitative Methods." In *The SAGE Handbook of Social Science Methodology*, eds. William Outhwaite and Stephen Turner. London: Sage.

Dervan, Lucian E., and Ellen S. Podgor. 2016. "Investigating and Prosecuting White-Collar Criminals." In *Oxford Handbook of White-Collar Crime*, eds. Shanna R. Van Slyke, Michael L. Benson, and Francis T. Cullen. Oxford: Oxford University Press.

Diehl, M., and W. Stroebe. 1987. "Productivity Loss in Brainstorming Groups: Toward the Solution of a Riddle." *Journal of Personality and Social Psychology* 53(3): 497–509.

DiMaggio, Paul, and Walter Powell. 1983. "The Iron Cage Revisited: Institutional Isomorphism and Collective Rationality in Organizational Fields." *American Sociological Review* 48(2): 147–160.

Domhoff, G. William. 1979. *The Powers That Be.* New York: Random House.

Dunning, Thad et al. 2019. "Voter Information Campaigns and Political Accountability: Cumulative Findings from a Preregistered Meta-Analysis of Coordinated Trials." *Science Advances* 5(7): 1–10.

Durand, Francisco. 2018. *Odebrecht: La empresa que capturaba gobiernos.* Lima: Fondo Editorial PUCP.

Easton, David. 1975. "A Re-Assessment of the Concept of Political Support." *British Journal of Political Science* 5(4): 435–457.

Eilstrup-Sangiovanni, Mette, and Jason C. Sharman. 2022. *Vigilantes beyond Borders: NGOs as Enforcers of International Law.* Princeton: Princeton University Press.

Epp, Charles R. 1998. *The Rights Revolution: Lawyers, Activists, and Supreme Courts in Comparative Perspective.* Chicago: Chicago University Press.

2009. *Making Rights Real: Activists, Bureaucrats, and the Creation of the Legalistic State.* Chicago: Chicago University Press.

Epstein, Lee, and Jack Knight. 1998. *The Choices Justices Make.* Washington, DC: CQ Press.

Falcone, Giovanni, and Giuliano Turone. 1982. "Tecniche di indagine in materia di mafia." *Rivista di studi e ricerche sulla criminalità organizzata* 1(1): 116–153.

Fearon, James D. 1999. "Electoral Accountability and the Control of Politicians: Selecting Good Types versus Sanctioning Poor Performance." In *Democracy, Accountability, and Representation*, eds. Adam Przeworski, Susan C. Stokes, and Bernard Manin. Cambridge: Cambridge University Press.

Ferejohn, John. 2002. "Judicializing Politics, Politicizing Law." *Law and Contemporary Problems* 65(3): 41–68.

Fernández-Vázquez, Pablo, Pablo Barberá, and Gonzalo Rivero. 2016. "Rooting Out Corruption or Rooting for Corruption? The Heterogeneous Electoral Consequences of Scandals." *Political Science Research and Methods* 4(2): 379–397.

Ferrajoli, Luigi. 2013. *Poderes salvajes: La crisis de la democracia constitucional.* Minima Trotta.

Ferraz, Claudio, and Frederico Finan. 2008. "Exposing Corrupt Politicians: The Effects of Brazil's Publicly Released Audits on Electoral Outcomes." *Quarterly Journal of Economics* 123(2): 703–745.

Figueroa, Valentín. 2021. "Political Corruption Cycles: High-Frequency Evidence from Argentina's Notebooks Scandal." *Comparative Political Studies* 54(3–4): 482–517.

Finkel, Jodi. 2008. *Judicial Reform as Political Insurance: Argentina, Peru, and Mexico in the 1990s*. Notre Dame: University of Notre Dame Press.

Fisman, Raymond, and Miriam Golden. 2017. *Corruption: What Everyone Needs to Know*. Oxford: Oxford University Press.

Forsyth, Donelson R. 2014. *Group Dynamics*. Belmont: Wadsworth Cengage Learning.

Fouirnaies, Alexander, and Anthony Fowler. 2021. "Do Campaign Contributions Buy Favorable Policies? Evidence from the Insurance Industry." *Political Science Research and Methods* 10(1): 18–32.

Freeman, Will. 2020. "Sidestepping the Constitution: Executive Aggrandizement in Latin America and East Central Europe." *Constitutional Studies* 6: 35–58.

Gailmard, Sean, and John W. Patty. 2007. "Slackers and Zealots: Civil Service, Policy Discretion, and Bureaucratic Expertise." *Journal of Politics* 51(4): 873–889.

Gallagher, Janice. 2017. "The Last Mile Problem: Activists, Advocates, and the Struggle for Justice in Domestic Courts." *Comparative Political Studies* 50(12): 1666–1698.

Gamson, William A. 1968. *Power and Discontent*. Homewood: Dorsey.

Gathii, James Thuo. 2019. "Recharacterizing Corruption to Encompass Illicit Financial Flows." *AJIL Unbound* 113: 336–340.

Gibson, James L., and Gregory A. Caldeira. 2009. *Citizens, Courts, and Confirmations: Positivity Theory and the Judgments of the American People*. Princeton: Princeton University Press.

Gibson, James L., Gregory A. Caldeira, and Vanessa A. Baird. 1998. "On the Legitimacy of National High Courts." *American Political Science Review* 92(2): 343–358.

Gibson, James L., Gregory A. Caldeira, and Lester Kenyatta Spence. 2003. "Measuring Attitudes toward the United States Supreme Court." *American Journal of Political Science* 47(2): 354–367.

2005. "Why Do People Accept Public Policies They Oppose? Testing Legitimacy Theory with a Survey-Based Experiment." *Political Research Quarterly* 58(2): 187–201.

Gillman, Howard. 1999. "The Court as an Idea, Not a Building (or a Game): Interpretive Institutionalism and the Analysis of Supreme Court Decision-Making." In *Supreme Court Decision-Making*, eds. Cornell W. Clayton and Howard Gillman. Chicago: Chicago University Press.

Gingerich, Daniel W. 2009. "Corruption and Political Decay: Evidence from Bolivia." *Quarterly Journal of Political Science* 4(1): 1–34.

2013. *Political Institutions and Party-Directed Corruption in South America*. Cambridge: Cambridge University Press.

Goldberg-Julie H., Jennifer S. Lerner, and Philip E. Tetlock. 1999. "Rage and Reason: The Psychology of the Intuitive Prosecutor." *European Journal of Social Psychology* 29(5–6): 781–795.

Gonzalez Ocantos, Ezequiel, Chad Kiewiet de Jonge, and David W. Nickerson. 2014. "The Conditionality of Vote-Buying Norms: Experimental Evidence from Latin America." *American Journal of Political Science* 58(1): 197–211.

Gonzalez-Ocantos, Ezequiel. 2016a. *Shifting Legal Visions*. Cambridge: Cambridge University Press.

2016b. "Evaluations of Human Rights Trials and Trust in Judicial Institutions: Evidence from Fujimori's Trial in Peru." *The International Journal of Human Rights* 20(4): 445–470.

2020. *The Politics of Transitional Justice in Latin America.* Cambridge: Cambridge University Press.

Gonzalez-Ocantos, Ezequiel, and Elias Dinas. 2019. "Compensation and Compliance: Sources of Public Acceptance of the U.K. Supreme Court's Brexit Decision." *Law & Society Review* 53(3): 889–919.

Gonzalez-Ocantos, Ezequiel, and Jody LaPorte. 2021. "Process Tracing and the Problem of Missing Data." *Sociological Methods & Research* 50(3): 1407–1435

Green, Paul E., Abba M. Krieger, and Yoram Wind. 2001. "Thirty Years of Conjoint Analysis: Reflections and Prospects." *Interfaces* 31(3 suppl.): S56–S73.

Groenendyk, Eric. 2011. "Current Emotion Research in Political Science: How Emotions Help Democracy Overcome Its Collective Action Problem." *Emotion Review* 3(4): 455–463.

Grosskopf, Anke, and Jeffery J. Mondak. 1998. "Do Attitudes toward Specific Supreme Court Decisions Matter? The Impact of Webster and Texas v. Johnson on Public Confidence in the Supreme Court." *Political Research Quarterly* 51(3): 633–654.

Guarnieri, Carlo. 2003. "Courts as an Instrument of Horizontal Accountability: The Case of Latin Europe." In *Democracy and the Rule of Law*, eds. Jose M. Maravall and Adam Przeworski. Cambridge: Cambridge University Press.

Gulzar, Saad, Miguel R. Rueda, and Nelson A. Ruiz. 2022. "Do Campaign Contribution Limits Curb the Influence of Money in Politics?" *American Journal of Political Science* 66(4): 932–946

Guthmann, Yanina. 2019. "El Ministerio Público Fiscal (MPF) en Argentina: Actors y prácticas. Apuntes de investigación." *Revista Argentina de Ciencia Política* 1(2): 59–80.

Hagopian, Frances. 2016 "Delegative Democracy Revisited: Brazil's Accountability Paradox." *Journal of Democracy* 27(3): 119–128.

Hainmueller, Jens, and Daniel J. Hopkins. 2015. "The Hidden American Immigration Consensus: A Conjoint Analysis of Attitudes toward Immigrants." *American Journal of Political Science* 59(3): 529–548.

Hainmueller, Jens, Daniel J. Hopkins, and Teppei Yamamoto. 2014. "Causal Inference in Conjoint Analysis: Understanding Multidimensional Choices via Stated Preference Experiments." *Political Analysis* 22(1): 1–30.

Hakhverdian, Armen, and Quinton Mayne. 2012. "Institutional Trust, Education, and Corruption: A Micro-Macro Interactive Approach." *The Journal of Politics* 74(3): 739–750.

Hammergren, Linn. 2008. "Twenty-Five Years of Latin American Judicial Reforms: Achievements, Disappointments, and Emerging Issues." *Whitehead Journal of Diplomacy and International Relations* 9(1): 89–104.

Hellwig, Timothy, and David Samuels. 2007. "Voting in Open Economies." *Comparative Political Studies* 40(3): 283–306.

Helmke, Gretchen. 2005. *Courts under Constraints.* Cambridge: Cambridge University Press.

Helmke, Gretchen, YeonKyung Jeong, Jae-Eun Kim, and Seda Ozturk. 2019. *Upending Impunity: Explaining Post-Tenure Presidential Prosecutions in Latin America.* Mimeo.

Helmke, Gretchen, and Steven Levitsky eds. 2006. *Informal Institutions and Democracy: Lessons from Latin America*. Baltimore: Johns Hopkins University Press.

Hetherington, Marc J. 1998. "The Political Relevance of Political Trust." *The American Political Science Review* 92(4): 791–808.

Hetherington, Marc J., and Joseph L. Smith. 2007. "Issue Preferences and Evaluations of the U.S. Supreme Court." *Public Opinion Quarterly* 71(1): 40–66.

Hibbing, John R., and Elizabeth Theiss-Morse. 1995. *Congress as Public Enemy*. Cambridge: Cambridge University Press.

Hilbink, Lisa. 2007. *Judges beyond Politics in Democracy and Dictatorship*. Cambridge: Cambridge University Press.

2012. "The Origins of Positive Judicial Independence." *World Politics* 64(4): 587.

Hilti, Martin. 2021. *Corporate Criminal Liability: Incomplete Legislation, Inadequate Enforcement, Serious Lack of Transparency*. Lausanne: Transparency Switzerland.

Hoekstra, Valerie J. 2003. *Public Reaction to Supreme Court Decisions*. Cambridge: Cambridge University Press.

Holland, Alisha C. 2021. *Creative Construction: The Rise and Stall of Mass Infrastructure in Latin America*. Unpublished Manuscript.

Hollis-Brusky, Amanda. 2015. *Ideas with Consequences: The Federalist Society and the Conservative Counterrevolution*. Oxford: Oxford University Press.

Human Rights Watch. 2006. *Lost in Transition: Bold Ambitions, Limited Results for Human Rights under Fox*. New York: Human Rights Watch.

Hunter, Wendy, and Timothy J. Power. 2019. "Bolsonaro and Brazil's Illiberal Backlash." *Journal of Democracy* 30(1): 68–82.

Ingram, Matthew C. 2015. *Crafting Courts in New Democracies*. Cambridge: Cambridge University Press.

International Crisis Group. 2011. *Learning to Walk without a Crutch: An Assessment of the International Commission against Impunity in Guatemala*.

Isbell, Linda M., Victor C. Ottati, and Kathleen C. Burns. 2006. "Affect and Politics: Effects on Judgment, Processing, and Information Seeking." In *Feeling Politics*, ed. David P. Redlawsk. New York: Palgrave Macmillan.

Iversen, Torben, and David Soskice. 2019. *Democracy and Prosperity*. Princeton: Princeton University Press.

Jackson, John D., and Sarah J. Summers. 2012. *The Internationalisation of Criminal Evidence the Internationalisation of Criminal Evidence*. Cambridge: Cambridge University Press.

Janis, Irving. 1982. *Groupthink: Psychological Studies of Policy Decisions and Fiascos*. 2nd ed. Boston: Houghton Mifflin.

Joly, Eva. 2003. "Coping with High-Profile Judicial Cases: Experience of Prosecutors from Asia and the Pacific, and from Europe." In *Effective Prosecution of Corruption*, ed. Asian Development Bank. Manila: Asian Development Bank.

Jorge, Guillermo. 2019. "The Impact of Corporate Liability on Corruption in Latin America." *AJIL Unbound* 113: 320–325.

Justicia Viva. 2007. *Balance del subsistema anticorrupción a seis años de su creación (2000–2006)*. Lima: Justicia Viva.

Kapiszewski, Diana. 2012. *High Courts and Economic Governance in Argentina and Brazil*. Cambridge: Cambridge University Press.

Kaufmann, Daniel, and Pedro C. Vicente. 2011. "Legal Corruption." *Economics & Politics* 23(2): 195–219.

Kim, Hunjoon, and Kathryn Sikkink. 2010. "Explaining the Deterrence Effect of Human Rights Prosecutions for Transitional Countries." *International Studies Quarterly* 54(4): 939–963.

Kirchheimer, Otto. 1961. *Political Justice: The Use of Legal Procedure for Political Ends*. Princeton: Princeton University Press.

Klašnja, Marko, Andrew T. Little, and Joshua A. Tucker. 2016. "Political Corruption Traps." *Political Science Research and Methods* 6(3): 413–428.

Klašnja, Marko, Noam Lupu, and Joshua A. Tucker. 2021. "When Do Voters Sanction Corrupt Politicians?" *Journal of Experimental Political Science* 8(2): 161–171

Klašnja, Marko, and Joshua A. Tucker. 2013. "The Economy, Corruption, and the Vote: Evidence from Experiments in Sweden and Moldova." *Electoral Studies* 32 (3): 536–543.

Klinkhammer, Julian. 2013. "On the Dark Side of the Code: Organizational Challenges to an Effective Anti-corruption Strategy." *Crime, Law and Social Change* 60(2): 191–208.

Krosnick, Jon, and Donald Kinder. 1990. "Altering the Foundations of Support for the President through Priming." *American Political Science Review* 82(2): 497–512.

Kunda, Ziva. 1990. "The Case for Motivated Reasoning." *Psychological Bulletin* 108(3): 480.

Kupatadze, Alexander. 2016. "Georgia's Break with the Past." *Journal of Democracy* 27(1): 110–123.

Lagunes, Paul, and Jan Svejnar eds. 2020. *Corruption and the Lava Jato Scandal in Latin America*. London: Routledge.

Langer, Máximo. 2004. "From Legal Transplants to Legal Translations: The Globalization of Plea Bargaining and the Americanization Thesis in Criminal Procedure." *Harvard International Law Journal* 45(1): 1–64.

Langer, Màximo. 2007. "Revolution in Latin American Criminal Procedure." *The American Journal of Comparative Law* 55: 617–676.

Leeper, Thomas J., Sara B. Hobolt, and James Tilley. 2020. "Measuring Subgroup Preferences in Conjoint Experiments." *Political Analysis* 28(2): 207–221.

León, Rafaella. 2019. *Vizcarra: Retrato de un poder en construcción*. Lima: Debate.

Lerner, Jennifer S., and Dacher Keltner. 2001. "Fear, Anger, and Risk." *Journal of Personality and Social Psychology* 81(1): 146–159.

Lessa, Francesca. 2019. "Operation Condor on Trial: Justice for Transnational Human Rights Crimes in South America." *Journal of Latin American Studies* 51(2): 409–439.

Levine, John M., and Richard L. Moreland. 1998. "Small Groups." In *The Handbook of Social Psychology*, eds. D. Gilbert, S. Fiske, and G. Lindzey. Boston: McGraw-Hill.

Levine, John M., Richard L. Moreland, and Hoon-Seok Choi. 2001. "Group Socialization and Newcomer Innovation." In *Blackwell Handbook of Social Psychology: Group Processes*, eds. Michael A. Hogg and Scott R. Tindale. Oxford: Blackwell Publishers.

Levitsky, Steven. 2013. "Peru: The Challenges of a Democracy without Parties." In *Constructing Democratic Governance in Latin America*, eds. Jorge Dominguez and Michael Shifter. Baltimore: The John Hopkins University Press.

Levitsky, Steven, and Maxwell A. Cameron. 2003. "Democracy without Parties? Political Parties and Regime Change in Fujimori's Peru." *Latin American Politics and Society* 45(3): 1–33.

Levitsky, Steven, and María Victoria Murillo eds. 2005. *Argentine Democracy: The Politics of Institutional Weakness*. University Park: Penn State University Press.

Levitsky, Steven, and María Victoria Murillo 2009. "Variation in Institutional Strength." *Annual Review of Political Science* 12(1): 115–133.

Levitsky, Steven, and Mauricio Zavaleta. 2016. "Why No Party-Building in Peru?" In *Challenges of Party-Building in Latin America*, eds. Steven Levitsky, James Loxton, Brandon van Dyck, and Jorge Dominguez. Cambridge: Cambridge University Press.

Limongi, Fernando. 2017. "Impedindo Dilma." *Novos Estud. CEBRAP*: 5–13.

Luna, Juan Pablo, and David Altman. 2011. "Uprooted but Stable: Chilean Parties and the Concept of Party System Institutionalization." *Latin American Politics and Society* 53(2): 1–28.

Lupu, Noam. 2016. *Party Brands in Crisis: Partisanship, Brand Dilution and the Breakdown of Political Parties in Latin America*. Cambridge: Cambridge University Press.

Machado, Fabiana, Carlos Scartascini, and Mariano Tommasi. 2011. "Political Institutions and Street Protests in Latin America." *Journal of Conflict Resolution* 55(3): 340–365.

Magaloni, Beatriz. 2003. "Authoritarianism, Democracy and the Supreme Court: Horizontal Exchange and the Rule of Law in Mexico." In *Democratic Accountability in Latin America*, eds. Scott Mainwaring and Christopher Welna. Oxford: Oxford University Press.

2008. "Enforcing the Autocratic Political Order and the Role of Courts: The Case of Mexico." In *Rule by Law*, eds. Tom Ginsburg and Tamir Moustafa. Cambridge: Cambridge University Press.

Malarino, Ezequiel. 2010. "Activismo judicial, punitivización y nacionalización. Tendencias antidemocráticas y antiliberales en la Corte Interamericana de Derechos Humanos." In *Sistema interamericano de protección de los derechos humanos y derecho penal internacional*, ed. Kai Ambos. Montevideo: Fundación Konrad Adenauer.

Manzetti, Luigi. 2014. "Accountability and Corruption in Argentina during the Kirchners' Era." *Latin American Research Review* 49(2): 173–195.

Manzi, Lucia. 2018. "The Effective Judicial Prosecution of Systemic Political Corruption: Italy." Unpublished Ph.D. Dissertation, University of Notre Dame.

March, James G. 1991. "Exploration and Exploitation in Organizational Learning." *Organization Science* 2(1): 71–87.

Marcus, George, Russell Neuman, and Michael MacKuen. 2000. *Affective Intelligence and Political Judgment*. Chicago: Chicago University Press.

Martini, Maíra. 2015. *Fighting Grand Corruption*. New York: Transparency International.

Mayka, Lindsay. 2019. *Building Participatory Institutions in Latin America*. Cambridge: Cambridge University Press.

McCann, James A., and Jorge Domínguez. 1998. "Mexicans React to Electoral Fraud and Political Corruption: An Assessment of Public Opinion and Voting Behavior." *Electoral Studies* 17(4): 483–503.

McCoy, Jennifer L., and Heather Heckel. 2001. "The Emergence of a Global Anti-corruption Norm." *International Politics* 38(1): 65–90.

van der Meer, Tom. 2010. "In What We Trust? A Multi-level Study into Trust in Parliament as an Evaluation of State Characteristics." *International Review of Administrative Sciences* 76(3): 517–536.

Meierhenrich, Jens, and Devin Pendas. 2017. "'The Justice of My Cause Is Clear, but There's Politics to Fear': Political Trials in Theory and History." In *Political Trials in Theory and History*, eds. Jens Meierhenrich and Devin Pendas. Cambridge: Cambridge University Press.

Meléndez, Carlos. 2019. *El mal menor: Vínculos politicos en el Perú posterior al colapso del sistema de partidos*. Lima: IEP.

Meléndez, Carlos, and Carlos León. 2009. "Perú 2008: El juego de ajedrez de la gobernabilidad en partidas simultáneas." *Revista de ciencia política* 29(2): 591–609.

Metz-McDonnell, Erin. 2017. "Patchwork Leviathan: How Pockets of Bureaucratic Governance Flourish within Institutionally Diverse Developing States." *American Sociological Review* 82(3): 476–510.

Meyer, John W., John Boli, George M. Thomas, and Francisco O. Ramirez. 1997. "World Society and the Nation-State." *American Journal of Sociology* 103(1): 144–181.

Michel, Verónica. 2018a. *Prosecutorial Accountability and Victims' Rights in Latin America*. Cambridge: Cambridge University Press.

2018b. "Public Prosecutors' Offices in Latin America." In *Routledge Handbook of Law and Society in Latin America*, eds. Rachel Sieder, Karina Ansolabehere, and Tatiana Alfonso. London: Routledge.

Michel, Verónica, and Kathryn Sikkink. 2013. "Human Rights Prosecutions and the Participation Rights of Victims in Latin America." *Law & Society Review* 47(4): 873–907.

Miller, Arthur H. 1974. "Political Issues and Trust in Government: 1964–1970." *American Political Science Review* 68(3): 951–972.

Mishler, William, and Richard Rose. 2001. "What Are the Origins of Political Trust?" *Comparative Political Studies* 34(1): 30–62.

Mondak, Jeffery J. 1990. "Perceived Legitimacy of Supreme Court Decisions: Three Functions of Source Credibility." *Political Behavior* 12(4): 363–384.

Moons, Wesley G., Naomi I. Eisenberger, and Shelley E. Taylor. 2010. "Anger and Fear Responses to Stress Have Different Biological Profiles." *Brain, Behavior, and Immunity* 24(2): 215–219.

Moreira Leite, Paulo. 2015. *A outra história da Lava-Jato: Uma investigação necessária que se transformou numa operação contra a democracia*. São Paulo: Geração Editorial.

Morgan, David L. 1996. "Focus Groups." *Annual Review of Sociology* 22(1): 129–152.

Moro, Sergio. 2004. "Consideraçoes sobre a operaçao Mani Pulite." *Revista CEJ* 26: 56–62.

2018. "Preventing Systemic Corruption in Brazil." *Daedalus* 147(3): 157–168.

Morris, Stephen D., and Joseph L. Klesner. 2010. "Corruption and Trust: Theoretical Considerations and Evidence from Mexico." *Comparative Political Studies* 43(10): 1258–1285.

Mota-Prado, Mariana, and Marta Rodriguez-Machado. Forthcoming. "Using Criminal Law to Fight Corruption: The Potential, Risks and Limitations of Operation Car Wash (Lava Jato)." *American Journal of Comparative Law*.

Mungiu-Pippidi, Alina. 2015. *The Quest for Good Governance*. Cambridge: Cambridge University Press.

Muñoz, Paula. 2019. *Buying Audiences: Clientelism and Electoral Campaigns When Parties are Weak*. Cambridge: Cambridge University Press.

2021. "Peru's Democracy in Search of Representation." In *Divisive Politics and Democratic Dangers in Latin America*, eds. Thomas Carothers and Andreas Feldman. Washington, DC: Carnegie Endowment for International Peace.

Muñoz, Paula, and Eduardo Dargent. 2016. "Patronage, Subnational Linkages, and Party-Building: The Cases of Colombia and Peru." In *Challenges of Party-Building in Latin America*, eds. Steven Levitsky, James Loxton, Brandon van Dyck, and Jorge Dominguez. Cambridge: Cambridge University Press.

Murillo, María Victoria, Steven Levistky, and Daniel Brinks. 2021. *La ley y la trampa en América Latina: por qué optar por el debilitamiento institucional puede ser una estrategia política*. Buenos Aires: Siglo XXI Editores.

Nabi, Robin L. 1999. "A Cognitive-Functional Model for the Effects of Discrete Negative Emotions on Information Processing, Attitude Change, and Recall." *Communication Theory* 9(3): 292–320.

Naim, Moisés. 1995. "The Corruption Eruption." *The Brown Journal of World Affairs* 2(2): 245–261.

Nelken, David. 1996. "The Judges and Political Corruption in Italy." *Journal of Law and Society* 23(1): 95–112.

Nicholson, Stephen P., and Thomas G. Hansford. 2014. "Partisans in Robes: Party Cues and Public Acceptance of Supreme Court Decisions." *American Journal of Political Science* 58(3): 620–636.

Nicholson, Stephen P., and Robert M. Howard. 2003. "Framing Support for the Supreme Court in the Aftermath of Bush v. Gore." *Journal of Politics* 65(3): 676–695.

O'Donnell, Guillermo. 1993. "On the State, Democratization and Some Conceptual Problems: A Latin American View with Glances at Some Postcommunist Countries." *World Development* 21(8): 1355–1369.

1998. "Horizontal Accountability in New Democracies." *Journal of Democracy* 9(3): 112–126.

Okonjo-Iweala, Ngozi. 2018. *Fighting Corruption Is Dangerous*. Boston: MIT Press.

Oliveros, Virginia, and Christian Schuster. 2018. "Merit, Tenure, and Bureaucratic Behavior: Evidence from a Conjoint Experiment in the Dominican Republic." *Comparative Political Studies* 51(6): 759–792.

Olvera Rivera, Alberto Javier. 2019. "Regime Crisis, Subnational Authoritarianism and Justice Reform in Mexico." *Perfiles latinoamericanos* 27(53): 1–25.

Ortellado, Pablo, and Esther Solano. 2016. "Nova direita nas ruas? Uma análise do descompasso entre manifestantes e os convocantes dos protestos antigoverno de 2015." *Perseu: História, memória e política* 11: 169–180.

Ortiz Ortiz, Richard. 2018. "Los problemas estructurales de la Constitución ecuatoriana de 2008 y el hiperpresidencialismo autoritario." *Estudios constitucionales* 16(2): 527–566.

Ottati, Victor, Nayda Terkildsen, and Clark Hubbard. 1997. "Happy Faces Elicit Heuristic Processing in a Televised Impression Formation Task: A Cognitive Tuning Account." *Personality and Social Psychology Bulletin* 23(11): 1144–1156.

Paiva, Luan Correa de. 2019. *A criminalização político-ideológica da esquerda: Uma explicação crítica para o recente caso brasileiro*. São Paulo: Editora Dialectica.

Pari, Juan. 2017. *Estado corrupto: Los megaproyectos del caso Lava Jato en Perú*. Lima: Planeta.

Patterson, M., and R. E. Schaeffer. 1977. "Effects of Size and Sex Composition on Interaction Distance, Participation, and Satisfaction in Small Groups." *Small Group Research* 8: 433–442.

Pavão, Nara. 2018. "Corruption as the Only Option: The Limits to Electoral Accountability." *The Journal of Politics* 80(3): 996–1010.

Pei, Minxin. 2018. "How Not to Fight Corruption: Lessons from China." *Daedalus* 147 (3): 216–230.

Petersen, Roger D. 2011. *Western Intervention in the Balkans: The Strategic Use of Emotion in Conflict*. Cambridge: Cambridge University Press.

Piper, William E. et al. 1983. "Cohesion as a Basic Bond in Groups." *Human Relations* 36(2): 93–108.

Pires, Roberto R. C. 2010. "Beyond the Fear of Discretion: Flexibility, Performance, and Accountability in the Management of Regulatory Bureaucracies." *Regulation and Governance* 5(1): 1–27.

Popova, Maria, and Vincent Post. 2018. "Prosecuting High-Level Corruption in Eastern Europe." *Communist and Post-Communist Studies* 51(3): 231–244.

della Porta, Donatella. 2001. "A Judges' Revolution? Political Corruption and the Judiciary in Italy." *European Journal of Political Research* 39(1): 1–21.

della Porta, Donatella, and Alberto Vannucci. 2007. "Corruption and Anti-corruption: The Political Defeat of 'Clean Hands' in Italy." *West European Politics* 30(4): 830–853.

Power, Timothy, and Matthew Taylor eds. 2011. *Corruption and Democracy in Brazil: The Struggle for Accountability*. Notre Dame: University of Notre Dame Press.

Praça, Sérgio, and Matthew M. Taylor. 2014. "Inching toward Accountability: The Evolution of Brazil's Anticorruption Institutions, 1985–2010." *Latin American Politics and Society* 56(2): 27–48.

Pulecio-Boek, Daniel. 2015. "The Genealogy of Prosecutorial Discretion in Latin America: A Comparative and Historical Analysis of the Adversarial Reforms in the Region." *Richmond Journal of Global Law and Business* 13(1): 67–144.

Rhodes-Purdy, Matthew, and Fernando Rosenblatt. 2021. "Raising the Red Flag: Democratic Elitism and the Protests in Chile." *Perspectives on Politics*

Rich, Jessica A. J. 2019. *State-Sponsored Activism: Bureaucrats and Social Movements in Democratic Brazil*. Cambridge: Cambridge University Press.

Ríos-Figueroa, Julio. 2007. "Fragmentation of Power and the Emergence of an Effective Judiciary in Mexico, 1994–2002." *Latin American Politics and Society* 49(1): 31–57.

2015. "Judicial Institutions." In *Routledge Handbook of Comparative Political Institutions*, eds. Jennifer Ganhi and Ruben Ruiz-Rufino. New York: Routledge.

2019. "Independence in Judicial Hierarchies: Civil-Law Systems." In *Research Handbook on Law and Courts*, eds. Susan Sterett and Demetrius Walker. London: Elgar Publishing.

Roca, David. 2019. *Lava Jato en el Congreso: detrás de cámaras de un debate*. Lima: Revuelta Editores.

Roht-Arriaza, Naomi. 2009. "Prosecutions of Heads of State in Latin America." In *Prosecuting Heads of State*, eds. Ellen L. Lutz and Caitlin Reiger. Cambridge: Cambridge University Press.

2015. "After Amnesties Are Gone: Latin American National Courts and the New Contours of the Fight Against Impunity." *Human Rights Quarterly* 37(2): 341.

Rose-Ackerman, Susan. 1999. *Corruption and Government*. Cambridge: Cambridge University Press.

Rose-Ackerman, Susan, and Bonnie J. Palifka. 2016. *Corruption and Government*. 2nd ed. Cambridge: Cambridge University Press.

Rotberg, Robert. 2017. *The Corruption Cure: How Citizens and Leaders Can Combat Graft*. Princeton: Princeton University Press.

Rothstein, Bo. 2011. "Anti-corruption: The Indirect 'Big Bang' Approach." *Review of International Political Economy* 18(2): 228–250.

Rothstein, Bo, and Aiysha Varraich. 2017. *Making Sense of Corruption*. Cambridge: Cambridge University Press.

Rousseau, Stéphanie, and Eduardo Dargent. 2019. "The Construction of Indigenous Language Rights in Peru: A Language Regime Approach." *Journal of Politics in Latin America* 11(2): 161–180.

de Sa e Silva, Fabio. 2020. "From Car Wash to Bolsonaro: Law and Lawyers in Brazil's Illiberal Turn (2014–2018)." *Journal of Law and Society* 47: 90–110.

Sadek, Maria Tereza, and Rosângela Batista Cavalcanti. 2003. "The New Brazilian Public Prosecution: An Agent of Accountability." In *Democratic Accountability in Latin America*, eds. Scott Mainwaring and Christopher Welna. Oxford: Oxford University Press.

Sakwa, Richard. 2017. "The Trials of Khodorkovsky in Russia." In *Political Trials in Theory and History*, eds. Jens Meierhenrich and Devin O. Pendas. Cambridge: Cambridge University Press.

Samuels, David J., and Cesar Zucco. 2018. *Partisans, Antipartisans, and Nonpartisans*. Cambridge: Cambridge University Press.

Sanchez-Badin, Michelle R., and Arthur Sanchez-Badin. 2019. "Anticorruption in Brazil: From Transnational Legal Order to Disorder." *AJIL Unbound* 113: 326–330.

Sberna, Salvatore, and Alberto Vannucci. 2013. "'It's the Politics, Stupid!': The Politicization of Anti-corruption in Italy." *Crime, Law and Social Change* 60(5): 565–593.

Scartascini, Carlos, and Mariano Tommasi. 2012. "The Making of Policy: Institutionalized or Not?" *American Journal of Political Science* 56(4): 787–801.

Scheb, John, and William Lyons. 2000. "The Myth of Legality and Public Evaluation of the Supreme Court." *Social Science Quarterly* 81(4): 928–940.

Schedler, Andreas, Larry Diamond, and Marc Plattner. 1999. *The Self-Restraining State: Power and Accountability in New Democracies*. Bounder: Lynne Rienner Publishers.

Segal, Jeffrey A., and Harold J. Spaeth. 1993. *The Supreme Court and the Attitudinal Model*. Cambridge: Cambridge University Press.

Seligson, Mitchell A. 2002. "The Impact of Corruption on Regime Legitimacy: A Comparative Study of Four Latin American Countries." *The Journal of Politics* 64(2): 408–433.

Sergi, Anna. 2016. *"Three Tales / Two Threats"*. *Prosecutors in Italy, England and the United States Narrate National and Transnational Organised Crime*. Mimeo.

Sewell, William H. 1996. "Historical Events as Transformations of Structures: Inventing Revolution at the Bastille." *Theory and Society* 25(6): 841–881.

Shen-Bayh, Fiona. 2018. "Strategies of Repression." *World Politics* 70(3): 321–357.

Shipan, Charles R., and Craig Volden. 2008. "The Mechanisms of Policy Diffusion." *American Journal of Political Science* 52(4): 840–857.

2012. "Policy Diffusion: Seven Lessons for Scholars and Practitioners." *Public Administration Review* 72(6): 788–796.

Sifuentes, Marco. 2019. *K.O. P.P.K.* Lima: Planeta.

Sikkink, Kathryn. 1993. "Human Rights, Principled Issue-Networks, and Sovereignty in Latin America." *International Organization* 47(3): 411–441.

2011. *The Justice Cascade: How Human Rights Prosecutions Are Changing World Politics*. New York: W.W. Norton & Co.

Singer, Peter. 2011. *The Expanding Circle: Ethics, Evolution and Moral Progress*. Princeton: Princeton University Press.

Silva, Cátia Aida. 2000. "Brazilian Prosecutors and the Collective Demands: Bringing Social Issues to the Courts of Justice." Paper Presented at the Annual Meeting of the Latin American Studies Association, Miami.

Simmons, Beth A. 2001. "The International Politics of Harmonization: The Case of Capital Market Regulation." *International Organization* 55(3): 589–620.

Simpser, Alberto. 2013. *Why Governments and Parties Manipulate Elections*. Cambridge: Cambridge University Press.

Smith, Steven M. 2003. "The Constraining Effects of Initial Ideas." In *Group Creativity: Innovation through Collaboration*, eds. B. Paulus Paul and Bernard A. Nijstad. Oxford: Oxford University Press.

Smulovitz, Catalina. forthcoming. "Del 'descubrimiento de la ley' al 'lawfare' o cómo las uvas se volvieron amargas." *Revista SAAP*.

Soifer, Hillel. 2020. "Shadow Cases in Comparative Research." *Qualitative & Multi-Method Research* 18(2): 9–18.

Solaz, Hector, Catherine E. de Vries, and Roosmarijn A. de Geus. 2019. "In-Group Loyalty and the Punishment of Corruption." *Comparative Political Studies* 52(6): 896–926.

de Sousa Santos, Boaventura. 1995. *Toward a New Common Sense: Law, Science and Politics in the Paradigmatic Transition*. New York: Routledge.

Spiller, Pablo T., and Mariano Tommasi. 2007. *The Institutional Foundations of Public Policy in Argentina*. Cambridge: Cambridge University Press.

Spink, Kevin S., and Albert Carron. 1992. "Group Cohesion and Adherence in Exercise Classes." *Journal of Sport and Exercise Psychology* 14(1): 78–86.

Stockemer, Daniel, and Lyle Scruggs. 2012. "Income Inequality, Development and Electoral Turnout – New Evidence on a Burgeoning Debate." *Electoral Studies* 31 (4): 764–773.

Stoyan, Alissandra T. 2020. "Ambitious Reform via Constituent Assemblies: Determinants of Success in Contemporary Latin America." *Studies in Comparative International Development* 55(1): 99–121.

Sugiyama, Natasha Borges. 2012. "Bottom-up Policy Diffusion: National Emulation of a Conditional Cash Transfer Program in Brazil." *Publius: The Journal of Federalism* 42(1): 25–51.

Sullivan, John L., James Piereson, and George E. Marcus. 1979. "An Alternative Conceptualization of Political Tolerance: Illusory Increases 1950s–1970s." *American Political Science Review* 73(3): 781–794.

Sutherland, Edwin H. 1983. *White Collar Crime*. New Haven: Yale University Press.

Taber, Charles S., and Milton Lodge. 2006. "Motivated Skepticism in the Evaluation of Political Beliefs." *American Journal of Political Science* 50(3): 755–769.

Taylor, Matthew M. 2018. "Getting to Accountability: A Framework for Planning & Implementing Anticorruption Strategies." *Daedalus* 147(3): 63–82.

Teitel, Ruti G. 2003. "Transitional Justice Genealogy." *Harvard Human Rights Journal* 16: 15–94.

Teles, Steven. 2012. *The Rise of the Conservative Legal Movement*. Princeton: Princeton University Press.

Tonry, Michael. 2012. "Prosecutors and Politics in Comparative Perspective." *Crime and Justice: Review of Research* 41: 1–34.

Travaglio, Marco, Peter Gomez, and Gianni Barbacetto. 2012. *Mani Pulite: La Vera Storia*. Roma: Chiarelettere.

Truth and Reconciliation Commission. 2003. *Informe Final: Tomo III*. Lima: Comisión de la Verdad y Reconciliación.

Tversky, Amos, and Daniel Kahneman. 1981. "The Framing of Decisions and the Psychology of Choice." *Science* 211(4481): 453–458.

Tyler, Tom R. 2004. "Enhancing Police Legitimacy." *The ANNALS of the American Academy of Political and Social Science* 593(1): 84–99.

United States Department of Justice. 2016. *Case Information File: United States V. Odebrecht*.

Uslaner, Eric M. 2008. *Corruption, Inequality, and the Rule of Law*. Cambridge: Cambridge University Press.

Valentino, Nicholas A. et al. 2011. "Election Night's Alright for Fighting: The Role of Emotions in Political Participation." *The Journal of Politics* 73(1): 156–170.

Valentino, Nicholas A., Krysha Gregorowicz, and Eric W. Groenendyk. 2009. "Efficacy, Emotions and the Habit of Participation." *Political Behavior* 31(3): 307–330.

Vannucci, Alberto. 2009. "The Controversial Legacy of 'Mani Pulite': A Critical Analysis of Italian Corruption and Anti-corruption Policies." *Bulletin of Italian Politics* 1(2): 233–264.

2016. "The 'Clean Hands' (Mani Pulite) Inquiry on Corruption and Its Effects on the Italian Political System." *Em Debate* 8(2): 62–68.

Vera, Sofia B. 2020. "Accepting or Resisting? Citizen Responses to Corruption across Varying Levels of Competence and Corruption Prevalence." *Political Studies* 68(3): 653–670.

Vergara, Alberto. 2018. "Virtue, Fortune, and Failure in Peru." *Journal of Democracy* 29(4): 65–76.

Vergara, Camila. 2020. *Systemic Corruption: Constitutional Ideas for an Anti-Oligarchic Republic*. Princeton: Princeton University Press.

Volosin, Natalia A. 2019. *La máquina de la corrrupción*. Buenos Aires: Aguilar.

de Vries, Catherine E., and Hector Solaz. 2017. "The Electoral Consequences of Corruption." *Annual Review of Political Science* 20: 391–408.

Wallander, Lisa. 2009. "Twenty-five Years of Factorial Surveys in Sociology: A Review." *Social Science Research* 38(3): 505–520.

Wang, Ching-Hsing. 2016. "Government Performance, Corruption, and Political Trust in East Asia*." *Social Science Quarterly* 97(2): 211–231.

Warren, Mark. 2004. "What Does Corruption Mean in a Democracy?" *American Journal of Political Science* 48(2): 328–343.

Webster, Steven W. 2017. "Anger and Declining Trust in Government in the American Electorate." *Political Behavior* 40(4): 933–964.

2020. *American Rage*. Cambridge: Cambridge University Press.

Weyland, Kurt. 2005. "Theories of Policy Diffusion Lessons from Latin American Pension Reform." *World Politics* 57(2): 262–295.

2009. "Institutional Change in Latin America: External Models and Their Unintended Consequences." *Journal of Politics in Latin America* 1(1): 37–66.

Whitehead, Laurence. 2021. "Democratic Delinquencies in Latin America." *Journal of Democracy* 32(3): 78–93

Whiteley, Paul, Harold D. Clarke, David Sanders, and Marianne Stewart. 2016. "Why Do Voters Lose Trust in Governments? Public Perceptions of Government Honesty and Trustworthiness in Britain 2000–2013." *The British Journal of Politics and International Relations* 18(1): 234–254.

Widmeyer, W. N., L. R. Brawley, and Albert V. Carron. 1990. "The Effects of Group Size in Sport." *Journal of Sport and Exercise Psychology* 12: 177–190.

Wittenbaum, Gwen M., and Richard L. Moreland. 2008. "Small-Group Research in Social Psychology: Topics and Trends over Time." *Social and Personality Psychology Compass* 2(1): 187–203.

World Bank. 1997. *Helping Countries Combat Corruption: The Role of the World Bank*. Washington, DC: World Bank.

Woods, Patricia J., and Lisa Hilbink. 2009. "Comparative Sources of Judicial Empowerment." *Political Research Quarterly* 62(4): 745–752.

Zechmeister, Elizabeth J., and Daniel Zizumbo-Colunga. 2013. "The Varying Political Toll of Concerns about Corruption in Good versus Bad Economic Times." *Comparative Political Studies* 46(10): 1190–1218.

Zink, James R., James F. Spriggs, and John T. Scott. 2009. "Courting the Public: The Influence of Decision Attributes on Individuals' Views of Court Opinions." *The Journal of Politics* 71(3): 909–925.

Zunino, Marcos. 2019. *Justice Framed*. Cambridge: Cambridge University Press.

Index

Cambridge Studies in Law and Society

Books in the Series

For EU product safety concerns, contact us at Calle de José Abascal, 56–1°,
28003 Madrid, Spain or eugpsr@cambridge.org.

www.ingramcontent.com/pod-product-compliance
Ingram Content Group UK Ltd.
Pitfield, Milton Keynes, MK11 3LW, UK
UKHW020359140625
459647UK00020B/2555